Developments
in Russian
Politics

Developments in Russian Politics

Henry E. Hale, Juliet Johnson, Tomila V. Lankina

DUKE UNIVERSITY PRESS   Durham and London   2024

This edition published by Duke University Press in 2024

First published by Bloomsbury Publishing in Great Britain in 2024

Cover design: Eleanor Rose
Cover image: © AFP/Getty Images

Library of Congress Cataloging-in-Publication Data

Names: Hale, Henry E., [date] editor. | Johnson, Juliet, 1968– editor. |
Lankina, Tomila, editor.
Title: Developments in Russian politics 10 / Henry E. Hale,
Juliet Johnson, Tomila V. Lankina.
Other titles: Developments in Russian politics ten
Description: Tenth edition. | Durham : Duke University Press, 2024. |
Includes bibliographical references and index.
Identifiers: LCCN 2024005053 | ISBN 9781478026020 (hardcover)
ISBN 9781478030256 (paperback)
Subjects: LCSH: Russia (Federation)—Politics and government—1991– |
BISAC: POLITICAL SCIENCE / World / Russian & Soviet | SOCIAL SCIENCE / Reference
Classification: LCC DK510.763 .D48 2024 | DDC 947.08—dc23/eng/20240202
LC record available at https://lccn.loc.gov/2024005053

Printed in the United States of America on acid-free paper ∞

Contents

Contributors

Vladimir Gel'man is Professor of Russian Politics at the Aleksanteri Institute, University of Helsinki, Finland. His research interests focus on analysis of political regime dynamics and patterns of governance in post-Soviet Russia and Eurasia. His most recent book is *The Politics of Bad Governance in Contemporary Russia* (University of Michigan Press, 2022).

Grigorii V. Golosov is Professor and Head of the Political Science Department at the European University at St Petersburg, Russia. His research interests focus on political parties, elections, sub-national and multilevel politics, political science methods, and comparative authoritarianism. He has published more than sixty articles on these topics in international political science journals. His most recent book is *Authoritarian Party Systems: Party Politics in Autocratic Regimes, 1945–2019* (World Scientific, 2022).

Henry E. Hale is Professor of Political Science and International Affairs at George Washington University, USA, where he directs the Institute for European, Russian, and Eurasian Studies (IERES). His books include *The Zelensky Effect* (with Olga Onuch, Hurst/Oxford University Press, 2022) and *Patronal Politics: Eurasian Regime Dynamics in Comparative Perspective* (Cambridge University Press, 2015). His work has won two prizes from the American Political Science Association. Specializing in political regimes, public opinion, ethnic politics, and post-Soviet politics, he is also editorial board chair of *Demokratizatsiya: The Journal of Post-Soviet Democratization*.

Yoshiko M. Herrera is Professor of Political Science at University of Wisconsin-Madison, USA. Her research focuses on Russian politics, identity, and political economy. She is author of *Imagined Economies: The Sources of Russian Regionalism* (Cambridge University Press, 2004) and *Mirrors of the Economy: National Accounts and International Norms in Russia and Beyond* (Cornell University Press, 2013).

Marat Iliyasov is a fellow at George Washington University's Russian Global Academy program, Institute for European, Russian, and Eurasian Studies

(IERES). His research interests focus on political developments in postwar Chechnya and the Chechen diaspora abroad. He has published on Chechen demographic growth during and after the Russo-Chechen wars, Chechen collective identity and memory politics, radicalization, and religious governance in Chechnya and Russia. His most recent research analyzes memory politics in authoritarian Chechnya.

Kristy Ironside is Associate Professor of Russian History and William Dawson Scholar at McGill University, Canada. She is the author of *A Full-Value Ruble: The Promise of Prosperity in the Postwar Soviet Union* (Harvard University Press, 2021) and numerous articles on the Soviet Union's social and economic history. Her current research is focused on Russia's and the Soviet Union's international engagements, in particular on economic cooperation with the capitalist West in the last years of the Soviet system and during the post-communist transition.

Debra Javeline is Associate Professor in the Department of Political Science, an affiliate of the Environmental Change Initiative, and a fellow of the Kroc Institute for International Peace Studies, Kellogg Institute for International Studies, and Nanovic Institute for European Studies at the University of Notre Dame, France. Her research has been published in *Climate Policy, Climatic Change, American Political Science Review, Comparative Political Studies, Perspectives on Politics, Public Opinion Quarterly, Natural Hazards Review, Bioscience*, and other journals. She is the author of *After Violence: Russia's Beslan School Massacre and the Peace That Followed* (Oxford University Press, 2023).

Juliet Johnson is Professor in the Department of Political Science at McGill University, Canada, an Elected Fellow of the Royal Society of Canada, and Network Director of the Jean Monnet network *Between the EU and Russia (BEAR)*. She is the author of the award-winning *Priests of Prosperity: How Central Bankers Transformed the Postcommunist World* (Cornell University Press, 2016) and *A Fistful of Rubles: The Rise and Fall of the Russian Banking System* (Cornell University Press, 2000), and served as president of the Association for Slavic, East European, and Eurasian Studies (ASEEES) in 2023. Her research focuses on the politics of money and identity, particularly in post-communist Europe, and has appeared in numerous scholarly and policy-oriented articles.

Tomila V. Lankina is Professor of International Relations at the London School of Economics and Political Science, UK. She has worked on democracy and authoritarianism, mass protests, and historical drivers of human capital and political regime change in Russia and other countries; she has also analyzed the propaganda and disinformation campaigns in the wake of Russia's annexation of Crimea and aggression in Ukraine. Her latest research is on social structure and inequality. Her *The Estate Origins of Democracy in Russia: From Imperial Bourgeoisie to Post-Communist Middle Class* (Cambridge University Press, 2022) won the 2023 J. David Greenstone Prize for best book in the Politics and History section of the American Political Science Association (APSA), the 2023 Davis Center Book Prize, and 'Honorable Mention' for the Sartori Book Award of the APSA's Organized Section for Qualitative and Multi-Method Research.

Evgeniya Mitrokhina is a PhD student in Comparative Politics at University of Wisconsin-Madison, US. Her work focuses on the role of bureaucracies in authoritarian regime persistence. Prior to joining UW-Madison, she studied political science and sociology at the Higher School of Economics in Moscow.

Jeremy Morris is Professor of Russian & Global Studies at Aarhus University, Canada, Denmark. He is the author of *Everyday Postsocialism: Working-class Communities in the Russian Margins* (Springer, 2016) and co-editor of *Varieties of Russian Activism: State-Society Contestation in Everyday Life* (Indiana University Press, 2023).

Maria Popova is Associate Professor of Political Science at McGill University, Canada. She is the author of *Politicized Justice in Emerging Democracies: A Study of Courts in Russia and Ukraine* (Cambridge University Press, 2012) and articles on rule of law and corruption in Russia, Ukraine, and post-communist EU members. She edits the Cambridge Elements Series in Politics and Society from Central Europe to Central Asia. With Oxana Shevel, she co-authored *Russia and Ukraine: Entangled Histories, Diverging States* (Polity, 2023).

Gulnaz Sharafutdinova is Professor of Russian Politics and Director of the Russia Institute at King's College London, UK. She is author of *The Afterlife of Soviet Man: Rethinking Homo Sovieticus* (Bloomsbury, 2023), the award-winning *The Red Mirror: Putin's Leadership and Russia's Insecure Identity* (Oxford University Press, 2020), *Political Consequences of Crony Capitalism Inside Russia* (Notre Dame University Press, 2010), and numerous articles. Her current research focuses on issues of the social psychology of collective ressentiment, authoritarian governance and legitimation, and public opinion in Russia.

Oxana Shevel is Associate Professor of Political Science at Tufts University, US and Vice President of both the Association for the Study of Nationalities (ASN) and the American Association of Ukrainian Studies (AAUS). She is co-author (with Maria Popova) of a book on the root causes of the Russo-Ukrainian war, *Russia and Ukraine: Entangled Histories, Diverging States* (Polity, 2024). Her earlier book, *Migration, Refugee Policy, and State Building in Postcommunist Europe* (Cambridge University Press, 2011) won the AAUS prize for best book in the fields of Ukrainian history, politics, language, literature, and culture. She has published numerous articles and chapters on nation building and identity politics in Ukraine, Russia, and the post-Soviet region.

Valerie Sperling is Professor of Political Science at Clark University, US. Her research interests lie mainly at the intersection of Russian politics and gender studies. Author of the award-winning *Sex, Politics, and Putin* (Oxford University Press, 2015), she has published on Russian women's movement activism, gender- and LGBTQ+ discrimination, and globalization. Her most recent book, co-authored with Robert Boatright, is *Trumping Politics as Usual: Masculinity, Misogyny, and the 2016 Elections* (Oxford University Press, 2020).

Kathryn Stoner is the Mosbacher Director of the Center on Democracy, Development, and the Rule of Law at Stanford University, US, where she is also a Senior Fellow at the Freeman Spogli Institute for International Studies and a Professor of Political Science and Senior Fellow at the Hoover Institution (both by courtesy). Her most recent book is *Russia Resurrected: Its Power and Purpose in a New Global Order* (Oxford University Press, 2021).

David Szakonyi is Associate Professor of Political Science at George Washington University, US, and co-founder of the Anti-Corruption Data Collective. His academic research focuses on corruption, authoritarianism, and political economy in Russia, Western Europe, and the United States. His book *Politics for Profit: Business, Elections, and Policymaking in Russia* (Cambridge University Press, 2020) examines why businesspeople run for political office and how their firms benefit.

Katerina Tertytchnaya is Associate Professor of Comparative Politics at the University of Oxford, UK. Her research interests include protest and public opinion with a focus on contemporary Russia. She has published work on the effect of protests on public opinion and the ways in which contemporary autocrats use propaganda and repression to lower the costs of staying in power.

Preface

On 24 February 2022, the Russian Federation launched a full-scale invasion of neighbouring Ukraine, sharply escalating its assault on that country which began in 2014. This war has killed tens of thousands, wrought immeasurable destruction, provoked sharper divisions than ever before between Russia and the West, and set off a competition for support from other countries ranging from India to Brazil.

The invasion presents a major challenge for Russian studies. For one, it has demonstrated the imperative to search for better ways to understand Russia. At the same time, the war has spotlighted Russian imperial ambitions and colonial attitudes toward countries around it and ethnic minorities within it, raising uncomfortable questions about whether our own views of these countries and peoples reflect this biased Russian gaze. Many call for 'de-centering' Russian studies by paying more attention to previously marginalized voices and perspectives, denying Russia and ethnic Russians the often unquestioned pride of place they have traditionally occupied in global research and education.

Developments in Russian Politics 10 reflects these new approaches to Russian studies. Understanding Russia is more important than ever and fresh perspectives are needed. In putting this volume together, one of our key goals has been to give readers access to diverse perspectives through a team of top-notch authors who reflect this diversity. We also break with a common tradition of organizing volumes on Russian politics primarily around formal institutions like parliament, the judiciary, or political parties that play more marginal and/or different roles in increasingly authoritarian Russia than they do in the wealthiest industrial democracies. This enables us to give due emphasis to societal factors and informal structures and processes that underpin support for Russia's political regime.

Chapter 1 frames the flow of post-Soviet Russian politics by emphasizing that informal institutions, networks, and practices can be as important as formal ones, clarifying the role of societal factors in it. Vladimir Putin's rise and long-term dominance, for example, cannot be understood without attention to all of this. The book then unfolds with four chapters examining fundamental influences on contemporary Russian politics, including Russian history, culture, and identity. Building on this foundation, the subsequent five chapters address how Russia's political system actually works. By 'actually', we mean that we focus primarily on the logic by which it functions – a logic hinging on a complex interaction between formal and informal politics that is often misunderstood in the West – rather than on the many ways in which it falls short of democratic ideals. The remaining chapters each address specific topics that we believe are important for courses on Russian politics to cover. These include not only a dedicated chapter on the Russia-Ukraine war and another on Russian foreign policy more generally, but also chapters on Chechnya, marginalized groups within Russia, Russia's protest movement and civil society, and climate change.

By putting Russian history, culture, and identity first, however, we remain duly attentive to the crucial fact that these too are influenced powerfully by politics. This is true even of history. While the 'facts' of what happened cannot change, how people remember and interpret them surely can. The effort to shape Russian collective memory has been a major part of what many now call 'Putinism', including his efforts to legitimate the invasion of Ukraine. To be sure, one of the greatest challenges of compiling a textbook is that the factors that drive Russian politics influence each other and are influenced by politics itself. We hope, though, that our attempt to break this down for readers into a set of discrete, focused chapters provides a readable, understandable entrée into this reality, helping simplify the complicated without sacrificing nuance and debate.

The politics of any country, especially one as volatile as Russia has been in the past century or two, is always a moving target. We aim to provide readers with a conceptual toolkit for understanding the dynamism of Russian politics, rather than a static understanding of how Russia looks at a particular moment. We hope that our volume will continue to be useful for understanding Russian politics regardless of what the future may bring. And if there is one thing we can predict based on Russian history, it is that something unpredictable is sure to happen.

Henry E. Hale
Juliet Johnson
Tomila V. Lankina

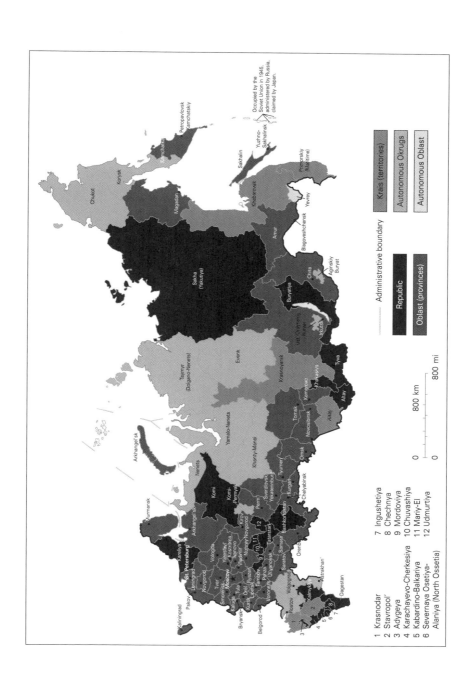

1 Krasnodar
2 Stavropol'
3 Adygeya
4 Karachayevo-Cherkesiya
5 Kabardino-Balkariya
6 Severnaya Osetiya-
   Alaniya (North Ossetia)

7 Ingushetiya
8 Chechnya
9 Mordoviya
10 Chuvashiya
11 Mariy-El
12 Udmurtiya

Administrative boundary

Republic

Oblast (provinces)

Krais (territories)

Autonomous Okrugs

Autonomous Oblast

0   800 km
0   800 mi

Occupied by the
Soviet Union in 1945,
administered by Russia,
claimed by Japan.

Putin and the Dynamics of Russia's Political System

Henry E. Hale

Russian politics does not easily reduce to many concepts that people frequently use to describe it. Simple terms like 'authoritarianism' and 'dictatorship' do a good job of telling us that Russia is not a democracy, but risk creating the impression that all we really need to know is what the autocrat (currently Vladimir Putin) wants to do. While sometimes this may be the case, in other instances it is clearly not. That is, thinking in terms of an autocracy–democracy binary does not tell us much about how a political system like Russia's *actually works* in practice. More colourful terms like 'kleptocracy' or 'fascism' do satisfy the urge to condemn odious regime behaviours and accurately describe important parts of the system, but neglect others. Labelling it 'imperialist' tells us something important about the worldview currently driving much of Russian political behaviour, but says little about regime mechanics and dynamics. And calling Putin Russia's latest 'tsar' highlights important continuities in symbolism and geography, but deemphasizes many ways in which his regime is quintessentially 'modern' in attaining and exercising dominance.

Rather than start with concepts developed largely to describe Western polities or that orientalize others, it can be helpful instead to begin with some basic principles about the context in which politics happens as Russia's citizens in all their diversity actually experience it. This begins with conceptualizing Russia's most important political actors and thinking about what drives their behaviour, and then looking at the implications without initially worrying about whether the result fits well with familiar categories like, for example, 'democracy' or 'autocracy'. Such an approach yields a vision of Russian politics as a system in which powerful, loosely hierarchical networks of people compete with each other while penetrating both the economic and political worlds when the rule of law is weak and corruption is high. This form of politics may at first seem exotic, but it is in fact very common throughout the world, and Westerners will find many of these patterns familiar in their own past and present politics.

The story of contemporary Russian politics, then, is at core a dynamic one about how these networks arrange and rearrange themselves politically, and how this process shapes and is shaped by the public. It takes us from the chaotic competition of the 1990s to the tightly fit machine that ultimately mobilized a full-scale invasion of neighbouring Ukraine in 2022, a brutal act that has killed thousands and is still wreaking carnage at the time of this writing. To focus on networks as political actors is not to discount the importance of ideology, ordinary people, or formal institutions like parliaments or political parties. All play their roles. But these roles are often deceptively different than those played in polities like the US or the UK. It is one goal of this book to explain how.

A social context of patronalism

Russia shares with much of the world a social context that I have called *patronalism*. The technical definition of patronalism is a social equilibrium in which people pursue their political and economic goals primarily through extended and roughly hierarchical networks of actual acquaintance, and often by meting out concrete, personalized rewards or punishments (Hale 2015). In short, this is a context in which personal connections matter to a degree that would seem extreme to most people growing up in the US or Britain. In the latter countries, connections can matter greatly for getting a job or obtaining good tickets to a show but, for example, people usually do not feel they need a personal connection to the leadership of a charity organization before they can be confident enough in it to donate money. Nor do they consider it common for doctors to expect personal rewards for providing needed medical services, or for professors to take payments of some kind for good grades or recommendations.

Patronalism is an 'equilibrium', because its practice is self-reinforcing when it is widespread, and therefore it is very hard to root out even when people are well-intentioned. While not all patronalism is corruption, an example involving corruption shows how this is the case. Suppose you are a mayor and it is widely believed that you need to pay off various officials to get a new regional medical facility located in your town. You can decide to be honest and refuse to make the payments, but if you take the proverbial high road, some other ambitious mayor is likely to go ahead and make the payments and get the facility located in their region instead. The result is that your constituents will be deprived and may even blame you for not doing what was necessary. But if you make the payment and satisfy your voters by getting the facility in your town, you are contributing to the expectation that 'this is just how things work', making others more likely to do the same when they have a chance.

At the level of national leadership, the practice is even more deeply rooted. Leaders tend to find it comfortable, convenient, and effective to hand out individualized rewards and punishments through personal connections to get done whatever they want to get done. They thus have little incentive to do the very hard work necessary actually to change things fundamentally. Thus, while all three of Russia's post-Soviet presidents have talked about the need to root out corruption and modernize the state, this has remained more talk than real action.

Power networks in Russian politics

One implication of the centrality of personal connections in Russia is that the key 'players' in the country's political arena are often not 'parties' or even formal institutions like the parliament, but extended networks of actual personal acquaintance led by powerful 'patrons'. At the very least, this is how many political insiders in Russia see it. And despite the term's gendered root (patron), patronalism is not necessarily gender-exclusive. That said, in Russia, it is nevertheless intimately intertwined with patriarchal structures and a performative masculinity that Putin has brilliantly mastered, as Chapter 5 discusses in detail.

The most important power networks in Russia today fall into at least three main categories. One set of networks grew out of the economy, building vast business empires by gaming the post-Soviet privatization process and then translating this wealth into political clout in ways examined in Chapter 7. These networks, led by figures widely known as 'oligarchs', would get 'their' people into positions all across Russian political society and often gained control of important mass media. In the 1990s, oligarchs like Boris Berezovsky, Mikhail Khodorkovsky, and Vladimir Gusinsky were household names and thought to be among only a handful of men who essentially ran the country during President Boris Yeltsin's final term in office.

Another category might be called 'regional political machines', networks based in peripheral regions in which a strongman could use his (or, rarely, her) leverage as governor to gain control over local economic assets, media and legislatures. These assets could then be mobilized to deliver large shares of the province's votes to themselves or whomever they chose, leverage they could convert into influence in federal politics. Major political machines in regions like Tatarstan and Primorsky Krai were thus highly sought after allies by national politicians, though the biggest and most famous of all political machines was the one led until 2010 by mayor Yuri Luzhkov in Russia's capital metropolis, Moscow.

A third type of network consists of those with home bases in the state itself, figures that Bálint Magyar and Bálint Madlovics (2021) have called *poligarchs* (politicians whose reach extends deeply into the economy). The most prominent example today is that of Vladimir Putin, who turned an array of personal and professional acquaintances (many acquired during his days in the KGB or as a St Petersburg city official) into an extensive network that now dominates key posts in the state (most obviously, Putin himself serving as president), the economy (e.g. Igor Sechin controlling the oil company Rosneft), mass media (e.g. Yuri Kovalchuk founding the National Media Group), and multiple political parties with diverse ideologies (e.g. Putin's St Petersburg associate Dmitry Medvedev atop the United Russia Party). This network started to come together as a coherent power network of national importance in the late 1990s, as Putin was finally reaching the pinnacle of Russian power, and it is now unquestionably the country's dominant network.

The emergence of Russia's single-pyramid system

The process through which nearly all major power networks came to be arranged into a single 'pyramid' of power, recognizing the primary authority of a single patron, began in the 1990s under Yeltsin. The USSR's collapse had left that country's most powerful networks in a state of disarray, leaving myriad emerging regional political machines and budding oligarchs to compete intensely with each other – and with the Kremlin – for power with only a weak institutional framework to govern this contestation. While Putin supporters today often exaggerate the degree to which the 1990s were a period of chaos and economic collapse, there certainly was a much higher rate of disorder than any fully functioning state would tolerate. By one count, as many as half of all regional acts were found to be inconsistent with the federal constitution as provincial networks and oligarchs often colluded to pursue their own interests without paying much heed to 'the centre' (Stoner-Weiss 2001, p. 121).

It was in this context that Yeltsin took moves that ultimately helped unify the country more through informal than formal means. Yeltsin laid the cornerstone in late 1993 when he defeated the Congress of People's Deputies in a dispute over the Constitution that turned violent, putting before voters a referendum question that effectively forced them to choose either a new basic law that strongly favoured the president or no constitution at all. He then employed a variety of methods to win over (or coerce) at least some major regional political machines to his side and to strike deals with key oligarchs. The most infamous deal, 'loans-for-shares', allowed figures like Khodorkovsky and Berezovsky to obtain some of Russia's most valuable assets, including oil, in return for providing the cash-strapped Kremlin with badly needed funds (Johnson 2000, 185–87). With a presidential election looming in 1996 and Yeltsin trailing badly in the polls, the Russian president opted against cancelling elections and instead (for the first time in post-Soviet Russia) successfully mobilized a broad coalition of regional political machines and newly enriched oligarchs to win a national election. Rallying against the candidate who had been favoured by many to win at the start of the year, Communist Party leader Gennady Zyuganov, the regional machines in Yeltsin's corner delivered huge numbers of votes his way (sometimes reversing outcomes between the first and second rounds of voting) while oligarch-controlled media warned of a dark communist restoration while burnishing Yeltsin's own image in their news and other programming.

Yeltsin eked out a victory, convincing many that the money, media, and machines he controlled could elect anyone president of Russia. These included some key people who ultimately helped Yeltsin pick Putin as prime minister, an appointment that effectively designated the little-known FSB (Federal Security Service) chief Yeltsin's successor in August 1999. One reason Yeltsin chose Putin is that the latter was steeped in the 'hardball' methods that Yeltsin and many around him thought were needed to bring Russia's independent-minded oligarchs and political machines to heel. The seeds of Putinism in the 2000s were thus sown in the 1990s.

The problem of presidential succession

Before the hastily assembled machine from 1996 could be kicked into gear again, however, it nearly fell apart due to one of the central problems single-pyramid systems face: succession. With Yeltsin physically ailing and running up against a constitutional term limit, many of the political machines and oligarchic networks that had backed Yeltsin's re-election in 1996 now started to think ahead to a future without him, seizing the opportunity to try and proactively shape that future in ways that suited them. The most dramatic event was the emergence of a major new challenger to Kremlin power, the Fatherland-All Russia (FAR) bloc. FAR was a coalition of some of Russia's mightiest political machines (including Moscow, St Petersburg, Tatarstan, Bashkortostan) and powerful oligarchic networks (including Gusinsky's 'Most' network and even the state-owned Lukoil), with the popular former prime minister Yevgeny Primakov as its leader. As of summer 1999, this opposition was the odds-on favourite to win the December 1999 parliamentary elections and after that the 2000 presidential race.

This challenge forced the Kremlin to scramble, ultimately winning the presidency for Putin only after an absolutely wild set of events took place in the second half of 1999. At this time, a series of mysterious explosions killed hundreds of people in ordinary residential buildings in different regions of Russia and terrorized the nation. As detailed in Chapter 11 of this volume, Putin responded by sending the Russian military into Chechnya, a small restive region that he identified as the source of the problems, and many believe elements in the Russian state orchestrated the apartment bombings precisely to justify this action and help Putin gain power. It was not hard to convince Russia's majority that Chechens were guilty, given how the former tended to view the latter through an 'orientalizing' lens, as they did many other ethnic minorities.

The military assault on Chechnya proved highly popular. Demonstrating strong leadership after years of seeming chaos and incapacity at the top, Putin quickly shot up the presidential standings until by December 1999 he was already polling well above 50 per cent in the presidential race, more than double that of his closest competitor. In parliamentary elections that same month, a brand-new Unity bloc created just three months earlier surged to a surprisingly strong second place after backing Putin unequivocally. This proved Putin's electoral appeal. Then Yeltsin sealed Putin's status as presidential front-runner by resigning on New Year's Eve, a move that made Putin (as prime minister) the new acting president and required presidential elections to be held early, in March 2000. Seeing the writing on the wall, some of the key networks in the opposition coalition started to withdraw or even lend their support to Putin in the presidential race. In patronal politics, it is imperative to figure out quickly who will win so as to always wind up on the winner's side: To be on the losing side, without independent courts to protect you, is to risk political and economic annihilation at the hands of the victors.

Tightening the political machine

One of the things Putin clearly learned from the 1999–2000 succession crisis was that one of the most serious potential threats to Kremlin power is the 'defection' of a coalition of regional political machines and oligarchs, especially those controlling mass media, to the opposition. Some of his very first moves, therefore, were to attack sources of gubernatorial and oligarchic power.

Targeting governors, as described in Chapter 10, he removed them from the upper house of parliament (the Federation Council), carved the country up into seven new 'federal districts' led by presidential envoys who could undercut gubernatorial power, and, starting in 2005, replaced direct elections for governor with a system that analysts generally treat as a form of presidential appointment. While the Kremlin restored direct elections in response to a wave of pro-democracy protests in 2011–12, they came with a big catch: to get on the ballot, a candidate had to obtain the signatures of a large share of deputies in lower-level councils, which were usually dominated by Putin supporters. This system, which came to be known as the 'municipal filter', was designed to ensure that no unwanted candidates could challenge the Kremlin's choice for governors, and indeed, only in a few instances has its choice lost (most recently in 2023, when a Communist Party candidate won the governorship of Khakasiya). To ensure that these Kremlin-friendly governors faced little challenge at home, mayoral elections have been steadily eliminated, to the point at which direct elections for mayor remained in place in only six regional capitals by the end of 2022 (Tubridy 2022). At the same time, to make sure that governors do not wield local power bases strong enough to challenge the Kremlin, governors are frequently installed who have little connection to the region. As Chapter 10 describes, to a great extent Russia now remains a federation in name only.

This process has also involved a strengthening of Russian ethnic dominance over its minority peoples. Some of the country's most powerful regional political machines, as in Bashkortostan and Tatarstan, had long advocated minority language rights and upheld locally important symbols of their distinct histories. Under Putin, however, central authorities steadily constrained the ability of the federation's ethnic minority homelands ('republics' in official Russian legal terms) to promote local languages and identities through education and state symbols. Some republics, notably Chechnya and Tatarstan, have managed to bargain for more such autonomy than others, but they remain striking exceptions. At the same time, the Kremlin has not gone so far as to completely eliminate the minority ethnic symbolism of its republics. Instead, Putin's strategy has been to quietly promote linguistic and symbolic russification and assimilation while publicly professing a vision of a 'multi-ethnic' and 'multiconfessional' Russian Federation that is nevertheless 'led' by the ethnic Russian people (Chapters 4, 11). This sense of ethnic Russian privilege also shapes the state's response to the many migrants who in the 1990s started pouring into Russia for work from the South Caucasus and Central Asia. This response has afforded them ample opportunities to work and send remittances home to their relatives, but also leaves them highly vulnerable to abuse and exploitation (Chapter 12).

As for the oligarchs, as described in Chapter 7, Putin early on forced the two with the biggest media assets (Berezovsky and Gusinsky) into de facto exile and offered a deal to the rest by which they could keep their property so long as they did not go against the Kremlin's political interests and economic priorities. He punctuated this 'proposal' with an emphatic 'or else'. What 'else' meant became clear in 2003 with the arrest of Yukos chief Khodorkovsky, at the time Russia's richest man, who appeared to be flouting Putin's preferred arrangement. As Putin's power grew, it also became evident that he could send a company's stock price plummeting merely by mentioning its owner's disloyalty and hinting at a new Yukos scenario, as the firm Mechel painfully discovered in 2008 (*The Economist* 2008). Additionally, oligarchs were increasingly enlisted to perform certain social functions aimed at preventing social explosions, as illustrated when Putin personally scolded oligarch Oleg Deripaska for neglecting his firm's obligations to the local population of the town of Pikalevo in 2009 (Barry 2009). Especially in the 2010s, figures with deep roots in Putin's own personal network rose to new economic heights, controlling massive economic assets ranging from the oil giant Rosneft to private trading companies like Gunvor and reputedly siphoning off billions for their (and potentially Putin's) personal use (Dawisha 2014). Since the latter 2000s, then, oligarchic networks have not been a source of challenge for the regime, and many of them were in fact quite eager to demonstrate willingness to play ball. Inequality in Russia, therefore, remains high, with little emphasis on redistribution, leaving many groups marginalized in a precarious existence (see Chapter 12). This appears not to have changed despite the fact that Western sanctions have explicitly tried to impose costs on the oligarchs for their support of Putin as the latter presided over the annexation of Crimea, militarily backed an insurgency in eastern Ukraine, and ultimately launched an all-out invasion of Ukraine (Chapters 6 and 15).

Sealing these moves against oligarchs and governors was another key move: the formation of a dominant party, described in Chapter 8. By 2002, a new United Russia party was founded that included not only core Putin supporters, but former opponents like Moscow Mayor Luzhkov acting on the old maxim 'if you can't beat 'em, join 'em'. Governors soon rushed to join the party, which served a crucial purpose of helping bind elites to the regime. With the 2007–08 election cycle, credible reports emerged that the Kremlin was effectively directing even the financing of *opposition* parties, telling specific oligarchs which opposition or systemic parties they should fund (Morar' 2007). Of course, it hardly goes without saying that close Putin network associates have been in firm control of the 'force agencies' throughout his period in power. Even there, though, he has kept them divided in ways that would seem to ensure that no one figure could orchestrate a major challenge by himself even if such an unlikely idea happened to enter into his head, as Chapter 9 describes.

Finally, and perhaps even most importantly, Putin also learned from his rise to power that one of the surest ways to navigate a succession crisis and more generally to stay in power is to maintain popular support. Yeltsin lost public support during his time in office, incentivizing major networks in his power pyramid to break with him and form opposition coalitions, while Putin won popular support and thereby had a much easier time putting the coalition back together and incorporating new allies. Indeed, if a leader is genuinely popular, then calls by opposition leaders for 'democracy' lose their sting and hence their attractiveness since the opposition would likely lose even if democracy were granted. As we have already established, powerful patronalistic networks do not want to back the losing side of a power struggle, even if they may agree with its ideas. Furthermore, when a country's chief patron wields popular support, it is harder to rally people to the streets in opposition and less costly for the regime to counter-mobilize or suppress, as Chapter 13 makes clear. And a truly popular president like Putin – one with demonstrated 'political coattails' – can alter balances of potential electoral power by his mere verbal backing, as when he sent his associate Dmitry Medvedev's standing in presidential ratings soaring when endorsing him to succeed him as president in the 2007–08 election cycle.

The Kremlin has thus paid a great deal of attention to Putin's public standing at the same time that it has sought to narrow the channels through which opposition could translate into regime vulnerability. This phenomenon appears in many of the chapters in this volume, explaining Putin's attention to national identity construction (Chapter 4), his decision to undertake military action (Chapters 4, 11, and 15), his performative masculinity (Chapter 5), his attention to the economy (Chapter 6), his regime's nuanced strategy for staying in power (Chapter 9), the way he has manipulated the formal institutions of democracy (Chapter 8), and the challenges he has faced from political protesters (Chapter 13).

Dilemmas of governance facing Putin

These lessons that Putin learned from his rocky rise to power and the actions he took in response, however, are fraught with dilemmas, and these are a constant source of dynamism in the regime (Petrov, Lipman, and Hale 2014). On one hand, popularity has been the crucial underpinning of stability in the system he established, enabling him to rise to power in the first place and also to move in and out of the presidency while still maintaining control. The best way to be popular is to give people what they want, and not to give them what they explicitly do not want. This does not necessarily require governing effectively and democratically; instead, the key is simply to appear to do so in the eyes of the public.

On the other hand, even creating the appearance of governing effectively and democratically can have the side effect of creating institutions and practices that can limit the discretion of the ruler and possibly even produce challenges to their hold on power. There is always the risk that fake opposition political parties intended to create the illusion of democratic competition, for example, could 'come to life' and become real opposition, or at least start to advance interests distinct from the Kremlin's own. Many of Putin's actions in office can be understood as his wrestling with just such dilemmas. This can involve attempts to strengthen certain institutions and constitutional regularities at the same time as others are weakened in favour of the flexibility that working through personal connections and individualized rewards and punishments can bring. Richard Sakwa has characterized this combination of the formal and informal institutional realms as Russia's 'dual state' (Sakwa 2010).

Putin's appeal

Indeed, as several chapters in this volume show, along with all of the moves discussed above to stifle political competition and negate potential sources of opposition, Putin and his supporters presided over a number of positive changes in the way average Russians live – at least, prior to throwing much of this away initially in 2014 and then even more decisively in 2022 by invading Ukraine. First and foremost is the rapid economic growth of the 2000s, which proved a major boon to many Russians throughout the country, even though a wealthy few benefited disproportionately (Chapters 6, 7, and 12). Research has consistently shown that Putin has benefited politically from this economic progress (McAllister and White 2008). Research has also found that Putin's appeal, as well as resistance to his rule, has fascinating societal roots in communist and even pre-communist history (Chapter 3).

In part, Putin was lucky that his early years in power largely coincided with a surge in world oil prices, and he also benefited from a ruble devaluation in 1998 that had led the economy to return to growth shortly before he arrived in office. While it may not have been his policies that caused the economic growth during his first years in office, it is clear that his policies did not mess things up too badly in the 2000s despite the corruption at the heart of his regime. In fact, Putin oversaw a number of economic reforms that are hard to explain through a logic of kleptocracy and that have been widely recognized as making positive contributions to economic growth (Chapter 6). These include the institution of a 13 per cent flat tax and the creation of stabilization and investment funds to manage Russia's incoming oil wealth, funds that arguably helped Russia weather the 2008–09 global financial crisis relatively successfully. His regime has also found ways to perform economically despite Western economic sanctions since 2014. His longtime central bank chief, Elvira Nabiullina, was named best central bank governor of 2015 by *Euromoney*, reflecting the strong performance of the Central Bank of Russia despite its corrupt surroundings and growing economic isolation.

Putin's public appeal has not been limited to economic performance, however, as was made clear when his popularity did not collapse after the period of rapid growth ended in the major economic contraction of 2009. From the very beginning, Putin's most fundamental source of support has been his image as an in-command, dynamic leader, something that has historically been much more important than where he has actually been leading the country. His surge in popularity in 1999 reflected a nearly euphoric sense that Russia was finally getting a take-charge, tough-talking, evidently competent, can-do leader determined to end what seemed to be Russia's ongoing decline and collapse after decades (in their view) of a doddering Leonid Brezhnev, a bumbling Mikhail Gorbachev, and an erratic, ill, or drunk Boris Yeltsin who were widely seen as better at destroying the USSR than building anything new in Russia. Moreover, Putin is widely associated in citizens' eyes with broad policy orientations that have at least plurality support in Russia, including favouring a deepening of market reform over returning to socialism (Colton and Hale 2014).

Putin did, though, shift his strategy for securing legitimacy after his support seemed to be slipping and the economy slowed in the early 2010s. In 2012, in the wake of the largest opposition protests his regime had yet seen, the Kremlin came newly to emphasize 'traditional values' as part of what is best described as an aggressive, illiberal 'imperial nation-building' project centred on Putin as the fatherly 'leader of the nation' (Chapters 4, 5). This shift, which experts frequently call the Kremlin's 'conservative turn', tapped into substantial public support for expanding Russian influence and territory. It soon produced the 2014 annexation of Crimea, a wildly popular move that sent the Russian president's approval ratings skyward. Scholars now debate whether the 2022 full-on invasion of Ukraine has had a similar effect. Many polls indicate overwhelming public support for both the war and Putin. But some analysts suspect many Russians are dissembling and find evidence that the invasion has instead caused anxiety and negative emotions to spike, dividing society between a segment of hardline imperialist or neo-Soviet warriors and a population either deceived by the regime's propaganda barrage or cowed into submission by its powerful repressive machinery (Chapter 15).

The Kremlin's work in the realm of ideas, and its efforts accordingly to claim legitimacy, are by no means divorced from the patronal nature of Russian politics. In fact, the Kremlin actually works through different oligarchs or state-based patrons who fund and curate their own 'ideological ecosystems' that typically include everything from idea-generating scholars or philosophers to clubs, institutions, publishing houses, and media outlets that disseminate their ideas (Laruelle 2017). For example, former state railroads chief and longtime Putin friend Vladimir Yakunin and oligarch Konstantin Malofeev support such ecosystems promoting ideas related to religious Orthodox conservatism or great-Russian imperialism. There are both conservative and liberal ecosystems in the Kremlin's realm, and they frequently espouse visions that compete with or even contradict each other. This suits the Kremlin just fine, since it can pick and choose from the ideas that this competition generates depending on the situation it faces. The conservative turn, therefore, mainly reflected a new empowerment of one set of ideational entrepreneurs, with media and other Kremlin supporters drawing on them more frequently to justify Russian government actions at home and abroad.

Putin's strong-hand rule

To be sure, Putin's deadly 2022 Ukraine gambit also brought a massive crackdown on opposition at home, bringing repression to levels unprecedented since the Soviet era (Chapters 9 and 13). For almost two decades, Putin had practised a much more nuanced form of political domination, recognizing that he did not have to ban opponents in order to defeat them. Instead, more subtle mechanisms usually sufficed, instruments that are less costly or risky than attempting to establish a Soviet-style totalitarian state or practising ballot-box fraud on a truly massive scale. With economic actors (including media owners) understanding that their fortunes hinged upon not 'crossing' Putin and his allies politically, it could be very hard for opposition politicians to raise money, get media coverage, or even find premises in which to campaign – even without any explicit repressive orders from the top. Similarly, state employees could be mobilized to vote for the regime by communicating to them that their firms might be in peril if the precincts in which they were located did not produce strong votes for the desired candidates or parties (Frye, Reuter, and Szakonyi 2014).

Buttressing such practices, the most influential media skilfully delivered messaging that the Kremlin calculated worked in its political favour, led by the trio of state-controlled national television channels on which the large majority of potential voters continue to rely for political information: First Channel, Rossiya-1, and NTV (Chapter 9). With television so dominant, feisty independent sources of information like the investigative weekly magazine *The New Times* or the free-wheeling *Ekho Moskvy* radio station could be tolerated even when they reported on egregious regime corruption or voiced harsh opposition narratives, as long as they remained in certain 'ghettos' where funding was scarce and the effective audience minimal. Since most Russians (like ordinary people everywhere) gravitate to the kind of highly professional and attractive entertainment programming that can be found in Russia primarily on the country's main television channels, they are likely to stay there for their news as well. News shows just had to retain a good ear in spinning events in ways that both amplified pro-Kremlin narratives and resonated with the public. Some social scientists have branded this style of rule 'informational autocracy' because of its reliance on manipulating information (Guriev and Treisman 2019).

In fact, until the 2020s, Russia's leadership saw little need to institute the most brutal forms of repression found elsewhere in the world. Even today, unlike China and Saudi Arabia, prisoners (not to mention political ones) are generally not executed, though they can be badly mistreated or even tortured. And for the Putin regime's first decade in office, the number of political prisoners was very low, rising significantly primarily since 2012 (Gel'man 2015). Only the most recent wave of repressions, those coming along with the 2022 full-scale invasion of Ukraine, compares with the scale of the crackdowns in Turkey after the anti-Erdoğan coup attempt in July 2016 or in Egypt following the Arab uprising and the ouster of President Mohamed Morsi in July 2013, not to mention routine repression in China and many other longstanding hard-core autocracies.

Moreover, when it comes to elections, Putin's regime has actually taken care *not* to strip them of all meaning by eliminating every form of opposition. Instead, some kind of actual alternative has been on the ballot in almost every major national election in Russia, including at least a candidate from the Communist Party, which while having reached a comfortable arrangement with the Kremlin that retains its status as the second largest bloc in parliament, does represent something genuinely different for which people can vote. Even after the events of 2022, the pro-democracy and fiercely anti-Putin (and anti-invasion) Yabloko Party has avoided being banned, something the Kremlin feels it can allow due to the party's low public appeal. This does not mean the Kremlin allows every opposition candidate on the ballot who goes for it. Far from it. The 'weeding out' of candidates through various judicial decisions and technicalities remains an important tactic for shaping electoral outcomes, as Chapter 9 discusses. For example, would-be contender Alexei Navalny was kept off the presidential ballot of March 2018 after the authorities hung clearly trumped-up criminal convictions on him (they ultimately jailed him in 2021). What all this means is that Russian voters are almost always given the *appearance* of at least *some* choice. And while independent (especially Western) media frequently report credible instances of fraud in Russian elections (perhaps most egregiously turnout figures over 100 per cent in occasional localities!), in reality the scale has rarely been high enough to dramatically shape electoral outcomes. The really important manipulation occurs before people ever get to the ballot box.

So tight has this system become that Putin has felt emboldened to embark on radical policies that did not have clear prior popular support and that would bring his own population economic decline and (for some) even death. Thus, while one December 2021 poll found only 8 per cent thought Russian troops should be sent to fight in Ukraine (Hale et al. 2022), Putin was clearly confident he could use his propaganda machine to sell the population a false narrative justifying the war based on a particular vision of Russian identity, and ramp up his repressive apparatus to manage any discontent.

While the scale of this move was a shock to many, it did not come out of the blue. Russia had grown more assertive in international relations throughout the Putin era, after an initial period of surprisingly extensive cooperation with the United States and its Western allies (Chapters 15 and 16). With 2014, however, Russia increasingly challenged Western (especially American) dominance. It did so not only by invading Ukraine, but also in such actions as sending troops to Syria, developing a military presence in Africa, supporting the regime in Venezuela, and actively attempting to influence election outcomes everywhere from the United States to France. Importantly, this was not always the work of the Foreign Ministry or even Russia's extensive intelligence services. As can be expected from high-patronalism countries, the Kremlin also exercised influence informally through some of the political–economic networks in its coalition. This has included the networks of Yevgeny Prigozhin and his Wagner Group, Chechen strongman Ramzan Kadyrov, as well as nationalist oligarchs like Konstantin Malofeev, all of whom are playing very direct roles in Russia's invasion of Ukraine (Chapters 11, 15). This did not always end well for the networks involved. In 2023, long-standing tensions between Prigozhin and top military brass led the former to launch an armed 'march on Moscow', to abort it after Putin labeled this treasonous, and then to die in a mysterious plane crash several weeks later.

Conclusion

Major debates remain about how firmly Putin controls the machinery of Russia's state. Some, like Timothy Frye (2021), characterize Russia's leader as a 'weak strongman', someone who faces significant constraints from public opinion and the different political coalitions upon which his power depends. Others see an extraordinarily powerful leader who has shaped the worldviews not only of key Russian elites, but also of much of the population to such an extent that they can hardly conceive of a Russia without him (Sharafutdinova 2020; Taylor 2018).

What we can conclude now, though, is that Putin, building on a foundation set in the Yeltsin era, has managed to establish a tight single-pyramid system in Russia and has now used it to pursue an aggressive course of territorial expansion that would negate the very existence and statehood of one of Europe's largest peoples, Ukrainians. At the same time, what we see today is surely not a 'consolidated' system of government. Instead, one of the most important lessons of post-Soviet Russian politics is that its system has constantly changed. Change, in fact, is arguably an essential feature of the system as Russia's chief patrons constantly recalibrate both institutions and ideas in order to hold their coalitions of rivalrous political-economic networks together.

They are very creative in performing such recalibrations, and they do not always move in the same direction. For example, when United Russia's popularity was at a peak in 2007, the Kremlin replaced the district-based first-past-the-post component of elections for the State Duma with party-list voting that would weaken the regional political machines it was still undercutting at the time. But after United Russia's popularity dropped in the early 2010s, the Kremlin restored district-based elections so that the Kremlin could compensate for a lower United Russia party-list result with pro-Kremlin candidates whose district victories could be engineered by regional political machines that were now more firmly under Putin's control. Putin's own ceding of the presidency to Medvedev during the tandem period can also be understood as a successful regime recalibration; it was during this time that the balance of people thinking the country was going in the right as opposed to the wrong direction reached its peak, one that was not surpassed even with the annexation of Crimea (Colton 2017, 14–15). Between 2012 and 2014, the regime recalibrated with its 2012 'conservative turn', its 2014 occupation of parts of Ukraine, and a sharp uptick in repression. And in February 2022, of course, Putin initiated the most far-reaching recalibration of all, launching his all-out invasion of Ukraine and putting his repressive apparatus on steroids. Russia has continually surprised us, and a careful look back at Russian political history should lead us to be open-eyed about the possibility that Russian politics may again take us in directions that at the moment may seem unthinkable.

At the same time, an understanding of the network dynamics that lie at the heart of Russian's single-pyramid system should give us some tools for making the unthinkable at least a little bit more thinkable. For the near future, it suggests we need to keep a careful eye on the politics of succession, and to expect Putin as he ages and faces at least the formality of elections to pay particularly close attention to public opinion as a key resource influencing how much control he will be able to exercise over the succession process. We should also expect him to be highly concerned about the relationship among different networks that are now integrated into his political system but could, with possible succession looming, quickly go their own ways should their patron's political future suddenly seem in doubt. How the war plays out could powerfully influence all of these factors. These are likely to be among the crucial questions for students of Russian politics in the years ahead.

Questions for discussion

1 What role do networks play in contemporary Russian politics?
2 What are the main sources of Vladimir Putin's power?
3 How powerful is Putin; can he essentially do anything he wants?
4 Does public opinion matter in an authoritarian system like Russia's?
5 How likely is Russia's current political system to change?

Recommended reading

Frye, Timothy. 2021. *Weak Strongman: The Limits of Power in Putin's Russia*. Princeton: Princeton University Press.

Hale, Henry E. 2015. *Patronal Politics: Eurasian Regime Dynamics in Comparative Perspective*. New York, NY: Cambridge University Press.

Magyar, Bálint, and Bálint Madlovics. 2021. *The Anatomy of Post-Communist Regimes: A Conceptual Framework*. Budapest: Central European University Press.

Sharafutdinova, Gulnaz. 2020. *The Red Mirror: Putin's Leadership and Russia's Insecure Identity*. Oxford, New York: Oxford University Press.

Taylor, Brian D. 2018. *The Code of Putinism*. New York: Oxford University Press.

2

Russian and Soviet History

Kristy Ironside

The emergence of socialism and the creation of the Soviet Union in the wake of the collapse of the Russian Empire were, in many ways, surprising historical developments. The Russian Empire was far from the first place Karl Marx envisioned a revolution taking place. Tsarist autocracy, in which the monarch's right to rule with unquestioned authority was presented as God-given, resembled medieval feudalism more so than a modern 'bourgeois' political system. The same could be said for its economy. The Russian Empire started its industrial capitalist phase late, in the last decades of the nineteenth century and over one hundred years later than much of Western Europe: as a result, its working class was small, though militant. The vast majority of its Slavic population consisted of illiterate and deeply religious peasants only recently emancipated from serfdom. Much of the non-Slavic parts of the empire, gained over the course of roughly 300 years of imperial conquest, was also economically underdeveloped and had a colonial relationship to the centre. In sum, Russia's working class was far from a mass of conscious proletarians ready to rise up and cast off their chains.

Yet, what it lacked in formal requirements for revolution, it made up for in sentiment: Late imperial Russia was a hotbed of political discontent, from liberals who wanted representative government, to populists who saw the future in Russia's collective peasant ways, to Marxists who thought that, with the right 'vanguard' in charge, they could spur a socialist revolution in their lifetimes. The most radical strain of Russia's Marxists, the Bolsheviks, did just that when they seized power on behalf of the working class in October 1917. They would spend virtually the rest of the twentieth century trying to reconcile the contradiction of jumpstarting a 'world-historical' process that was supposed to emerge organically from the crises of capitalism but began in 'backward' Russia largely at the instigation of its radical intelligentsia. It would not be the only contradiction they had not resolved by the time the Soviet Union, itself, collapsed.

Revolutionary Russia

Imperial Russia underwent sweeping changes beginning with Tsar Alexander II's Great Reforms of the 1860s–70s, which put an end to serfdom, modernized the legal, military and educational systems, and created the *zemstva*, local semi-representative governmental bodies. These changes, intended to modernize the country and raise its prestige in the wake of its humiliating loss in the Crimean War, caused Russia's feudal structures to rapidly break down, bringing on increased social mobility and urbanization. A growing chorus of voices called for greater popular participation in Russia's political system, but Alexander II refused to cede his autocratic prerogatives. Revolutionary political movements emerged, many of them populated by the beneficiaries of his reforms. Alexander II did not take challenges to his authority lightly, arresting, jailing, exiling and executing his critics. Toward the end of his life, he backtracked on some of his liberal reforms, including clamping down on universities, which he believed had become hotbeds of radicalism.

In 1881, Alexander II was assassinated by populist terrorists including the future Soviet leader Vladimir Lenin's older brother, who was hanged for his part in the plot. Following the murder of his father, Tsar Alexander III believed his spiritual mission was to bolster autocracy, which he portrayed as a uniquely Russian institution supported by a majority of the population. Alexander III oversaw the dramatic expansion of Russia's secret police, which rooted out the country's revolutionaries. Repression and surveillance had the effect of pushing their political activity underground and abroad. At the same time, capitalist industrialization began in earnest under Alexander III's rule, leading to the creation of a more robust working class and a growing audience for Marxist and other radical ideas, which remained in circulation despite stiffened censorship.

Russia's last Tsar, Nicholas II, would prove even less willing to embrace the country's changing circumstances. Like his father, he believed autocracy was his sacred inheritance. He took hesitant steps in the direction of representative government only grudgingly, in response to widespread unrest in the wake of Russia's failed 1904 war against Japan, as well as the infamous 'Bloody Sunday' incident in January 1905 when he authorized gendarmes to fire on a peaceful workers' march to the Winter Palace to issue him a petition. During the October 1905 revolution, Nicholas granted Russia's first parliament, the Duma, and the following year, Russia's 'Fundamental Laws,' or first constitution, granted limited civil rights. However, Nicholas proved resistant to working with the Duma, repeatedly dissolving it and refusing to consent to even limited restrictions on his power.

Russia's political unrest boiled over during World War I. Nicholas joined the conflict on the side of the Allies, believing it would be a short and glorious war, but the Russian war effort turned out to be disastrous. The Tsar borrowed heavily abroad and printed rubles to pay for the war, sinking the country into debt and inflation. Living standards declined. Nicholas' solution to humiliating military defeats was to appoint himself commander of the armed forces, making him responsible for its failures. His German-born wife Alexandra also fell under the spell of the charismatic holy man Grigory Rasputin, whom many believed exerted undue influence over the Tsarina and indirectly over the Tsar. Even many members of Russia's nobility withdrew their support for the royal couple. By the fateful year of 1917, many within Russian society had come to seriously doubt not only Nicholas' competence, but the system over which he presided.

On 23 February (8 March N.S.), bread riots in the streets of Petrograd (contemporary Saint Petersburg), evolved into mass protests and city-wide strikes. Nicholas responded by dissolving the Duma and ordering troops to fire on the protesters; however, discontent with his leadership had grown so much that, before long, both the Duma and much of the military were in open rebellion against him. Amid calls for his abdication, Nicholas eventually agreed to step down and hand over power to his son, Alexei, but the latter was young and in poor health. Nicholas then offered the throne to his brother, the Grand Duke Michael, who refused. Although the precise status of the monarchy in Russia remained unsettled – some pushed for a constitutional monarchy – Russian autocracy had finally come to an end.

Russia's political future remained unclear after the February Revolution. Two centres of power emerged in its wake. First, there was the Provisional Government, an outgrowth of a coalition of reform-minded Duma deputies that was supposed to govern until an elected Constituent Assembly determined Russia's new political system. The Provisional Government was recognized abroad and by the Allies, but it was unpopular at home, in large part because it committed to staying in the war and fighting toward the Tsar's original war aims. Second, there was the Petrograd Soviet, an institution that was first established by Russia's Marxists to represent workers' interests and to steer strike activity. The Petrograd Soviet held more de facto power on the ground in the city and enjoyed substantial support from the military.

Russia's Marxists were enthused by the February Revolution, seeing it as an important milestone on the way to the 'real' socialist revolution, but they were divided on how to proceed. Following a 1903 split in the Russian Social Democratic Labour Party, Russia's precursor to the Communist Party, they were divided into more moderate Menshevik (minority) and more hardline Bolsheviks (majority) wings. The Petrograd Soviet was initially dominated by Mensheviks, who advocated for cooperation with the Provisional Government and adopted a wait-and-see approach; the Bolsheviks, led by Lenin, refused to accept its legitimacy and pushed for an immediate uprising against it.

That uprising occurred on the night of 24 October (7 November N.S.), 1917. By then, Lenin had become convinced that the Provisional Government was tottering and, if the Bolsheviks did not seize power now, they would miss their chance. That evening, the Petrograd Soviet's Military-Revolutionary Committee demanded the surrender of the Provisional Government, whose ministers were inside the Winter Palace on the banks of the Neva River. The battleship Aurora, under Bolshevik orders, fired a warning shot and, a few hours later, Red Guards stormed into the Palace and arrested the Provisional Government. Although Russia's October Revolution was later portrayed in Soviet films and other propaganda as a shoot-out between the Reds and Palace guards and as a triumphant seizure of power by the masses, it was in fact relatively quick, bloodless, and involved very few workers. Some historians have argued it is better categorized as a coup d'état (e.g. Pipes 1990). Others have emphasized that the Bolsheviks rode to power on a wave of social and economic grievances (e.g. Suny 1983).

Civil war, war communism, and the new economic policy

At a meeting of the Second All-Russian Congress of Soviets in the early hours of the morning of 25 October, 'all power to the soviets', a Bolshevik slogan between February and October, was declared accomplished. But it was by no means clear that the Bolsheviks were in charge. Elections to the Constituent Assembly were still scheduled to proceed, and these took place in November. The Bolsheviks were confident they would do well in these elections, and that electoral victory would legitimize their actions in October. To their dismay, they came in second behind the Socialist Revolutionaries, a political party that grew out of Russia's nineteenth-century populist movement. When the first session of the Constituent Assembly took place in January 1918, the Socialist Revolutionaries refused to acknowledge the Soviet government; in return, Lenin locked them out of the palace where the meeting took place and signed a decree dissolving the Constituent Assembly.

The Bolsheviks' aggressive and uncompromising tactics in early 1918 put them on a collision course with the country's rival political forces. The tipping point came when they pulled Russia out of World War I. The Provisional Government remained committed to staying in the war, while the Mensheviks wanted to stay in until they could pull out on more favourable terms in a strategy of 'revolutionary defensism'. Lenin, by contrast, had long condemned Russia's participation in this 'imperialist' war and wanted out of the conflict as soon as possible on any terms, even if that entailed losses. The Bolshevik (majority) wings unilaterally reached out to Germany, and, in the treaty of Brest-Litovsk of March 1918, accepted major territorial concessions in the country's western borderlands in exchange for the cessation of hostilities. Their domestic enemies, as well as Russia's international allies, were outraged, accusing Lenin of being a German agent – amid Russia's political turmoil the previous year, and seeking to turn it to its advantage, Germany had helped Lenin, then hiding from authorities abroad, travel back to Russia on an armoured train.

Over the next four years, Russia was embroiled in a deadly and destructive Civil War. The main conflict, but by no means the only one, was between the Reds, the Bolsheviks and their allies, and the Whites, a loose coalition of anti-Bolshevik forces including monarchists, liberals, and other types of socialists. Other political groupings, such as anarchists, peasant Greens, and the Black Hundreds, an ultra-rightwing nationalist movement, also joined the fray. During the Civil War and under the leadership of Leon Trotsky, the Red Army grew to around five million men. The Whites' forces, led by former imperial generals, were more decentralized by comparison. Seeking to oust the Bolsheviks and potentially capitalize on Russia's political turmoil, the Allies intervened in the Russian Civil War and sent in their own troops.

Both the Reds and the Whites, as well as the Allies, used extreme violence against their opponents, including executions, internment in concentration camps, and assassinations. Lenin himself was shot in a failed assassination attempt by a Socialist Revolutionary in 1918. Among the Communists, the use of 'Red Terror' soon led to disillusion and unrest in their ranks: in March 1921, sailors at the Kronstadt naval base in northwestern Russia mutinied against the Soviet government and issued a list of political demands, including freedom of speech and the release of political prisoners. Failing to negotiate with the mutineers, the Bolsheviks put down the uprising by force, killing thousands in the city.

The Kronstadt incident prompted a reevaluation of the Bolsheviks' heavy-handed methods, which many felt strayed far from their core ethical principles; moreover, by then, it was becoming clear that the scales were tipping in their favour in the Civil War. By 1921, the Allies were pulling out their troops and the Whites' main forces were in retreat. Military skirmishes continued over the next five years, especially in the Far East, but the Reds had emerged victorious by the end of 1922. It was a pyrrhic victory: the Civil War resulted in millions of deaths, a huge wave of emigration, the near collapse of the economy, and Soviet Russia's international political isolation.

During the Civil War, the Bolsheviks forged ahead with their communist plans which had, as Sheila Fitzpatrick notes, 'a wildly impractical and utopian streak', despite their conviction that Marxism was 'scientific' and thus 'immune from utopianism' (Fitzpatrick, 2017, 84). On the economic front, that included expropriating capitalist businessmen, nationalizing industry, repudiating the Tsar's foreign debt, and introducing experimental economic policies like the abolition of money, as well as the elimination of private trade. In the countryside, they resorted to violent confiscatory measures to extract what they needed from the peasantry. These policies proved disastrous: they lost access to foreign credit, workers walked off the job, and peasants refused to cooperate with the new authorities. Industrial and agricultural production plummeted.

Already before the Civil War was over, the Bolsheviks began to pull back on the policies associated with 'War Communism' and, in 1921, introduced the New Economic Policy (NEP). That entailed a mixed public–private system in which socialist economic forms like state enterprises, as well as top-down planning methods, coexisted with decentralized private small-scale enterprises and market mechanisms. Rationing, which they had resorted to during the war and which some saw as a move in the direction of communism, came to an end, and the abolition of money was postponed. The government also eased off on its aggressive methods in the countryside. The NEP was a pragmatic move designed to give the Bolsheviks breathing space, build an 'alliance' (*smychka*) between peasants and workers, and better provision Russia's working class while it developed its lacking proletarian consciousness.

A union of republics on the ruins of empire

Though they had long criticized the Tsarist imperial system for oppressing ethnic minorities, with Lenin going so far as to call the Russian Empire a 'prison house of nations', the Bolsheviks did not break up the Russian Empire after there was no longer a Russian emperor. Instead, as it became clear that revolutions were not breaking out across the world in the wake of their own as expected, and as the policy of 'national self-determination' was rolled out in Europe after World War I, creating nation states from the former Austro-Hungarian and Ottoman empires, they turned to defending what the October Revolution had 'achieved' in the former Russian Empire.

That meant holding this territory together as a federal structure composed of national republics, hence the title 'Union of Soviet Socialist Republics' or USSR (*Soiuz sovetskikh sotsialisticheskikh respublik, SSSR*). These republics would be 'national in form, socialist in content'. Each republic was named after the 'titular nationality' that lived there, that is, the dominant ethnic group in that region. The Soviet Union was officially created in December 1922 by the Russian, Ukrainian, Belarusian, and Transcaucasian (Georgia, Armenia, and Azerbaijan combined) republics. More republics were added through the 1930s. Each republic had its own government that mirrored the All-Union 'commissariats' (renamed ministries in 1946) for domestic matters like health and education, while foreign affairs, defence, and other top-level functions of state were governed at the All-Union level. Below the level of the republic, special administrative statuses were granted to smaller ethnic minorities in the form of autonomous regions, *okrugs*, and *krais*. Technically, each republic was equal; in reality, as the largest republic, and as the one that contained the Soviet capital, which was moved to Moscow in 1918, the Russian Soviet Socialist Federative Republic (RSFSR), remained at the top of an implicit hierarchy.

As communist internationalists, the Bolsheviks scorned Russian nationalism and put little stock in 'nation' as a source of identity. Many Bolsheviks were themselves ethnic minorities in the Russian Empire, notably Joseph Stalin (born Iosif Dzhugashvili), a Georgian revolutionary who became the Communist Party's first Commissar of Nationalities in 1918 and held the position until just after the USSR was created. Stalin was considered an important authority on this subject. In an early treatise, he argued that a nation was 'not merely a historical category but a historical category belonging to a definite epoch, the epoch of rising capitalism', and that, during this era, national struggle was 'struggle of the bourgeois classes among themselves' (Stalin 1913). Nationalism disguised class conflict, in other words, and it was a phenomenon that would be superseded after the revolution.

The Bolsheviks nevertheless grasped the power of national identity for spreading revolution to non-Russian peoples who had been oppressed in the Tsarist Empire. Some Soviet leaders argued for instrumentalizing national versions of socialism, especially in areas in which the Bolsheviks had a weaker grip on power, such as Georgia, which formed a short-lived democratic republic in 1918 that was ruled by Mensheviks, and which was invaded and quashed by the Red Army in 1921. Lenin also argued against what he saw as a problematic holdover from the Tsarist period, that is, 'Great Russian chauvinism', or the belief that ethnic Russians were culturally superior and thus should dominate political life (Lenin 1922).

In order to spread the revolution to non-Russian areas, during the 1920s, the Bolsheviks implemented a policy of 'indigenization' (*korenizatsiia*, literally 'taking root'), entailing promoting ethnic minorities into leadership positions in local Party organizations, governments, enterprises, and other institutions. These individuals were often brought to Moscow for training and were given priority access to university education. Terry Martin argues that in these years the Bolsheviks implemented something akin to the 'affirmative action' programme in the United States (Martin 2001). Schools taught in local languages, non-Russian languages were standardized, and literature, art, and culture in those languages were promoted. This was not necessarily done out of respect for non-Russian cultures. According to the Bolsheviks, ethnic minorities, who had been left to linger in poverty and ignorance by the Tsars, needed to go through a national phase within the confines of the Soviet Union, before they discarded their national identities and became internationalist proletarians.

The rise of Stalin

The 1920s were difficult and uncertain times in Soviet Russia. Living standards remained low, and many workers were aggrieved that 'NEPmen', petty entrepreneurs who took advantage of opportunities for private trade, were still profiting long after the capitalists had supposedly been overthrown. Homeless children roamed the streets, many of them war orphans. Agriculture rebounded, but peasants remained deeply suspicious of the Bolsheviks, who had come to power promising them land reform and quickly reneged on their promises. Russian peasants, who remained deeply committed to their faith, also chafed at the Bolsheviks' attacks on the Russian Orthodox Church and their policy of official atheism.

The Bolsheviks were divided on how long the NEP should last. This prompted increasingly bitter in-fighting within the Communist Party. All agreed that industrialization was the Soviet Union's top priority, but the Party cleaved into 'Left' and 'Right' oppositions that fought bitterly over how to accomplish it: The Left Opposition, led by Trotsky, argued for rapid industrialization fuelled by squeezing the peasantry for more grain to sell on the international market for hard currency. The Right Opposition, led by Nikolai Bukharin, one of the Party's economic experts and one of its favourites, argued for a more gradual and moderate approach and for strengthening the alliance with the peasantry.

These factional disputes were not just about industrialization: After a series of strokes, in January 1924, Vladimir Lenin died, sparking a succession crisis. Before his death, Lenin wrote a 'Testament' hoping to avoid this outcome; however, in it, he criticized virtually all the main contenders for the job (Lenin 1923). That included Trotsky, whom many assumed was his logical replacement, and the General Secretary of the Communist Party, Joseph Stalin. By then, a fierce power struggle already existed between Stalin and Trotsky. Stalin skillfully manoeuvred this conflict and built up an entourage of loyal supporters along the way. Although Trotsky was widely seen as a brilliant orator, intellectual and theorist, and enjoyed international prominence, he was less skilled at, and less concerned about, matters of domestic governance; by contrast, Stalin was popular among the Party's rank-and-file, newcomers, and less intellectual types, and was seen by many as a political moderate. Unlike Trotsky, who often made bombastic statements and held tenaciously to his opinions, Stalin's views were harder to pin down and he often switched sides (Fitzpatrick 2015).

In the mid-to-late 1920s, the Party attempted to put an end to these factional disputes, which were seen as an unproductive distraction. An alliance against Trotsky, whom many believed had amassed too much power, had emerged by 1927; however, before too long, members of that alliance, namely Grigory Zinoviev and Lev Kamenev, began to worry that it was, in fact, Stalin who was building up too much power. They, along with Trotsky, moved against Stalin. It did not work: Trotsky, Zinoviev, and Kamenev's factionalism was condemned, and all three were kicked out of the Party. Zinoviev and Kamenev recanted and were eventually allowed back in; Trotsky refused to do so and was sent into exile. Stalin did not forget his grudge against Trotsky. He organized multiple attempts to assassinate him, succeeding in 1940.

Technically, Stalin remained merely General Secretary of the Communist Party, not the Soviet Union's official head of state – that was Mikhail Kalinin, a long-time Bolshevik of peasant origins, who was head of the All-Russian Central Executive Committee, renamed the Supreme Soviet in 1936, the country's highest governmental body. However, by the time of Stalin's fiftieth birthday in 1929, there was little question that he was in charge: That year, massive celebrations were held in his honour across the country. The cult of Stalin, which expanded upon an existing cult of Lenin, and saw Stalin's image plastered virtually everywhere in Soviet society, was by then in full swing. Stalin feigned a lack of interest in it, but as Jan Plamper has shown, he, in fact, actively participated in his cult's construction (Plamper 2012).

Stalin preferred to rule via informal channels of power. He instrumentalized the Politburo, a special emergency committee within the Party dealing with issues that were considered too urgent to go through the formal process of being considered by the Central Committee, the Party's executive leadership (Khlevniuk 2008). The Politburo's members cycled in and out – in the Stalin years, depending on who was in his good graces at any given time – and its decrees had the force of law. This predominance of the Party over the government, and this reliance upon informal over formal channels of power, established a precedent in Soviet political life that would last until Mikhail Gorbachev's reforms of the late 1980s.

Industrialization and collectivization

Back in the mid-1920s, Stalin was on the 'Right' of the industrialization debate, but after forcing out Trotsky, he veered hard to the 'Left'. In 1928, the NEP was dismantled and replaced by a command economy, entailing top-down plans and steep production quotas. Thereafter, economic life was organized according to five-year plans that extended to all branches of the economy; in total, there would be thirteen five-year plans during the Soviet Union's existence. The first five-year plan (1928–32) envisioned the rapid industrialization of the Soviet economy and the build-up of heavy industry such as mining, metallurgy, and machine building.

During the NEP there was a great deal of unemployment; the first five-year plan, by contrast, created a massive labour shortage. Millions of Soviet citizens, including peasants and women, became industrial workers and moved into urban areas at this time. Wholly new workers' settlements and cities were built, such as Magnitogorsk, which was organized around the region's iron and steel works. Stalinist authorities cast aside their earlier communist notions about egalitarianism and radically differentiated wages, rewarding those in the so-called 'leading industries', and they encouraged 'socialist competition' and Stakhanovism (hyper-productive labour) to incentivize productivity. Soviet workers were allegedly so enthusiastic about the first five-year plan that it was completed in only a little over four years.

Rapid industrialization necessitated obtaining a firm grip on the food supply, both to feed these new workers and to export grain to pay for needed industrial technology purchased in hard currency abroad, since the Soviet ruble was nonconvertible. Soviet authorities thus took a more uncompromising approach in their dealings with the peasantry at the end of the decade. They had long suspected that peasants deliberately withheld deliveries from them, seeking to negotiate higher prices or divert their products to what was left of the private sector. After a disappointing harvest in 1928, which forced the government to bring back rationing, the Soviet government turned to the 'Urals-Siberian method', named after the region in which it was first implemented. This was a throwback to the Bolsheviks' confiscatory tactics during the Civil War, in which noncompliant peasants were subject to steep fines, confiscation, arrests and deportation.

Seeking to further restrict peasants' ability to withhold deliveries, in 1929, the Soviet government embarked upon the full-scale 'collectivization' of Soviet agriculture. That entailed expropriating peasants' personal land, tools and livestock, now to be held in common by the collective farm. Joining the collective farm was portrayed as a voluntary act but, in fact, it was largely forced upon peasants by outsiders, that is, Party members and activists. Many peasants fiercely resisted it: Collectivization seemed to them a second serfdom because it demanded their similarly forced and uncompensated labour and expropriated their land. Rather than hand over their property, many peasants intentionally destroyed it. Lynne Viola argues that, though it was portrayed as socialist construction, collectivization was 'in reality a war of cultures, a virtual civil war between state and peasantry, town and countryside' (Viola 1999, p. 3). Soviet authorities interpreted resistance to collectivization as sabotage, spurred on by insidious forces in the village like priests and 'kulaks', that is, wealthy peasants who allegedly tried to convince poor and 'middle' peasants not to join the collective farm. As a result, the state embarked on a campaign of 'dekulakization': Peasants deemed to be kulaks were arrested, expropriated, and sent to forced labour camps or to so-called 'special settlements' in distant parts of the country.

Collectivization wreaked havoc on the country's food supply and contributed to a deadly famine primarily affecting Ukraine, Kazakhstan, and southwestern Russia in the early 1930s. To the present day, historians debate whether this famine was intentional or unintentional and the extent to which national considerations were behind it. Some have argued that Ukraine was deliberately targeted, and that the 'Holodomor' (terror famine) can be considered a genocide (Conquest 1986; Naimark 2010; Graziosi 2015; Applebaum 2017). Others suggest the famine was more the product of unrealistic quotas and the Soviet state's refusal to believe the true state of the grain supply (Fitzpatrick 1999). Economic historians have pointed to grain yield trends and climactic conditions as the culprit (e.g. Wheatcroft 2018), while others have concluded that weather is not a main explanation (e.g. Naumenko 2021). In the case of Kazakhstan's 'Asharshylyk', it was also an outcome of the forced sedentarization of its nomadic population (Cameron 2018). The famine remains important to national identity in both contemporary Ukraine and Kazakhstan.

Repression and terror

Although some willingly cooperated with Soviet authorities' plans, often drawn to the opportunities for social mobility they presented, they also generated discontent and not only in the countryside. If, in the early 1920s, the Soviet government frequently attributed resistance to a lack of education or political consciousness, by the 1930s, it increasingly interpreted it as the work of its 'enemies'. The government expanded surveillance and policing of the population in the 1930s to root out perceived threats. As of 1932, all Soviet citizens were required to have a passport indicating their personal information, residence, and nationality. Major cities and regions were 'passportized', restricting travel to and legal residence in them. Collective farmers were denied passports. Police regularly conducted sweeps of major cities, rounding up and exiling people without passports, as well as so-called 'socially harmful elements', including recidivist criminals, but also a range of socially marginalized individuals (Shearer 2009).

Millions of those arrested were sentenced to hard labour. They were sent to the 'gulag', forced labour camps that dated back to the Tsarist period but were expanded by the Bolsheviks and placed under the authority of the internal security system, first the Joint State Political Directorate (*Ob"edinennoe gosudarstvennoe politicheskoe upravlenie*, OGPU), later merged into the People's Commissariat of Internal Affairs (*Narodnyi kommissariat vnutrenykh del*, NKVD) in 1934, a precursor to the Committee on State Security (*Komitet gosudarstvennoi bezopasnosti*, KGB). The Soviet government boasted of the progressive qualities of its prison system and the unique opportunities it offered to be rehabilitated (Barnes 2011). However, free forced labour was increasingly inputted into its economic plans (Khlevniuk 2013). Prisoners performed backbreaking and often dangerous labour the Soviet state struggled to convince ordinary workers to do in remote and inhospitable, but resource-rich, parts of the country like Siberia and the Far North. Living and working conditions in the camps were atrocious, and many died due to accidents, malnutrition and illness (Alexopoulos 2017). Many prisoners remained there long after their sentences were completed, subject to administrative restrictions that prevented them from going home.

By the late 1930s, the Soviet leadership was wracked by paranoia about both internal and external threats. In December 1934, Sergei Kirov, head of the Leningrad Communist Party organization, was assassinated by a lone gunman in his office. Many believed his death was the product of a conspiracy because the gunman was previously known to the security services and was able to sneak past the building's guards. Some have suggested it was Stalin who arranged for his assassination because he viewed Kirov as a threat to his leadership (Conquest [1968] 2008). No conclusive evidence supports this theory, but what can be said conclusively is that Stalin used Kirov's death to unleash a campaign of terror against the country's perceived enemies, arguing that they needed to be even more aggressively purged from Soviet life (Lenoe 2010).

In 1936, Nikolai Yezhov, who headed up the investigation into Kirov's murder, was appointed head of the NKVD and oversaw a mass campaign of arrests, imprisonment, and executions – in Russian, the 'Great Terror' is known as the *Yezhovshchina* after Yezhov. Steep quotas were set for purging enemies within the Party and in society at large. That included individuals accused of harbouring oppositionist political sentiments: many of the so-called 'Old Bolsheviks' who had participated in the October Revolution in Russia back in 1917, including Zinoviev, Kamenev, and Bukharin, were purged in show trials in which they 'confessed' under pressure to sabotage, spying, and even conspiring to kill Lenin, and were executed. Most ordinary victims of the purges were meted out summary justice on charges such as sabotage, spying, 'bourgeois nationalism', and 'anti-Soviet agitation'. In 1938, Stalin abruptly called off the Terror and purged the NKVD, including Yezhov, who was arrested in 1939 and shot the following year. The precise number of victims of Stalinist repression remains unclear but it is estimated to run into the millions (Nove 1993).

Among historians, the Stalinist 1930s have generated fierce debate about the ideological underpinnings of the system and the extent of popular participation in it. Scholars in the 'totalitarian school' of thought, some of them political scientists, viewed this period as paradigmatic, emphasizing that Soviet society was controlled and terrorized from above by a Communist Party professing an inherently illiberal and repressive ideology (e.g. Friedrich and Brzezinski 1965; Conquest [1968] 2008; Malia 1994). Their work was often inflected by the ongoing Cold War. In the 1970s and 1980s, 'revisionist' historians, some of them sympathetic to the left, sought to move away from Cold War paradigms and introduced social science concepts into the study of the Soviet system, for example, how social mobility influenced popular support (Fitzpatrick 1978; 2007). After the collapse of the Soviet Union, and with the opening up of its archives, some scholars returned to the totalitarian school's preoccupation with ideology. The 'subjectivity school' focused on the discursive power of the Stalinist system which produced true believers, as well as others who merely 'spoke Bolshevik', all of whom participated in building, as Stephen Kotkin put it, a 'Stalinist civilization' (Kotkin 1997).

The Great Patriotic War

Stalin and the Bolsheviks long believed that war was coming: The Soviet Union's 'capitalist encirclement' worried them from the 1920s onward (Davies and Harris 2014). By the mid-1930s, war seemed increasingly probable on the European continent. They thus shifted resources into weapons production and reorganized labour along military lines in anticipation of this conflict. The Soviet Union also began attacking its neighbours, allegedly to shore up its borders. In August 1939, the Soviet

Union signed a non-aggression pact with Nazi Germany, the 'Molotov-Ribbentrop Pact', named after their respective foreign ministers, which contained secret protocols that divided Central and Eastern Europe between them. In September, the Nazis invaded Poland from the west and, two weeks later, the Soviets invaded and occupied Eastern Poland. They next occupied the Baltic states. By late 1939, Stalin was increasingly convinced that Finland posed a security risk and, after demanding concessions and border adjustments, the Soviet Union attacked it. The 'Winter War' lasted for all of three months but proved extremely costly: The Soviet Union was kicked out of the League of Nations and, though it was smaller and outgunned, Finland put up a fierce fight. Disproportionately more Soviet than Finnish soldiers died and more Soviet than Finnish tanks were destroyed.

The Soviet Union's poor showing in the Winter War may have led Adolf Hitler to believe that he faced a weak adversary in Stalin and in the Red Army. He viewed Soviet territory as part of Nazi Germany's 'living space' (*lebensraum*) to be included into an expanded Third Reich. Despite multiple intelligence warnings about Hitler's intentions that Stalin refused to believe, the Soviet Union was caught off guard when, on 22 June 1941, Nazi Germany launched Operation Barbarossa and invaded its territory through occupied Poland. By the end of 1941, the Nazis were occupying Ukraine, Belarus, and large swathes of southwestern Russia. Beginning in September of that year, they surrounded and besieged Leningrad for 872 days.

The Soviet war effort went extremely badly in its first stages. Many members of the Red Army's top brass had been purged during the Great Terror, leaving it with generals with limited direct combat experience. Millions of ordinary people were hastily conscripted into the military, the vast majority of them peasants, and they were given only rudimentary training and weapons that paled in comparison to those of the Wehrmacht. Chaos and confusion led to very low morale. Some soldiers defected to the Nazis, while many more simply deserted, leading Stalin to issue an order that treated any unsanctioned retreat as tantamount to desertion, punishable by death.

The home front was fully mobilized toward the war effort. Many citizens, as well as whole factories, were evacuated away from the front in the Western parts of the country and to more distant locales in Siberia and Central Asia. Much of what was left behind was burned or destroyed to avoid leaving anything useful behind for the Germans. All human and material resources were poured into the war machine, leading to a precipitous drop in living standards. Rationing was brought back but centralized food distribution all but stopped; Soviet civilians were largely left to their own devices to feed themselves. The Soviet government enforced harsh wartime labour laws that criminalized even small infractions on the job. The gulag swelled in these years as millions of people were prosecuted for labour violations.

The Soviet government tried to boost both frontline and home-front morale by allowing greater freedom of religion, in large part to appease the peasantry, and, despite the multinational character of the Soviet Union, by stoking Russian patriotic sentiment. World War II became known as the 'Great Patriotic War', a sequel to the first 'Patriotic War' against Napoleonic France back in 1812, which had famously awakened a sense of Russian national identity. Pre-revolutionary heroes were celebrated: The Order of Aleksandr Nevsky, named after the thirteenth-century Novgorodian prince who won an important battle against the Swedes not long after the Mongol invasion of the Russian lands, was given to Red Army soldiers who demonstrated great bravery in battle.

The tide turned in the war after the Soviet Union won the Battle of Stalingrad. From August 1942 to January 1943, the Red Army and the Wehrmacht fought a bloody battle there, involving air raids but also street combat, that resulted in the latter being surrounded and capitulating. After this, the Red Army pushed the Germans all the way back to Berlin, winning a decisive tank battle at Kursk in 1943 and liberating Ukraine and Belarus from occupation in 1944. In early 1945, the Red Army liberated the Auschwitz concentration camp. On 2 May 1945, Soviet troops hoisted a hammer-and-sickle flag over the Reichstag, and on 9 May 1945, the Soviet Union celebrated its victory in the war. It was yet another pyrrhic accomplishment, however: Much of the country lay in ruins and its population was decimated.

Until the 2000s, the war was largely neglected as a topic of study by Soviet historians, though, as Amir Weiner points out, it 'transformed the Soviet polity physically and symbolically ... forever divid[ing] Soviet history and life into two distinct eras' (Weiner 2000; 2001, p. 7). In recent years, historians have explored the combat experiences of soldiers in the Red Army (Merridale 2006) as well as the experiences of everyday life on the beleaguered home front (Filtzer and Goldman 2021). Scholars have also looked at how a cult of the war emerged in the late Soviet period, particularly under Brezhnev, when victory was portrayed as one of the Soviet Union's most important achievements, to a certain extent eclipsing even the revolution (Tumarkin 1994). This cult of the war persists to the present day in post-Soviet Russia.

The Cold War and postwar Stalinism

The Soviet Union joined the Allies to defeat Nazi Germany, resulting in a brief improvement in its relationship with Western capitalist countries, especially with the United States. However, tensions persisted even as they were outwardly united. From the early days of its entry into the war, Soviet authorities pushed for the opening of a second front, however, British Prime Minister Winston Churchill and American President Theodore Roosevelt were hesitant to commit troops. Stalin suspected they wanted the Soviet Union to shoulder the burden of fighting the Nazis all on its own. At the 1945 Teheran, Yalta, and Potsdam conferences, the Soviet government's aggressive demands for reparations, POW labour, and the complete demilitarization of Germany raised eyebrows. By the time the Americans dropped atomic bombs on Japan in August 1945, the Soviets had already infiltrated the American nuclear programme and were stepping up their plans to develop the Soviet Union's own nuclear capacity.

Relations between the erstwhile Allies quickly deteriorated in the wake of the war. Roosevelt died in April 1945 and was replaced by Harry S. Truman, a former military general who was staunchly anti-communist and increasingly alarmed by the Soviets' expansionary moves on the continent. Indeed, the Soviet Union had emerged from the war with more territory and a much larger sphere of influence. Latvia, Lithuania, and Estonia became Soviet republics after they were 'liberated' from Nazi occupation by the Red Army. Germany was divided into four zones at the Potsdam conference, and the Soviets wasted no time in installing a socialist regime in their zone. One-party socialist systems emerged in Poland, Hungary, and Czechoslovakia through fraudulent elections and coups that were unsubtly backed by the Soviets. The Soviet Union's satellite states were barred from receiving aid from the American government under the Marshall Plan for postwar recovery.

The 'superpowers' in the emerging Cold War prepared for a confrontation. Under the 'Truman doctrine', the US government pledged to provide aid to 'free people who are resisting attempted subjugation by armed minorities or by outside pressures'. Most immediately that meant Greece, then in the throes of a civil war and which had a significant communist movement, but it more broadly referred to any country that was perceived as vulnerable to falling into Moscow's orbit. The US was the driving force behind the creation of the North Atlantic Treaty Organization (NATO), a military alliance directed at the Soviet Union, in 1949. The Soviets would later create the Warsaw Pact, a military alliance of Soviet satellite states, as a counterweight to NATO.

Despite popular hopes for greater political and social liberalization after the war, the postwar Stalinist government made it clear that nothing had changed and set about rebuilding the pre-war system (Zubkova 2005). Living standards in the cities remained extremely low. The countryside, ravaged by warfare and by the departure of millions of peasants for the Red Army, was left in an even more abysmal state. Another deadly famine hit the country in 1946–48. Stalin pushed domestic economic reforms to the backburner and focused his attention almost exclusively on the international situation in these years, although he increasingly delegated tasks to Soviet officials who devised reforms around him (Gorlizki and Khlevniuk 2005). His paranoia and antisemitism also grew to dangerous levels. Toward the end of his life, Stalin appeared to be ramping up toward another major purge: The 'Leningrad affair' saw several top Party leaders accused of gaining too much power and executed and, in 1952, trumped-up charges were brought against Jewish doctors in Moscow who were accused of trying to kill the Soviet leader. Stalin died of natural causes on 5 March 1953, and the charges against the doctors were quietly dropped.

Khrushchev and the Thaw

After Stalin's death, the Soviet Union was ruled by a collective leadership that realized reforms were crucially needed in many areas of Soviet life. That group included Lavrenty Beria, head of the NKVD; Georgy Malenkov, the second-highest ranking member of the Politburo after Stalin; and Nikita Khrushchev, First Secretary of the Communist Party. Beria quickly tried to move into Stalin's shoes and even launched liberalizing reforms, including releasing many prisoners from the gulag. Worried that Beria was gaining too much power, in December 1953, Party leaders had Beria arrested and convicted on charges of treason, terrorism and counterrevolutionary activity and summarily executed. In the wake of Beria's death, a rivalry emerged between Khrushchev and Malenkov, with both launching economic reforms designed, in part, to bolster their candidacy for the job (Zubkova 2008).

Khrushchev threw a curveball at the Twentieth Party Congress in February 1956 when he made the unprecedented move of condemning Stalin publicly in his famous 'Secret Speech'. In it, he criticized Stalin's dictatorial streak and admitted that many 'honest and dedicated' communists had become victims of Stalin's despotism during the Terror. Though it was supposed to be heard only by the Party, the speech quickly leaked to the public and was widely discussed in Soviet society. In the wake of the speech, a group within the Party including Malenkov came to believe Khrushchev was gaining too much power and tried to oust him. However, drawing upon support from the military, Khrushchev managed to thwart this so-called 'Anti-Party' group. Its members were kicked out of the Party and sent into exile; however, in a break with the past, none were executed.

The Secret Speech kicked off a period in Soviet history known as 'the Thaw'. A campaign of de-Stalinization was rolled out, in which Stalin's leader cult was dismantled: His statues were taken down and his body was moved out of Lenin's mausoleum on Red Square. Censorship was relaxed. The writer Alexander Solzhenitsyn, who was sent to the gulag during the war for 'anti-Soviet agitation' after a letter in which he criticized Stalin was intercepted, published his famous novella *One Day in the Life of Ivan Denisovich* with state support. The story, a partly biographical tale about a day in the life of a gulag inmate, caused a sensation both within and outside the Soviet Union. Interest in it stemmed from current events: Millions of gulag inmates were then being released from the camps (Dobson 2011). Many people who had been victims of the Great Terror were also rehabilitated in these years, posthumously in the case of those who were executed.

In the first half of Khrushchev's leadership, he explicitly promised to raise living standards, acknowledging that the Soviet government had allowed them to decline. Of peasant origins himself, Khrushchev was especially committed to improving conditions in the countryside. He launched a mass housing campaign; millions moved into their first-ever private homes in these years. He sought to settle distant 'uncultivated' lands in Central Asia and Siberia during the 'Virgin Lands' campaign and he embarked on an ambitious project to grow corn, primarily to serve as fodder for a growing body of livestock. He pledged to catch up to the US in the per capita production of meat and milk. Khrushchev assured Soviet citizens that, given its promising progress, communism could be attained 'in the main' in the Soviet Union by 1980.

However, in the second half of his time in office, Khrushchev's reforms faltered. His Sovnarkhoz reform, which aimed to decentralize the economy by devolving oversight and decision making to the local level, produced a loss of control instead of better information to input into plans (Kibita 2015). Shortages of virtually everything, especially meat, emerged. Wage reforms launched in 1956–62 proved to be a glorified pay cut. In 1962, the government put up the prices of meat and milk, allegedly to increase the prices paid to peasants for their deliveries and to boost production; workers in the town of Novocherkassk, whose wages had recently been cut, launched a wildcat strike in response to the price hikes. The government responded by sending in troops and killing many of the protesters and hushed up the massacre until the late 1980s (Baron 2002).

On the international front, Khrushchev forged a more productive relationship with the West, especially with the US, under the banner of 'peaceful co-existence'. He travelled to the US in 1959, the first Soviet head of state to do so. Simultaneously, the Soviet Union and the US competed for power and influence around the globe in proxy wars, such as Vietnam's civil war. In the summer of 1962, Khrushchev agreed to move missiles that were capable of hitting American territory into Cuba in response to the Bay of Pigs incident, when American-backed paramilitaries had tried to overthrow Fidel Castro's communist regime. After tense negotiations that brought them to the brink of nuclear warfare, an agreement was reached between President John F. Kennedy and Khrushchev to dismantle the missiles. Khrushchev's 'revisionism' about Stalin, rapprochement with the capitalist West, as well as his perceived bungling of the Cuban Missile Crisis, contributed to a split between the Soviet Union and the People's Republic of China under Mao Zedong.

By the early 1960s, many within the Communist Party had developed grave doubts about Khrushchev's competence. He was widely seen as a 'harebrained schemer', who made impulsive decisions and was prone to bragging and bluster. His folksy public behaviour, especially on the world stage, was often viewed as embarrassing. Beginning in the spring of 1964, a group of top Party officials, led by Leonid Brezhnev, began to make plans for Khrushchev's removal. In October 1964, Khrushchev was called in for a meeting and informed that he was retiring. He was banned from political activity and spent the rest of his life as a pensioner, working on his memoirs.

Much of the historiography on the Khrushchev period has been influenced by the 'cultural turn', which expanded the scope of sources used and topics explored: Scholars began to study daily life and the domestic realm, as well the government's handling of dissent and the effects of de-Stalinization upon Soviet culture and society (Dobson 2011). Scholars looked at the ways in which the Khrushchev-era government broke with the Stalinist past. It took a less overtly repressive, albeit more intrusive, approach when it came to handling nonconformity (Kharkhordin 1999). It also re-embraced internationalism and opened up to the outside world after years of 'anti-cosmopolitan' isolation (Kozlov and Gilburd 2013). Yet, the popular image of the Thaw as a period of relaxed control is, as Stephen V. Bittner (2008) has pointed out, partly a product of Soviet intellectuals looking back fondly on it during the more stifling Brezhnev years that followed.

Brezhnev, late socialism, and the height of the Cold War

Leonid Brezhnev would go on to be the longest serving Soviet leader, in power from 1964 until 1982. He came to power promising to restore collective rule, trust within the Party, and 'cadre stability', that is, an end to the disruptive reshuffling caused by Khrushchev-era reforms (Schattenberg 2021). He argued that the Soviet Union could linger in a state of 'developed socialism': In other words, Soviet citizens could enjoy a peaceful, predictable, and normal life after almost fifty years of tirelessly striving toward communism. In Russia to the present day, his rule is often viewed as the Soviet Union's 'Golden Age'. The period was characterized by rising living standards, the expansion of the Soviet welfare state, and an enhanced emphasis on consumption – paid for with the hard currency earnings the Soviet government made from its massive and lucrative oil reserves.

The Thaw and de-Stalinization came to an end under Brezhnev. Censorship was increased, especially of the country's 'dissidents' – individuals who publicly criticized the government and the Soviet system. After the Soviet Union signed the Helsinki Accords in 1975, many Soviet dissidents called on the Soviet government to live up to its principles when it came to freedom of conscience, movement and speech. Dissidents' works often circulated clandestinely in self-published (*samizdat*) manuscripts at home or were published abroad (*tamizdat*). The government clamped down on both. After enjoying prominence in the Khrushchev era, Solzhenitsyn ran afoul of the censors with his newer writings and was stripped of his Soviet citizenship and sent into exile abroad in 1974. Andrei Sakharov, a Soviet nuclear scientist who won the Nobel Peace Prize in 1975 for his peace activism, was internally exiled to Nizhnii Novgorod in 1980.

Brezhnev never considered himself a foreign relations expert; he was critical of Khrushchev's brinksmanship, on full display in the Cuban Missile Crisis, and he wished to deescalate tensions in the Cold War (Zubok 2007).

He thus pursued a policy of détente in the Soviet Union's relations with the West, especially with the US. Nixon and Brezhnev signed agreements on arms control. The Soviet Union sought to expand foreign trade relations with capitalist states. It dominated its satellites in the East bloc, however. After Czechoslovakia tried to implement liberal reforms, the Warsaw Pact invaded in the summer of 1968, a move that was retroactively justified as preserving the unity of socialist states, the so-called 'Brezhnev Doctrine'. In 1979, the Soviet government applied that doctrine once again and invaded Afghanistan to prop up its fledgling communist regime, a move that was met with international condemnation. American President Jimmy Carter imposed an embargo on shipments of grain to the Soviet Union in response. Many countries, starting with the US, boycotted the Moscow Olympics the following year in response. After Ronald Reagan was elected President in 1980, he abandoned détente and sought to contain the 'evil empire' by building up the armed forces, ramping up weapons production, and banning trade in strategic goods. The Soviet Union entered into a costly and distracting arms race with the US, one which it could not win.

Much of the stability and normalcy associated with the Brezhnev years was on the surface only. Soviet economic growth slowed to a near standstill in these years. Although they outwardly complied with the Soviet system and professed their belief in communism, many Soviet citizens quietly broke the rules and flirted with alternative ideas, and, as Aleksei Yurchak has famously argued, lived outside the Soviet Union in their minds (Yurchak 2005). The Party, meanwhile, grew ossified; many Party officials were well beyond the age of retirement. Following the death of Brezhnev in 1982, the Soviet Union went through two new leaders in rapid succession, Yuri Andropov and Konstantin Chernenko, both of whom were terminally ill at the time of their appointment and quickly died on the job. By early 1985, it was clear that change was desperately needed, in particular to solve the country's increasingly undeniable economic problems.

At the same time, just as assessments of the Thaw were, in part, the product of discontent with the Brezhnev period, the characterization of the latter as one of 'stagnation' was retroactive. It was Mikhail Gorbachev who popularized the term in 1986 when expressing his frustration with Soviet bureaucracy and to justify the radical transformation of the economy he sought to initiate (Fainberg and Kalinovsky 2016). Scholars have, of late, begun to question whether the Soviet Union, in fact, lost its dynamism and simply succumbed to decay during this period. Dina Fainberg and Artemy Kalinovsky have argued it was not 'one endless monolith' and they challenge the assumption that 'the period as a whole was characterized by rampant cynicism and decline of faith in the socialist creed', emphasizing that popular engagement with socialist ideology persisted (Fainberg and Kalinovsky 2016, vii, xiv).

Gorbachev, perestroika, and the collapse of the USSR

In March 1985, Mikhail Gorbachev was appointed General Secretary of the Communist Party. He was chosen for the job because of his age – at fifty-four, he was the youngest leader since Stalin – as well as his promising track record on economic issues. Gorbachev proceeded to lay out an ambitious reform agenda under the banner of 'perestroika' or 'reconstruction'. That entailed new investments into technology aimed at 'accelerating' economic growth and achieving greater efficiency, an anti-alcohol campaign aimed at producing healthier and more productive workers, and encouraging workers to take more interest in, and speak up more about, what was going on in their workplaces and in Soviet society. Gorbachev wanted to harness the 'human factor', in other words each human being's potential to improve the system. His campaign of 'openness' (*glasnost*') also involved liberalizing culture, allowing for greater freedom of speech and of the press, and revisiting some of the country's darker moments: it became possible for the first time in over two decades to openly discuss the Great Terror and to criticize Stalin, and another round of political rehabilitations occurred.

Gorbachev wanted to put an end to informal channels of power and the predominance of the Communist Party over the government. He thus created a new legislative body, the Congress of People's Deputies, which held its first elections in March 1989. The dissident Andrei Sakharov, newly returned from exile to Moscow, was elected as one of its deputies. In 1990, seeking to reduce the Party's power to block his reforms, Gorbachev created the position of the Presidency and the Congress of People's Deputies elected him, the sole candidate, to it. He simultaneously stayed on as General Secretary of the Communist Party.

Gorbachev's decentralizing and liberalizing reforms inadvertently undermined many of the foundations of the Soviet system. Instead of promoting innovation, productivity and growth, his economic reforms starved the state budget of revenue and opportunities to cheat, steal and embezzle from workplaces and from the state proliferated. Gorbachev contemplated, but ultimately stopped short of implementing market reforms under the '500 Days Programme', including making the ruble convertible and deregulating prices; this, in turn, limited his access to Western economic aid, which Gorbachev began asking for and which was denied by G7 countries until these structural reforms were completed.

Glasnost emboldened critics of Gorbachev, Soviet power, and communism. His economic reforms produced widespread shortages and privation, leading to worker strikes. Hardline communists argued that perestroika and glasnost were straying very far from the Party's core tenets: In 1988, Party activist Nina Andreeva published a damning open letter, tacitly endorsed by Central Committee member and Gorbachev critic Yegor Ligachev, criticizing Gorbachev for criticizing the 'trailblazers of communism', that is, the older generation that had built the Soviet system from the ground up. Glasnost also invigorated Russian nationalists, whose ideas has been circulating increasingly openly since the Brezhnev years – though the government often clamped down on other republics' nationalist tendencies, in particular that of Ukraine, in the name of protecting internationalism. Russian nationalists supported the imperial nature of the Soviet state, and opposed perestroika and market reform, and thus lent their support to conservative elements in the Party who were trying to preserve a multinational empire, an authoritarian form of government, and the command economy (Brudny 1998).

Meanwhile, the increased opportunities for independent political association afforded by glasnost, combined with Gorbachev's refusal to intervene militarily as the satellite states of Central and Eastern Europe went through revolutions in which their communist regimes were ousted from power beginning in 1989, emboldened nationalist movements in the Soviet titular republics. They had long harboured grievances about the predominance of Russian language and culture despite the government's professed 'Soviet' and 'internationalist' values, and about their political and economic subordination. In the case of the Baltic republics, for example, some held their inclusion in the Soviet Union to be little more than a form of Russian occupation. Many, moreover, simply saw no future for the Soviet Union. Popular front parties emerged pushing for national self-determination. The right to secede had always been included in the 1922 treaty that created the Soviet Union; they now sought to exercise it. Beginning with the Baltic republics, they declared sovereignty – even the RSFSR declared itself sovereign in June 1990. These declarations were not, in all cases, peacefully accepted by

Soviet authorities in Moscow: Lithuania and Latvia declared independence in March and May of 1990, respectively, only to face violent responses by Soviet military forces who sought to overthrow the nascent independent movements. In January 1991, fourteen people were killed and over one hundred were injured in Vilnius in clashes between the military and civilians.

By the summer of 1991, hardliners in the Communist Party had decided that perestroika and glasnost had gone off the rails and the blame lay mostly with Gorbachev. They were concerned by his recent proposal to create a new Union treaty allowing for a looser confederation, a last-ditch attempt to hold the Soviet Union together. Several Soviet republics refused to participate in drafting the new agreement, wanting nothing less than full independence. Hardliners, for their part, believed it was tantamount to allowing the Soviet Union to unravel. They decided to oust Gorbachev, who was on holiday in Crimea at the time, from power before he could return to Moscow to sign the agreement. Gorbachev was placed under house arrest and the plotters declared a state of emergency.

To their great surprise, however, many people spontaneously gathered at the government's headquarters in Moscow and protested their actions. Boris Yeltsin, the leader of the RSFSR and once a supporter of Gorbachev's, but by then one of his critics, famously stood up on a tank and delivered a speech in which he declared that an 'anti-government coup' had taken place. Within just three days, the coup was put down, but the damage had been done. Gorbachev resigned as General Secretary of the Communist Party. More republics proceeded to declare their official independence from the Soviet Union. On 8 December 1991, representatives of the three signatories to the 1922 treaty on the creation of the Soviet Union (Belarus, Russia, and Ukraine) met outside Minsk and signed the Belavezha Accords declaring that the Soviet Union had ceased to exist 'as a subject of international law and geopolitical reality'. On 25 December 1991, Gorbachev resigned as President and the Soviet Union officially collapsed.

Historians are still hotly debating the causes of the collapse. Martin Malia emphasized that 'total collapse' was only possible in a 'total society' in which everything was subordinated to the Party-State's aims, and that communism was ultimately unreformable as a system (Malia 1991). Stephen Kotkin also emphasizes ideological factors: In his view, Gorbachev was, unlike many of his predecessors, a 'true believer' in communism who failed to grasp that violence and coercion held the Soviet system together and, when he refused to resort to them, the whole system fell apart (Kotkin, 2008). More recent histories have stressed economic factors in their explanations (Miller 2018; Zubok 2021). Vladislav M. Zubok (2021) has likened Gorbachev to a 'sorcerer's apprentice', who aimed to strengthen the socialist system through his decentralizing and liberalizing reforms, but ultimately proved 'unable to control the destructive forces he had unleashed'.

Conclusion

The Soviet Union was an ambitious experiment in building a utopian, egalitarian society free of exploitation, a supranational fraternity, and a rationally planned economic system. However, these ideals proved extremely difficult to realize in the former Russian Empire. Instead, the Soviet system contained a number of contradictions from the outset, flowing from a tension between ideology and pragmatism.

The Bolsheviks consistently leaned in the direction of pragmatism. Having been some of autocracy's most vehement critics at the turn of the twentieth century, in their efforts to industrialize and modernize as quickly as possible, they proceeded to similarly reject pluralism and implemented an undemocratic political system that facilitated dictatorship. Much like the Tsarist regime, they consistently repressed their critics. Although many Soviet citizens genuinely embraced the Soviet project, large swaths of the population, especially in the countryside, remained unmoved – at best, the Soviet government could obtain their forced or grudging compliance through the very kinds of violence and coercion that were not supposed to exist in a socialist system. Despite the formal equality of all citizens, hierarchies persisted, including an implicit ethnic hierarchy. Ethnic differences were consistently reinforced, and non-Russian ethnic minorities were often treated paternalistically, the 'little brothers' in the 'brotherhood of nations'. When it came to the command economy, it was beset with chronic shortages and inefficiencies that made it extremely difficult to provide a consistently reasonable standard of living to the population as a whole. Over time, this nudged Soviet authorities back in the direction of the market mechanisms they, as communists, rejected. These mounting contradictions helped to undermine the Communist Party's monopoly on truth, sapped support for Soviet power, and contributed to the collapse of the Soviet system.

Questions for discussion

1 Was the Soviet project doomed to fail, given that imperial Russia did not have the necessary socioeconomic prerequisites for a revolution in 1917?

2 Why, despite their anti-imperial politics, did the Bolsheviks effectively hold together the Russian Empire?

3 Why, despite claiming to be creating a more just and ethical system benefiting the working class, did the Soviet government use coercion and force to obtain the population's compliance with their plans?

4 Why did World War II become so central to late Soviet and post-Soviet Russian identity?

5 Did Gorbachev cause the Soviet Union to collapse by liberalizing and decentralizing politics and the economy?

Recommended readings

Edele, Mark. 2020. *Debates on Stalinism*. Manchester: University of Manchester Press.

Fitzpatrick, Sheila. 2017. *The Russian Revolution*, 4th edition. Oxford: Oxford University Press.

Fitzpatrick, Sheila. 2022. *The Shortest History of the Soviet Union*. New York: Columbia University Press.

Gorlizki, Yoram and Oleg V. Khlevniuk. 2005. *Cold Peace: Stalin and the Soviet Ruling Circle, 1945–1953*. Oxford: Oxford University Press.

Zubok, Vladislav. 2021. *Collapse: The Fall of the Soviet Union*. New Haven: Yale University Press.

3

How Russia's Past Influences Current Politics

Tomila V. Lankina

One of the major theoretical fault-lines that emerged after the disintegration of communism was between scholars who highlighted the significance of historical legacies in understanding political institutions and regimes, as well as the foreign policy of, present-day Russia and other countries with a legacy of communism, and those who emphasized the role of more recent developments (see discussions in Kopstein and Reilly 1999; Ekiert and Hanson 2003; Pop-Eleches 2007). In the former camp were scholars who drew attention to elements of historical development – such as imperial and communist autocratic institutions, a historically weak civil society, limited experience of private property ownership and market capitalism, the long historical processes of the diffusion of ideas among neighbouring countries or influences that came from being under the tutelage of specific imperial powers, and the record of imperial expansion and domination over neighbouring nations and states. In the latter camp were those who argued that the more recent processes accompanying the demise of communism, such as institutional choices – for instance, a parliamentary or a strong presidential system – electoral outcomes in the first competitive elections, the role of leaders like Gorbachev or Putin, or other contingencies, matter for the political regime trajectories of Russia and the other countries with a legacy of communism.

This chapter presents a case for the significance of the long reach of history in making sense of Russia's domestic politics and elements of foreign policy. While Chapters 2, 4–6, and 11 discuss in detail the development of specific institutions, values, and historical processes, my objective here is to provide a more general outline of some of the key political-institutional and societal historical legacies from the Tsarist, communist, and the more recent post-communist past that impinge on politics in the present. This perspective is not meant to deny the significance of recent political institutional choices, processes and leadership. The aim is also not to provide a simplistic take on Russia's politics that orientalizes and exoticizes Russia by claiming that it is stuck in an autocratic rabbit hole, something that Henry Hale's introductory chapter in this volume warns us against. In fact, among the other complex and multifaceted historical legacies that span the various epochs that I discuss, I emphasize how different regions and social groups came to develop preferences that are at odds with the broader autocratic tendencies of the central state. In this chapter, I use the term 'historical legacy' both to capture the reproduction of the same broad phenomenon or institution across distinct political regimes and epochs, such as centralization or autocracy, and to refer to the (re-)appearance of a phenomenon in a modified form, for instance, elements of Tsarist social inequalities that re-emerged in Bolshevik Russia.

There are considerable challenges in establishing causal links between institutions and processes far removed in time. Two phenomena might appear similar across different times, but this does not always mean that there is a direct causal link between them even if they are correlated in a statistical sense. Russia's present-day authoritarian institutions, for instance, may resemble the autocratic institutions of Tsarist or Bolshevik Russia. But the present-day institutions may be a product of a complex constellation of factors related to elite choices in the present. And one historical phenomenon may trigger a chain of developments that need to be carefully unpacked. Simply postulating correlation between the past and present would not be enough, for we need to grasp *how* it came to matter so much despite the long gaps in time between phenomena. For instance, the share of adherents of the Protestant faith in Russian regions in the Tsarist period might correlate with political openness in a district in the post-communist period. But the causal mechanisms linking the two variables are likely to be quite complex, not least because the Bolsheviks persecuted religious institutions and believers. The variable of share of Protestants may capture, for instance, geographic proximity to Western Europe, which in turn may be linked with economic development, to give one example. Or it might proxy for literacy rates – Protestants had some of the highest literacy in the Russian Empire – and literacy is in turn associated with economic development, education, and demand for democracy. The discussion that follows summarizes some of the processes that link together distinct epochs and help us analyze how the legacy is reproduced. For an in-depth discussion of the concepts and legacies used here and further citations to important works in the comparative research on legacies, see Lankina 2022; Simpser et al. 2018; Kotkin and Beissinger 2014; Wittenberg 2012.

The chapter proceeds as follows. First, I discuss in what way historical legacies of Russia's state-building might matter for politics in the present. Next, I provide a brief overview of key elements in state formation and expansion in the Tsarist period, followed by a section with an overview of the Soviet period and relevant legacies, and then a section on the period of transition from communism in the 1990s. The various subsections also dwell at some length on the historical legacies of entrenched socio-economic and status inequalities in Russia which in turn derive from Tsarist period social institutions, religious influences on society, and the different patterns of settlement in Russia's regions. These legacies are not discussed very often in textbooks on Russian politics. I nonetheless consider them pivotal for understanding the social bases of support for autocracy and challenges to it. This angle in turn is based on a new approach to Russian politics that argues against the artificial separation of politics, society, and social history (Lankina 2022).

Which of Russia's historical legacies should we care about and how might they matter for politics?

We have all heard the adage that history matters. But how exactly does it matter for Russia? And *which* of the histories should we care about when trying to make sense of the effects of the past on the present? There is the *pre-communist* part of Russia's history that spans centuries. Historians parcel the history that preceded the watershed of the Bolshevik Revolution into multiple distinct epochs. Pre-communist histories include the Rus period, during which multiple principalities vied for power over territories that comprise the Central, South-Western, and North-Western lands of the Eurasian landmass, but which Russia's autocratic leader Vladimir Putin has made central to his pseudo-historical visions about the origins of Russia's modern statehood. Mongol invasion and centuries of tributary rule were also consequential for Russia's subsequent political development. There are the epochs encompassing the emergence of a unified Russian state in the sixteenth–seventeenth centuries; the westernization agenda of Peter the Great (ruled 1682–1725) and the Empress Catherine II (reigned 1762–96) in the eighteenth; and in the nineteenth, the emancipation of serfs and other progressive reforms of Alexander II (ruled 1855–81), and the proliferation of radical and terrorist movements and peaceful impulses for democratic change that eventually brought down the monarchy in 1917. The *Soviet* period of Russian history is relatively short, but likewise has informed politics in the present.

With the dramatic demise of communism in Europe in the 1980s–90s, yet another era began. The Soviet Union fell apart in 1991 and the republics that comprised it, including the Russian Soviet Federative Socialist Republic (RSFSR), became sovereign states. Political scientists and historians – eager to make sense of the complex and messy amalgams of developments by creating neat temporal categories – now call this period *post-Soviet* or *post-communist*. Then there is the period known as the transition period, with the word transition capturing the unfulfilled hopes that Russia would not only embrace capitalism but become a consolidated democracy. It encapsulates the political and economic reforms of the 1990s. Russia's leaders like the first popularly elected President Boris Yeltsin (elected twice; president in the period 1991–99) and his aides and ministers built on the reforms aimed at liberalizing politics and the economy that the last Soviet leader, Mikhail Gorbachev (1985–91), had initiated. Competitive elections were held, there was a proliferation of free press and news channels, and the courts were reformed to bring the rule of law to Russia. There were also far-reaching reforms aimed at the quick dissolution of a state-run socialist economy and the emergence of market capitalism. This transition period itself can be considered as engendering another *historical legacy,* something that helps us make sense of how a combination of the long-gone, but also the more recent, epochs impinge upon the politics of the present.

Historians take great care to establish the facts, events and sequences of happenings in the past without necessarily thinking about their implications for the present. But students of politics do care about the long reach of history for what goes on now. We worry about the stickiness of political institutions that originated centuries ago but retain their grip on the present. Some of us still believe that we cannot understand Russian political culture – a set of societal values consequential for how citizens regard political authority and see their own individual role in society and the public sphere – without a deep dive into the religious practices, societal divides, and even the legacies of exile and repressions under the Tsars. And even though communism had been a mere blip compared to the pre-communist history in a temporal sense – just seventy years – we think that it too has left a deep imprint on how Russia is governed now. This is because of the structural peculiarities of the Soviet economy and the untransparent and inequitable ways in which assets were privatized in the post-Soviet epoch. Relatedly, we give careful thought to the possibility that the process of transition from one phase of history to the next – like the communist transition – had been deeply traumatic for many people. Consequently, these legacies continue to impinge upon the voting decisions of ordinary people, their levels of support for market capitalism, or the trust that they have in domestic politicians and western powers whose promises about democracy and prosperity have not materialized for most Russians.

Of course, as political scientists we ought to be equally concerned with the immediate – or contingent – influences on Russian politics and processes that could lead to any number of outcomes. With all our knowledge of history, could we anticipate, for instance, that an unknown former KGB operative would become president and would then proceed to rule Russia for nearly twenty-five years and eventually become a despot who would invade Ukraine, a sovereign country, and bring unimaginable suffering to its people? Chance may well have played a role in Putin's dramatic rise to power – such as a lucky encounter with the right people and at the right time, who supported his candidacy as Prime Minister and then Presidential nominee. There are also other immediate drivers of political processes and indeed global influences that are beyond the control of ordinary Russian people and politicians. Economic downturns or commodity price shocks may well matter for what happens in Russia. And when ordinary citizens decide for whom to vote, they respond to 'pocketbook' logics – that is, considerations of current economic wellbeing – these may result from a combination of present-day domestic happenings and external influences and 'shocks.'

But history is never too far away even when we consider the day-to-day inputs into political processes that ultimately shape the 'big' outcomes like the nature of Russia's current political regime, political institutional configurations, and societal challenges to strongman rule. What seems like 'chance' or 'contingency' may well have a deeper historical explanation. The security apparatus that spawned Putin had a notorious grip on Soviet domestic and foreign policy and the KGB remained in place even after communism collapsed. And the special police and security forces that are associated with notorious crimes of Stalinism and, following Stalin's death, with the persecution of dissidents and the crushing of dissent at home and abroad, in turn built on the practices of the Tsarist *Okhrana* police (Soldatov and Borogan 2022). Likewise, history matters for understanding the divisions among social groups when it comes to the kinds of politicians that they like to see in power, the political parties that they vote for, the values that they hold dear, and the principles that they would want to uphold even if it entails risks to their lives and to those of their loved ones.

The trouble with history is that it is like the proverbial needle in a haystack. The deeper it sinks into the hay, the harder it is to grasp. But the task is not impossible. And making sense of history to understand politics in the present is deeply rewarding. For as we unpeel the layers and layers of time, we begin to see that 'temporally proximate' (Pop-Eleches 2007) explanations of political phenomena do not fully account for the puzzling variations in political regimes, institutions, and citizen values, not just among nations but even between localities within one country.

Pre-Soviet history and legacies

Russia's historical development as a state shaped: the nature of the country's political institutions; relations between Russia's rulers and the people; social divisions and citizen rights and obligations towards the state; and, relatedly, how Russia sees itself and its role in the world. Accounts of the key milestones in Russian state building usually highlight several building blocks. Among them is the imperative to create unity out of disunity during the Rus period in the eleventh–thirteenth centuries. Rus, the embryonic state in the lands presently part of Ukraine, Belarus, and Russia, had originated as a loose conglomeration of principalities; it acquired the contours of a proto-state when in the ninth century the Varangian (Viking) Prince Rurik – so the legend goes – accepted the invitation of the native Slavic tribes to reign over their divided lands. Among the rulers in the Rurik dynasty, Prince Vladimir (ruled in 980–1015) is one of the best known. Not only did Vladimir the Great, as he became known, consolidate Rus's rule over the East Slavic tribes and the Volga Bulgar people, but in 988 he had himself baptized and decreed Eastern Christianity to be the religion of the realm, laying the foundation for Rus's ties with Byzantium rather than Rome.

But the fragile unity of Rus could not spare it from subjugation by superior Mongol armies in the mid-thirteenth century. The Mongol Golden

Horde vassalage of major cities that had been part of Rus – Kyiv, Moscow, Novgorod, Tver, and others – endured until as late as the fifteenth century for some of the conquered lands, long after the Battle of Kulikovo in 1380 which began the erosion of Mongol rule. The Mongols left lasting legacies impinging upon the state-building of territories over which they had control, not least the creation of a space with uniform institutions of taxation, the development of a postal road network, and the implementation of some of the first censuses. Moscow also emerged as one of the more powerful of the conquered cities; and it displaced Kyiv as the seat of Rus's Orthodox Christianity, for the savvy rulers of Moscow took sides with the Mongols against other rivals. But Mongol rule, coupled with the embrace of Eastern Christianity, cut off Muscovy from Western parts of Europe and developments that lay in times ahead – not least the Enlightenment intellectual currents and the various movements for church reforms that came to be known as the Protestant Reformation. After the defeat of the Mongols, Ivan III, also known as Ivan the Great (reigned 1462–1505), proceeded to establish control over prominent city states and principalities. This process involved violent subjugation of self-governing city-states and communities like Novgorod that did not want to be ruled by Moscow, not least because they cherished their proto-democratic forms of government. To aid his expansionist ambitions, Ivan III married the princess of Byzantium, Sofia Paleologue, and went on to propagate the myth of Russia as the Third Rome, that is, successor to the Roman Empire's 'First Rome' of the Western part of the Roman Empire, and to the 'Second Rome' or Constantinople in the East, the seat of Byzantium until Constantinople fell to the Ottoman Empire in 1453 (Neumann 1996).

As noted above, Mongol rule had spurred the beginnings of a bureaucratic state with a uniform set of administrative institutions. But it also encouraged successive Russian Tsars to seek to strengthen their hold over the various territories and protect their territorial possessions from hostile incursions. Over the centuries, Russia developed into an expansionist and centralizing state where the Tsars sought to reign supreme over their realm. In the seventeenth and eighteenth centuries, Russia's rulers, notably Peter the Great and Catherine II, recognized that their country had come to lag behind major Western powers when it came to systems of government, the economy, and the development of skills such as engineering and shipbuilding. Consequentially, they sought to modernize the state's bureaucratic apparatus, government structures and education systems. A growing number of educated subjects from among aristocratic circles in particular, but also an emerging stratum of the less privileged mixed-title men and women – the so-called *raznochintsy* – joined the civil service and the professions. These groups were gaining increasing exposure to European education and ideas and were growing impatient with how far Russia had fallen behind the more enlightened and liberal monarchies of Western Europe when it came to granting citizens basic civil liberties. In the nineteenth century, a vibrant intellectual movement emerged that proposed various solutions – from radical to moderately reformist – to deal with the country's absolutism and social backwardness.

Even the most enlightened monarchs, however, resisted attempts to liberalize the political system although contemplating social reforms. They hesitated to set up parliamentary institutions at the national level; and they regarded with suspicion the institutions of local governance and civic groups that would not only mediate the relations between state and society but would ease the burdens of managing a large and expanding empire. A particular cause for concern among Russia's liberal intelligentsia, including many nobles, had been their country's pre-modern social relations. While in Europe, serfdom was on the wane by the late eighteenth century, Russia's rulers breathed new life into it by granting special privileges to the nobility and confirming the landed gentry's hold over serfs, who were only emancipated in 1861.

The Great Reforms of Tsar Alexander II, notably the emancipation of the serfs, also included the setting up of locally elected bodies called the *zemstva* which decided on local expenditures and social services provision. Jury trials were also introduced. But as with his other liberal reforms, the Tsar came to see these institutions as incubators of radical political dissent. Consequentially, as Kristy Ironside discusses in Chapter 2 of this volume, even the limited reforms like the expansion of the franchise and the setting up of national representative institutions were followed by backsliding, the scaling down of reform, and reaction. Towards the end of the nineteenth century, many Russian cities featured a vibrant associational life and a mushrooming of political dissent. But state censorship, the persecution of political activists, and arbitrary justice against them, which often relied on personal decisions by the Tsar rather than the courts, led to the emergence of movements that saw the end of the monarchy – and even political terrorism – as the only way to liberalize the country. The assassination of Tsar Alexander II in 1881 led his son, the successor to the throne, Alexander III, who reigned until his death in 1894, to endow the secret police with unprecedented powers to spy on and mete out administrative justice over his subjects, and act essentially beyond the control of even the bureaucratic apparatus. The draconian measures against even the mildest of opposition to the monarchy remained in place until the Bolsheviks took power in 1917 and proceeded to install their own version of a police state built on violence, terror and repression (Neumann 2008, p. 142).

Meanwhile, Russia's incessant territorial expansion and brutal conquests, notably in Siberia, Central Asia and the Caucasus, contributed to the mounting challenges of autocratic governance. The Tsars' expansionist and colonial policies over the centuries resulted in a vast empire with a landmass that stretched from Poland and Finland in Europe to the Pacific coast in the Far East. Not only did expansion make governing the realm a huge headache for the Tsars – for they had to supply scores of loyal and skilled bureaucrats to govern the provinces – but the sovereign faced numerous revolts and dissent from the colonized nations, notably Poles, Ukrainians, and the peoples in the Caucasus. Russian leaders justified their hold over colonized territories either by highlighting defence imperatives or posing as protectors of the native peoples of Siberia, the Caucasus, Central Asia, and Central Europe.

Russian rulers past and present have argued that the country's geography made it vulnerable to attack, more so than would be the case with nations like the United States of America, for instance, which is flanked by oceans on both sides. Conservative Russian thinkers also used culturalist arguments to legitimize colonial policies, arguing that Russia itself is not a straightforwardly European nation and power. It absorbed rich cultural influences from both the West and the East, and the Mongols and other peoples of the Eurasian landmass have had a lasting positive influence on Russia's unique development (Laruelle 2008). Contradicting the narrative that Russia regards its Asian heritage in a benign way, are notions that to protect itself against incursions from the East and attain strategic access to the Pacific Ocean, Russia has had to absorb the lands that stood in the way. In Siberia, for instance, the process of conquest involved brutally subjugating the Siberian peoples – the Khanty, the Tungus, Koryaks, Chukchi, the Buryats, Yakuts, and the Turkic-Mongol states of the lands like the Khanate of Sibir. As with the European settlers' colonization of North America, aside from the slaughter of indigenous populations with superior weapons, a significant proportion of native populations were wiped out by diseases that the colonizers brought with them. Russian invaders also sought to erase the cultural identity of the native peoples through forcible conversion to Christianity, mass rape, and displacement of women and children (Lincoln

2007). The notion that Russia is a benign power that looks both East and West also clashed with impulses for political and administrative centralization in the conquered territories.

But colonial legacies would come to haunt Russia. In the North Caucasus, the legacies of General Yermolov's brutal wars of subjugation in the 1800s would reverberate when Chechnya proclaimed independence from Russia in the 1990s and the federal authorities had to fight two wars to re-establish control over it (see Iliyasov, Chapter 11 of this volume). And in the Middle Volga, the *Jadidi* reform movement spurred impulses for sovereignty among the Turkic peoples of the Empire (Sidel 2021, p. 77). Whether Tatar or Ukrainian, Jew or Pole, the peculiar histories of subjugation and discrimination of the diverse imperial populations created national consciousnesses that would shape politics in the epochs that lay ahead. The colonized groups also developed skills of campaigning, organizing, and building civic networks to resist Tsarist oppression. Jews, Poles, Tatars, Germans, and many Ukrainians were also detached from the grip of the Russian Orthodox Church, which became the pillar of the monarchy, unless, of course, they opted, or were forced, to convert. Furthermore, some communities – notably in the western territories of present-day Ukraine – had limited experience of serfdom. Historically, some nations and communities also had higher literacy rates than did the enserfed peasants in the Central Black Earth regions of Russia. In turn, these legacies have led Russia's neighbours and formerly colonized nations which became independent from Russia's rule after communism's collapse to look West, not East; they regarded with suspicion the attempts of Vladimir Putin to create new Russia-led regional political organizations and opted to seek NATO and EU membership instead.

Another element of Russia's state building that left lasting legacies impinging on politics in the present pertained to Russia's embrace of Eastern Christianity at the end of the tenth century. This event affected the nature of Russia's political system and the country's relations with other powers and nations. And Russian Orthodox Christianity added to the development of the insular and expansionist tendencies of Tsarist rulers, a tradition that post-communist leaders like Putin have also exploited relying on the Orthodox Church to project influence abroad. Religion became an important element in the foundation myths and in the overarching political narrative about cultural identity that Russian leaders have propagated. Russia remained relatively insulated from the religious conflicts within Western Christianity and the fusion between Orthodoxy and the monarchy remained enshrined as a pillar of Russia's statehood. Meanwhile in Europe, the religious wars against the authority of Rome that both political rulers and ordinary believers fought would have profound and lasting effects on the European state system and the societal values that would take hold in the centuries to come.

But Russia's national religion also indirectly shaped how citizens related to political authority, the spread of education, and even economic enterprise. Aside from the erosion of the political hold of the Catholic Church on many European rulers and peoples, among the indirect societal consequences of the Protestant Reformation was the emergence of an embryonic social consensus around notions of *tolerance of difference*, not least because of the dark, violent, and savage wars and witch hunts which had taken place in Europe in the name of religion. But the Protestant Reformation also encouraged the spread of basic literacy and the technology of mass book printing, for the faithful were meant to have direct access to the word of God without the mediating role of the clergy. Russia stayed largely on the sidelines of these developments in Europe.

It is important to note that despite the centralizing impulses of the national state and the social control that the Orthodox Church came to exercise over Russian citizens, Russia had its own record of religious dissent and there were religious minorities and sects distinct from the mass of Russian Orthodox population in the various regions. The religious schism within the Orthodox Church created a community of Old Believers, who resisted Patriarch Nikon's reforms of the Orthodox Church in the 1650s–60s and who were branded as heretics. Many Old Believers retreated into the frontier territories where they could practice their faith and ritual without state interference. There were also religious sectarians similar in outlook to the Protestant communities in Europe, for instance, the Molokans (milk drinkers) or the Dukhobortsy (spirit fighters) – they maintained a proud separation from the established Church.

Inadvertently, Russian rulers also invited the process of the dissemination and germination of ideas, worldviews, and practices that emerged in the furnaces of Europe's religious wars. These processes affected some regions more than others. In the eighteenth century, Catherine II encouraged citizens from Germanic lands to settle in Russia. Catherine saw the European settlers as valuable assets from the point of view of Russia's economic development: The farming skills of these labourers were superior to those of Russian serfs who relied on old-fashioned practices of land cultivation and harvesting.

Another historical legacy of Russian state building pertained to the pre-modern organization of society into the so-called estates or *soslovie*. The estate system evolved gradually over the centuries to reward the nobility's service to the Crown, facilitate taxation, generate recruits, and generally maintain state control over citizens. The Bolsheviks abolished this system of social divides, but it left important legacies with implications for citizen capacity to resist state power and challenge authority. Serfdom is the best-known feature of this system. But serfdom, which became legally enshrined in a series of edicts in the late sixteenth century (Mironov 2015, 21), had been one element in an elaborate pre-modern institution of *soslovie* that profoundly shaped all aspects of social relations in Russia. The *soslovie* divided citizens into the majority of serf subjects and other peasants at the very bottom of society, the tiny group of hereditary aristocracy and life peers or nobles at the top, the small population of the relatively free hereditary category of the clergy, and a large layer of urban burghers with various rights and obligations towards the state, roughly one in ten citizens of the realm.

The urban burghers, alongside the much smaller layer of scions of the clergy and nobility of more modest means, by the end of the nineteenth century came to constitute the proto-middle class in Tsarist Russia. Catherine II granted a special charter to townsmen, divided into the categories of merchants, artisans, and *meshchane*. They enjoyed modest privileges in trade in their towns and governed their affairs in urban estate councils encompassing those ascribed to these various categories of burghers. Peasants, especially those on the serf estates and in the peasant commune after emancipation, were deprived of many of the rights and opportunities of the urban burghers and coveted the status of *meshchane*; their rights and status had also been far removed from that of the habitually well-educated and free estates of clergy and nobility. The estate structure consolidated the wedge – or as some have called it *chasm* – between the people, the *narod* and the more privileged nobility, clergy and urban burghers. Because of the legacies of serfdom, large swathes of the peasantry remained poorly educated and retained paternalistic values well into the Soviet period, undermining the capacity of this most disadvantaged social stratum to challenge state authority.

But serfdom and towns evolved unevenly across Russia. The various territories came to vary considerably in terms of their social make-up, levels of development, and even the political freedoms that citizens could enjoy. To rule Siberia and the Far East, the Crown created incentives for peasants to resettle. One such incentive was freedom from serfdom. Some communities, like the Protestant and Catholic settlers on the Volga from Germanic lands, enjoyed special rights of self-government. And the European settlers made good use of their rights to cultural autonomy too – they set up churches and schools where both boys and girls were taught numeracy and literacy – a prerequisite for mastering the Bible. Over time, the European settlers received acclaim locally for their farming skills, such that Russian peasants in surrounding villages would be inspired to emulate them and even become curious about the precepts of their non-Orthodox Christian faiths.

Following the collapse of the USSR, countries that had been held together by force under both the Tsars and the communist dictatorship were quick to exhibit variations in citizen democratic tendencies, civic activism, and the propensity to challenge corrupt or autocratic rulers – a contrast visible for instance between Ukraine and Russia and between Russia and the Baltic nations. But scholars of Russian regions were also quick to note the stark variations in regional politics *within* Russia – one of the USSR's constituent republics that emerged as a sovereign state (McMann and Petrov 2000). Some regions emerged early on as champions of a free press, electoral integrity, and civil society. Others became known as the 'red belt' – a group of regions where citizens continued to vote for the Communist Party, even as Russians in other regions were embracing politicians with a pro-Western, pro-democracy, agenda. Still other regions became 'authoritarian enclaves' where regional strongmen tightly controlled the local populations, repressing media freedoms, electoral integrity and dissent (see Gel'man, Chapter 10 of this volume). Analysts have pondered whether the red belt regions and those that became autocratic enclaves are those where the legacies of serfdom left a deep mark on how people vote or more generally position themselves vis-à-vis political authority, or whether the more democratic regions might be those where literacy had been higher historically and where a combination of circumstances spurred the development of a bourgeoisie and middle class that is supportive of democracy and rule of law (Lankina and Libman 2021). Sceptics would argue, however, that the more distant Tsarist past does not matter so much as the events that happened after the watershed of 1917, the Bolshevik Revolution, which by many accounts swept away the vestiges of the old order. I now turn to discussing this other bundle of *communist* legacies.

Communist history and legacies

After the Bolsheviks took power in 1917, they quickly proceeded to build a centralist autocracy ostensibly ruled by a 'dictatorship' of the proletarian masses (for a detailed treatment of Soviet history, see Ironside, Chapter 2 of this volume). While holding together by force many of the territories that had been colonized under the Tsars, during World War II the Soviet state annexed parts of Central Europe and forcibly incorporated into the USSR the sovereign Baltic countries. It also set up puppet communist regimes and sought to maintain a tight grip on them until the 1980s, when Mikhail Gorbachev embarked on far-reaching reforms of Soviet foreign policy.

Although the word democracy featured prominently in the labels that the Bolsheviks attached to Soviet institutions, what became the Communist Party of the Union of Soviet Socialist Republics had been forged in the secretive, conspiratorial, and violent tactics that the Bolsheviks embraced under the repressive Tsarist autocracy. The Bolsheviks set up a political system based on the principles of 'democratic centralism', whereby citizens ostensibly participated in elections to local, regional, and national soviets or councils and assemblies. But the Communist Party faced no competition from other parties and the system was democratic only in name.

To deal with their 'class enemies' and pursue their ruthless policies of industrialization, Vladimir Lenin and his associates set up a brutal apparatus of state coercion, building upon, but also expanding the repressive machinery of the Tsarist state. As early as the 1920s, well before the purges of the Joseph Stalin period of rule (1924–53) that saw tens of thousands executed and millions incarcerated, deported, and exiled to remote regions, the new leaders also established slave labour camps known as the gulag. Although Nikita Khrushchev (leader in 1953–64) eased political repressions after Stalin's death in 1953, the state security apparatus under Khrushchev and his successors Leonid Brezhnev (leader in 1964–82) and Yuri Andropov (leader in 1982–84) never ceased to pursue surveillance over dissidents and others who dared to challenge the Communist Party's grip on power or demand basic human rights and political freedoms.

The peculiarities of Soviet industry, economy, and planning also created lasting legacies that continue to matter for politics in Russia now. The Soviets created large vertically integrated industrial conglomerates and built whole towns where the citizenry became dependent on the state for jobs and welfare. Although ideologically, the Soviet state had been committed to state-led planning and production, Lenin tactically allowed for a brief period of market freedoms that came to be known as the New Economic Policy or NEP, in the 1920s. But by 1926 Joseph Stalin proceeded to methodically obliterate private enterprise and set the foundations for rapid state-led industrialization and an economy based on centralized economic planning.

These legacies contributed to what Henry Hale calls the emergence of 'patronal politics' in post-communist Russia, and to various forms of workforce dependencies which in the post-communist period made citizens vulnerable to manipulations by political bosses during elections (Rosenfeld 2021; Frye et al. 2014; Hale 2015). Aside from the structural peculiarities of the Soviet economy, there were important influences on how citizens came to regard the role of the state in their welfare and their expectations about political authority and relations with it. Bolshevik leaders were ideologically committed to full employment and cradle-to-grave social welfare, including universal public education and socialized medical care. Even if the realities were different – there were school fees that citizens had to pay during the early years of Soviet rule, and slave labour in the gulag made a mockery of notions of employment rights – many citizens internalized the message of state welfarism and paternalism.

There were also other elements of Soviet social and economic policy that left lasting legacies impinging on citizen orientations towards the political system. Soviet policies inadvertently helped consolidate inequalities in society – something that went against the very foundation myths of the communist state that was supposed to level out centuries-long social inequities. By the 1930s, even communist sympathizers and fellow travellers were calling out the new inequalities whereby the party apparatchiks became the 'new class' with access to specialized shops with gourmet food inaccessible to other Soviet citizens, luxury sanatoria – set up in the expropriated mansions of merchants and aristocrats – and trips and holidays abroad denied to most citizens. Meanwhile, Soviet leaders discreetly moderated their witch hunts against the co-called class enemies once they realized that they needed doctors, engineers, scientists, artists, and writers to fulfil their grand proclamations about modernization and to propagate Soviet ideology at home and abroad. But these professionals and anyone who was reasonably well educated in the 1920s and 1930s came mostly from the estates that the Bolsheviks proclaimed as reactionary and who were granted no place in the Soviet class scheme that glorified the proletariat as the revolutionary vanguard, and the peasantry as its ally. Although in the Soviet state, peasants enjoyed far more rapid social mobility than they had under the Tsars, social uplift for collective farm workers often came via the party cadre route. Most peasants, nonetheless, remained far less advantaged in a socio-economic sense compared to the privileged intelligentsia of the old regime because many were trapped in collective farms after Stalin pursued a brutal campaign of coerced collectivization in the late 1920s.

Although communist rule lasted a mere seventy years, it arguably created a lasting imprint on the political system and citizen values after communism's collapse. For instance, Grigore Pop-Eleches and Joshua Tucker (Pop-Eleches and Tucker 2017) drawing on large public opinion surveys found that citizens in countries with a legacy of communist rule have different political values from citizens with comparable levels of development in states that had not experienced communism. And Alexander Libman and Anastassia Obydenkova have found that individuals who used to be members of the Communist Party in the Soviet period in post-Soviet Russia have exhibited values and political preferences that are different from those of citizens who had not been party members or those whose families did not have such ties in the past (Libman and Obydenkova 2021). These ground-breaking works have provided us with useful signposts that we should look for when we evaluate the weight of communist legacies.

But we have also seen how Soviet legacies built upon and interacted with the legacies of the pre-communist past. And there were important variations in how different social groups, ethnic and religious communities, and different regions in Russia experienced communism, not least because of the cultural, societal, and communal values that survived the communist experiment and which may even have been strengthened. Lankina and Libman precisely find that Tsarist legacies, like the uneven distribution of the various estates across Russia's territories, mattered for regional democratic outcomes in the 1990s–early 2000s, along with Soviet legacies of development (Lankina and Libman 2021).

The transition period in the 1990s and the legacies of transition

In the early 1990s, Russia embarked on a process of political and economic reforms led by the charismatic leader Boris Yeltsin. But Russia's democracy was short-lived. When the communist-era deputies in the national assembly mounted opposition to Yeltsin's reforms and fought his attempts to rule by decree, a showdown ensued between the President and parliament in September–October 1993. Yeltsin ordered the dissolution of the parliament, and when the parliamentarians refused to abide by the decision, Yeltsin approved the storming of the White House, the building housing the parliament, where deputies had barricaded themselves. To many, this tragic episode symbolized the beginnings of the death of Russia's short-lived post-communist democratization process. The presidential elections, in which Yeltsin emerged victorious for the second time, in 1996, were marred by irregularities, and were skewed towards the incumbent. The elections also lubricated the rise of a new group of 'oligarchs' – individuals who became phenomenally rich and obtained preferential access to state resources in exchange for loyalty and kickbacks to Yeltsin and his family and the other government figures around them. Under Yeltsin, many regions embarked on a bargaining process with the Kremlin, demanding greater powers from the centre and withholding revenue, not least because the privatization of the 1990s allowed regional oligarchs to establish control over lucrative resources and industries like the petrochemical, precious metals and minerals, and diamond industries. The regional political bosses' control over local economies allowed them to establish political fiefdoms and construct structures of patron–client relationships, which undermined the integrity of the electoral process (see Hale; and Gel'man, Chapters 1 and 10 of this volume).

The weak institutionalization of Russia's democratic process and the social ills that accompanied the transition from state-led economies to market capitalism led to social disillusionment with Russia's post-communist political system. Although similar sentiments were widespread in the other formerly communist countries in Europe, unlike in Russia, the prospect of, and for many, quick EU membership, helped cushion the economic burdens of transition while also putting pressure on the political class to sustain democratic momentum. Not only did it become clear that Russia lacked such prospects, but growing resentment emerged among the political class and wider citizenry about being treated unjustly and exploitatively by the West. Russia's diminished status in the world following the collapse of the USSR and loss of control over Central European states provided ammunition to politicians who exploited citizens' nostalgia. As Sharafutdinova writes in this volume (see Chapter 4), Russia's leaders started to engage in identity politics that exploited and amplified perceptions of exceptionalism and superiority not only in Russia, but also among Russian speakers in the newly independent states. The USSR's victory over Nazi Germany in World War II became particularly important in the symbolic arsenal of the glorification of the memories of empire. Putin would come to rely on these symbols to project a form of 'soft power' to justify his expansionist ambitions (Soroka and Krawatzek 2021); see also Popova and Shevel, Chapter 15; and Stoner, Chapter 16 of this volume).

The social consequences of transition are particularly consequential for making sense of popular support for autocracy and anti-Western orientations of many citizens. To many citizens, the collapse of communism was such a traumatic process that it put them off democracy and free markets. Many fell into precarity and poverty of the kind that Russians had not witnessed since the dark days of the privations of the 1920s–30s, World War II, and the early postwar years of the late 1940s–50s (see also discussion by Morris, Chapter 12 of this volume). Transition became associated in many people's minds with the impoverishment of a sizeable chunk of the population and the rapid enrichment of an often well-placed small minority of citizens. Enterprise managers were strategically placed to benefit from the poorly executed privatization process. Functionaries in the party apparat and the Komsomol, the party's youth branch, as well as elite scientists and members of the intelligentsia were able to leverage their connections and networks and monetize their skills. For most citizens, though, so painful had the process of transition been that Pop-Eleches and Tucker, in their book about the legacies of communism, had to take great care to demonstrate to their readers that citizens' attitudes towards democracy and capitalism were not merely an artefact of the transition from communism, but rather the legacy of communism per se.

There are singular historical events that become etched in people's memory – like the assassination of JFK and 9/11 in America. And then there are epochs that go beyond the singular event but may leave a lasting – and painful – imprint on cognition. To many Russians, what became known as the 'wild 1990s' became just such an epoch. Most Russians have stories of how the transition affected their families and their life changes, whether positive or negative – and often negative for the older generation. For one KGB officer called Vladimir Putin, the memory of transition was facing the angry mob besieging the Russian diplomatic outpost in the East German city of Dresden where he was stationed. By many accounts, Putin never got over his fear of mass uprisings of the kind that toppled the East German communist dictatorship. And he came to regard the demise of the USSR as 'the greatest geopolitical catastrophe of the twentieth century', justifying his drive for Russia's re-centralization in the 2000s with reference to the near disintegration of Russia in the 1990s that might have followed the scenario of the USSR collapse.

Scholars who are conscious of the imprint of history on the present pay careful attention to collective memory. Collective memory is made of historical events that citizens in one place experience together and that affects them profoundly. Politicians may refrain from capitalizing on certain events, while amplifying the significance of others. Putin became very skilful at manipulating history and historical memory, engaging in 'memory wars' that glorified Russia's Imperial and communist past, and stressing the role of Soviet leaders in defeating Nazism and stigmatizing other nations for their alleged Nazi sympathies. But he also exploited the painful memories that ordinary Russians who lived through the transition shared – the quest for basic foodstuffs and toilet paper, the jobs lost, the savings wiped out. He blamed Russia's pro-democracy politicians and the West for bringing this upon Russia. And he brought back the cult of strongmen idols from the Tsarist and Bolshevik past to help him consolidate his personal grip on power at home and to pursue expansionist ambitions abroad. Putin also relied on the Russian Orthodox Church to accentuate Russia's separation from the West and to advance his agenda of social conservatism, not least the persecution of the LGBTQ+ communities (see Sperling, Chapter 5 of this volume).

Putin also skilfully manipulated social sentiments to garner support for his regime. Windfall revenues from oil and gas in the first decade of the 2000s allowed him to create a form of social contract with the Russian people. Though the transition provided different opportunities to citizens depending on their education, skills and family backgrounds, under Putin many citizens benefited from burgeoning public sector employment and welfare payments to needy citizens. But as Bryn Rosenfeld writes, in autocracies like Russia, public sector jobs create incentives for employees to support the political regime in power (Rosenfeld 2021).

While the employment structure intrinsic to the current regime matters for understanding political processes in Russia now, so too are the social legacies of the more distant past. As noted above, despite the economic restructuring of the post-Soviet era, giant industrial conglomerates survived, and continued to be major employers in some company towns. In a legacy of state paternalism, citizens rely on social welfare and other perks attached to the enterprise. Enterprise managers and employers often put pressure on employees to vote for the incumbent autocrat, as do school principals (Frye et al. 2014; Hale 2015; Lankina 2004). Of course, many citizens have the option to become entrepreneurs, artists, or scientists, which might provide a reasonable degree of insulation from state pressures to conform. But whether in Tsarist Russia, in the Soviet Union, or in Russia under Putin, only a small minority of citizens are able and willing to openly challenge the autocracy; and some regions are more open and civically active than others. The legacies of territorial variations in settlement, human capital, and ethnic minorities' resistance to colonial rule, as well as the inequalities from times past, continue to matter beyond the recent experiences of post-communist transformations.

Conclusion

In trying to make sense of Russia's turbulent political development and regime dynamics over the last three decades, political scientists rightly pay attention to present-day political institutions and the immediate political choices that leaders made at the juncture when communism collapsed. But many explanations do not fully account for the big puzzles – like political and economic variations among post-communist states, between regions in Russia, and among Russian citizens – these are often hard to explain if we look only at temporally proximate factors.

History matters because the peculiarities of Russian state building – and colonial expansion – have shaped the ways in which the Russian state had come to govern its subjects, the freedoms that it had been prepared to grant its citizens and minority ethnic groups depending on the imperatives of the consolidation of Russia's hold over its colonized domains, and the grip that the divisions of society into *soslovie* retained over society long after they had waned in the more developed parts of Europe. The uneven patterns of colonization of the frontier meant that regional economies developed heterogeneously and that citizens across Russia came to exhibit very different values and orientations towards political authority. And throughout Russian history, there were religious minorities and divides within the Orthodox Church that led some communities to establish settlements and worldviews independent of state authority and the prevailing Church dogma.

The Bolsheviks never succeeded in exterminating all vestiges of the past order, and the social divisions, values, and memories from the times past continued to matter. Their state institutions also replicated some of the institutions of the past order, such as the security and repression apparatus aimed at crushing popular dissent against autocracy. The transition period of the 1990s amplified some of the historical social divides and made it easy for politicians to exploit the painful memories of the collapse of the Soviet Union. In the 2000s, Russia became a centralizing autocracy, echoing the patterns of state rule from centuries past. But different social groups and different regions have exhibited distinct patterns of voting, civic life, and protest, and these patterns too could be linked to the historical development of territories.

The complex history and legacies are a cautionary tale against arguments that read too much into the present moment – as when Russia appeared to be on the way to becoming a democracy in the 1990s but developed quickly into a consolidated autocracy, something that could partly be linked to the long chain of inter-related legacies from the distinct epochs covered in this chapter. But equally, it would be wise to avoid embracing simplistic historical narratives that are not attuned to the rich and complex historical texture of Russian society, economy, and polity.

Questions for discussion

1   Which historical legacies are important for understanding Russian politics?
2   Does the history of state building over many centuries help explain the failure of democracy to take hold in Russia in the present, or should we focus more on the role of individual politicians and contingencies?
3   Are social inequalities important when we try to make sense of the 'big' politics of Russia in the post-Soviet period? And is *soslovie* a useful concept to understand social inequalities and their imprint on Russian politics now?
4   In what ways do historical memories matter for making sense of the views of politicians and ordinary citizens in Putin's Russia?
5   Would political scientists studying Russia benefit from careful attention to history, or is history best left to historians?

Recommended readings

Darden, Keith, and Anna Grzymala-Busse. 2006. 'The Great Divide: Literacy, Nationalism, and the Communist Collapse'. *World Politics* 59(1): 83–115.
Jowitt, Ken. 1993. *New World Disorder: The Leninist Extinction*. Berkeley: University of California Press.
Kopstein, Jeffrey. 2003. 'Review Article: Postcommunist Democracy: Legacies and Outcomes'. *Comparative Politics* 35(2): 231–50.
LaPorte, Jody, and Danielle N. Lussier. 2011. 'What is the Leninist Legacy? Assessing Twenty Years of Scholarship'. *Slavic Review* 70(3): 637–54.
Zhuravskaya, Ekaterina, Sergei Guriev, and Andrei Markevich. 2022. 'New Russian Economic History'. CEPR Press Discussion Paper no. 17244.

4

Nationalism, Identity, and the Russia-Ukraine War

Gulnaz Sharafutdinova

Writing about the national identity of a country waging an aggressive war with its neighbour is treacherous. Balance, neutrality, and objectivity in political analysis are hard to achieve even in more settled times. In a historical moment of collective angst and unprovoked military violence unleashed against a neighbouring state, neutrality seems impossible and hard to forgive. One cannot live in historical times and be autonomous from the events and processes that make up the present. The impossibility of objectivity and neutrality, however, does not mean that we should not try to comprehend the reality with the knowledge that can help us make sense of the present. The important thing to remember is that we should not use such an exercise to distance ourselves from our own roles as historical agents involved in the battles shaping that present.

The war on Ukraine provides a predominant angle from which the Russian nation is viewed and judged by the public today. The public focus on the issues of shame, guilt, and collective responsibility is inevitable until those responsible for the crimes against humanity perpetrated by the Russian military in Ukraine are tried and convicted and the destroyed cities are rebuilt. War simplifies judgement. The view of the Russian nation with all its diverse ethnic communities, historical legacies, and contested identities all collapses today under the public gaze into a single, undivided collective body underpinned by the Russian state, its military, and its leader. Favourable views of Russia have dropped to record lows in many parts of the world. The Pew Research Center reported in June 2022 that a median of

85 per cent across eighteen countries had a very unfavourable opinion of Russia.[1] In Russia itself, Putin, the nation and the state merged into the imagined 'we' as the existential challenge raised by the war actualized the 2014 propagandistic slogan: 'no Putin, no Russia'. Only the end of this war is likely to break this widely presumed unity and allow for a different configuration of the Russian state, the Russian nation, and the country's leadership.

The war has significance from an analytical standpoint. How will analysts integrate it into social science analysis? What is this war a case of? Is it primarily a case of a personalist dictator losing touch with reality and undertaking a suicidal adventure driven by megalomaniacal ideas and aspirations? Is it a case of a colonial war fought by an empire over the territory it formerly controlled? Is it an attempt by an insecure, corrupt autocratic regime to stay in power relying on nationalist sentiments and patriotic consolidation effected by war's existential threat? Each of these alternatives provides a plausible angle through which we can grapple with the tragic reality. In this chapter I will advance an interpretation of war as the culmination of the national identity politics that the Kremlin initiated in earnest in 2013 (although its first expressions emerged even earlier). Such a view allows me to engage the most recent contributions to comparative studies of nationalism and embed the current political developments in the region as well as developments in Russian history in existing knowledge and approaches to nationalism and collective identity.

A recent juxtaposition of nationalism in settled and unsettled times builds on the recognition of the ubiquity of nationalism on one hand and different forms of its expression, on the other. There is nationalism that is more tranquil and taken-for-granted; it is seemingly invisible and silent for long stretches of time (Bonikowski 2016). And then there is 'hot' nationalism that is loud, expressive, and even violent (Goode, Stroup and Gaufman 2022). The Russian nationalism we observe today is of the latter type, reflecting the unfinished character of nation-building processes in Russia combined with the regime's reliance on national identity politics to promote its political aims. To illustrate this argument, I review Russia's modern experience with nationalism and identity politics and focus specifically on: (a) the historically prevalent strategies and models of national and state consolidation in Russia; (b) the effects of a more recent experience of state collapse on Russian national identity politics; and (c) the main lines of contestation in modern Russian nationalism.

Nationalism in settled vs. unsettled times

Nationalism as a political ideology and a social movement emerged in modern Europe to affirm the national community as the essential bearer of sovereignty and legitimacy for the state, replacing the traditional source of rule associated with royal dynasties (Gellner 2008, Hobsbawm 2002, Anderson 2020). Over more than two centuries, nationalism turned into a powerful social and political force that transformed the globe, ending the age of empires and creating the 'imagined communities' for which individuals could, at times, sacrifice their lives. Grounded in the organizational and ideological prowess of the state, nationalism turned into the dominant form of modern political subjectivity (Malešević 2019). It is enacted, often unreflexively, in daily interactions, routines, and rituals, in consumption patterns and media communication, and in mundane choices people make every day (Fox and Miller-Idriss 2008). It is pervasive, omnipresent, and often banal (Billig 2005).

The banality of nationalism naturalizes the world that has been historically constructed. The struggles and contestation involved in nation-building are either forgotten or presented from the winner's point of view in school textbooks, while the territorial and national boundaries of the national community are taken for granted (Billig 2005). Susan Condor notes that the banality of nationalism and national symbols is also a 'social accomplishment': It emerges in local interactional contexts (2000, 179).

National communities find themselves in different states of the taken-for-granted nature of specific, socially shared meanings of national belonging. The evolution of such meanings – often understood under the term *national identity* – is a politically and socially mediated process that could be ruptured by historical events such as state collapse, war, or economic crisis at a national level that interfere with shared beliefs and practices and undermine the sense of continuity of a national community (Mitzen and Larson 2017, Ejdus 2018). Therefore, nationalism is more banal in settled times and more politicized, contentious, and emotional in unsettled times and places.

Domestically, politicians can use the openings provided by historical experiences to advance the rhetoric that politicizes national identity and frames various problems and their potential solutions in identity terms. Such identity politics engages with people based on deeply entrenched and emotionally resonant ideas and a sense of belonging, community, and self, which then can easily spill over into the realm of foreign policymaking. Most wars, violence, and inter-community hatred are perpetrated in relation to groups and inter-group relationships (Elcheroth and Reicher 2017). Russia's war on Ukraine – starting with the 2014 annexation of Crimea and developing into a full-blown military invasion in February 2022 – is not an exception. It should be viewed as the culmination of the Kremlin's political survival strategy that took a big turn towards identity politics and nationalism after Vladimir Putin returned to power in 2012. That political return occurred on the back of political protests in Russia, and the turn towards national identity politics signified the Kremlin's new strategy of managing dissent (Smyth and Soboleva 2014).

Politicians operate in historical conditions they inherit from others. Russia's inheritance from the past includes a strong imperial and expansionist ambition that underpinned Russia's pre-Soviet and Soviet era developments (Lieven 2000). As important is the country's peripheral condition in relation to the West. Relations with Europe and the West, more generally, have been central to Russia's collective identity and represented a continuous source of resentment and consternation (Morozov 2015; Neumann 2013). The format and nature of these relations, as defined by Russia's political leaders and intellectual elites, have changed over time but have always been interdependent with domestic and foreign policies as well as with the specific identity narratives adopted by the elites (as I illustrate below). The deep-rooted nature of these narratives is an important factor of their resonance and, therefore, political potency in newly unsettled times.

Between empire and nation

Modern Russia emerged as a new state from the ruins of the Soviet Union in 1991. The Soviet collapse brought an end to the communist ideology and institutions that underpinned the construction of the Soviet nation and therefore raised a challenge of creating new ground for post-Soviet Russian nation-building. More than thirty years into these processes, it is now clear that Russia's war on Ukraine symbolizes a massive failure of post-Soviet nation-building and the end of the most recent historical attempt of the country's elites to bring Russia onto the path of development and institutions modelled on the West. Already from the beginning of his presidency, Russia's second president demonstrated a lack of commitment to the political choices and values buttressing the emergence of the new Russian state in 1991. Upon his return to power in 2012, he initiated a new political project for Russia returning the narratives of Russian civilizational exceptionalism and the threat the nation faces from the West.

Political leadership and the regime imperative might be the most proximate explanation for Russia's current condition. However, a historical perspective that sets the Russian experience against the experience of other European states is instructive for highlighting the broader context in which one can position the sources of Russia's nation-building failure. Russia's Soviet experience stands out in terms of its uniqueness vis-à-vis other European states. Understanding the lasting legacies of this experience in contemporary Russia and Russian nationalism is one of the challenges that analysts have grappled with over the years since the Soviet collapse. Additionally, it is also important to consider where Russia was in terms of nation-building before the Soviet government embarked on the path of building the Soviet nation.

For many new states emerging from the Soviet collapse, their earlier historical experience with state and nation-building were important in terms of the political and institutional choices new elites made. The Baltic states of Estonia, Latvia, and Lithuania, as well as Ukraine, Armenia, and Georgia all had nationalist movements and independent states established as republics in the wake of the 1917 Bolshevik Revolution. Even if these statehood experiences were short-lived, they provided national elites with their 'history of independence' and 'republicanism' to which they reverted when the opportunity arose in 1991. Even those new states that did not have independent, modern statehood experiences (such as those in Central Asia), still experienced nationalist movements in the late nineteenth and early twentieth centuries. For Russian Muslims in the Tsarist Empire mobilization occurred along religious and Turkic lines. Muslim Turkic intellectuals in Central Asia, the North Caucasus, and the Volga region developed a Muslim cultural reform movement – Jadidism – that sought to modernize education among the Muslims in order to be able to compete with the West (Khalid 1999). A short-lived autonomous attempt at nation-building in Tatarstan in the 1990s and early 2000s, for example, involved an intense intellectual attention to the Jadidist movement framed as an example of Euro-Islam and used in support of Tatarstan's 'state sovereignty' project (Dannreuther and March 2010).

Russia did not have the convenience of falling back onto the pre-existing institutional and ideological state format. The USSR was built on the back of the Russian Tsarist Empire that imploded under the weight of its own unresolved economic, political, social, and ethno-national problems. In

Tsarist Russia, society was divided into estates and each estate had its own relations with the state. While the Slavophiles and Westerners engaged in heated discussions about Russia's civilizational belonging in the 1840–50s and the meanings attached to being a Russian, the more conservative ideas linking Russia to autocracy and supporting the more traditional and patriarchal relationships between the people and the state became more entrenched over the course of the nineteenth century. Sergei Uvarov, sometimes seen as a founder of Russian conservatism, was a minister of education under Tsar Nicholas I. He is also an author of the official doctrine 'Orthodoxy, autocracy, and nationality' that turned into the ideology of the Russian state in the nineteenth century (Robinson 2019).

After the military defeat in the Crimean war in 1854, the soul-searching intellectual elites unearthed the concept of 'Moscow as the Third Rome', which posits Moscow as the rightful inheritor of Byzantium and the saviour of Christianity. This exceptionalist vision of Russia's mission and place in the world, highlighting Orthodox faith and spirituality, remained very popular well into the twentieth century. As the Russian Empire incorporated new lands and peoples in Central Asia in the nineteenth century, it followed the patterns of European colonial history, underpinned by notions of modern and progressive Europeans bringing civilization and development to backward and primitive non-Europeans.

Meanwhile, the ideas of popular sovereignty and the state as a reflection of such sovereignty that drove nationalism in other parts of Europe did not find fertile ground in Russia. While the core ethnic group in the Russian Empire was becoming increasingly enchanted by the doctrine of Russian exceptionalism, the early twentieth century also saw the emergence of ultra-nationalist, far-right political parties espousing anti-liberalism and antisemitism. At the same time, the Tsarist government had to contend with the rising historical and national consciousness of its subjects in the periphery: Poles, Finns, Latvians, Lithuanians, Estonians, Armenians, Georgians, Russian Muslims, and others.

World War I brought an end to the Russian Tsarist Empire along with the Ottoman, Austro-Hungarian, and German Empires. Many of the diverse ethno-national communities that emerged out of the imperial collapse proceeded in the direction of building their nation-states. However, the Soviet Union, which incorporated most of the territories of the Tsarist Empire, did not develop as a nation-state. Formally, the Soviet Union was a multinational state. The early Bolsheviks used an anti-imperialist stance to woo the diverse national liberation movements on the territory of the

Russian Empire to the Bolshevik side (Slezkine 1994). Incorporating these political movements left an imprint on the structures of the Soviet state: It was constructed based on the national-administrative principle 'national in form and socialist in content'. This principle served as a cornerstone for Soviet culture and for the Soviet state, more generally. But, anti-imperialist rhetoric notwithstanding, as state-building progressed, the Soviet Union restored pre-existing ethno-national hierarchies that privileged Russian culture and language (Brandenberger 2002). In that, the Soviets built on the legacies of the Russian Tsarist Empire and the presumed (though unstated) superiority of the Russian 'core' ethnicity.

The alternative view of the USSR as 'an affirmative action empire' that invested in the development of national elites and institutions in its peripheries suggested that the Soviet Empire was one of a kind (Martin 2001). The Soviet state embraced multinationalism and diversity, proclaimed support for internationalism, sponsored national folk festivals, and allowed millions of Soviet citizens to identify simultaneously with their own ethnonational heritage and the big Soviet citizenry (Norris and Sunderland 2012). Nonetheless, deep ethno-national injustices took place and hierarchies were rebuilt. Some nations were deemed disloyal and deported (i.e. Chechens, Crimean Tatars, Germans, Ingush, etc.); anti-Jewish policies continued on the official level; xenophobic attitudes spread widely in Soviet society.

In short, the establishment of the Soviet Union, a communist state underpinned by the universalist, Marxist ideology, did not result in the most common path of civic or ethnic nation-building characteristic of modern states in Europe and beyond (Hirsch 2014; Suny and Martin 2001). The Soviet path to modernity represented an alternative historical route. It did involve a more centralized process of constructing the sense of Soviet belonging before World War II and more grassroots driven campaigns (at least, they were officially presented that way, while also placed under the control of the party) to create new rites, rituals and festivals for performing Soviet-ness after the war (Baiburin 2012, 94–95). Unlike nation-building processes in other states, it emphasized universalism over particularism and Soviet exceptionalism. The Soviet consolidation rested on this socially shared and institutionally nurtured sense of exceptionalism combined with the idea that the Soviet state was permanently encircled by external enemies (Sharafutdinova 2020). The ethno-national aspect of Soviet consolidation was turned on and off, depending on political exigencies. The dominant strategy was that of advancing russification, when possible, and relying on Russian historical and cultural figures to show the historical continuity of the state (Brandenberger 2002). As Ron Suny suggested eloquently, 'A supranational but Russified patriotism was grafted onto Leninist internationalism, replacing the class element with a new primacy placed on Russia's past' (Suny 2001, 27). This political formula emerged ever-more victorious after World War II and existed side by side with the institutional structure of the Soviet state that incorporated the national principle in its *raison d'être* and which, in the end, turned into the boundary-delimiting factor.

New Russia

The Russian state that emerged in 1991 was multinational, even after shedding the fourteen other Soviet republics that obtained independent statehood. There was an ambiguity in relation to the past from the onset. While ideologically the new government disavowed communism, the Russian state was viewed from the outside (and, indeed, from the inside) as the inheritor of the Soviet Union. It meant that, in the absence of a very clear understanding of the purpose behind breaking up the Soviet state and a strong commitment to the mission of the new Russian state, the elites and the masses would face a strong inclination to compare Russia to the USSR and to refer to Soviet experiences and geopolitical standing as a yardstick for measuring the success of the new state.

Although the Russian state had the predominant ethnic group of Russians (*russkie*) that comprised around 80 per cent of the population (relative to 50 per cent in the Soviet Union), the Russian state emerged as an ethno-federal state and left the ethnic principle as a fundamental feature of the state composition, a Soviet legacy. The Russian Federation today claims to consist of eighty-nine 'federal subjects', six of which are not recognized by the international community and are contested by Ukraine. Two subjects (the city of Sevastopol and the Republic of Crimea) were annexed in 2014 and four other Ukrainian territories were declared to be part of the Russian Federation on 30 September 2022, as the People's Republics of Donetsk and Lugansk, and the regions of Kherson and Zaporozhye. Besides these occupied territories, the federation consists of twenty-one ethnic republics, forty-six *oblasts* (regions), nine *krais* (territories), four autonomous *okrugs* (districts), one autonomous *oblast*, and two federal cities (Moscow and St Petersburg).

Boris Yeltsin's reformist government built on the narrative of Russia's return to the highway of modern history – from its Soviet detour back into the family of civilized nations. However, we could see in hindsight that the Russian government did not treat the problem of political communication and civic education as a serious state matter. Yeltsin personally deemed ideology to be a thing of the Soviet past. Symbolic issues inevitably crept into policymaking in the early 1990s; but the debate on symbolic issues turned into a reflection of the political struggle between the reformist government and national-patriotic forces opposed to reforms. The opposition seized on Soviet symbols and the reformist government adopted a hotchpotch of symbols from pre-Soviet Russia, trying to fit them into the new democratic era. Values associated with democratic choice were, for the most part, assumed to be widely held and shared by virtue of Yeltsin's having won the presidency by popular vote. The new economic and political system was expected to bring prosperity to the people and thereby reinforce the new values and institutions created by the reformists. In the midst of falling living standards and a growing sense of chaos, anarchy, and rule of greed, the prospects for democratic state and nation-building wore ever thinner and hinged on the political commitment of Russian elites to democracy.

On the question of the Russian nation, the Yeltsin government adopted and promoted the more inclusive concept of Russia as a civic nation – adopting the term *rossiyane* (Russian citizens) – a multi-ethnic community unified by the Russian state. This conceptualization was, arguably, only politically plausible in the context of the ethnic, religious and cultural diversity in Russia. According to the latest 2021 census, 194 ethnic groups live in Russia today, although only six of these groups have a population of over one million (Russian, Tatar, Chechen, Bashkir, Chuvash, and Avar). The four state-recognized, traditional religions in Russia are Orthodox Christianity, Islam, Judaism, and Buddhism. There are non-traditional faiths professed in Russia as well, including Catholicism, Protestantism, and Shamanism. Foreign proselytizing by various new religious movements, mostly from a variety of Christian sects, was active in Russia in the first half of the 1990s. From the mid-1990s on, the growing criticism from the Moscow Patriarchate of such competitive trends coalesced with the state's more restrictive approach to religious expression and the focus on the more historically rooted religions to preserve 'ethno-religious balance' and the 'cultural and spiritual foundations of the state' (Shterin 2001, 315).

The overall civic nation-building project of the Yeltsin government turned into a failure, underscoring the fact that Russia has never been a nation-state and opening the path towards more ethno-centric and imperialist projects of nation-building (Goode 2019). Goode argued that this failure resulted from institutional instability and the personalist nature of the Yeltsin regime. Between 1991 and 1999, Russia's Ministry of Nationalities was reorganized eight times and changed its leadership as many times (ibid). Such top-down ambivalence and organizational instability was paralleled by the absence of good solutions at the grassroots level. Russia's federal subjects have been engaged in their own, regional or republic-level, consolidation projects (Graney 2009). It was symptomatic that the search for a new Russian national idea, announced by Yeltsin in 1996 through the government-controlled *Rossiiskaia gazeta*, did not produce any original formulations.

The broader socio-political context of the 1990s was not prone to producing symbolic consolidation around a specific idea of the nation either. The Yeltsin government spearheaded economic reforms that resulted in deep political polarization between the reformist government representing Russia's 'democratic choice' and conservative forces that opposed radical 'shock therapy' reforms and coalesced in the parliament (the Supreme Soviet). These conservative forces, which included the reformed Communist Party of the Russian Federation (KPRF) under the leadership of Gennady Zyuganov and the increasingly popular Liberal Democratic Party of Russia (LDPR) led by Vladimir Zhirinovsky, also represented the 'nationalist choice' of Russia which opposed liberal reforms and Russia's Western orientation. Instead, this national-patriotic camp called for the defence of Russia's own, Eurasian continent-centred interests, perceived to be in opposition to the interests of the Atlantic nations and particularly the United States.

Without the culture of democratic competition that can keep political conflicts within civil bounds and in the absence of national consolidation, the opposed political forces engaged in an existential struggle in which each side tried to symbolically annihilate the other (Urban 1994). Fearful of communist and nationalist throwback, the West was vested in Boris Yeltsin and the reformist government. This political battle turned into a stand-off between the executive and legislative branches of the Russian government, which was ultimately resolved with the deployment of the military in September 1993. The seat of parliamentarians in the White House was shelled by tanks and, a few weeks later, the Kremlin proceeded with the adoption of a new Constitution which installed a 'super-presidential' system of power.

Russia's economy did not fare well in the 1990s. GDP contracted by over 40 per cent, and hyperinflation wiped out people's savings, only to be followed by a restrictive monetary policy producing a crisis of payments and fragmenting Russia's economic space. The August 1998 financial crisis that saw government defaulting on its debts and the ruble devaluing by 400 per cent was the last nail in the coffin of the reformist wing in the Russian government. Yevgeny Primakov, one of the last survivors in the government from Gorbachev's time, replaced Sergei Kirienko as prime minister in September 1998 and formed a new government, inviting former communist officials such as Nikolai Ryzhkov and Yuri Masliukov.

These economic and political challenges unfolded in an era of political liberalization and opening carrying over from the late 1980s and into the early 1990s that allowed for the emergence of more radical Russian nationalist groups and leaders. They advocated for very different visions of the Russian state (*russkoe gosudarstvo*) – whether defined in imperial terms by people nostalgic for the Soviet state such as Eduard Limonov and Aleksandr Prokhanov or, in more ethnic and Slavic terms, by those such as Aleksandr Solzhenitsyn, who returned to Russia from exile in 1994. Solzhenitsyn's nationalist views had already been outlined in Soviet times, when he advocated for the congruence of political and national units and called for Russia to separate itself from other nations in the Soviet Union (Rowley 1997). Still more radical nationalists included a neo-Nazi party Russian National Unity (*RNE*) founded by Aleksandr Barkashov in 1990, after he broke off from the extremist nationalist society *Pamyat* that rose to prominence in the late Soviet Union (Horvath 2013).

The nationalist political organizations in the 1990s were in radical opposition to Yeltsin's government and Russia's new, Western orientation. Opposed to Western liberal ideas and values, they drew on Russia's traditional faith – Russian Orthodoxy – and advocated for the preservation and protection of Orthodox spirituality and cultural values (Mitrofanova 2017, 106). Many nationalist groups in Russia sought support from the Russian Orthodox Church (ROC), but the Church's position has been more nuanced, especially in the 1990s. The ROC was itself not homogenous: Liberal clergy who followed Alexander Men's teachings (killed in 1990) opposed nationalist elements in the Church (Knox 2005). But the more conservative and xenophobic forces were more powerful, as Patriarch Alexei II soon realized after his election by the Church in 1990 (Knox 2005). Ultimately, the widespread political and social support for linking Orthodox faith to Russia's national identity worked to align national-patriotic forces with support for the ROC. This linkage characterized Zyuganov's rhetoric in the 1990s as much as Putin's rhetoric in the 2000s (Knox 2005).

Putinism as national identity politics

Russia's political evolution in the 2000s witnessed a reversal of fortunes between liberals and national-patriotic forces. Over a period of two decades the Kremlin came to appropriate the key messages of conservative and nationalist forces, while discrediting and marginalizing liberal views and policies. Such reversal did not happen overnight. Russia's second president started out as a leader committed to market forces and viewed Russia as part of Western civilization (Hale and Laruelle 2020). At the same time, he also quickly revealed his preoccupation with symbolic issues and a preference for historical continuity in national symbols. The return of the Soviet anthem with revised lyrics in January 2001 and a gradual return of top-down patriotic education in schools indicated the Kremlin's new orientation on the symbolic front (Daughtry 2003).

The symbolic aspect of policymaking in the first decade of the twenty-first century was still secondary to the more pragmatic goals of restoring the 'power vertical' (a common term for the Russian power structure from Putin on down) and establishing control over key political and economic elites. Extensive research was done on how the Kremlin rebuilt its relationships with powerful oligarchs, recalcitrant governors, and political opposition parties in the State Duma. The authoritarian reversal, reflected in various aspects of political and social life in Russia, progressed and intensified over the years of Putin's long presidency, interrupted only for four years between 2008–2012 (but even then, measures were taken to ensure continuity). In 2004, for the first time since the Soviet break-up, Freedom House downgraded Russia's ranking to the status of 'not free'.[2]

The Kremlin's symbolic policymaking also evolved in the first two decades of the twenty-first century in the direction of intensification, radicalization, and a full-blown identity politics that began in earnest in 2013, supplanting the Kremlin's other legitimation strategies (Smyth and Soboleva 2014). The Kremlin's early focus was on memory politics and historical falsification issues. In 2009, Dmitry Medvedev (then Russian president) created a new commission 'to counteract attempts to falsify history to the detriment of Russia' (Kolstø 2019). This was an early indication of how Russian political elites viewed history and memory as an arena of political struggle and recognized its central role in nation-building. With that in mind, the government focused on promoting government-approved historical interpretation in official textbooks, tightening control and reversing the more liberal school teaching practised in the 1990s. One of the important drivers of these actions was a perceived threat from alternative historical interpretations in post-communist Eastern European countries that were earlier incorporated into or controlled by the Soviet Union. These newly sovereign states built their political foundations on the exposure of Soviet crimes against their people (Budryte 2017). The Kremlin-approved version of history tried to minimize these crimes, while at the same time advancing the memory of the Soviet Union as a liberator from fascism.

The memory of World War II played a particularly significant role as a mechanism for legitimation and national consolidation in Russia (Walker 2018, Wood 2011). In *The Red Mirror* (2020), I used Vamik Volkan's term 'the chosen glory' to acknowledge the political and social significance of this memory for Russia's national consolidation as a historical moment that helps in building faith and pride in the nation. Russian sociologists have also noted the disproportionate importance of World War II and the cult of victory constructed around it (Gudkov 2005). This cult had already been constructed in the 1960s, but in the twenty-first century it obtained new rituals around it and a new significance. One such new public ritual is the Immortal Regiment parade on 9 May, when Russian families march on the streets holding a portrait of their relatives (mostly but not exclusively fathers, grandfathers, and great-grandfathers), who fought in the war.

Besides the memory of World War II leveraged as a moment of glory, the Kremlin had also chosen this historical moment in the country's history to construct a sense of collective trauma. Such a 'chosen trauma,' in Volkan's terms, is another crucial pillar required for consolidating the national community. Alas, the trauma the Kremlin chose to emphasize was not Stalinism and the Soviet history of totalitarianism that repressed hundreds of thousands – even millions of Soviet citizens, if we take into account its entire duration. The tragedy of Soviet history was sidelined from public attention and replaced by widely shared nostalgia for late-Soviet stability and economic security (albeit at very low levels). As Aleksandr Etkind showed in his important book on post-Gulag memory, the mourning over the dead that was reflected in post-catastrophic Soviet art, film, and literature remained of a 'warped' nature (2013). While society-wide reflection and reassessment of these issues started during the period of perestroika and glasnost, memory and nation-building work around tragic Soviet history was not completed. These processes were cut short by the Soviet collapse and the ensuing transformation that enveloped all aspects of life in Russia, creating new adjustment challenges. In the end, individual tragedies were never incorporated into the collective sense of a catastrophe around which Russia's new national identity could have been constructed, which in turn could have enabled both national success for Russia and peaceful co-existence with its neighbours. Instead, Kremlin political technologists politicized the difficult period of the 1990s to enable Putin's electoral victory in 2000. This electoral strategy then transformed into a bigger legitimation strategy over the following years because the early economic and administrative successes of Putin's presidency could be conveniently juxtaposed with the economic contraction, hyperinflation, and non-payments of the 1990s, along with other regional and national challenges Russians had faced (Wijermars 2018; Malinova 2021).

The Kremlin's choice of a national consolidation strategy came with opposition to liberal reforms and reformers, political pluralism, competition, and political parties and opposition not controlled or managed by the Kremlin. Starting with the Pussy Riot affair in 2013, Russia's leadership invested heavily in promoting civilizational and traditional values-based discourse, positing Russia's difference *and* moral superiority as compared to the West. In his 2013 Valdai speech, Putin referred to Russian philosopher Konstantin Leontyev and his idea of Russia as 'as a state-civilisation, reinforced by the Russian people, Russian language, Russian culture, Russian Orthodox Church, and the country's other traditional religions'.[3] Meanwhile, 'the Euro-Atlantic countries are actually rejecting their roots, including the Christian values that constitute the basis of Western civilisation'.[4] Such a juxtaposition of Russian virtues and Western vices turned into the central message circulated in Russia's state-controlled media environment.

The intense rallying around the flag and around the leader that followed the 2014 annexation of Crimea highlighted the political dividends of identity politics that could come from such perceived foreign policy successes (Alexseev and Hale 2016). Arguably, the decision to invade Ukraine in February 2022 depended strongly on the political effects of the earlier foreign policy choices vis-à-vis Ukraine, underpinned by national identity politics. War against Ukraine could therefore be seen as a culmination of identity politics and a mechanism of regime survival for Russia's current political establishment.

Regime, state and war

The war brings national identity to the forefront, making it the most salient and central vantage point for forming individual-level political attitudes and worldviews. The Russian public thus responded to the invasion in a way that has been described as 'defensive consolidation', even though public support for military resolution of the conflict in Donbas was very low as late as December 2021, just over two months before the invasion (Morris 2022). Even if many Russians fled the country and, among those who stayed, some engaged in anti-war protests and activism, the dominant public reaction differed ('Hidden Resistance'). After the initial shock of the invasion, many Russians 'closed ranks' in support of the Russian army and the government. More often than not, these were people who did not see any possibility of alternative responses (such as leaving the country or protesting). More than a year into war, it is evident that the Kremlin relies on a combination of the politics of fear and repression and war-induced social consolidation dynamics to maintain regime stability (Yusupova 2022).

But what happens if Russia loses the war? The heroic Ukrainian resistance accompanied by the moral consolidation in the West revealed the military weakness of the Russian state. The arguably tight linkage between the war and regime fortunes poses a challenging question regarding the potential consequences of this war not only for the regime, but also for the Russian state.

What goes around, comes around, a proverb suggests. If the war produced social consolidation (whether 'naturally' occurring or forced by fear), military defeat is likely to be associated with subsequent political contestation that might create disintegrative forces tearing the state apart. The history of the Soviet collapse and the role of the nationally defined state structure in turning nationalism into a relevant force are instructive (Beissinger 2009). In his analysis of the role of nationalism in the Soviet collapse, Mark Beissinger (2009, 337) highlighted the fused nature of the Soviet state and the communist regime and the subsequent difficulty of separating anti-regime activity from challenges to the Soviet state. Such regime-state fusion is evident in modern Russia as well, only instead of the communist regime there is a personalist regime associated with Russia's president.

There are important structural differences that distinguish the Russian ethno-federal state from the Soviet state: Russia does not have one core group embedded in the state structure institutionally as the Soviet state did, where Russian nationalism played into Soviet disintegration (Hale 2004). Nonetheless, the strong decolonizing narrative that is in the process of gaining public momentum in other post-Soviet states, especially in Central Asia, might catch up within minority national groups in Russia very quickly and powerfully, if political conditions allow. The sham referenda held on 30 September 2022 in the occupied territories in Ukraine brought into sharp relief the imperial and expansionist nature of the war, reinforcing the perception of Russian imperial nationalism as the driver and motivator of the Kremlin's actions. The anti-imperial and decolonizing impulse might eventually turn into a strong mobilizing force among Russia's many indigenous ethnic minorities.

This trajectory is not yet palpable, but dramatic changes might take place after the war ends, depending on political conditions at that point. There are a number of underlying conditions that might make such mobilization feasible. Since the early 2000s the Russian federal state has been centralized, federalism effectively abolished, and regional elites' autonomy gains of the 1990s lost. Any cases of minority group nationalism and political activism inside the country were repressed. These processes took place in an environment when the Kremlin faced a challenge from radical Russian nationalism, neutralizing it by a combination of repression and co-optation of (Kolstø 2016). The Russian ethnic group was recognized in Russia's amended Constitution in 2020 as a people playing the leading role in the creation and existence of the Russian state. But this important move was made without fanfare, and after a failed 2016 law on the 'Russian nation' endorsed by Russia's president, which would have defined the term legally. The opposition to this law came from Russia's ethnic minorities.[5]

The war in Ukraine exposed the intersection of ethnic and economic inequalities in the country. Therefore, possible defeat in war and the end of the regime might open up long-festering fissures exacerbated by the war and the crisis that is likely to follow. In that situation, the strategies and decisions in Russia's regions and, especially ethnic republics, would depend on the type of elites that would control power in Moscow and their appetite for compromise in governing Russia in a more decentralized and federal format.

Conclusion

The Russian state that emerged from the ruins of the Soviet state contained the early ideological impetus for developing into a Western-style nation-state and creating a multinational community unified by its historical choice. More than three decades later we are witnessing not only the failure of this nation-building project, but the revival of a revanchist imperialist aggression spearheaded by the leader of a personalist autocratic political regime controlling the Russian state. The discussion above has highlighted the different drivers of such a transformation. Crucial among them are the economic, political, and institutional challenges of the 1990s that produced the social circumstances enabling political leadership to move in the direction of authoritarianism, victimhood-driven, and ressentiment-ful identity politics. Such politics was also politically effective for the Kremlin because it unfolded in the context of the historical legacies of Russian and Soviet exceptionalism and the ambiguities of Russian national identity associated with the country's imperial heritage. The combination of national identity politics and an autocratic leadership interested primarily in political survival brought about a war against Ukraine that has been unimaginable in scale and the level of atrocities. While fought against Ukraine's aspirations to be a Western-oriented state integrated into Western political and security institutions, the Russian leadership has effectively put the future of the Russian state and the Russian nation in line at the service of their unachievable political goals.

Questions for discussion

1 In what ways do the historical legacies of national consolidation in Russia influence the politics of national identity today?
2 Can nations be built from the top down? Who or what should we blame for the failed nation-building processes in Russia?
3 In what ways can Russian nationalism be seen as banal and settled? In what ways is it still unsettled?
4 How can war contribute to a nation-building process? When do wars destroy nations?
5 How is Russia's current top down, imperialist nationalism linked to regime survival?

Recommended readings

Beissinger, Mark R. 2002. *Nationalist Mobilization and the Collapse of the Soviet State*. Cambridge University Press.
Curanović, Alicija. 2021. *The Sense of Mission in Russian Foreign Policy: Destined for Greatness!* Routledge.

Gaufman, Elizaveta. 2023. *Everyday Foreign Policy: Performing and Consuming the Russian Nation after Crimea*. Manchester University Press.

Laruelle, Marlene. 2009. *In the Name of the Nation: Nationalism and Politics in Contemporary Russia*. Springer.

Smith, Kathleen E. 2018. *Mythmaking in the New Russia*. Cornell University Press.

5

Russia's Gendered Politics[1]

Valerie Sperling

Putin subdues a Siberian tiger! Putin drives a Formula One racecar! Putin flies a jet fighter! Putin defeats opponents in martial arts displays! Putin fishes and rides horseback – shirtless! As Vladimir Putin consolidated power during his first three terms in office – the first two as president, and the third as prime minister – the Russian media regularly painted him as a macho superhero. Putin's masculinity became a political trademark of his regime starting almost immediately after his ascent to power as Russian president in 2000 (Sperling 2015a). Deep into his fourth presidential term (2018–24), Putin's image remained that of a tough and – after Russia's full-scale invasion of Ukraine in February 2022 – increasingly brutal political leader. And while the current regime relies more on repression than on footage of macho stunts to undergird Putin's power, gender norms have become even more central to the regime's legitimation strategy.

This chapter examines gender politics in Russia in several aspects. It analyzes gender as an element of political legitimacy, exploring masculinity and political leadership in Russian domestic and foreign policy, paying particular attention to the ways that traditional gender norms and queerphobia have underlain Russia's 'conservative turn' in Putin's third and fourth presidential terms, and have been used to legitimate Russia's war against Ukraine. The chapter also highlights resistance to sexism and LGBTQ+ oppression via civic activism.

Gender and political legitimacy in Russia

Masculinity in politics is pervasive. Political leaders compete with one another at home and abroad in a multitude of fields, from personal charisma to public policy positioning – but always on the terrain of masculinity. From early on in Vladimir Putin's tenure at the top of Russia's political hierarchy, masculinity has been central to the Putin regime's legitimation strategy (Sperling 2015).

When he first ascended to the presidency, image-makers used Putin's KGB background and penchant for physical fitness to frame him as a macho strongman who could reverse Russia's waning power and 'remasculinize' the country after a decade of supposed geopolitical flaccidity in the wake of the Soviet collapse (Riabov and Riabova 2014). From the famous photos of the shirtless Putin fishing and horseback-riding to Putin's tough talk against Chechen terrorists (promising as Prime Minister in 1999 to 'waste them' in their outhouses), Putin reassured his domestic audience that Russia would no longer be pushed around by Western states hoping to permanently weaken the fatherland. Putin's machismo was a way to broadcast both his legitimacy and Russia's strength.

Public displays of masculinity are hardly a new development in political leadership. In 1966, China's Communist Party chairman Mao Zedong sought to demonstrate his virility at age seventy-two by swimming in the Yangtze River accompanied by a fully dressed military detachment, Chile's Augusto Pinochet – like Putin, a martial artist – broke bricks in public, and Benito Mussolini readily revealed his own hairy chest for Italian public consumption (Antola Swan 2016). Political leaders in more democratic states are decisively not immune to reliance on masculinity for legitimation. Donald Trump's repeated disparagements of his political competitors as weak, 'little', and low-stamina constitute recent reminders of this fact; indeed, politicians across the political spectrum in the United States regularly wield masculine gender norms in their campaign advertisements – both to bolster their own support and to undermine their opponents (Boatright and Sperling 2020).

The conservative turn

Gender norms became important in additional ways for the Russian regime's political legitimation in Putin's third and fourth presidential terms (2012–

18, 2018–24), as Putin adopted an increasingly conservative line that drew on traditional masculine and feminine gender norms (stereotypical understandings of masculinity and femininity), as well as an increasingly explicit homophobia and transphobia.

Putin's third term began against the backdrop of widespread, prolonged popular protests against electoral fraud in Russia's December 2011 parliamentary elections. During Putin's annual hours-long TV call-in show on 15 December 2011, Putin jested that he thought the protestors' white ribbons (which stood for clean elections) looked like condoms and that perhaps the vast crowd of protestors were actually AIDS activists. His remarks were intended to paint the protestors as gay, thereby rendering them objects of ridicule in the context of Russian state-sponsored homophobia. Putin's opposition responded in the same vein. Protestors at a mass rally on 24 December compared Putin himself to a condom in a variety of their posters; one showed a line drawing of a condom, and the words 'You're one, yourself'. Another depicted Putin along with a condom, and the caption, 'Not for re-use' – suggesting that voters deny Putin a third presidential term at the March 2012 elections. A joke playing on homophobia and the condom theme also circulated at that time: Putin and Medvedev enter a drugstore together, approach the counter, and say to the pharmacist, 'Two condoms'. 'Yes, I know', responds the pharmacist. 'What can I do for you?' (Sperling 2015a).

Concerned that he had lost the support of Russia's educated, professional middle class, Putin shifted to the right. This conservative turn was embodied in a series of policies that attacked women's and LGBTQ+ rights, and in anti-Western and anti-American political rhetoric lambasting the Western societies that supposedly embraced those rights and sought to undermine the Russian government. This effort to re-legitimate the Putin regime drew support from conservative, right-wing actors like the Russian Orthodox Church, ultranationalist parents' groups like Parents' Control (*Roditel'skii kontrol'*), and conservative oligarchs like the railroad tycoon Vladimir Yakunin and banker Konstantin Malofeev, as well as from some portion of the Russian population outside of the largest cities (Johnson, et al. 2021; Novitskaya, et al. 2023).

Attacks on women's rights and LGBTQ+ rights

Gender and sexuality were central to the 'conservative turn'. Women's rights were rolled back in several important areas. In 2011, the regime restricted abortion rights, establishing a waiting period for abortion on demand (permitted up to twelve weeks), limiting the permissible reasons for second-trimester abortion to rape and medical issues, and introducing psychological consultations as part of the visit to an abortion clinic (Sperling 2015, 256). Russia has no law specifically criminalizing domestic violence. In 2016, battery – the statute typically used by Russian women who try to bring charges against abusers – was demoted from the Criminal Code to an administrative offence, but feminist activists were able to persuade legislators to keep battery against 'close persons' (i.e. family members) in the Criminal Code. In 2017, however, activist pressure by conservatives insisting on the right to 'slap' one's children or spouse resulted in first-time battery by 'close persons' also being decriminalized (Johnson 2017). After Russia's 'foreign agent' law was passed in 2012 (see Chapters 9 and 13), various feminist organizations, including two groups opposing domestic violence and a handful of gender studies centres, were labeled 'foreign agents' (several of the latter then closed). Renewed emphasis was placed on addressing Russia's demographic 'problem' – a low birthrate that the government sought to reverse by means of financial rewards to women who had more than one child (a policy initially established in 2006). Presumably, if Russia's female population could be shielded from feminism and gender studies, rewarded for childbirth, encouraged to remain in intimate relationships with men (even those who used violence to control their partners), and prevented from getting *some* abortions, the birthrate might rise, meeting one of the regime's ostensible goals.

LGBTQ+ rights fared no better under Russia's new 'traditionalism'. The hallmark of state-sponsored homophobia was a federal law passed in 2013, outlawing the promotion of 'non-traditional sexual relations' to minors. What this meant was that same-sex relationships could not be presented in a positive light – or as equivalent in value to heterosexual ones – in front of children. Commonly referred to as the 'gay propaganda' ban, the law's passage was followed by prosecutions and an increase in homophobic violence (Kondakov 2022). This inequality was enshrined in law anew when one of Russia's constitutional amendments in 2020 proclaimed that marriage could be defined only as a relationship between a man and a woman. And in November 2022, the 2013 law was expanded to ban any positive or neutral mention of LGBTQ+ topics (including gender affirmation surgery) in front of audiences of any age, leading to charges against book publishers, and, potentially, bars or nightclubs catering to LGBTQ+ communities, and even individuals, simply for being queer in public.

These efforts to re-legitimate the regime on a more conservative basis were not far out of step with Russian public opinion. While a nationwide

Russian survey conducted in spring 2021 found the population nearly unanimous in thinking that a husband hitting his wife or girlfriend could not be justified (97 per cent), which suggests that there would be popular support for criminalizing domestic gender-based violence, the population was split evenly on whether abortion could be justified (with 46 per cent saying yes, and 47 per cent saying no). Public opinion on LGBTQ+ rights was far less tolerant, with 69 per cent of the population saying they would not want 'sexual minorities' as neighbours, and 89 per cent agreeing that marriage should only be between a man and a woman (LegitRuss Survey 2021). These differences likely represent echoes of the Soviet era, during which the government rhetorically supported women's equality and made abortion available (except from 1936 to 1955), while criminalizing gay male sex entirely from 1933 onward (Novitskaya et al. 2023).

Anti-Westernism

Having argued baselessly that the tens of thousands of Russian protestors had been paid by the US State Department to take to the streets in December 2011, Putin likewise blamed the popular overthrow of his ally in Ukraine, Viktor Yanukovych, in early 2014, on US State Department operatives, rather than recognizing the long-standing frustration of Ukrainians with their president's refusal to sign a financial trade agreement with the European Union; Yanukovych had promised to do so, but signed a loan agreement with Russia instead. Unfounded rhetoric about Ukraine's new 'fascist' government and its Western supporters – supposedly in cahoots to use Ukraine as a forward base from which to weaken and attack Russia – bloomed on Russian state-run television. Eight years later, Putin would make the extraordinary claim that the need to 'de-Nazify' Ukraine was high on the list of reasons for Russia's invasion, despite the fact that Ukraine's democratically elected president, Volodymyr Zelensky, was Jewish, and that the right-wing nationalist parties on the Ukrainian political spectrum regularly polled no more than 3 per cent support in the post-Soviet period (Mierzejewski-Voznyak 2018, 862).

Gender norms and foreign policy

Gender norms frequently arise in foreign policy rhetoric, and Russia's foreign policy under Putin is no exception. Following Ukraine's first pro-democracy revolution in 2004, Russia raised the price of gas exported to Ukraine. On Russian television, Ukraine was then painted as America's female mistress, a 'greedy, kept woman', and Russian protestors' posters outside the US embassy in Moscow instructed the US to pay Ukraine's subsequent debts to Russia: 'A Gentleman Always Pays for his Girlfriend'. Putin likewise used homophobic terms to dismiss Georgia's Rose Revolution in 2003, responding to a reporter's question by saying: 'A rose revolution – next they'll come up with a light blue one' (Riabov and Riabova 2014). In Russian, 'light blue' or *goluboi* is slang for 'gay male'. Putin's ally in that conflict, the president of South Ossetia, likewise remarked of Georgia's president, 'Saakashvili is far from having democratic values – not to speak of male ones – he doesn't have any of those at all' (Sperling 2015, p. 78).

Kremlin-sponsored 'astroturf' youth groups also adopted the notion that Putin's toughness and strength were changing Russia's power relationship to its international competitors. An art show organized by the youth wing of the United Russia party in 2014 included paintings of Putin dominating American President Barack Obama in martial arts and disciplining him like a child for supposedly trying to get his hands on Ukraine (Riabova 2014). Similarly, for Putin's sixty-second birthday that year, a pro-Putin group called Network (*Set'*), produced two gifts emphasizing Putin's achievements as an unshakeable national leader navigating a hostile international environment. The first gift was an art exhibit featuring renderings of 'The Twelve Labors of Putin' (modeled after the Twelve Labors of Hercules). Here, among other things, a well-muscled, sword-wielding Putin could be seen shielding Russia from the economic sanctions imposed by the European Union, Canada, Japan, and the US after Russia's illegal annexation of Crimea – where the sanctions were portrayed as the Hydra, a multi-headed serpent, and where Putin had chopped off the hydra-head labeled 'USA'. Network's second gift was a series of giant patriotic murals painted on exterior walls in seven Russian cities (including Sevastopol, in the newly annexed Crimea), each illustrating one of Putin's achievements for Russia: Strength, Remembrance, Arctic, Sovereignty, History, Security, and Olympics – which composed an acronym for the Russian word *spasibo* (thank you). As Network's press secretary explained, under Putin, Russia was *winning*. With Putin in charge, the state, like its leader, was now seen as a strong state that would not hesitate to use force, ostensibly in self-defence against incursions by the 'collective West'.

Gender norms, queerphobia, and Russia's 2022 invasion of Ukraine

Another means of mobilizing gender norms in politics – at home and abroad – is to use femininity and female sexuality in the service of male political authority. Putin's image-makers embraced this tactic. This began with the release of a catchy pop music video in 2002 called 'Someone Like Putin' performed by a duo of attractive young women who complained about a boyfriend's failings and voiced their desire instead for a man 'like Putin' who would be 'full of strength' who didn't drink alcohol, and who wouldn't run off. A male politician's 'manly' image can thus be enhanced via women's public – and, often, sexualized – support. The most famous example of this was a calendar published in October 2010 as a gift for Putin's fifty-eighth birthday, featuring twelve female students and alumni of Moscow State University's prestigious journalism department wearing lingerie, each woman suggesting herself as a potential lover for Mr Putin. 'You put the forest fires out, but I'm still burning', smiled a student illustrating the month of March (Sperling 2015, p. 1).

Gender norms have been used in Russia in this and other ways to justify Russia's annexation of Crimea in 2014 and broader war against Ukraine since that time. In January 2015, Mashani, a Russian female pop singer, introduced a catchy new song, 'My Putin' (*Moi Putin*), whose lyrics laud Putin for his fearless ability to face the 'war that threatens on all fronts' and his willingness to 'challenge' those who stand in the way of his goals. In the music video, a tall, slender woman with ribbons in her long hair wears a tricolour dress patterned after the Russian flag, and proclaims her delight that Putin has appropriated Crimea and – more surprisingly – that he's going to 'revive the [Soviet] Union'. She is also shown in a blue-and-yellow dress – the colours of the Ukrainian flag – looking alarmed and sad, trapped inside a bombed-out brick building, seeking help from Putin. The chorus, which she sings in the guise of both 'Ukraine' and 'Russia' in her different outfits, visually and lyrically justified Putin's illegal annexation of Crimea and military incursions into the Donbas, combining support for Putin's foreign policy and his appeal as a man: 'You're Putin/I want to be with you/I'm calling after you/My Putin, my dear Putin/Take me with you/I want to be with you' (Sperling 2015a). In light of Russia's full-scale assault on Ukraine starting in February 2022, the false and propagandistic claims in these lyrics – that the West was threatening to attack Russia, and that Ukraine's citizens would welcome a Russian military 'rescue' – are even more disturbing.

In the months preceding the 2022 invasion, Putin's public language became increasingly homophobic and transphobic. For years, the 'West' (Europe and the US in particular) had been painted by Russian conservatives as sites of moral decay, linked in particular to feminism and homosexuality, while Russia, by contrast, was praised as a bastion of traditional values (as further discussed below). But Putin himself, in the first two decades of his annual speeches to the Russian public, had said nothing explicitly anti-feminist, aside from one complaint in 2013 at his annual Big Press Conference about Pussy Riot, the members of which had 'dishonored women,' he noted: In order to stand out and promote themselves in some way, they crossed every line' with their protest song in Moscow's Cathedral of Christ the Saviour in 2012.

Nor had Putin said much about LGBTQ+ issues in those speeches, having made only two remarks on the subject (Johnson, et al. 2021, 10). In 2007, when asked at his annual Big Press Conference whether he agreed with Moscow's then mayor, Yuri Luzhkov, that gay parades were 'the work of Satanists', Putin had replied, 'My attitude toward gay pride parades and sexual minorities is simple. It has to do with the fulfilment of my official duties and the fact that one of this country's biggest problems is demographic.' And on his 'Direct Line' television call-in show in 2013, when a reporter noted that Putin had spent considerable time talking about 'same-sex marriage and pedophilia' while on recent trips to Germany and the Netherlands, Putin responded: 'You are indeed correct that during my last trip a lot of discussion time was dedicated to the rights of sexual minorities and other such issues. But, you see, they have their own standards, and I talked about it there and can say it again here: If in Holland a court allowed the activities of an organization involved in the spread of pedophilia, why must we adopt these standards?' (Novitskaya, et al. 2023).

While these statements – especially the latter, which conflated homosexuality and paedophilia – can be considered homophobic, Putin's rhetoric opposing LGBTQ+ rights escalated as Russia's full-scale attack on Ukraine approached. At the October 2021 meeting of the Moscow-based Valdai Discussion Club, Putin remarked that teaching children about gender fluidity was 'truly monstrous' and 'verging on a crime against humanity'. And at his December 2021 nationwide news conference, Putin announced, 'I uphold the traditional approach that a woman is a woman, a man is a man, a mother is a mother, and a father is a father' (Sperling et al., 2022).

Such declarations continued following the invasion. In March 2022, Putin's ally at the head of the Russian Orthodox Church, Patriarch Kirill, proclaimed in a sermon that gay pride parades were a 'loyalty test' demanded by the West – one that the separatists in the Donbas had 'fundamentally rejected'. The Patriarch further justified Russia's so-called 'special military operation' as a necessity in order to prevent the influx of socially liberal Western values, including gay rights, saying, 'If humanity accepts that sin is a variation of human behaviour, then human civilization will end there' ('Russian Church Leader' 2022).

In a speech in late September 2022, when Putin announced the annexation of four regions of Ukraine that Russia had partially and temporarily occupied – Donetsk, Luhansk, Kherson, and Zaporizhzhia (a week or so later, Russian troops were forced to pull out of Kherson) – he included similarly homophobic and transphobic remarks: 'Do we want to have here, in our country, in Russia, "parent number one, parent number two and parent number three" (they have completely lost it [over there]!) instead of mother and father? Do we want our schools to impose on our children, from their earliest days in school, perversions that lead to degradation and extinction? Do we want to drum into their heads the ideas that certain other genders exist along with women and men and to offer them gender reassignment surgery? Is that what we want for our country and our children? This is all unacceptable to us. We have a different future of our own' ('Signing of Treaties' 2022). This language clearly implied that Russia was obliged to invade Ukraine to prevent the irrational and immoral ('perverse') Western incursions on Russia that would ostensibly take place if Ukraine remained an independent state.

Putin's sexist remarks

While Putin has not been the worst global offender with regard to misogynist statements (here he faces fairly intense competition from Rodrigo Duterte, Jair Bolsonaro, Donald Trump, and others), he has donated several unforgettable nuggets of sexism to the political-rhetorical storehouse. During her first run for the Democratic presidential nomination in 2008, when Hillary Clinton joked that Putin, as a KGB officer, 'doesn't have a soul' (contra George W. Bush's experience of looking into Putin's eyes and reportedly getting a 'sense of his soul' as a 'very straightforward and trustworthy' man), Putin retorted that 'At a minimum, a head of state should have a head'. Likewise, when Putin falsely claimed that the Russian takeover of Crimea in March 2014 was necessary to 'save a largely Russian speaking population from Ukrainian government violence', and Clinton then compared the Russian annexation of Crimea to Hitler's moves into Poland and Czechoslovakia in the 1930s to supposedly protect German minorities, Putin's response called upon gender stereotypes as a means to dismiss Clinton's criticism, remarking that it was 'better not to argue with women' and that 'When people push boundaries too far, it's not because they are strong but because they are weak. But maybe weakness is not the worst quality for a woman.' And in the course of filming Oliver Stone's 2017 documentary, *The Putin Interviews*, Putin explained that he never had 'off' days as president because he was 'not a woman' and thus did not suffer the – in his view – inevitable hormonal impairments that plague women's abilities to do their jobs (Sperling 2022).

Putin's sexist comments also include rape jokes. In 2006, he lauded the Israeli president, who was accused and later convicted of rape and sexual harassment, as a 'mighty man' who 'raped 10 women'. And at a press conference shortly before Russia's invasion of Ukraine, Putin remarked that Ukrainian President Volodymyr Zelensky did not like the Minsk Accords (a ceasefire agreement reached in 2014 to end the fighting between Ukraine and the Russia-backed separatists in the Donbas region), adding, 'Like it or not, my beauty, you have to put up with it' – suggesting that Zelensky would have to 'put up with' Russia's violation of Ukraine, the same way that women are supposed to 'put up with' sexual assault or rape without complaint. Notably, a Ukrainian artist, Andrei Yermolenko, responded to Putin's remark with a poster showing a Ukrainian woman putting a gun in Putin's mouth and saying in Ukrainian, 'I'm not your "beauty"' – symbolically dominating and violating Putin, and thereby eroding his masculinity-based authority (Sperling 2022).

Resistance

Feminists and LGBTQ+ activists have protested in response to the conservative turn, although the state's repression of free speech and assembly (with large fines for participating in demonstrations without a permit, and an increased likelihood of beatings, arrest and jail for protestors) has suppressed street protest considerably and moved much of it online. In this section we will briefly examine feminist and LGBTQ+ organizing in the late-Soviet, post-Soviet, and contemporary periods.

Feminist and queer activism

The first instance of feminist activism under Soviet rule was a dissident publication (*samizdat*) of a collection of essays called *Almanac: For women, about women* in 1979. The *Almanac*'s contents raised difficult issues like the poor conditions and maltreatment of women in Soviet maternity hospitals and the grisly and humiliating details of abortion procedures. Because any publication not approved by the Soviet censors was illegal, the *Almanac*'s authors came to the attention of the Soviet secret police (the KGB) and several were exiled from the country.

In the late 1980s, a new opening for feminist organizing arose under Soviet General Secretary Mikhail Gorbachev's policy of glasnost (the reduction of censorship). At that time, there had been only one legal women's organization – the Soviet Women's Committee – which was subordinated to the Communist party and had little in common with the idea of defending women's rights or improving women's status in the Soviet Union. But with glasnost, tiny feminist organizations also began to appear, especially in Moscow and Leningrad. These groups largely took the form of consciousness-raising clubs, and then expanded, offering seminars on women's issues and publishing occasional feminist newsletters and journals.

By 1991, several dozen small women's organizations had dared to form in the USSR, and activists in this nascent women's movement organized the first national women's conference, independent of state and Communist party control. The conference was called the First Independent Women's Forum, and it was held in March 1991, in Dubna, a town outside of Moscow, where more than 200 women gathered for the event. At that time, however, state monitoring of grassroots organizing was not yet a thing of the past. On the eve of the conference, rumours were spread in a popular newspaper that the conference would be a dangerous meeting of 'overexcited lesbians', and people were warned to keep their children off the streets. When the conference began, there were representatives of the police and KGB in the auditorium. But no arrests were made, and although the organizers feared they might lose their jobs, that did not happen, either. By the time the Second Independent Women's Forum conference was organized, toward the end of 1992, the Soviet Union itself was gone, and concerns about the repression of women's organizations had largely disappeared along with it.

Russian women's organizing in the post-Soviet 1990s was diverse, and most of it was not explicitly feminist. By the mid-1990s, in addition to some self-identified feminist discussion clubs, rape and domestic violence crisis centres and hotlines, gender studies research institutes, and advocacy groups that sought to influence government policy, many other women's organizations and charitable groups sprang up to help address women's unemployment and other negative economic effects of Russia's transition to capitalism. Small LGBTQ+ associations appeared as well, such as the Moscow Organization of Lesbian Literature and Art (which offered mutual support and organized women's concerts). These groups increased queer visibility in an extremely homophobic society by starting newspapers, sponsoring queer-friendly discos, and organizing occasional queer-themed conferences (Essig, 1999). Women's groups seeking money to support their activities found that the opportunities for domestic fundraising were extremely limited. In 1990s Russia, there was no such thing as chequebook activism, where people support organizations by sending them money; people in Russia at that time did not yet have chequebooks, credit cards were rare, and using the post office to do a 'direct mail' campaign to raise funds for a civic group was completely unheard of. In short, because there were no independent social movement groups under the Soviet regime, there was no economic infrastructure in post-Soviet Russia to support them. Feminist groups in the 1990s therefore competed with one another for funding from Western foundations and governments that were interested in building 'civil society' in Russia.

The unfortunate side effect of that competition, especially in big cities like Moscow and St Petersburg, was to fractionalize the movement, creating incentives for people to form their own small women's groups and compete for scarce resources. This made cooperation among the groups difficult. To win grants, organizations had to show their foreign donors successful, measurable outcomes, which in turn made the organization of women's conferences and seminars a priority, rather than organizing public protest against gender discrimination, or doing outreach to potential constituents and trying to build a grassroots feminist movement. By the end of the 1990s, with foreign funding for Russian civil society drying up, many groups became inactive, and, as the twenty-first century began and the relative political freedom of the 1990s began to recede into the past, feminist organizing declined.

The first fifteen years of Putin's leadership changed several factors for social movement organizing in Russia, the most important of which was the rise of the Internet as a means of communication and an organizational tool. Feminists took advantage of these opportunities, starting websites and discussion boards on Russia's new social media platforms. By 2015, feminist activism looked quite different than it had in the first post-Soviet decade.

The Putin-era wave of Russian feminist activism in the public space began in 2010 after a young male artist in Moscow was jailed for rape, and, while in jail, was awarded a prize for 'moral support' by a chic Moscow art gallery. Feminist activists organized a protest and awarded the *gallery* a prize for 'amoral support'. That kicked off a wave of street actions by feminists in Russia over the next few years. They objected to sexist commercial advertising and violence against women, and they joined anti-Putin protest marches. They also protested for reproductive choice, a campaign that accelerated in 2011 in response to proposed (and implemented) restrictions on abortion access.

Feminists also demonstrated for LGBTQ+ rights, holding a 'March of Burning Hearts' in 2012 together with LGBTQ+ groups and a variety of left-wing and human rights organizations. The March was organized after a prominent Russian journalist stated that gay people should not be allowed to donate their organs in the event of fatal accidents, and that their organs should be burnt instead – thus guarding against their receipt by unwitting (presumably heterosexual) transplant patients. As the event organizers explained, 'Bigots burn with hatred and fear, but our hearts burn with anger and indignation. They burn with the thirst for justice and are capable of igniting the hearts of others' (Sperling 2015, 262).

Promoting LGBTQ+ rights publicly at that time was challenging. Starting in 2006, annual efforts to get Moscow's city authorities' permission to hold a yearly gay pride parade failed; when activists gathered for the event regardless, in 2011, for example, they were physically attacked by Russian Orthodox extremists. A year later, in a burst of homophobic efficiency, a Moscow court banned gay pride events in the city for the next hundred years (Sperling 2015, 199).

One feminist group at that time started a 'Sexist of the Year' competition where prizes were virtually awarded to public figures in Russia who made sexist remarks. In 2014, one of the prizes went to a pundit, Yegor Kholmogorov, who commented: 'When we take over America, the first thing we'll do is pass a secret decree giving American men who hear the word "sexism" permission to punch whoever says it in the face. And for those who tell me that it's not proper to punch women in the face, I'll say that as soon as a woman pronounces the word "sexism", she ceases to be a woman and becomes a second-class object.'

Unlike the situation with the Russian women's movement in the 1990s, during Putin's third presidential term (2012–18), feminists continued to organize small rallies – especially around International Women's Day on 8

March. For the most part, those gatherings were permitted to occur, although in March 2013 a feminist rally in Moscow was disrupted by Russian Orthodox Church activists who shouted at the rally's speakers, calling them perverts and Satanists, and even squirting syringes filled with what they claimed was urine at them. Police took away the women's leaflets and a banner reading, 'Feminism is liberation', and arrested some of the attendees. This worrisome development provoked some activists to retreat and foreshadowed the repression that evolved over Putin's next decade in power.

Despite growing repression, feminists continued protesting. For instance, on May Day in 2015, a colourful and lively feminist contingent joined the annual labour-rights rally in St Petersburg. They carried posters critiquing a spate of advertisements plastered on the walls and spray painted on the sidewalks of St Petersburg, offering 'wife for an hour' (prostitution) services; they brought posters noting that women and men played merely functional roles for the state in that women produce babies and men are recruited to die in wars; and they marched with a clever see-through banner objecting to the glass ceiling that renders women's promotion in the workplace so difficult.

Pussy Riot and the political repression of feminist activists

The most well-known feminist group in Russia at that time was Pussy Riot, the self-identified feminist punk group of young women in colourful balaclavas who, in February 2012, entered Moscow's Cathedral of Christ the Saviour and sang about forty seconds of what they labeled a 'Punk Prayer' – a song calling upon the Virgin Mary to help get rid of Putin – before being bodily removed from the premises. Three of the group were caught and jailed a few weeks later. Yekaterina Samutsevich appealed her sentence successfully and was released on probation in October of that year, while Nadia Tolokonnikova and Masha Alekhina remained imprisoned until they were released two months ahead of schedule in December 2013 in advance of the Russia-hosted Sochi Olympics.

The punishment Pussy Riot received for their Punk Prayer and other public criticisms of the Putin government and its patriarchal alliance with the Russian Orthodox Church highlighted the regime's animus toward feminism. Although Marina Syrova, the judge in Pussy Riot's trial, found them guilty of the crime of 'hooliganism motivated by religious hatred', in her lengthy written sentence, she claimed that Pussy Riot's belief in 'feminism' was at the heart of their anti-religious sentiments, and thus was the motivator for their crime. In essence, the women of Pussy Riot were jailed for their feminism (Sperling 2015, 287–89).

Political repression hampered the activity of other women's groups in Russia, too, in Putin's third and fourth presidential terms, especially in connection with the 'foreign agent' law and his administration's general turn toward anti-American and anti-Western-European sentiment. The foreign agent law overtly targeted groups endorsing human rights and rule of law, and groups that the regime thought might organize citizenry in a way that could – however hypothetically – threaten the political status quo. Putin's government used the foreign agent law to target several feminist groups, either to deprive them of their Western funding, or to delegitimate them by forcing them to identify as foreign agents. Russia's foremost network of organizations bringing attention to the widespread issue of domestic violence – the ANNA Centre, headquartered in Moscow and founded in 1993 – was among the civic groups labeled as a foreign agent in 2016, as was the anti-domestic-violence support and advocacy group *Nasiliu.net* (No to Violence), in December 2020.

A new Putin-era feminist collective, Eve's Ribs (*Rebra Evy*) – a combination of mutual support and feminist consciousness-raising group and shared workspace in St Petersburg that also held an educational feminist summer school and an annual feminist film and theatre festival shedding light on gender-based discrimination – also drew the regime's ire in May 2019 for a project promoting 'feminitives' (a way of making nouns in the thoroughly gendered Russian language less sexist). On 1 May 2019, half a dozen Eve's Ribs activists were arrested on their way to a Labour Day demonstration; the police also confiscated their hand-drawn posters. Each poster featured a single noun describing a profession like 'doctor' (*vrach*) or 'lawyer' (*iurist*) but adding a grammatically 'female ending' to the noun – like 'doctoress' (*vrachinia*) or 'lawyeress' (*iuristka*) – that would not usually be there because those professions are grammatically gendered male. The activists were released after several hours, but their posters were retained until the activists came to the police station a week later to demand their return, at which point they were told that the police were holding on to the posters to carry out an expert analysis and determine whether they constituted 'extremism'.

Individual feminist and LGBTQ+ activists have also been targeted by the Putin regime. In August 2020, for instance, feminist activist Daria Apakhonchich was arrested in St Petersburg for participating in the street performance of a 'vulva ballet' (the dancers held cardboard vulvas bearing phrases like 'My vulva is my vulva') in support of feminist and LGBTQ+

activist Iulia Tsvetkova, who was charged with distributing criminal pornography in 2020 in response to her body-positivity website featuring diverse drawings of female genitalia.

Activism against domestic violence

Domestic violence emerged as a particularly hot-button feminist issue during Putin's third and fourth terms. In part, the visibility of this issue was due to several particularly brutal and sensationalized cases of domestic or family violence that gave rise to street protests. In December 2017, Margarita Gracheva's husband took her into the woods and chopped off both her hands with an axe. He had previously accused her of cheating on him, and threatened her with a knife, but when Gracheva turned to the police for help, they did not take it seriously. The second case of 'family violence' garnering enormous public attention was that of the Khachaturyan sisters – three teenagers living in Moscow who killed their father in July 2018 after years of suffering physical and sexual violence at his hands. The case brought out the details of the violence, and, again, of police inaction, so that when the daughters were charged with murder and faced the possibility of long jail sentences for their act of self-defence, people went onto the streets to protest. In November 2019, the public was shocked again when it emerged that a twenty-four-year-old student at Saint Petersburg State University had been killed and dismembered by her partner, who was also her history professor; he was caught when trying to rid himself of her body parts in the Moika river.

The emergence of social media platforms during the Putin era enabled digital forms of feminist activism to counter gender-based violence. In 2016, a year ahead of the emergence of the viral #MeToo hashtag campaign in the US, feminist activists in Ukraine created a bilingual Ukrainian and Russian campaign called 'I am not afraid to talk [about it]' (#яНеБоюсьСказати/#я НеБоюсьСказать) that spread rapidly across the Internet. Another viral hashtag campaign arose on Instagram in 2019, initiated by feminist activist Alena Popova and blogger Alexandra Mitroshina, called 'I didn't want to die' (#Янехотелаумирать), which successfully boosted support for an online petition demanding that the Russian government adopt a domestic violence law. The campaign featured graphic photos submitted by women who wrote the slogan on their faces or bodies along with makeup mimicking injuries consistent with domestic abuse. The petition gathered over 900,000 signatures. Digital activism is harder to suppress than in-person protests in an autocratic environment – and thus became even more important for feminists and LGBTQ+ activists after Russia's full-scale invasion of Ukraine began in February 2022.

Feminist and queer anti-war activism

When Russia's massive attack on Ukraine began in late February 2022, the combination of popular outrage and accelerated state repression of public protest produced creative responses on the part of antiwar activists. Feminist and LGBTQ+ activists played a vanguard role in protesting against the war. A group called *Kvir Svit* (which means Queer World in Ukrainian), created by two Afro-Russian women, a Ukrainian woman, and a Ukrainian man, formed in order to help people of colour and queer people who were forced by the war to leave Ukraine, or to leave Russia to avoid mobilization; the organization initially offered funds as well as advice on housing and legal issues associated with relocation, but demand for funding soon exceeded supply.

The Feminist Anti-War Resistance (FAR) – an egalitarian, non-hierarchical network of autonomous cells inside and outside of Russia – formed just after Russia's full-scale invasion of Ukraine and directed particular attention to the impact of the war on women and queer people. FAR's manifesto explicitly condemned the war, explaining that, as feminists and Russian citizens, they vehemently opposed Russia's war of aggression and upheld Ukraine's sovereignty, and urged feminists in Russia and abroad to 'actively oppose the war and the government that started it' (Feminist Anti-War Resistance, 2022).

Early on, FAR's actions included street demonstrations, but as the Russian government rapidly escalated its repression, activists turned more to internet-based protest. With tens of thousands of followers on their social media channels, FAR posted images of protest actions around the country. These included artistic street actions like Mariupol-5000, where participants made grave markers and photographed them in the courtyards of their apartment buildings, to symbolically represent the burials of citizens killed in Russia's devastating attacks on the Ukrainian city of Mariupol (those attacks made it nearly impossible for people to venture out and bury their relatives in cemeteries). Other eye-catching protest tactics included 'guerilla' stickering and other creative methods of countering Russian propaganda about the war, such as writing 'no to war' on Russian coins and banknotes and featuring Ukrainian women's stories on FAR's social media. FAR also organized psychological support and humanitarian aid for Ukrainians forcibly relocated to Russia, and helped Russian antiwar activists safely exit the country when faced with government persecution. FAR also took an actively decolonial perspective, critiquing discrimination against non-Russian ethnic groups inside Russia as well as Russian imperialism abroad. None of this activism went unnoticed; in December 2022, the Russian Ministry of Justice added the Feminist Antiwar Resistance to the foreign agent list.

Conclusion

The repression of feminist and LGBTQ+ activism has been part and parcel of Putin's third and fourth presidential terms amidst the conservative turn, because such activism threatens his regime's legitimacy by questioning the validity of binary and traditional gender norms. While feminist actions and public assertions of LGBTQ+ rights may appear harmless or even beneficial to the public, political leaders who depend on masculinity know that they can only survive in power if gender stereotypes and the pervasive notion that masculinity and its associated characteristics are superior to femininity remain unquestioned (Chenoweth and Marks 2022). As the Russian government becomes more and more a personalistic dictatorship, feminism and expressions of LGBTQ+ rights will likely be increasingly vilified by the regime.

We cannot understand Russian politics – or the politics of any country – without understanding its gender dimensions. Fortunately, there are many ways to study these issues. Social scientists use multiple methods to research the intersection of gender and politics, such as participant observation, activist interviews, scrutiny of discussions on social media (Perheentupa 2022; Sperling 2015), analyzing politicians' speeches for content having to do with gender equality and LGBTQ+ rights and comparing them with popular attitudes captured by survey data (Johnson, et al. 2021; Novitskaya, et al. 2023), and studying court cases that involve gender and LGBTQ+ discrimination (Sundstrom, Sperling, and Sayoglu, 2019). Taking a fine-grained intersectional approach that considers not only gender, but relevant variables like race or ethnicity and social class – and how these factors interact – adds richness to our understanding.

This chapter has made the argument that gender norms – alongside sexism and queerphobia – matter in politics. Our ideas about gender, about masculinity and femininity, have an impact on the way people feel about political figures and evaluate their legitimacy. As Putin's fourth term wears on – and especially if he avails himself of the opportunity to run for and win the fifth and sixth terms to which the current Russian constitutional rules entitle him – his macho, tough, decisive, protective image will wane as he ages and his perceived masculinity declines.

Questions for discussion

1 Putin's machismo has been a big part of his overall image as a political leader. Is Russia unusual in this regard?
2 How and why do voters take the masculinity and femininity of their political leaders into account when they consider which ones to support?
3 If you were a feminist activist in Russia today, what issues would you prioritize?
4 If you were an LGBTQ+ activist in Russia, what strategies do you think you would use to try and counter state-sponsored (and societal) queerphobia?
5 Why has the Putin regime used homophobia and, especially, transphobia to help justify Russia's illegal war against Ukraine?

Recommended readings

Buyantueva, Radzhana. 2022. 'Cultural and Geopolitical Conflicts between the West and Russia: Western NGOs and LGBT Activism.' *Connexe*, 8: 148–67. https://oap.unige.ch/journals/connexe/article/view/1031/748.
Goretti, Leo and Sofia Mariconti, 'Let's Learn Judo with Putin: Sport, Power and Masculinity in 21st Century Russia.' *Istituto Affari Internazionali Papers*, 23/03 (January 2023), www.iai.it/sites/default/files/iaip2303.pdf.
Kondakov, Alexander. 2022. *Violent Affections: Queer Sexuality, Techniques of Power, and Law in Russia*. London: University College London Press.
Sperling, Valerie, and Alexandra Novitskaya, Janet Elise Johnson, Lisa McIntosh Sundstrom. 2022. 'Vladimir Putin, the Czar of Macho Politics, Is Threatened by Gender and Sexuality Rights.' *The Conversation*, 11 April. https://theconversation.com/vladimir-putin-the-czar-of-macho-politics-is-threatened-by-gender-and-sexuality-rights-180473.
Temkina, Anna. 2020. 'Neither Harmless Nor Distant: How Russian State Conservatism Combines Emancipation and Tradition to Undermine Women's Rights and Suppress Sexual Awareness.' *Meduza*, 23 November. https://meduza.io/en/feature/2020/11/24/neither-harmless-nor-distant.

6

Russia's Economic Policies

Juliet Johnson

Russia's economic system has two main characteristics. First, the state owns or significantly influences the largest companies, particularly in the financial and natural resource sectors. Second, it uses this control to support an extensive web of patronage-based political and economic relationships. This system privileges informal rules and a small group of loyal elites to the detriment of small business and foreign investors, and relies upon natural resource revenues funnelled through a centralized financial system to maintain the regime.

Some scholars have described Russia's economy as a contemporary version of *state capitalism*. Governments in state capitalist systems play a direct role in economic management, and reciprocal relationships of loyalty and trust bind state–business coalitions that cooperate and compete with one another (Mizobata and Hayashi 2022, Viktorov and Abramov 2022). State-owned enterprises (SOEs) still produce at least one-third of Russia's economic output. This puts the Russian economy in the same category as countries like China, Brazil, India, and Indonesia (Kurlantzick 2016). Neil Robinson (2011) has dubbed Russia's system *patrimonial capitalism*, a form of illiberal capitalism in which elite interests dominate, personal connections are paramount, and formal and informal rules actively work against one another (see Herrera and Mitrokhina in this volume for more on Russia's informal economy). Scholars have also argued that since the 2014 annexation of Crimea, Russian economic policies have increasingly turned towards *financial nationalism* (Johnson and Köstem 2016) or *conservative developmental statism* (Bluhm and Varga 2020), systems in which political elites use illiberal economic means to pursue national identity and status goals. This view compares Russia to countries like Hungary under Prime Minister Viktor Orbán.

This chapter provides an overview of Russian economic policymaking since the Soviet collapse. It begins with a brief description of the major challenges that Russia's post-Soviet leaders have faced, and then discusses the evolution of the contemporary Russian economic system over four time periods: (1) transformation, 1992–99; (2) managed liberalism, 2000–07; (3) failed modernization, 2008–13; and (4) retrenchment and realignment, 2014 to the present.

Post-Soviet economic challenges

Russian leaders faced three fundamental economic challenges after the breakup of the Soviet Union. First, Russia had to make the transition away from the *command economy*, a system in which the government centrally controls ownership, prices, and distribution. While Soviet leader Mikhail Gorbachev's policies began this transition process, the results were so chaotic and contested that they contributed significantly to the Soviet collapse (see the chapter by Ironside in this volume). Post-Soviet Russian leaders attempted to create the institutions necessary to support a market economy while also liberalizing prices, establishing a more stable domestic economic environment, and transferring state property into private hands. Battles over how to do so, who would benefit, and what role the state should ultimately play in the economy profoundly shaped the post-Soviet political landscape.

Second, Russia had to transform its economic relationships with other countries. Russia's post-Soviet integration into global capitalist trade and financial networks affected everything from the availability of goods to the value of the ruble. In addition, the Soviet Union itself had been highly economically integrated, sharing a single currency as well as a production and distribution infrastructure. Russian leaders had to navigate the breaking, loosening, and renegotiation of these ties with the fourteen other Soviet successor states. Russian government attempts over the years to formally reintegrate much of this economic space under its own leadership met with only limited success. At the same time, as the region's largest economic power and its former imperial core, Russian policies and developments have strongly impacted its closest neighbours. For example, Russia has the fourth largest migrant population in the world, dominated by economic migrants from Central Asia (United Nations 2017).

Finally, the Russian economy depends heavily on revenues from the production and export of oil, gas, and other natural resources. Energy sales alone accounted for about half of Russia's export income in 2021.[1] This represents both a significant source of wealth for Russia and a challenge for economic management. The government budget, the ruble's exchange rate, and Russia's trade balance all fluctuate in response to international oil prices, making the economy vulnerable to price shocks. Resource dependence can lead to *Dutch disease*, a phenomenon in which resource exports drive up the currency's exchange rate, undercutting manufacturers for the domestic market by increasing the competitiveness of imports. Researchers also argue that significant resource wealth can reinforce tendencies toward political centralization and authoritarianism (Ross 2001). Dealing with the benefits and challenges of Russia's natural resource abundance has been a continuous preoccupation of Russian policy makers.

Transformation (1992–99)

Today many Russians look back on the 1990s as a painful time of 'capitalism without limits' that made a few Russians obscenely wealthy while impoverishing the country as a whole. Jokes about rich 'New Russians' and their shallow materialism captured the perceived ethos of the era. In one well-known joke, a New Russian crashes his car, and as he drags himself bleeding from the wreckage, he laments 'Oh no, my Mercedes!' A bystander, noticing that the man has lost an arm, shouts 'Forget your Mercedes, what about your arm?' The New Russian looks down and wails, 'Oh no, my Rolex!' The Russian economy in the 1990s underwent a massive transformation that upended people's lives and led to significant socioeconomic inequality that has persisted to this day (see Morris in this volume). The fall in Russia's Gross Domestic Product (GDP) in the 1990s was far more severe than the United States experienced during the Great Depression of the 1930s.

Modern market economies are highly complex and are underpinned by a wide range of supporting institutions and practices, both formal and informal. Transforming a command economy into a capitalist one is no easy task, as it demands at least six fundamental changes. First, it requires liberalization of prices and trade. Prices must be mostly set by the marketplace rather than the state, and people must be relatively free to engage in trade both internally and across borders. Second, it requires privatization. State-owned property such as enterprises, housing, and land must be at least partially transferred from state control and a system to enable non-state exchange and entrepreneurship must be established. Third, it requires a market-oriented financial system. This means creating a relatively stable and convertible currency, a modern central bank, and a network of commercial banks, insurance companies, and other financial institutions to facilitate economic transactions. Fourth, it requires establishing *hard budget constraints*. This means that in most cases, enterprises can no longer count on a government bailout if they run into trouble. They must cover their operating costs from their own profits or else risk going under. Fifth, it requires setting up a legal and regulatory framework to support capitalist exchange and protect property rights. Finally, it requires the creation of a new tax system. Once enterprises are privatized and most people no longer work for the state, the government must rely on taxation to collect the revenue necessary to fund its activities.

So, how to move from one type of system to another? At the time, the main scholarly debate was between advocates of *shock therapy* and *gradualism* (Ghodsee and Orenstein 2021). Shock therapy, or the 'big bang' approach, means the rapid and simultaneous liberalization of prices and trade, large-scale privatization, and pursuing macroeconomic stabilization through tight monetary and fiscal policies. Proponents argued that even though this approach would cause an initial spike in inflation and a severe economic downturn, the economic pain would end quickly and would set Russia on a sustainable and irreversible path to a market economy. Gradualists argued that carrying out massive liberalization before putting institutional structures in place to support a market economy was a recipe for disaster. They advised taking a more measured approach and often invoked the example of China's successful gradual economic transformation. Metaphorically, while shock therapists argued that 'you can't cross a river in two leaps', gradualists countered that one should 'cross a river by feeling for the stones underfoot'. In practice, Russia's economic transformation took place not according to a master plan, but through trial and error, contestation, compromise, opportunism, and unexpected consequences.

With the Soviet collapse imminent, in November 1991 the Russian Congress of People's Deputies overwhelmingly voted to grant President Boris Yeltsin and his prime minister, economist Yegor Gaidar, the emergency powers necessary to embark on a shock therapy programme. The economic situation at the time was dire. Production was down, shortages were rampant, and inflation had accelerated to over 160 per cent per year. Low international oil prices contributed to the Soviet government's financial woes. Although little formal privatization had yet occurred, in practice well-connected individuals and groups across the Soviet Union had taken advantage of perestroika-era policies and the uncertainty they introduced to appropriate state-owned resources, in a process Steven Solnick (1998) famously dubbed 'stealing the state'. Gaidar and Yeltsin believed that only rapid reform could set the Russian state on a better economic path and make the market transition irreversible. Modelling their policies after Poland's 1989–90 economic reforms, they promised that although at first inflation would rise and production would drop, by late 1992 there would be tangible improvement in the economy.

Yeltsin's decree liberalizing most prices came into force on 2 January 1992, followed quickly by trade liberalization, tighter monetary policy, and more restrictive government spending. The Russian government also officially made the ruble convertible to US dollars for trade in goods and services, first internally and then externally. After political infighting and delays, in June 1992 Yeltsin introduced a key decree that allowed his privatization chief Anatoly Chubais to begin the process of privatizing Russian enterprises.

As expected, inflation spiked, Russia experienced cash shortages and production disruptions, and goods soon returned to the stores. However, the reform attempts quickly ran into serious trouble as the Russian government could not restrain the money supply. Instead of peaking quickly and then receding, Russia experienced *hyperinflation* of over 2,500 per cent in 1992. In the end, Russian officials would not manage to get inflation under control until 1995. Gaidar himself believed that the main reason for this failure was the decision of the International Monetary Fund (IMF) not to provide a foreign currency stabilization fund to back up the ruble's value during the price liberalization process. Others have pointed to the serious political opposition that arose in Moscow as soon as the dire initial effects of the reforms became clear, reflected in the replacement of Yeltsin's chosen central bank governor with the former head of the Soviet central bank, Viktor Gerashchenko, in May. But the failure to stabilize Russia's macroeconomy had deeper systemic roots, ones that would have been difficult to overcome under any circumstances.

After price liberalization, Russian enterprises quickly entangled themselves in what became known as the *interenterprise debt crisis* (Ickes and Ryterman 1992). State-owned enterprises raised prices in response to price liberalization, but when the Central Bank attempted to restrict access to state credit, companies then found it difficult to pay their suppliers. In addition, the centralized Soviet economic structure meant that many companies were monopolies and monopsonies, making it challenging to set 'market' prices. The SOEs responded by issuing what became a massive, interlocking network of IOUs in the (correct) assumption that the government would eventually clear their debts. Although SOEs lost the ability to issue these IOUs after the debt-clearing in July 1992, the process involved a significant increase in the money supply and sabotaged the stabilization effort.

Moreover, many Russian regions refused to cooperate with the stabilization programme. In the face of rising prices, some regional governments reintroduced price controls in defiance of Moscow, while others issued their own parallel currencies, lottery tickets, or debt instruments to compensate for the shortage of cash. Some regions also introduced restrictions on trade, prohibiting key locally produced goods from leaving the area. This should not have been surprising, as Russian regional governments had already begun demanding greater autonomy and withholding revenue from the central government before the Soviet collapse, trends that continued throughout the early 1990s.

But of all the factors that scuttled Russia's early macroeconomic reforms, the *ruble zone* looms largest. Russia had taken over the former Soviet central bank and its ruble printing presses, but in January 1992 all fifteen Soviet successor states still used the ruble as a common currency and had created their own central banks from the Soviet-era branches in their republics. Both the IMF and the Russian government initially supported maintaining the ruble zone, believing that its dissolution would complicate commerce across the newly international borders. Currency unions require a single monetary policy, however, and the Russian government had not consulted the other ruble zone members before undertaking its liberalization and stabilization efforts. When prices in Russia shot up and it became more difficult to get cash rubles as the Russian government attempted to restrict the money supply, the other countries were forced to react. Estonia and Latvia rapidly introduced their own currencies and broke with the ruble zone entirely, but many others issued their own currencies (or coupons) to circulate in parallel with the ruble, effectively increasing the money supply. Even more damaging to Russian efforts, many post-Soviet central banks began independently issuing large amounts of ruble credit to local SOEs. The companies, in turn, used this credit in transactions with Russian SOEs, again increasing the money supply. Ukraine's policies proved the most damaging to Russia, as it was the second-largest post-Soviet economy and heavily issued both parallel currencies and ruble credits. By the time the Central Bank of Russia shut down these inflationary conduits by introducing an independent Russian ruble in

July 1993, the damage to Russia's macroeconomic stabilization programme had been done.

Russia's privatization efforts had unexpected consequences as well. Following the Czech model, the Russian government undertook a *mass privatization* programme intended to redistribute ownership in most SOEs. Although the programme excluded the largest and most politically sensitive SOEs in natural resources, finance, medicine, and defence, by the programme's end in July 1994 over 15,000 SOEs had been privatized (Blasi, et al. 1996). In October 1992 every Russian citizen received a voucher with a face value of 10,000 rubles that could be used to acquire company shares in privatization auctions. Managers and employees of enterprises undergoing privatization received first crack at acquiring shares in their own companies, but the companies were required to make shares available for purchase through voucher auctions as well. In practice, after privatization the former company managers typically ended up in control of their enterprises once again, but this time with formal ownership rights. While this process did divest much property from the state, it did so without adding new resources, value, or expertise to the privatized companies. It also spawned pyramid schemes masquerading as voucher investment funds. The most infamous such scheme, MMM, eventually collapsed having robbed its many citizen 'investors' of multi-millions of US dollars.

The struggle to gain and maintain control over property in both industry and agriculture raged throughout the country as the development of institutions to govern property rights lagged behind (Barnes 2006). During these early years of economic instability, individuals, companies, and even local governments fled the ruble. While Russia's GDP plummeted, diverse monetary surrogates and barter appeared widely (Woodruff 1999). Many cash-strapped companies paid their workers in kind with the products they made, including items such as dildos, coffins, and bras. Russia also developed one of the world's highest *dollarization* rates (Johnson 2008). Dollarization means that much economic exchange in a country occurs in US dollars rather than the local currency. In the 1990s, more US $100 bills circulated in Russia than anywhere except the US itself. By 1998 perhaps as much as half of all exchange in industry relied on alternatives to the ruble.

While industry and agriculture suffered, the financial sector thrived. Russian banks, both newly created and descended from the Soviet banking system, made money in the 1990s through connected lending, currency trading, state financing, and other speculative activities (Johnson 2000). With their relative wealth, Russia's bankers began to enter the political system as campaign financiers, lobbyists, and even candidates. Institutional deficiencies encouraged state agencies to place their funds in commercial banks in a process that became highly politicized. Ironically, as enterprises became increasingly cash-starved, money became heavily concentrated in the banking system. The largest and most influential banks, led by the so-called 'oligarchs', expanded their activities to become *financial-industrial groups* (FIGs). Financial-industrial groups join banks and enterprises through shared ownership under a main holding company.

Under the circumstances, the cash-strapped Yeltsin government turned to the banking system for funds. Mass privatization, low international oil prices, and the proliferation of non-monetary exchange had made it difficult for the Russian government to finance its budget. In 1993 the Finance Ministry started issuing government bonds known as GKOs, which quickly became a major revenue source for the central government. At first the GKO market was restricted to the politically influential domestic banking sector, which benefited from very high yields. Eager for even more funding, the government opened the GKO market to foreign investment in 1996 and the money flooded in once Yeltsin had secured re-election in the tight presidential race that year. The government's search for funding and the oligarchs' political influence also led to the most controversial economic policy of the Yeltsin era, the 1995 *'loans-for-shares'* privatization auctions. In these rigged auctions, leading Russian FIGs snapped up controlling shares in major natural resource companies for a fraction of their real market value. Although many saw these auctions as a quid pro quo for the oligarchs' support for Yeltsin in the hotly contested 1996 presidential elections, the oligarchs already had every incentive to back Yeltsin in his successful campaign against their mutual antagonist, Communist Party leader Gennady Zyuganov.

After a brief post-election period of apparent economic stability, in 1998 Russia's house of cards collapsed in a major financial crisis. With ongoing tribulations in industry and agriculture, the Russian government's financial dependence on oil revenues, foreign GKO investors, and the politically connected FIGs had left it highly vulnerable. The 1997 Asian financial crisis led foreign investors to pull their money out of Russian markets at the same time that international oil prices were falling rapidly. This put increasing strain on the overvalued ruble and on the biggest Russian banks. Despite an emergency IMF loan in July, the Yeltsin government could not forestall the crisis and defaulted on its debt in August. The ruble's value plummeted, inflation rose, GKOs became virtually worthless, the stock market crashed, and imported goods once again became out of reach for many. Despite government bailout efforts, the crisis forced the banks at the centre of key FIGs either to go under or to restructure significantly. Prime Minister Sergei Kirienko, a market liberal who had been appointed earlier that year, resigned in the wake of the default.

The 1998 crisis signalled the end of Russia's first attempt at economic transformation and represented the nail in the coffin for the reputation of beleaguered president Boris Yeltsin. In August 1999 he appointed former intelligence officer Vladimir Putin as his third new prime minister since Kirienko's resignation. On New Year's Eve 1999 Yeltsin himself resigned, naming Putin acting president and announcing presidential elections for March 2000. In his farewell speech, an emotional Yeltsin apologized to Russians for the state of the economy:

> 'I want to ask your forgiveness – for the dreams that have not come true, and for the things that seemed easy but turned out to be so excruciatingly difficult. I am asking your forgiveness for failing to justify the hopes of those who believed me when I said that we would leap from the grey, stagnating totalitarian past into a bright, prosperous, and civilized future. I believed in that dream, I believed that we would cover the distance in one leap. We didn't.'[2]

Managed liberalism (2000–07)

After handily winning the March 2000 election, President Vladimir Putin moved to reassert state control over Russia's monetary and fiscal situation to set the stage for economic recovery and growth. The searing experience of the 1998 crisis encouraged Putin and his economic team to emphasize macroeconomic stability and monetary sovereignty. The first order of business was to remonetize the economy and build a more secure tax base to secure a steady revenue stream for the government. His plan for doing so involved conservative monetary and fiscal policies combined with reasserting state influence over natural resources and finance.

The aftermath of the 1998 financial crisis presented a golden opportunity to rebuild the state's position in the economy. The December 1999 parliamentary elections brought in a legislature that supported the new Putin government. The ruble's collapse had sparked a wave of import substitution that boosted Russian industry, leading to the first meaningful growth in Russia's GDP since the 1980s. State-controlled banks once again led the financial sector. International oil prices rose and kept rising for the next decade, providing a cushion for reform efforts as windfall energy revenues turned massive budget deficits into surpluses.

But most importantly, the crisis had shifted the balance of power between the oligarchs and the state. With their finances in tatters and their influence significantly reduced, Putin informed the oligarchs that they could keep their empires if they stayed out of politics and cooperated with state efforts to stabilize the economy. Integral to this plan was introducing a tax system that would direct far more oil industry profits to the state. Despite resistance from oil companies that naturally preferred to keep their windfall profits, the newly empowered Putin government decisively won this conflict (Johnson and Woodruff 2017). The Putin government also introduced a simplified 13 per cent flat tax on personal income in 2001, after which tax compliance significantly improved (Appel 2018).

Along with securing its tax base, the Putin government moved quickly to reassert monetary sovereignty in Russia. A more liberal exchange-rate regime and conservative central bank monetary policy brought inflation to the low double-digits and led to the re-monetization of the economy. Barter, monetary surrogates, and dollarization receded as the ruble reasserted its central position in the financial system. The government dealt with the exchange-rate pressures of high oil prices by paying off its foreign debt and accumulating foreign exchange reserves. Russia's reserves rose from less than $13 billion before the 1998 crisis to nearly $600 billion by mid-2008. Although some within the Russian state lobbied to spend the windfall oil profits on economic development projects, the Putin team's dual desire to rein in inflation and to build a wall of money as a shield against future oil price shocks won out. The Ministry of Finance created a *sovereign wealth fund* called the Stabilization Fund in 2004 to hold excess oil tax revenues. Sovereign wealth funds can serve a variety of purposes, but in oil-rich states they are primarily risk-management tools used to diversify investments, guard against Dutch disease, and protect the state budget from oil price volatility. By 2008 the Stabilization Fund had grown so large that it was split into the Reserve Fund and the National Wealth Fund.

Putin saw oil and gas as vital tools for economic development, political patronage, and foreign policy. Indeed, his academic research in the late 1990s had envisioned a statist economy in which large Russian natural resource companies could compete with their Western counterparts, provide social benefits, and enhance Russia's influence abroad (Balzer 2005).

But to effectively wield that tool, the state had to control Russia's energy resources. After stabilizing the economy and consolidating political power, the Putin government moved to establish firmer state influence over Russia's natural resource industries. Putin put his political allies on the boards of key companies and folded the Yukos oil company into state-owned Rosneft after Yukos owner Mikhail Khodorkovsky's arrest and imprisonment on tax evasion charges. The monopoly gas giant Gazprom acquired the Sibneft oil company from exiled oligarch Boris Berezovsky, as well as taking in other key defence and natural resource companies. In June 2005 the Russian government increased its stake in Gazprom to over 50 per cent, solidifying its control over the company.

In a sign of things to come, as Putin grew more statist and authoritarian in his second presidential term his government increasingly began to use natural resources as coercive foreign policy tools with its neighbours. For example, Russia had long provided cut-rate gas to Ukraine and Georgia as a means of maintaining economic influence in those countries. After the Georgian Rose Revolution in 2003 and the Ukrainian Orange Revolution in 2004 brought pro-Western, nationalist leaders to power, mutual relations cooled and the Russian government regularly threatened to cut off gas supplies to both countries if they did not accept price increases or agree to other economic concessions. The Putin government firmly believed that Russia should enjoy a privileged economic and political role in the former Soviet space and reacted negatively whenever these states expressed more interest in enhancing their ties with the West than with Russia.

The Russian economy grew by over 7 per cent a year between 2002 and 2008. Although the Putin government itself eschewed foreign debt, the booming economy and progressive capital account liberalization led to increased foreign borrowing by Russian companies and banks. With the ruble stabilized and well backed by foreign exchange reserves, Russian leaders began discussing the ruble as a possible international reserve currency and Moscow's development as an international financial centre. Some scholars argued that under the Putin government Russia had finally become a 'normal' middle-income country, one that had shed its Soviet past and set out on a path towards greater convergence with Western advanced industrial democracies (Shleifer and Treisman 2005). But others predicted confrontation rather than convergence, arguing that Russia's state-centered capitalism, patronage-based political economy, and heavy resource dependence made it more akin to a *petrostate* (Goldman 2008), or a non-Western authoritarian-patrimonial system (Rosefielde 2005, Batini and

Kopstein 2022). When the 2008 global financial crisis hit the Russian economy, it put these theories to the test.

Failed modernization (2008–13)

The global financial crisis came at a politically tricky moment for the Russian government. Having served his constitutionally permitted two terms as president, in late 2007 Putin tapped Gazprom board chair and first deputy prime minister Dmitry Medvedev to run for the presidency. Medvedev assumed office in May 2008 after his predictable victory and named Putin his prime minister, just in time for the crisis to hit. Russia's declining terms of trade, capital flight, and the rapid drop in international oil prices combined to plunge the Russian economy into turmoil by mid-2008. Oil prices fell from $147/barrel in July 2008 to under $50/barrel by November 2008, leaving a $150-million hole in the budget. The ruble's value declined steadily, sparking a domestic rush to convert rubles to dollars and euros. Russia's stock exchanges repeatedly halted trading during the autumn in the face of collapsing share prices. Russian banks and companies that had taken out foreign-currency loans were squeezed, and credit dried up. In September the government pumped $60 billion into its financial system to kickstart the credit market. The crisis continued through 2009, a year in which Russia's GDP fell by 7.9 per cent. The dramatic swing from nearly 8.5 per cent GDP growth in 2007 to -7.9 per cent in 2009 was among the largest in the world.

The Medvedev-Putin 'tandem' government responded to the crisis by carrying out massive fiscal expansion to stimulate the economy and currency intervention to ease the ruble's slide in value. Unlike August 1998, this time Russia had the foreign-exchange reserves necessary to act. In the process, it also bailed out politically connected oligarchs and firms such as the state oil company Rosneft, Alfa Group's Mikhail Friedman, and Oleg Deripaska, winner of the so-called 'aluminum wars' of the 1990s (see Barnes 2006). The bailouts and fiscal expansion led to further consolidation and state control over the energy and financial sectors, as well as to budget deficits as the government funneled cash towards defence, agriculture, and social assistance.

The global financial crisis's unexpectedly strong impact on Russia led Medvedev to declare *modernization* as the centrepiece of his presidential economic policy agenda. Modernization meant diversifying the economy to become less dependent on natural resource revenues and to nurture high-technology export industries and human capital. Medvedev published a prominent article entitled 'Go Russia!' in September 2009 that condemned Russia's 'economic backwardness', corruption, and paternalistic culture, and proposed an aggressive campaign of modernization as the way forward:

> 'Let's answer a simple but very serious question. Should a primitive economy based on raw materials and endemic corruption accompany us into the future? ... Achieving leadership by relying on oil and gas markets is impossible ... In the end, commodity exchanges must not determine Russia's fate; our own ideas about ourselves, our history and future must do so.'

This reinforced earlier calls by leading Russian economic liberals for the government to pursue diversification, transparency and the rule of law, and macroeconomic stability. The Ministry of Economic Development likewise posed a stark choice: Russia could either stagnate as an energy superpower (the conservative scenario), or grow by investing heavily in diversified high-tech industries, health and education, and transportation infrastructure (the innovation scenario).

However, the state-centric and patronage-based nature of the Russian economy made implementing such modernization policies difficult. Once strong domestic demand and rising oil prices kicked off an economic recovery in 2010, the government succumbed to the temptation to keep greasing the wheels of the existing system with resource revenues rather than making the tough choices necessary to transform it. By the autumn of 2011, Russia's reserves, which had fallen to almost $380 billion in early 2009, had returned to pre-crisis levels. Innovative high-tech industries typically flourish in countries with decentralized economic systems and open political systems, neither of which described Russia. The travails of the Skolkovo Innovation Centre on the outskirts of Moscow, the showpiece of Medvedev's modernization plan, demonstrated this problem well (Gel'man 2022). Initially projected to cost upwards of $4 billion and to feature a technopark, university, and start-up incubator, Skolkovo never fulfilled its promised role and as Medvedev's pet project was neglected after Putin returned to the presidency in 2012.

The modernization agenda ran fully aground with Putin's return in the context of a highly visible anti-authoritarian protest movement and restless political elites. Putin made extensive social and military spending commitments during his presidential campaign and leaned heavily on state resources to further consolidate and extend his political 'power vertical'. The renewed Putin government was thus not in a position to invest in new high-tech industries, to crack down on corruption, to reform the judicial system, or to reduce the state's hold on the economy. Oil and gas remained Russia's dominant industries, accounting for an overwhelming two-thirds of exports in 2013. Ongoing resource dependence and the increasing cost of fuelling the Putin regime's political patronage system proved to be a significant drag on economic growth. Instead of taking off after the economy had recovered from the crisis, Russian GDP trends stubbornly continued to follow the rise and fall of international oil prices.

As Russian domestic economic reforms stalled, the government's foreign economic policies became more assertive, especially once Putin returned to the presidency. Russian leaders saw the global financial crisis not only as the fault of the US, but as an invitation to challenge the privileged role of the West in the global economy. The Russian government redoubled its efforts to economically reintegrate the post-Soviet space in order to position Russia as the Eurasian pole of what they saw as an emerging multipolar world order. With Russian prodding, Russia, Belarus, and Kazakhstan entered a *customs union* in 2010. Countries in customs unions typically have free trade relationships with each other and a common set of tariff barriers for outsiders. Even after joining the World Trade Organization (WTO) in 2012, Russia's tariffs remained high for the region, and these tariffs were extended to the customs union. In January 2012 the customs union became the Eurasian Economic Space targeting the free movement of goods, labour, capital, and services. Putin lauded it as a precursor to an eventual Eurasian Economic Union modelled after the European Union, stating that 'only together do our countries have the ability to become leaders of global growth and civilizational progress'.[3] At the same time, Russia's partners resisted its overtures towards making the ruble a common regional currency and establishing Russian monetary dominance.

Beyond the region, the Russian government invested significant effort in transforming the *BRICS* economic group (Brazil, Russia, India, China, and – as of 2010 – South Africa) into more than just an informal talking shop. The central Urals city of Yekaterinburg hosted the first meeting of the BRICs Ministers of Foreign Affairs in 2008 and the first official BRICs leaders' summit in 2009. For Russian leaders, the BRICS group represented a way to collectively challenge the West's predominant role in the international economic system. Under Putin's renewed leadership, Russia also moved to increase its economic ties to the Asia-Pacific region more broadly. As Russia's 2013 Foreign Policy Concept argued, 'the ability of the West to dominate the world economy and politics continues to diminish. Global power and development potential is now more dispersed and is shifting to the East, primarily to the Asia-Pacific region.' Beyond the intellectual debate, one practical reason for this so-called 'Pivot to Asia' was to attract much-needed investment to Siberia and Russia's Far East. As the state's role in the domestic economy grew, authoritarian tendencies deepened, and Russian leaders became more frustrated with Russia's position in the global economic system, the stage was set for increasing confrontation with the West.

Retrenchment and realignment (2014–present)

Russian economic policy took a decisive turn after Ukraine's Revolution of Dignity in 2013–14 and Russia's subsequent annexation of the Crimean peninsula. Responding to Russian pressure, in November 2013 Ukrainian president Viktor Yanukovych abandoned plans to sign an agreement with the European Union that would have expanded EU–Ukraine trade and political ties. He later accepted an alternative deal with Russia that promised cheaper energy prices, economic aid, and the removal of bilateral trade tariffs on the implicit condition that Ukraine not pursue further economic integration with the EU. Protestors immediately filled Kyiv's central square waving EU flags and demanding that Yanukovych reconsider. The situation escalated over the following weeks until Yanukovych fled to Russia in late February 2014. The Russian government seized the opportunity to take over Crimea, formally incorporating the Ukrainian region into Russia after staging an illegitimate annexation referendum on 16 March. At the same time, the Russian government sparked conflict in the Donbas by backing separatist militias and attempting to detach the region from Ukraine. These actions made it clear that the Russian government had no intention of allowing Ukraine to independently choose its own economic or political path.

This incursion into Ukraine led to a mutually reinforcing spiral of Western *economic sanctions* and Russian financial nationalism. Sectoral sanctions introduced in the summer and autumn of 2014 increasingly restricted Russian access to Western finance. This led to a credit squeeze in the banking sector, to companies hoarding foreign exchange, and to downward pressure on the ruble. At the same time, international oil prices fell from a high of $115/barrel in June to below $70 in December. As the price of oil fell, the ruble fell along with it. Despite the Central Bank's reserve spending and interest-rate hikes, the dual pressure of sanctions and low oil prices led to a ruble crash in December 2014. Having learned from past experiences, the government quickly raised interest raises to a punishing 17 per cent, spent billions to back the ruble, imposed informal capital controls, prevailed upon the largest state-owned exporters to sell foreign currency reserves, and insisted that their future currency sales be coordinated with the government.

These efforts stabilized the ruble, but low oil prices and Western sanctions continued to put pressure on the economy. Although liberal Russian economic thinkers hoped that the economic downturn would spark a return to the modernization agenda, the Putin government instead pursued import substitution, food security, and increased investment in the military-industrial complex. As Russia turned defensive and inward, the government built what became known as 'Fortress Russia' to protect the domestic economy from the effects of sanctions. It created an independent national payments system and its own national credit ratings agency to reduce its reliance on existing international institutions. The Central Bank rebuilt Russia's foreign exchange reserves, diversified them from the traditional heavy reliance on the US dollar, and restrained inflation rather than boosting the ruble's exchange rate to make imports more affordable. It also pursued a major clean-up of the banking sector, contributing to the growth and diversification of domestic bank lending. GDP growth remained relatively stagnant.

Facing an understandably hostile Ukrainian government, Russia redoubled its efforts to build influence among its other neighbouring states. In 2015 the Eurasian Economic Space officially became the *Eurasian Economic Union* (EAEU), encompassing the original three states plus Armenia and Kyrgyzstan. The EAEU included a range of intergovernmental and supranational institutions that bore a superficial similarity to those in the EU, but Russia's overwhelming economic size compared to the other members led it to treat the EAEU primarily as a geopolitical tool. Meanwhile the Russian government continued to use economic levers to threaten recalcitrant neighbours. For example, it blocked key Ukrainian exports in July 2014 after the Poroshenko government signed the EU agreement that Yanukovych had previously rebuffed, and it replaced Ukraine's currency and financial services with Russian ones in Crimea and the separatist-controlled parts of Donbas. The Russian government also deepened its ties with other international challengers to Western-led international economic institutions. The BRICS launched the joint New Development Bank during its July 2015 summit in Ufa, Russia. That same year, Russia signed on to the new, China-led Asian Infrastructure Investment Bank (AIIB) as its third-largest shareholder. China had already been Russia's leading bilateral trade partner, with Russia primarily exporting oil and importing electronics and machinery. Western sanctions enhanced this trend.

The COVID-19 crisis of 2020–21 led to economic recession, supply-chain disruptions, and inflation around the world. Russia was no exception to this trend. Putin announced numerous economic subsidies and concessions to support those hit by the downturn. It dealt with rising food prices by introducing new price caps and export restrictions, including to its EAEU partners. The government also abandoned the flat tax regime, introducing a new 15 per cent rate for top earners as of January 2021. By mid-2021 the economy was recovering. Russia's GDP fell comparatively less due to the pandemic shock than in other resource-rich countries or in the advanced industrial democracies (World Bank 2021). The pandemic reinforced statist and nationalist trends in Russia, as Putin closed himself off to all but a handful of his most loyal political allies.

Russia's full-scale invasion of Ukraine on 24 February 2022 shook the world and prompted a sharp reaction. The immediate post-invasion Western sanctions were sweeping, and for Russia unexpectedly so. After the West's begrudging but implicit acceptance of its annexation of Crimea, the Russian government had not anticipated that harsh financial sanctions, including freezing over $300 billion of the Central Bank's foreign-exchange reserves, would be imposed in a rapid, unified way by countries across Europe and North America. Other sanctions included banning major Russian banks from the SWIFT messaging system, imposing targeted financial sanctions and travel bans on many individuals associated with the Russian government, and putting tariffs and import bans on many Russian goods. Thousands of private Western companies like IKEA, Renault, Volkswagen, Siemens, and McDonald's compounded the economic pain by shifting their financing and operations out of Russia. The first Russian McDonald's, which had opened to enthusiastic crowds in January 1990 on Pushkin Square in downtown Moscow, closed its doors in March 2022 and was later replaced by a Russian knock-off brand called *Vkusno – i tochka* (Tasty – and That's It).

The new sanctions led at first to a crash in the ruble exchange rate, an inflation spike, a temporary shutdown of the Russian stock market, capital flight, and predictions of a massive fall in Russian GDP. But the Russian economy bounced back from the initial hit, thanks in great part to skilful financial policy and planning by the Russian central bank and finance ministry as well as loopholes in the sanctions regime, particularly regarding oil and gas exports. Although Putin's team of economic liberals had warned him against the invasion and underlined the likely dire consequences, once the decision had been taken most stood by him, accepted the loss of their hard-earned Western ties, and did their best to limit the damage to the economy. Inflation and the exchange rate seemed to be under control, available reserves were not excessively depleted, and Russia's budget numbers remained solid through 2022. The Russian government leaned more heavily on its non-Western economic partners and proved adept at sanctions evasion.

As the war dragged on, however, the damage to Russia's economy, military capabilities, and international reputation accumulated. The sanctioning states maintained unexpected unity in the face of a drawn-out conflict and collateral economic damage. The West began closing loopholes in the sanctions regime as European countries reduced their dependence on Russian oil and gas. Russian monetary stability relied on extensive capital controls, stifling Russia's growth potential, and Russian exporters were required to turn over much of their foreign-currency revenue to the state. The sanctions-driven fall in imports propped up the current account but did not markedly increase import substitution domestically. Companies that relied on imported technology for their products, including defence-related companies, had trouble sourcing alternatives. Russia's better-than-expected GDP numbers reflected a wartime economy, with disproportionate spending on the military effort and on defence-related industry. Russian government statistics became less reliable, as basic data on capital flows, foreign investment, credit, and commodity exports were often not released. Its EAEU partners grew restless as well, as Russia appeared less economically supportive and more a potential threat to their own sovereignty. Most concerning for Russia's long-term economic future, since the full-scale invasion it has experienced a significant brain drain, become far more economically dependent on China, and lost access to important channels of international finance and trade.

Russia's economic policy dilemma

Russia's patriotic militarization, economic nationalism and imperialism, and overt challenges to the Western-dominated liberal order reflected the frustrations of an authoritarian and personalistic regime that aspired to a global leadership role but did not have the means to achieve it. As Russian elites have long understood, for Russia to become an international economic leader it must modernize and diversify its economy. However, Russia's patronage-based political system and resource wealth mean that undertaking such reforms in earnest could challenge the regime's stability. The war against Ukraine and Western sanctions have put Russia's goal even further out of reach, as it has become progressively cut off from important international finance, technology, and trade relationships that cannot easily be replaced. Russia faces a difficult economic policy road ahead.

Discussion questions

1 Why do many Russians remember the 1990s as a traumatic experience? Would different economic policies have led to a smoother transition from the command economy? If so, what else should have been done? If not, why not?
2 How did the August 1998 crisis and its aftermath shape economic policymaking in Russia?
3 What is state capitalism? Do you agree that Russia's economic system is best described as state capitalist? What are the main strengths and weaknesses of such a system?
4 The Russian economy is dependent on oil and gas exports. On balance, has this been more of a benefit or a 'curse' for Russia's economy and for its political system?
5 How and why has Russia's economic relationship with the West changed since the 2008 global financial crisis? What effects have Western sanctions had on the Russian economy?

Recommended readings

Balmaceda, Margarita. 2021. *Russian Energy Chains*. Columbia University Press.
Herrera, Yoshiko. 2017. *Mirrors of the Economy: National Accounts and International Norms in Russia and Beyond*. Cornell University Press.
Johnson, Juliet. 2016. *Priests of Prosperity: How Central Bankers Transformed the Postcommunist World.* Cornell University Press.
Logvinenko, Igor. 2021. *Global Finance, Local Control: Corruption and Wealth in Contemporary Russia.* Cornell University Press.
Wengle, Susanne. 2015. *Post-Soviet Power: State-led Development and Russia's Marketization.* Cambridge University Press.

7

Russia's Informal Economy

Yoshiko M. Herrera and
Evgeniya Mitrokhina

All economies include both formal and informal institutions and practices. However, whereas the formal economy can be studied through analysis of laws and government policies that regulate behaviour, the informal economy requires analysis from a different perspective and often relies on interviews, surveys, and analysis of observational data that go beyond official statistics. In addition, the informal economy might be studied from structural, institutional, and agentic perspectives. A structural perspective focuses on the structure or type of economic activity in a country as well as larger concepts such as culture. An institutional approach usually focuses on the rules, both formal and informal, that might push economic activity into the shadows. And an agentic approach considers the choices and decisions of individuals in engaging in the informal economy. In this chapter we analyze Russia's informal economy by focusing first on a discussion of the definition of the informal economy, and then we discuss three related concepts: the 'black market', corruption, and the rise of 'oligarchs', or wealthy elites with political connections. These themes illustrate the connections between Russia's economic and political systems. While somewhat complex, the system is not necessarily chaotic in nature but rather is related to institutions, norms, and the strategic choices of agents.

What is the informal economy?

Goods and services can be distributed in three ways: the market, the state, and through networks. Typically market and state distribution is large scale and works through formal institutions, laws, or written rules that regulate who gets what, and how. For example, there are market rules on what can be sold (e.g. alcohol, but not opium), where it can be sold (online, in some states or counties, on certain days, etc.), and to whom (adults, not minors). States can distribute goods and services (e.g. providing housing or healthcare), but often deal in payments (tax refunds) or obligations (taxes) to redistribute income and wealth. States may also regulate prices, even in 'market' economies.

In contrast to the state and markets, social or personal networks are another way of distributing goods and services. The family or household economy is the most common example: Parents take care of and provide for children, and most of this type of exchange is not monitored or regulated by the state or markets, and it is non-monetized. Moreover, this economy is based on specific social ties. Beyond households, larger family or social networks may form the basis for exchange of goods and services. The use of networks to obtain certain goods or services occurs in every society, but in different forms (e.g. the 'old boys' network or 'pulling strings' in the United States, or 'guanxi' in China). It almost goes without saying that all economies are gendered in that some kinds of economic activity are structured by power hierarchies of men, women, and other genders. In addition, distributional economic networks may overlap with ethnic groups and other social categories, and this is almost definitionally the case when kin groups form the basis of economic networks, but kin or ethnicity are not the only basis of economic networks.

Official statistics, such as Gross Domestic Product (GDP), which is a measure of all goods and services produced in year in a given country, focus on monetized transactions (i.e. things that are paid for). For this reason, if you cook your own dinner, watch your children, and mow your own lawn it does not count as contributing to GDP, but if you pay someone else to do these things they are counted in GDP. In addition, whereas the formal economy is based on mostly anonymous or arm's-length ties (i.e. a gardener might be hired on the basis of an advertisement), making dinner for family members is based on familial or close ties. Of course, there are many exceptions and nuances, but in general the informal economy is based on close ties or social networks.

A core part of the informal economy is the household, and is therefore a part of every economic system, though to varying degrees, but the informal economy extends beyond non-monetized transactions, and also includes norms and informal institutions related to economic exchange. Norms are behavioural prescriptions for given identity groups, and typically bring about social sanctions if they are broken. For example, in the US it is customary to leave a tip of around 15–20 per cent of a bill at restaurants, and not leaving a tip will be frowned upon by others. At the same time, it is not customary to bring gifts to doctors or teachers in exchange for services in the US, but that is common in other countries. Moreover, some kinds of informal exchange are legal, if largely ignored by the state (household labour), and others are illegal (selling certain drugs). While the informal economy exists in every society, these examples suggest that informal norms and the informal economy might differ across countries and that certain kinds of informality might be specific to certain countries or societies.

The informal economy in the Soviet Union

The USSR was a communist country and, as such, the state controlled most aspects of the economy including the production, distribution, and prices of nearly all goods and services. Because the system was not able to meet the demands of consumers, the prohibition on market-based mechanisms created tremendous demand for an alternative, namely the informal economy in which exchange was based on family, friendship and other social networks.

One way to think about the informal economy in the USSR is that it was an alternative mechanism of exchange, or even a 'survival strategy' in the context of shortages that arose due to problems with the planned economy. But some have argued that it was a deeper cultural practice, especially in the Soviet Union, and that the specificity of the communist system created both widespread reliance on informality and a specific kind of informal economy.

In a groundbreaking study, Alena Ledeneva (2009) described the practice of 'blat' networks which were pervasive in the USSR. In essence, blat was the use of personal networks to trade favours to obtain goods and services. Ledeneva explained that 'blat merged with patterns of sociability to such an extent that people were unable to distinguish between friendship and the use of friendship. The boundaries became particularly blurred as the exchanged favours were favours of a particular kind – 'favors of access'' (Ledeneva 2009, p. 258).

Where blat differs from mere non-market exchange is that it relies on reciprocal ties, friendship networks, which are not just based on profit motives. Prices in blat networks might be closer to the state prices (which were so low as to induce constant shortages in stores), but the availability of goods depended on being connected to the right network. According to Barsukova and Radaev (2012, p. 5), *blat* 'was neither a criminal activity nor an alternative to the planned economy, but rather a legitimate compensatory mechanism for economic failures of the planned economy. It enabled people to resolve their everyday problems such as obtaining desired commodities and services.' In this way the development of the informal economy in the Soviet Union was integrally tied to, or even dependent on state institutions rather than existing or developing completely apart from the state or formal economy.

Ledeneva's and other research on *blat* networks and informality in the USSR and Russia opened a window into studying governance from a different perspective, namely by focusing on informal practices and strategies people use to survive under authoritarianism and under harsh economic conditions. As it turns out, many of the informal practices from the Soviet era carried over into the post-Soviet era as well.

The persistence of informality in the post-Soviet era

According to surveys carried out by the European Bank for Reconstruction and Development (EBRD), even into the mid-2000s a majority of post-Soviet households relied heavily on informal private safety nets. That is, with the introduction of a market economy, rather than disappearing, some key elements of the Soviet informal economy persisted, albeit in new circumstances.

Two pillars of the transition from communism to a market economy in Russia were the privatization of previously state-owned assets and the liberalization or the relaxation of regulations on trade and commerce. In practice the economic transition in Russia was unfair, privileging certain insiders in the buying and selling of assets, and creating a set of government and legal institutions that sanctioned privileged access. Hence the 'market economy' in Russia never consisted of a level playing field where everyone had equal opportunity to participate in the economy. Instead, as in Soviet times, social networks, and in particular networks related to powerful government actors who controlled the economy and the economic transition, translated into opportunities for certain well-connected people to become enormously wealthy. Russia went from being a country with historically low income inequality to one of the most unequal countries in the world in record time in the 1990s.

This economic inequality, which was the direct result of the network-based, privileged access in the economic transition, laid the groundwork for the continuation of the informal economy in post-Soviet Russia. However, rather than the informal economy being focused on circumventing state shortages in consumer goods, network connections became the infrastructure of a corrupt market economy in the 1990s, and an even more corrupt state-directed market economy in the 2000s.

Under President Vladimir Putin, the state was steadily reasserted as the dominant force in the economy, where power was concentrated in Putin himself and connections to Putin became the *sine qua non* of economic power. Rather than *blat* or an 'economy of favours', under Putin Russia developed an economy dominated by Putin's sycophants, whose distinguishing characteristic is loyalty to the regime, in return for which they gained nominal control over vast economic resources.

What is the black market?

Like the informal economy more generally, the 'black market' is a phenomenon that occurs in all economies. The core definition of the black market is economic activity that takes place beyond the view of the state or formal economy, and is carried out so clandestinely because it violates formal rules or laws. The black market can include employment, manufacturing, or trade that is legal but off the books (e.g. hiring workers for cash payments), or illegal (e.g. trade in endangered animals), and it may be engaged in by individuals or firms. In most cases the black market is related to either tax evasion or prohibited activity. In the former case the activity itself may not be prohibited but is hidden from the state in order to avoid paying taxes, and in the latter case there are myriad reasons why states might prohibit certain economic transactions (public safety, health reasons, environmental reasons, international sanctions, national security concerns, etc.).

In any case, the relationship to the state is always significant for the development of black market activity, because black market activity involves hiding from or lying about economic activity to the state. A different set of state tax requirements may lead to different kinds of behaviour by individuals or firms, and what is considered reportable to the state may directly change the scale of informal or black market activity (e.g. if the state only requires reporting of transactions over a certain amount, an individual would neither hide nor report activity below that threshold). As noted above, most household labour is non-monetized, and not reported nor taxed by states, and hence while it is considered part of the 'informal economy' it is not typically considered 'black market' activity.

In extreme cases, a completely unregulated economy would have no black market because everything would be legal and not subject to taxes, and at the same time a highly regulated economy, such as existed in the USSR, would produce incentives for a lot of black market activity in transactions that are prohibited. For this reason, socialist economies are thought to have been particularly susceptible to black market pressures, but at the same time the development of black markets in socialist states was held in check by the high level of surveillance and control by government authorities over the population. The weakening of Soviet control during Mikhail Gorbachev's perestroika period (1986–91) allowed for an explosion of black market activity in the context of only partially reformed liberalization of the formal Soviet economy. Finally, given the risks associated with illegality and the black market, poor, marginalized, and otherwise vulnerable people who lack other, legal options for economic advancement are more likely to engage in certain kinds of black market activity.

The black market in the USSR and Russia

In the USSR, lying to the state about economic activity was endemic. The oft-repeated adage, 'They pretend to pay us, and we pretend to work' captures both the cynicism and dishonesty in the relationship between workers and the state. The informal practice of '*pripiski*' has been well documented in the USSR, and it refers to the reporting of invented production output in order to (falsely) meet Soviet economic plan quotas (Harrison 2018). The schemes for claiming overperformance were varied and sophisticated, and during the Cold War a lot of effort was devoted to uncovering true Soviet production values in contrast with official statistics. Barsukova and Radaev (2012) labelled this widespread practice of lying about output a 'fictitious economy', because the fraud had to do with claiming production that did not actually occur and it only made sense to do so in the context of state planning targets – absent those and the incentives that went along with them, there would be no need to exaggerate and overvalue output.

In addition to *pripiski*, another widespread informal black market practice in the USSR was stealing from the state. People who worked in stores took goods to distribute to friends and family, as discussed above in *blat* networks. However, the Gorbachev-era reforms opened a much wider frontier for theft because enterprise directors were allowed to open private businesses, sometimes within the same space as a state-owned enterprise. In this case state assets were stolen on a massive scale in order to produce 'private' goods that could then be legally sold by new firms under new perestroika-era laws. Small-scale 'shuttle traders', often from ethnically non-Russian regions of the USSR, also emerged in order to bring in imported goods from across Soviet borders to be resold by sketchy resellers within Russia. These traders and sellers were previously considered to be 'speculators' whose activity was illegal in Soviet times, but now became legal, if unregulated, under perestroika and in Russia in the 1990s. Shuttle traders were both highly disliked because of their high prices, and also needed because of the goods that they brought in, in the context of extreme shortages, which were exacerbated by both the breakdown of supply changes with the end of the USSR and the massive theft of state assets and the disintegration of state production plans.

A cash liquidity crisis in the 1990s gave way to a 'barter economy' in which goods and services were directly traded with limited ability of the state to monitor or regulate such transactions. Some estimates put the level of barter as high as 70 per cent of industrial output by the end of the 1990s (Barsukova and Radaev 2012). In addition, whereas in the USSR the black market had been a small part of household consumption, it became a primary resource for many households in the 1990s.

In contrast to the Soviet period, rather than overstating or inventing fictitious output, the black market in the 1990s evolved to focus on hiding real output from the state, i.e. vastly undervaluing real performance and output, primarily to obscure the stolen provenance of assets and also to avoid taxes. Tax evasion became so widespread that by the mid-1990s the Russian state was going bankrupt because of its inability to collect any tax revenue, and it tried to increase revenues by further sales of state assets, in the context of privatization, which as noted above mainly benefited well-connected individuals.

With privatization and the liberalization of trade in the 1990s, the black market proceeded in Russia in the 2000s along three paths: (1) massive attempts to hide otherwise legal revenue and output in order to avoid taxes; (2) continued and varied attempts to steal valuable assets; and (3) capital flight of ill-gotten gains abroad on an unprecedented scale.

Tax evasion took on many guises. A standard approach in many countries is to underreport revenue by selling some part of output 'on the books' and then some part 'off the books', so that the business owner only reports and pays taxes for the (lower) revenue that was on the books. In Russia another technique of 'black cash' (*chernaia nalichnost'*) also became widespread (Yakolev 2001). In this practice, firms over-report costs, which are not taxed or are taxed at a much lower rate, and hide revenue. They do so by working with sham firms that they pay for fictitious services (in order to inflate their costs), and the sham firms secretly repay the funds, minus a small percentage fee. In this way the firm can claim real costs and hide the black cash it received back from the sham firms, which it could use for off-the-books salary, bonuses or other purposes. Because the sham firms only exist for a month or so (they were referred to as '*odnodnevki*' or 'one-dayers'), they are very hard to audit or prosecute and were largely ignored by tax authorities. Another evasion scheme existed for money laundering and was essentially the reverse-black-cash scheme where firms contracted to sell rather than buy fictitious goods or services from sham firms, who then legally paid for the fictitious goods with money gained from other shady sources.

What is notable about the black cash tax evasion and money laundering schemes is that they return to the Soviet-era practice of fictitious economic activity, whereas the standard approach relies on hiding real activity from the authorities.

Corruption in Russia

Corruption has negative effects on economic growth by introducing costs (inefficiencies), as well as more uncertainty into interactions between economic actors. For example, the distribution of public procurement contracts to less efficient firms, on the basis of informal ties to public officials, has negative welfare implications. On a larger scale these ties have serious implications for the whole state.

While there is no agreement about a precise definition of corruption, there is consensus that corruption denotes acts when a public office is used for personal gain by violating existing rules of the game (Kaufmann and Siegelbaum 1997). In this sense some illegal actions, such as operations in the black market or fraud do not represent corrupt behaviour because they do not necessarily involve the use of public power. That is why corruption usually involves some conduct on the part of bureaucrats, public officials, politicians, or legislators. Conceptualized this way, corruption can be realized on different levels. The first concerns small-scale routine interactions between citizens and authorities and is usually defined as 'petty corruption'. 'Grand corruption' describes larger-scale interaction between businesses and the government. As a result of the abuse of power, corruption might even affect government policy to further particular individuals' economic interests at the expense of the common good (see the section on oligarchs below).

Discretionary power over resource allocation, income from corruption versus legitimate sources, the strength of political institutions, and penalties for corruption (including monitoring, the independence of courts, and law enforcement) are among the many factors that determine corrupt behaviour. To a certain degree, all of these factors are accounted for when measuring corruption. One of the most widely used indices is the Corruption Perception Index (CPI) by Transparency International, which concentrates on public sector corruption. Russia has always been near the bottom of the rankings (meaning worse levels of corruption). For example according to CPI, in 2021 Russia ranked 136 out of 180 countries, with a CPI score of 29/100. One of the distinctive features of corruption in Russia is its presence in various types of social relationships, including the economic and political spheres. For this reason, Levin and Satarov (2012) even call corruption in Russia an 'industry' when comparing estimated income from corruption in 2005 to export revenues from oil and gas.

Corrupt behaviour usually depends on the monopoly that actors have, what kind of job they perform, and the effectiveness of control and potential punishment. Barsukova and Radaev (2012) note that everyday corruption is inseparable from social practices such as bargaining, gift-giving, and even help. Existing rules and their application might vary depending on interpretation. For example, gift-giving in Russia and many other countries might imply various expectations and relationships. Reciprocal interactions sometimes create conditions when unlawful gift giving can be justified and the boundary between bribery and a standard practice of gift-giving becomes arbitrary. Moreover, differences in attitudes to informality and reliance on informal institutions might justify an abuse of power. Thus, while corruption is complained about by everyone in Russia, it also facilitates the smoother working of rigid state institutions.

Russia was the successor to the Soviet Union, which had a planned economy characterized by the absence of private property, a concentration of power in the state, and as with the informal economy, widespread petty corruption. These activities were supposed to compensate for numerous defects in central planning and management, as well as balance the contradictions between socialist ideas and the real existing Soviet economy. After the collapse of the Soviet Union the structure of everyday corruption did not change drastically. Russians still tolerate petty bribes, such as personal payments to traffic police for non-compliance with existing rules. Small businesses cope with uncertainties relating to the interpretation of rules by bribing public officials who are supposed to ensure compliance with such rules.

Corruption is stigmatized and disapproved of in society, but is still widespread. Paradoxically, corrupt behaviour exists at various levels of society (from bribing a policeman to government contracts worth millions of dollars), alongside an anti-corruption discourse and campaigns in Russia. This is not unique to Russia. Scholars find similar patterns in Mexico and Tanzania. The system continues to exist because of the availability of these practices that are activated as a response to challenges produced by the same system (the pervasive resolution of everyday problems by corrupt methods). At the same time, the fight against corruption becomes not only economic and social, but also a political problem.

Grand corruption in Russia, however, was significantly affected by the regime change at the end of the Soviet Union. Economic reforms introduced by Mikhail Gorbachev were characterized by economic ties between production managers and the party leadership. The transition period of the economy was characterized by the dissolution of older institutions and the weakening of legal regulations (Kaufmann and Siegelbaum 1997). The inability to enforce the rule of law during President Boris Yeltsin's government led to an increase in everyday corruption, as well as abuse of power during the large-scale privatization of state property. Consequently, the state was captured by large businesses and their owners (known as oligarchs) and became highly dependent on them (one example is the role that oligarchs played in funding Yeltsin's second presidential campaign in 1996). Moreover, some businessmen became legislators or took up positions in the executive branch.

Corruption increased even more during Vladimir Putin's presidency. The main reason for this was authoritarian backsliding and weakening of democratic principles (such as separation of powers and freedom of the media). Corruption was used by the Putin regime as a resource to buy the loyalty of the bureaucracy and the economic elite, which led to the formation of new corruption networks. At the same time, as the state was strengthening under Putin, business became controlled by the state. In 2004, Russia's richest man, Mikhail Khodorkovsky, was arrested on television, dragged off his personal plane with state TV cameras rolling, and sentenced to ten years in prison. It was widely assumed that the reason for the arrest was that Khodorkovsky had meddled in politics, and his arrest was a signal to other oligarchs to stay out of politics. After the Khodorkovsky case, the ability to control businesses depended on belonging to a clientelistic network ultimately controlled by Putin. Thus, the political system during Putin's reign became characterized by informal power networks and a wide array of privileges for insiders (Ledeneva 2013).

At the same time, as noted above, grand corruption has consistently been an important concern in post-Soviet Russian society. While around 20 per cent of respondents agree that sometimes giving a bribe is the only means to get something done (according to a Levada survey conducted in 2016), people name corruption as the number one form of immoral behaviour according to a VCIOM survey conducted in 2020. For this reason, the discourse relating to combating corruption remains an important part of the agenda for both the government and the opposition in Russia. One of the main opposition leaders in Russia, Alexei Navalny (who, after surviving various arrests and an assassination attempt by the government, is currently in prison in Russia) built his whole campaign and popularity by initiating anti-corruption investigations. In 2011, Navalny established a non-profit organization called the Anti-Corruption Foundation, which was labelled an extremist (terrorist) organization by the government in 2021. One of the Foundation's investigations, relating to the lavish lifestyle of the prime minister, was followed by country-wide street protests in 2017. While Navalny himself is not very widely supported by the masses, his organization's anti-corruption campaigns still reflect a growing public demand for change in Russian politics and society.

Thus, corruption was a building block of Putin's power, but it is also one of the vulnerabilities of the system. For this reason, the state, and not only the opposition, has initiated various anti-corruption campaigns and also suggested various reforms, including to the public procurement system, mandatory asset and income disclosures of bureaucrats, as well as investigations of top-level officials (e.g. Alexei Ulyukaev, who held the office of Minister of Economic Development, and Minister of Defense Anatoly Serdyukov). These actions allow the regime to promote the impression that it is actively engaged in the fight against corruption. However, on the state level, the seeming struggle against corruption is concentrated more on particular people who have fallen out with the regime, rather than on corruption as a systematic issue in itself.

Oligarchs

The classical definition of *oligarchy* emphasizes the rule by a few members of the economic elite, who rule based on their own interests (Guriev and

Rachinsky 2005). This conceptualization excludes rule by politicians, bureaucrats, and executive managers of public companies (such as Gazprom or Russian Railways), and hence Russia may not be an *oligarchy* per se, but it is thought to have *oligarchs*, who are extremely wealthy business people (mostly men) whose wealth is in part based on their government connections. While the issue of oligarchs as a post-Soviet phenomenon has been widely recognized, the debate about oligarchs and the role they play in national politics continues. The modern concept of oligarchs applied to Russia denotes private owners of capital 'who control sufficient resources to influence national politics' (Guriev and Rachinsky 2005, p. 32). At the same time, since Putin's presidency, oligarchs in Russia remain economically powerful, but as Putin's rule has become more personalistic, they have less and less influence on politics.

There are three main periods in the USSR and Russia that describe the emergence and persistence of oligarchs (Braguinsky 2009). First, Gorbachev's perestroika allowed some *nomenklatura* members to control Soviet-era enterprises, de facto converting them into privately owned companies. Some individuals worked in the government or other state agencies that were supervising or managing these enterprises. At the same time, the emergence of liberalization and a market economy created opportunities for people who were able to import goods to the country and sell them for profit. Therefore, there were individuals in Russia who gained some capital in various ways before 1992, when liberalization and privatization began (Guriev and Rachinsky 2005).

Many oligarchs emerged in the 1990s, and while their specific paths to wealth may have varied, they have in common the experience of obtaining control, one way or another, of very valuable assets, formerly held by the state, at bargain basement prices. Some well-connected entrepreneurs acquired their wealth as a result of the 'voucher privatization' programme. Vouchers were collected for a pittance and then exchanged for stakes in enterprises, although access to the process of exchanging vouchers for firms was limited to certain insiders.

In addition, there was a 'loans-for-shares' programme in which individuals or firms bid for stakes in newly privatized, very valuable firms in auctions. However the auctions were run by state-appointed insiders, and instead of bidding up prices on the privatized firms, the rigged 'auctions' allowed insiders to acquire firms at very low cost by giving loans to the government with firm stakes as collateral. In most cases, the government was unable to pay back the loans (because it was unable to collect tax revenue), and via default on the loans certain insiders acquired large stakes in companies at minimal cost. The loans-for-shares programme occurred around the time of the second Yeltsin presidential campaign and appeared to be a way of consolidating both resources and support for Yeltsin, who was facing a difficult campaign. In the loans-for-shares process, young men such as Roman Abramovich, Mikhail Khodorkovsky, and Vladimir Potanin became billionaires. Thus, ownership rights during this period were closely linked to political patronage, but the state remained too weak to control the process.

Starting with the 2000s, the relationship between the state and the oligarchs began to change. In February 2000, just before his first presidential election, Putin organized a meeting with oligarchs where he announced that as long as the president was not challenged by them, the state would not interfere with their businesses. Some of the oligarchs followed, others were punished, usually on charges of tax evasion. Two of the wealthiest and most powerful oligarchs of the Yeltsin era, Boris Berezovsky and Vladimir Gusinsky, left the country and avoided legal prosecution. Mikhail Khodorkovsky, however, as noted above, was arrested and spent ten years in prison. These criminal charges were seen to be politically motivated, and signalled a power struggle with President Putin, which Putin won. According to Braguinsky (2009), only half of the Yeltsin-era oligarchs had managed to keep their status by 2006 (Braguinsky 2009). Scholars also argue that Khodorokovsky's arrest signified the centralization and personalization of power in Russia.

However, despite political control over oligarchs under Putin, they still play a significant role in the Russian economy. Their business acquisitions and wealth depend on political loyalty to Putin, and oligarchs in the Putin era have increasingly relied on the centralized power of the state to increase their wealth. The process might be characterized as a return to 'state capitalism'. Political and economic stability during Putin's two terms in office allowed oligarchs who played by Putin's rules to increase their wealth, and they also benefited from the oil boom and increased metal prices. At the same time, new oligarchs who had personal relations with Putin became more visible (e.g. Arkady Rotenberg and Gennady Timchenko). As many anti-corruption investigations demonstrate, Putin personally benefited from the existence of a close circle of loyalists. Some of the most striking examples include the Ozero Dacha Cooperative and Bank Rossiya, which were used to divert state funds to build Putin's enormous gilded palace near Sochi.

Hence, during the Putin era, political connections still play an equal and perhaps even more important role in protecting ownership rights. Individual businesses or whole industries still needed to establish personal connections with government officials to promote their interests (e.g. on protective tariffs or tax reductions, as well as government contracts). Another distinctive feature of the Putin period is state corporatism. Large state-owned companies, whose supervisors and managers are loyal to Putin, are examples of this phenomenon (these corporations include Gazprom, Russian Railways, and Rosneft). Some of the board members in these companies have also been government representatives. Even though these companies are run on a commercial basis, some of the decision-making process is hidden and they are rumoured to be beholden to Putin.

After the annexation of Crimea and the full-scale Russian invasion of Ukraine, Putin's cronies and their money abroad were targeted by Western governments. One of the main goals of the sanctions was to impact the elites, to isolate them from global markets, and to induce them to reconsider their support for Putin and the war on Ukraine. While some Russian elites clearly worry about the sanctions, and some of them have taken elaborate precautions to protect or even hide their wealth abroad or to prevent it from being seized or frozen, only a very small number, such as Mikhail Fridman and Oleg Tinkov, have spoken out against the war. At the same time, we do not know their true motivations: They may be loyal to Putin, or they may reason that they have little or no influence on the increasingly isolated Putin regime, and be biding their time, hoping for the war to end and hoping they might be able to regain access to travel and their wealth abroad.

Conclusion

The process of Putin-led state control over the economy culminated in 2022 with the Russian invasion and war on Ukraine, which saw a record-breaking exodus of foreign companies from Russia and the cutting of trade ties (i.e. the de-globalization and de-privatization of the Russian economy as the state nationalized assets and became the primary source of investment). Rather than any sign of weakening of the network ties that constituted the Russian economy, the war has only made informal leverage and ties all the more important. Moreover, the sanctions and inflationary environment may return Russia to Soviet-era shortages of some goods and services, building great pressure for expansion of the informal economy, and possibly even a return to *blat* and other informal ways to deal with a state-run economy.

Instead of promoting and developing democratic institutions or a diversified economy, Putin and the people close to him created an authoritarian system that benefits a relatively small group of elites. Using the state to build an institutionalized corrupt system, they exercise widespread control over the economy, but while corruption in Russia generates loyalty and control over oligarchs, it is not necessarily a stabilizing factor. It generates enormous inequality and inefficiencies, and various groups within the regime including oligarchs, the bureaucracy, and the security apparatus compete for the same economic resources. Moreover, economic prosperity and stability were acclaimed as the key achievements of Putin's government, and therefore the regime is sensitive to economic crises. Thus, even though corruption is one of the main levers of control for the regime, it is also its weakest link.

Questions for discussion

1 What explains the emergence and persistence of the informal economy in modern Russia, especially after Putin came to power? What is different about the informal economy in Russia today compared to the USSR?
2 Do network-based exchange networks such as *blat* overall have a positive or negative effect on the formal economy?
3 What is the difference between the black market and corruption?
4 Where did oligarchs in Russia come from? How did they make their money and what power do they have today?
5 Could sanctioned businessmen put pressure on Putin to change policies and end the war in Ukraine? What means do they have to do so, and would they want to?

Recommended readings

Gel'man, Vladimir. 2012. 'Subversive Institutions, Informal Governance, and Contemporary Russian Politics.' *Communist and Post-Communist Studies*, 45(3–4), 295–303.
Johnson, Juliet. 2000. *A Fistful of Rubles: The Rise and Fall of the Russian Banking System*. Cornell University Press.
Ledeneva, Alena V. 1998. *Russia's Economy of Favours: Blat, Networking and Informal Exchange*. Cambridge University Press.

Rochlitz, Michael, Kazun, Anton, & Yakovlev, Andrei. 2020. 'Property Rights in
    Russia after 2009: From Business Capture to Centralized Corruption?'
    Post-Soviet Affairs, 36(5–6), 434–50.
Snegovaya, Maria, & Petrov, Kirill. 2022. 'Long Soviet Shadows: The
    Nomenklatura Ties of Putin Elites.' *Post-Soviet Affairs*, 38(4), 329–48.

8

Formal Institutions of Governance

Grigorii V. Golosov

Few authoritarian regimes of the past, and even fewer today, have been regimes of complete arbitrariness based on brute force. Typically, autocrats create or maintain systems of rules that govern how power is acquired, exercised and transferred. Such rules are political institutions. In this respect, autocracies are no different from democracies. But authoritarian institutions can be overtly different from democratic ones. During the twentieth century, some of the most stable institutional forms of authoritarianism were quite idiosyncratic, such as those of one-party regimes in the Soviet Union and elsewhere, from East Asia to Africa and Cuba, and those of absolute monarchies, such as the one that exists now in Saudi Arabia.

In the modern world, the most widespread variety of authoritarianism is electoral authoritarianism. The word 'electoral' in this term indicates that the formal source of power in such regimes is provided by elections, which makes these regimes look like democracy. Indeed, such regimes claim to be democracies. Basically, these claims are false. Authoritarian elections do not fulfil the main function that elections perform in a democracy: They do not ensure the turnover of power. Autocrats – to the extent that they remain autocrats – create conditions under which they cannot lose elections. Power remains in the same hands, or passes to a successor appointed by the current ruler, or, if for some reason a successor is not appointed by the current ruler himself, the issue of power succession is decided within a narrow circle of close associates of the former autocrat after his death. Quite often, power changes hands as a result of coups d'état or revolutions.

The fear of a coup d'état is one of the main reasons for the existence of formal institutions of government under authoritarian conditions (Geddes et al. 2018). Unlike the autocrats of the past, today's authoritarian leaders cannot justify their claim to power either by party goals related to the transformation of society or nation building, or by monarchical inheritance rights. This makes autocrats vulnerable to any political actors who have the ability to use force to seize power. Under such conditions, winning elections becomes useful if not indispensable. The holding of elections requires the creation of other institutions that are outwardly similar to democratic ones. This chapter is devoted to an examination of such institutions that exist in contemporary Russia.

Authoritarian institutions cannot serve as a principal instrument for any serious political change, in Russia or elsewhere. They are only to a very limited extent capable of restraining an authoritarian ruler. If some rules of the political game do not suit the autocrat, then he simply ignores them or changes them. However, only the autocrat himself or his close associates who have received such an entitlement from him can act as rule changers. For all other citizens, following these rules is mandatory, and if unauthorized deviations from these rules threaten the stable functioning of the regime, then the punishment can be swift and cruel.

Constitutional division of powers

The basis of any system of formal institutions of governance, both in democracies and electoral authoritarian regimes, is the model of division of powers between the political executive and the national representative assembly. In Russia, the word 'parliament' is used to refer to the national assembly, officially named the Federal Assembly (*Federal'noe Sobranie*) and consisting of two houses. The lower house is the State Duma (*Gosudarstvennaia Duma*), often simply called the Duma, and the upper house, Federation Council (*Sovet Federatsii*). Executive power is exercised by the president and the government. Unlike in the United States and many other presidential systems, the government is headed not by the president but rather by an official whose position is officially called the 'Chairperson of Government' (*Predsedatel' pravitel'stva*), often informally referred to as the prime minister. The president and the government jointly constitute the basic structure of executive power at the national level.

The model of division of powers, as established by the Russian constitution that was adopted in December 1993 and remains in force today with some amendments, the most important of which were enacted in 2020, establishes that the directly elected president plays a central role in appointing the prime minister and determining the composition of the government. At the same time, the candidacies of the prime minister and many other members of the government are subject to approval by the houses of the parliament. This model of dual responsibility means that Russia is not a presidential system, but rather belongs to a variety of semi-presidential systems that is referred to as the presidential-parliamentary system in the scholarly literature (Elgie 2011). Under such systems, the president is not the head of the government. He has the right to dissolve the lower house of parliament and call new legislative elections, which would be impossible in a purely presidential system.

According to the Constitution, the participation of the State Duma in the formation of the government is exercised as follows. After the elected president takes office, the powers of the former government cease, and the president must submit the candidacy of the prime minister to the Duma. If the candidates submitted by the president are rejected by the Duma three times in a row, then the president appoints an acting prime minister, dissolves the Duma, and calls new parliamentary elections. The same consequences occur in the following two situations. First, the Duma is entitled to pass a vote of no confidence in the government by a simple majority vote. The president has the right to ignore the move, but if a vote of no confidence is passed for a second time within three months, then the above provisions apply. The same happens if the Duma votes no confidence in a vote initiated by the president himself.

The 2020 amendments to the Constitution expanded the scope of the Duma's participation in the formation of the government, making not only the candidacy of the prime minister himself but also the candidacies of federal ministers proposed by the prime minister subject to approval by the Duma. The legal consequences of the Duma's refusal to approve more than a third of ministers are the same as those described above. However, this rule does not apply to the ministers in charge of defence, state security, internal affairs, justice, foreign affairs, prevention of emergency situations and elimination of consequences of natural disasters, and public security. These ministers, jointly referred to in Russia as the 'power block' of the government, are appointed by the President after consultations with the Federation Council. The Constitution does not regulate the procedures and consequences of such consultations.

Scholars specializing in the study of institutional design tend to negatively evaluate the political consequences of a presidential-parliamentary system.

Since this system makes the government accountable to both the president and the parliament, it creates the possibility of a situation where the two bodies of equal legitimacy cannot agree on the composition of the government because of irreconcilable political differences. This leads to new parliamentary elections, but such elections do not necessarily make the parliamentary composition more favourable to the president. Elections are called again and again, and the country is left without a properly functioning government for a long time, resulting in political destabilization. This sequence of events in literature is sometimes referred to as the 'Weimar scenario' because, in the final phase of the so-called Weimar Republic in Germany in the early 1930s, it contributed to a profound political crisis that led to the establishment of the Nazi dictatorship.

In this form, the 'Weimar scenario' has never materialized in the recent history of Russia. Moreover, during the entire period of Vladimir Putin's rule, the parliament has never rejected the candidates submitted by him for government positions and has not attempted to pass a vote of no confidence in the government. However, the presidential-parliamentary structure has contributed to the autocratization of Russia through a process that can be called the 'reverse Weimar scenario'. During the 1990s, Russia's ruling circles systematically witnessed the president's inability to secure stable support of parliamentary majorities. There was no such support even after the 1999 Duma elections. This potentially destabilizing situation served as an important incentive for the restriction of political freedoms that had already started to be observed in 2003–04, at the end of Putin's first presidential term. The resulting authoritarian system of government, in which the parliament is under the full political control of the president, rules out the 'Weimar scenario', but does so at the cost of abandoning democracy.

Thus, the main danger of the presidential-parliamentary system for political stability has been effectively neutralized by autocratization. At the same time, this form of government played a role in keeping Putin in power at a time when constitutional norms made his departure from the presidency almost inevitable. In 2008, Putin's second presidential term expired. The third term could become possible only after changing the Constitution, but at that time, Putin declined to opt for this method of retaining power. Putin's closest political associate, Dmitry Medvedev, was nominated for the presidency, while Putin himself took over as prime minister after the 2008 presidential election. The powers of the Russian president were great enough for allowing Medvedev to stay in power for a second term, which could be achieved by excluding Putin from participation in the 2012 presidential elections. However, this was practically impossible not only because of Medvedev's political weakness but also because the parliamentary majority controlled by Putin could have prevented such an outcome. In 2012, Putin returned to the presidency.

The 2020 constitutional amendments eliminated the problem of presidential term limits for Putin by establishing that, effective in 2024, he could be elected two more times. At the same time, the presidential-parliamentary system of governance has been formally preserved. Apparently, Putin has no doubt that during the entire period of his extended tenure in power, the Duma will remain under his control. Even in the unlikely event that Putin will not run for the presidency, a political safety net for him remains in the form of an opportunity to take the post of prime minister or, rather, to nominate a loyal supporter to this post. The 2020 amendments strengthened the formal powers of the presidency by expanding the government appointment powers of the president, but the basic model of separation of powers in Russia did not change.

The president

The Constitution stipulates that the president is the head of state and the 'guarantor of the Constitution', and that he determines the main directions of the domestic and foreign policy of the state. Thus the Constitution places the president at the top of the national political executive and endows him with sweeping legislative powers. Overall, so sweeping are the powers of the presidency that some scholars characterize Russia's institutional design as 'super-presidential' (Hale 2005). This is not in contradiction with its characterization as a semi-presidential system because presidential powers in such systems vary substantially, in some cases, and particularly in post-Soviet countries, greatly exceeding those seen in 'pure' systems with strong presidencies.

While the Constitution gives the Duma a certain role in the formation of the government, the role of the president is paramount. He not only proposes a prime minister to the Duma and appoints him by his decree after the approval of the Duma, but also has the right to chair government meetings, and, according to one of the amendments adopted in 2020, exercises general management of the work of the government. The president approves the structure of the government (which practically means that no ministerial positions in the government can be created without the president's consent) and appoints the members of the government after parliamentary approval.

The president has practically unlimited powers to change the composition of the government. Before the adoption of the 2020 amendments, the prime minister could be removed from office by resigning voluntarily or as a result of a no confidence vote in the Duma. The amendments establish that the president has the right to make a binding decision to dismiss the prime minister. Other members of the government can also be dismissed by the decision of the president and not on the proposal of the prime minister, as was the case before the adoption of the amendments.

In addition, the 2020 amendments completely removed the prime minister from appointing the 'power block' ministers, as listed in the previous section of this chapter. Thus, the issues of state and public security, defence and foreign policy in Russia are within the exclusive competence of the president. To the extent that the president deems it necessary to bring these issues up for discussion with other officials, they are discussed in the Security Council, a consultative body chaired by the president. The Security Council includes, in addition to the 'power block' ministers, the prime minister, several other members of the government, the chairpersons of the houses of the parliament and, on a non-permanent basis, presidential representatives in federal districts and some regional governors. The key positions on the Security Council are held by Putin's closest political supporters, Sergei Patrushev (secretary) and Dmitry Medvedev (deputy).

The president also has powers to appoint other state officials. He submits to the State Duma the candidacy of the chairperson of the Central Bank of Russia, and, to the Federation Council, the candidacies of the chairpersons of the highest bodies of the judiciary, and those of the head of the Accounts Chamber and half of its members. The appointment of the highest command of the armed forces is a prerogative of the president.

The Presidential Administration plays an important role in Russia's system of governance. The Presidential Administration is briefly mentioned in the Constitution as a body that ensures the exercise of presidential powers. Some divisions of the Administration do perform technical functions related to the observance of presidential protocol, taking care of the health of the president, and so on. However, other divisions perform important political tasks. This work is coordinated by the head of the administration (Anton Vaino) and his first deputies (Sergei Kirienko and Alexei Gromov). Particularly important is the Department of Internal Policy within the Presidential Administration, a body that oversees the activities of political parties, the conduct of elections, the work of the media, and the activities of the parliament. In effect, this department acts in Russia as a 'ministry of domestic politics'. In general, the Presidential Administration serves as a key tool for the Russian authorities in implementing the political restrictions upon which authoritarian control rests.

The president of Russia possesses significant legislative powers. He has the right to issue decrees and orders of binding force, even though the Constitution determines that decrees and orders of the president shall not contradict laws passed by parliament. The president has the right of legislative initiative, as well as the right to veto legislation, which is exercised as follows. A law adopted by the parliament comes into force only after signing by the president. If this does not happen within two weeks after receipt for signature, then the law is again sent to the Duma. It has the right to change it or adopt it in its previous form, which means overriding the presidential veto. However, this is only possible by a two-thirds majority vote in both houses of the parliament.

The term of office of the Russian president, which was originally four years, was extended to six years by amendments to the Constitution that were adopted in 2008. Since 2000, Putin has been elected president five times. Formally, all these elections were held by a simple majority electoral system under which a candidate who receives more than 50 per cent of the vote is recognized as the winner. If none of the candidates achieves such a result, then a second round of voting must be held between the two candidates who performed most successfully in the first round. In fact, however, Putin has always won on the first ballot. As a result of the 2020 constitutional amendments, Putin will be entitled to take part in the elections of 2024 and 2030.

The Constitution establishes that the president can be impeached, i.e. removed from office on the basis of an accusation of high treason or other serious crime brought by the State Duma. The accusation must be confirmed by the Supreme Court of Russia and supported by a two-thirds majority vote in the two houses of the parliament. The final decision to remove the president from office is made by the Federation Council. The upper chamber has the right to support the charges put forward by the State Duma, reject them, or abstain from voting on the issue of impeachment. If a vote in the Federation Council is not held within three months after the indictment, then the impeachment does not occur. In addition, the president can be removed from power in the event of his voluntary resignation or 'persistent inability for health reasons to exercise his powers'. The Constitution does not detail in what way, and by what authorized body, the president's persistent inability to exercise his powers can be established. It seems that the death of the president can serve as the only unambiguously applicable reason.

There is no office of vice president in Russia. The short-lived vice presidency of Aleksandr Rutskoi that existed in Russia in 1991–93, before the adoption of the 1993 Constitution, was marred by a bitter conflict between Rutskoi and then president Yeltsin, so that the office was abolished and never sought to be restored. According to current constitutional provisions, if the president loses power for any of the reasons mentioned above, then the execution of his powers is temporarily vested in the prime minister, and new presidential elections must be held within a period of not more than three months. The Constitution does not specify a further line of succession. It seems that if, for whatever reason, the prime minister does not assume the presidency, then one of his deputies takes the office. But the Constitution does not stipulate this directly. The vagueness of the legal provisions associated with the removal of the president from power testifies both to the fact that this prospect has never been considered as realistic, and that such an event, if ever it ever materialized, might lead to a serious political crisis.

The government

The Constitution defines the government of Russia as an executive body consisting of the chair (prime minister), the chair's deputies, and federal ministers. In addition, the government includes the heads of some other federal agencies who do not have the status of ministers. The main function of the government is the implementation of operational management of various spheres of public life, and above all the economy. In particular, the government submits a draft federal budget for approval by the State Duma. Like the president, the government has the right to issue binding legal acts that are called resolutions and orders. However, these legal acts can be revoked by the president. The government has the right of legislative initiative. In addition, some bills providing for expenditures covered by the federal budget can be submitted to the Duma only if there is a government opinion on the feasibility of such expenditures. The government manages federal property.

The basic structure of the Russian government includes more than twenty federal ministries and several other agencies, some of which are designated as services. The ministries are primarily responsible for policy implementation in their areas of competence. Since 2020, the government has been headed by Mikhail Mishustin, with Andrei Belousov serving as his first deputy responsible for financial and economic policy. In addition, Mishustin has several deputies (as many as ten in January 2023), most of whom coordinate the activities of ministries and other federal government agencies in wide policy areas, such as economic policy or agriculture, and at the same time perform coordination of federal agencies operating in federal districts. For example, Tatiana Golikova serves as deputy prime minister for social policy and culture, at the same time coordinating all federal agencies in the Northwestern Federal District.

The political role of the government in modern Russia is modest. Its members are viewed as 'technocrats' who do not make fundamental political decisions and are competent only in their areas of direct responsibility. As a rule, they are not members of political parties, and only a few of them have experience participating in elections. Taking into account that within the framework of the formal distribution of powers, the prime minister could be a very important political figure, this state of affairs is due to the fact that real executive power in Russia is entirely concentrated in the hands of the president. The current prime minister, Mishustin, has a reputation as an economist with particular skills in the field of fiscal policy, but he is not a public figure of high visibility and almost never speaks out on political issues.

The parliament

The appointment powers of Russia's bicameral parliament have been discussed in the previous sections of this chapter. Of course, as is the case with any national representative assembly, the main functions of the Russian parliament are related to legislation. A peculiarity of the Russian parliament is that, unlike national representative bodies in many other countries, it has very few control powers. These powers are limited to hearing the government's annual reports and to the right to send parliamentary inquiries to ministers and other state officials on issues within these officials' competence.

Most federal laws are adopted by a simple majority vote of the total number of deputies of the State Duma, even though some laws require two-thirds majority for adoption. Then the bill is submitted to the Federation Council. In the upper chamber, it can be approved by a simple majority of votes, or not considered, which is equivalent to adoption, or rejected. In the event of rejection by the Federation Council, the two chambers may create a conciliation commission to overcome the disagreements, after which the bill is subject to reconsideration by the Duma. As an alternative, a bill rejected by the Federation Council may be adopted by the Duma by a two-thirds majority.

The State Duma consists of 450 deputies. The work of the Duma is coordinated by its chair (speaker), Vyacheslav Volodin, and the Council of the Duma that includes several vice-speakers and the leaders of party factions. The Federation Council includes two members from each of the federal units of Russia. In both chambers of the parliament, there are committees and commissions. The primary functions of most of them are related to the preliminary consideration of bills submitted to these chambers. The political structure of the Duma is formed by the factions of political parties. There are five party factions in the Duma elected in 2021. The Federation Council does not have party factions. The chairwoman of the Federation Council is Valentina Matvienko.

A significant portion of the legislation adopted by the Russian parliament is initiated by the president or the government. Presidential bills are almost invariably adopted, while bills initiated by the government may be blocked by lobbyists in the Duma if some special interests are threatened. This happens almost exclusively to bills on narrow economic policies. Bills introduced by members of parliament themselves, especially by the members of opposition parties, are frequently rejected or stalled. Many bills are introduced by groups of deputies on a cross-partisan basis, which increases their chances of adoption. Normally, the content of such bills is either coordinated with the Presidential Administration or formed on its direct instructions.

The political composition of the parliament, within which the party controlled by the president has huge leverage, minimizes the possibility of passing bills that do not correspond to the preferences of the executive. In discussions on the assembly floor, criticism of the government is sometimes voiced, especially by members of opposition factions, but criticism of the president is unthinkable. As the then speaker of the Duma, Boris Gryzlov, said in 2003, 'the State Duma is not the platform where political battles should be held, and some political slogans and ideologies should be defended. This is the platform where constructive, effective legislative activity should be carried out.'

Deputies of the Duma are elected for a five-year term. The most recent election took place in September 2021. The 450 deputies are elected by a mixed electoral system, half of them by party-list proportional representation, with only parties that receive at least 5 per cent of the vote being eligible for representation (in Russia, this is called the '5 per cent barrier'), and the other half, by a plurality system in single-member districts ('first-past-the-post'). A mixed electoral system was employed in Russia in all Duma elections held from 1993 through 2003. In 2007, plurality district elections were abolished and a purely proportional system for electing all 450 deputies was introduced. The main goal of this reform was to facilitate the organizational strengthening of the main pro-government party. However, the 2011 elections showed that purely proportional representation placed a limitation on this party's share of parliamentary seats. This restriction is alien to the plurality system with its well-known technical ability to award a sizeable majority of seats to a party that has a lead, however little, throughout all electoral districts. Starting with 2016, a mixed system has been used in Russia again, to the effect that the pro-government party won more than two-thirds of the seats in the Duma in the 2016 and 2021 elections.

The Federation Council is not a directly elected body. One representative from each of the federal units of Russia is appointed by its governor, and the second is elected by the legislative assembly. In 2023, after the claimed annexation of four Ukrainian regions, the overall number of members reached 178. As shown in Chapter 10 of this volume, gubernatorial elections in Russia are designed in such a way that candidates supported by Putin are practically guaranteed victory. In the 2010s and early 2020s, large majorities of regional assembly seats have been won by the pro-government party in nearly all federal units. The 2020 constitutional amendments endowed the president with the power to appoint additional members of the Federation Council, up to a maximum of thirty, at his own discretion. In 2020–22, however, the president did not exercise this power. There has been no political need for such appointments.

Political parties

The Constitution contains formal guarantees of ideological pluralism and a multiparty system in Russia, but detailed legal regulation of party activities is carried out on the basis of laws. In the 1990s, this regulation was soft. At that time, numerous parties of various ideological persuasions formed in Russia. Many of them were in opposition to the executive. The most important of them was the Communist Party of the Russian Federation

(*Kommunisticheskaia partiia Rossiiskoi Federatsii*, KPRF). In the 1995 and 1999 Duma elections, the KPRF emerged as the largest party of Russia. Unlike the KPRF, which inherited most of its membership from the formerly ruling party of the Soviet Union, other parties, even if relatively successful in elections, consisted mainly of their leaders and small numbers of activists. Shortly after the 1999 elections, the Presidential Administration initiated and guided the formation of a new pro-government party, later to be known as United Russia (*Edinaia Rossiia*). In the 2003 elections, this party won just under a half of Duma seats, 223, and was able to form a majority faction by recruiting some deputies elected as independents.

Since 2004, the Presidential Administration has pursued a policy aimed at removing from the electoral arena those parties that were willing and capable, even if potentially, of challenging the political executive. The main instrument of this policy is legislation on political parties. In 2004, it was legally established that parties registered in Russia had to have at least 50,000 card-carrying members. Because of parties' inability to fulfil this requirement, the number of parties eligible to participate in elections was reduced to less than ten in 2011. In 2012, along with the reform of the electoral system, membership requirements were significantly relaxed, which led to the emergence of dozens of minor political parties. Many of these parties do not participate in national elections. Their role relates mainly to the fact that in some regions, they can be used for candidate nomination by locally influential groups that are loyal to the executive authorities but not associated with United Russia. Since such situations are rare, the political role of these parties is negligible. Many of them are used solely to cut off some of the votes from parties and candidates who pose a problem for United Russia in regional and municipal elections.

All these parties are controlled by the Presidential Administration. Although the membership size requirements were lowered in 2012, many other requirements, mostly of a technical nature, remain in place. Parties are required to maintain a network of regional organizations, provide extensive financial reporting on their activities, and hold regular organizational events, such as congresses and regional conferences. All these activities are closely monitored by the Ministry of Justice. It is widely believed that the Ministry's approach to monitoring party activities is heavily politically biased. Parties that are recognized as violators of the technical requirements of the law are subject to liquidation in court. It can be said that parties in Russia exist only insofar as the Presidential Administration allows them to exist.

These legal tools are used by the Presidential Administration to prevent the creation of parties that could pose a real threat to the political monopoly of the executive. A leading critic of Vladimir Putin's politics, Alexei Navalny, tried to register his own parties under different names three times between 2012 and 2018, but in the end, none of these passed all stages of the registration process. The official reasons for refusals to register have always been technical, arising from the fact that the registration authorities discovered certain violations in the preparation of party documents or in the conduct of founding conferences. In 2021, Navalny's attempts to register a party were brought to an end when all public organizations associated with him were declared extremist and banned.

The main parties running in Russian elections and winning almost all seats in the State Duma and other representative assemblies are generally loyal to the executive branch, although their degrees of loyalty vary. The main pro-government party is United Russia. It is not, however, a ruling party. The influence of United Russia on the executive branch is small. Putin has never been a member. In the overwhelming majority, members of the government are not members of United Russia either. The main function of United Russia is to represent the executive branch in elections and, having won majorities of seats in representative assemblies, to ensure the implementation of the legislative agenda of the executive. Many regional branches of United Russia function as political departments of regional administrations. United Russia is headed by Dmitry Medvedev.

The KPRF remains the second largest party of Russia. Due to its relative strength, it retains some limited degree of autonomy from the executive. The current ideological positions of the party can be characterized as a mixture of traditional Marxism-Leninism, nationalism, and social conservatism. Since 1993, Gennady Zyuganov has been at the head of the party. The Liberal Democratic Party of Russia (LDPR), contrary to its name, has always been nationalist and advocated the transformation of Russia into a centralized state. Much of its success was due to the political skills and personal appeal of its former leader, Vladimir Zhirinovsky. After his death in 2022, Leonid Slutsky assumed leadership.

A Just Russia (*Spravedlivaia Rossiia*, SR) party was created in 2006 by merging several pre-existing groups under the leadership of Putin's close associate, Sergei Mironov. The initial goal of the enterprise was to create a leftist party that would be more tightly controlled by the executive than the KPRF. Over time, however, SR moved to predominantly nationalist positions. In the 2021 elections, one small party of a presumably pro-business standing, New People (*Novye Lyudi*), was also able to win party-list seats in the Duma. Some other small parties and non-party members have achieved marginal representation in the Duma by winning district seats.

During election campaigns, these parties can criticize each other rather sharply, but they refrain from criticizing the president. Sometimes they speak against the economic policies of the government, often evaluating these policies as 'not patriotic enough'. However, the Kremlin's aggressive foreign policy is fully supported by all of them. During the Russian invasion of Ukraine, the KPRF, the LDPR, and SR occasionally assumed even more belligerent positions than those voiced by the official representatives of United Russia.

This model of government support is not characteristic of Yabloko, a party which was founded in 1993 and which has stood on fairly consistent pro-democracy positions ever since. However, Yabloko's organizational weakness, the personal unpopularity of its leader, Grigory Yavlinsky, as well as its unwillingness to co-operate with popular opposition politicians like Alexei Navalny, discredited Yabloko in the eyes of opposition-minded voters and pushed it to the margins of Russia's political life. Starting with 2003, Yabloko has never crossed the 5 per cent barrier in Duma elections.

Table 1 illustrates the relative importance of Russia's political parties by presenting the results of the 2021 Duma elections. A more detailed description of how the Russian executive achieves such results through controlled elections can be found in Chapter 9 of this volume, 'Authoritarian Mechanics'. The party system in Russia is different from the party systems of democracies where the huge predominance of one party over others occurs only in rare and exceptional cases. In modern autocracies, predominant party systems like the Russian one are common enough. They are characterized not only by the pro-government parties' lion's shares of seats,

Table 8.1 Results of the 2021 Duma elections

Party	Share of party-list vote, %	Number of party-list seats	Number of district seats	Share of all seats, %
United Russia	50.9	126	198	72.0
KPRF	19.3	48	9	12.7
LDPR	7.7	19	2	4.7
SR	7.6	19	8	6.0
New People	5.4	13	0	2.9
Yabloko	1.4	0	0	0.0
Other parties and independents	7.7	0	3	0.7
Total	100.0	225	225	99.0*

* Does not add up to 100 per cent because of rounding
Source: Central Electoral Commission of Russia, www.cikrf.ru/opendata/.

but also by the fragmentation of the opposition camp, so that none of the opposition parties can be viewed as a credible prospective challenger to the incumbent executive (Golosov 2022).

Courts

Under the Constitution, the judicial system of Russia consists of the Constitutional Court, the Supreme Court, federal courts of general jurisdiction, and arbitration courts. The main function of the Constitutional Court is to review federal and regional laws and other legal acts, including those issued by the executive, as well as international treaties before they come into force, for their conformity with the Constitution. The Constitutional Court is also entitled to resolve disputes on competence between different government structures.

The president, the houses of the parliament as a whole or large groups of their members (at least one-fifth of them), as well as the Supreme Court and regional authorities, have the right to initiate consideration of legal acts in the Constitutional Court. In addition, the Constitutional Court has the right to consider complaints coming from lower courts and individual citizens. The Constitution establishes that complaints from citizens are accepted for consideration only if the contested provisions relate to legal acts applied in a particular case, and only after all other judicial remedies have been exhausted. Because of this provision, the Constitutional Court refuses to consider a significant proportion of complaints from citizens. However, some of them do reach the Constitutional Court. For example, in 2014, twenty out of thirty-three rulings issued by the Constitutional Court resulted from citizen complaints.

If the Constitutional Court recognizes a legal act as inconsistent with the Constitution, then within six months after the publication of the decision of the Constitutional Court, the government is obliged to submit to the Duma a bill in which the inconsistencies with the Constitution are eliminated. In fact, the six-month deadline is not always respected by the government.

Until 2020, the Constitutional Court consisted of nineteen judges, but amendments to the Constitution reduced their number to eleven. All members of the Constitutional Court are appointed by the Federation Council on the proposal of the president. Since the Federation Council is the house of the parliament that is most tightly controlled by the executive branch, it is extremely unlikely that judges will be appointed who would be likely to diverge from the position of the president.

Meanwhile, the Constitutional Court is politically significant, and some of its decisions have played an important role in the authoritarian dynamics of Russia's political regime. The most important of these was a resolution that recognized the legality of the 2020 constitutional amendments, and in particular the amendment that allowed for the extension of Putin's term limits. In accordance with the wishes of the president, the Constitutional Court also ruled that the amendments could be approved by a 'popular vote', although the Constitution stipulates a different procedure. In 2022, the Constitutional Court recognized 'treaties' on the annexation of Ukrainian territories as consistent with the Constitution. In 2015, the chairman of the Constitutional Court, Valery Zorkin, started to argue publicly that the Russian Constitution should have priority over international legal norms. In 2020, such a provision was written into the Russian Constitution.

The political role of other federal courts in Russia is small. When cases of political significance are brought before the Supreme Court, its rulings are normally favourable to the executive branch. Such are the cases related to the contestation of election results by the opposition, the sentences of lower courts against protesters and opposition politicians, and bans on the activities of political parties and NGOs. The Supreme Court is constitutionally designated to play an essential role in the presidential impeachment procedure if it is initiated by the Duma, which is unlikely.

It is widely recognized that the Russian judiciary is strongly dependent on the executive. When describing this dependence, the expression 'telephone law' is often used, meaning that judges make their decisions in obedience to instructions that officials and law enforcement officers give them over the phone. This situation has negative consequences for the country in many ways, especially in its economic life, because it is arguably one of the main reasons for the lack of guarantees of property rights in Russia. This is discussed in more detail in other chapters of this volume. Speaking of the system of political governance, it is very difficult to characterize the judiciary as a separate branch of power in the same sense as in the US or in Western European countries.

Conclusion

It would not be an overstatement to describe the basic mechanics of political governance in modern Russia as follows. The president makes the main decisions and has the right to alter any decisions made by other authorities;

the government executes the decisions of the president and makes its own decisions on matters of less importance; the parliament adopts laws in accordance with the wishes of the executive; and the courts validate these laws and the political decisions based on them. Such a political mechanism can smoothly operate under any set of institutional arrangements. Personalist autocracies can exist in various institutional forms, and there is no reason to believe that if Russia were to shift to a purely presidential or a parliamentary institutional design without regime change, the practice of governance would be significantly different. Under authoritarianism, institutions are less important than they are in democracies.

However, authoritarian institutions do exert some impact on the political process. They define the specific ways in which authoritarian rulers hold and exercise power. For example, in parliamentary and presidential-parliamentary systems, in which control over the parliament is of crucial importance to the executive, it goes to great lengths not only to win colossal majorities of legislative seats but also to purge the parliament of any meaningful opposition. For many authoritarian regimes of the past that existed in the form of presidential systems (e.g. in Latin America), this task was important, but not a priority. Therefore, such regimes allowed genuine opposition parties to participate in parliamentary elections and were more willing to resort to individual repression against their leaders than to systematic restrictions on opposition activities. At the same time, the presidential-parliamentary system, unlike the parliamentary one, significantly reduces the autocrat's need to rely on the pro-government party, which explains the organizational weakness of the United Russia Party in comparison to the ruling parties of parliamentary autocracies such as Cambodia.

There have been historical instances when authoritarian institutions have assumed crucial importance in the process of regime change. When an authoritarian regime falls apart, the old political mechanisms fail, and the leading political actors begin to feel the need to interact according to some rules, as a result of which the old institutions may become important in a new and unexpected way. For example, democratization in Spain was largely, if not decisively, carried out by the government inherited from Francisco Franco's dictatorship and legislated by a parliament which, at the time of Franco's death, had no opposition members at all. Democratization in Mexico was also carried out by using institutional structures that had developed and functioned for a long time under authoritarian conditions. However, in many countries successful transitions to democracy were accompanied by complete breakdowns of the institutional structures of the former regimes, as happened in Portugal in the 1970s. It is difficult to predict which of these paths will be taken in Russia, if and when regime change ever occurs. Under the current conditions, the formal institutions of governance in Russia are fully adapted to the political mechanics of authoritarianism and serve the purpose of maintaining a personalist dictatorship.

Questions for discussion

1   What makes parliaments and political parties important for electoral authoritarian regimes?
2   What differentiates Russia's semi-presidential system from purely presidential systems?
3   What prevented Russia from entering the 'Weimar scenario'?
4   According to the Constitution, who will act as the president of Russia if Putin suddenly departs from power?
5   What were the reasons for major electoral system reforms in Russia?

Recommended readings

The Constitution of the Russian Federation adopted by popular vote on 12 December 1993, with amendments approved by all-Russian vote on 1 July 2020. http://rm.coe.int/constitution-of-the-russian-federation-en/1680a1a237.
Chaisty, Paul. 2006. *Legislative Politics and Economic Power in Russia.* Basingstoke: Palgrave.
Henderson, Jane. 2022. *The Constitution of the Russian Federation: A Contextual Analysis.* Oxford: Hart Publishing.
Remington, Thomas F. 2014. *Presidential Decrees in Russia: A Comparative Perspective.* New York: Cambridge University Press.
Shevchenko, Iulia. 2017. *The Central Government of Russia: From Gorbachev to Putin.* New York: Routledge.

9

Authoritarian Mechanics

David Szakonyi

Since coming to power in 1999, Vladimir Putin has overseen the transformation of Russia from a fledgling democracy into a tightly controlled authoritarian state. Putin's regime has consolidated power through a range of tactics, from the suppression of free speech and the persecution of political opponents to the manipulation of elections and the use of state-sponsored violence. This chapter will explore the mechanics of authoritarian rule in Putin's Russia. It will analyze the wide range of mechanisms used in Russian politics to repress, coerce, and co-opt, including the use and abuse of propaganda, the bolstering of security services, and the cultivation of a culture of fear. This authoritarian turn in Russian politics has been years in the making, but accelerated by the Colour Revolutions occurring across Eurasia and the 2011–12 protest cycle in Russia that demonstrated the extent of mass discontent with the regime. Over the past decade, Putin's authoritarian model has proved remarkably resilient, allowing the regime to weather economic, political, and social crises, including its horrific invasion of Ukraine which has isolated the country from much of the world.

Domestic media and propaganda

In the 1990s, Russia's media environment was chaotic but largely free from government influence, a breath of fresh air after decades of strict censorship under the Soviet Union. However, upon coming to power, Putin and his team recognized the political utility of establishing unchallenged control over the information environment. Intervening in the media sector has allowed the regime not only to micro-manage the news content and political messaging that Russians consume, but also to paint the regime's leadership in glowing terms and prevent the emergence of any sort of popular alternative to its rule.

Media manipulation and propaganda begin on television, which is still the dominant medium by which Russians receive information about the world. According to recent surveys, roughly 86 per cent of Russians consider television to be their main source of news. Most of that viewership is concentrated on a small number of federal channels that are universally available to the public. One of Putin's first actions after assuming the presidency in 2000 was to orchestrate a multi-pronged campaign to establish government control over these networks. In a series of moves against powerful media oligarchs Vladimir Gusinsky and Boris Berezovsky, within just four years the three most popular channels (Channel 1, Rossiya, and NTV) were either majority-owned by the Russian government or in the hands of Gazprom, a state-owned enterprise.

During the first decade of the Putin regime, the state appeared content with limiting its intervention to this so-called commanding heights of the media sector. But as the country's political and economic situation tightened, the government has increasingly inserted itself and its proxies into local media markets across the country, providing a combination of financial incentives and top-down pressure to bring a once quite pluralist and vibrant sector to heel. In addition to all three of the major television networks broadcast nationwide, the government or corporations closely linked to it control all the leading radio stations (including the ostensibly independent *Ekho Moskvy* (Echo of Moscow)), all of the country's national newspapers and the news agencies, and roughly two-thirds of over 20,000 periodicals published across the country. Roughly a quarter of the population still gets news from the radio, most likely due to a growing audience of car owners, and giving the state an additional microphone to influence Russians' news consumption. Thousands of regional TV and radio networks have also come under government influence, attracted by federal subsidies dealt in exchange for editorial influence. Those that tried to remain independent faced impossible working conditions. In 2015, authorities shut down the private TV network Tomsk 2, an award-winning regional broadcaster in Tomsk that enjoyed substantial local popularity while also criticizing the authorities.

Russia also boasts the largest Internet audience in Europe, known colloquially as the RuNet. As of 2022, over 85 per cent of the population, or roughly 124 million people, reported accessing the Internet on a regular basis. Once solely the turf of the younger generation, the Internet has slowly gained traction even among older users (a little under half of people over sixty-five use it daily), partly due to so many key government and entertainment services having moved online. Internet penetration has also improved as of late outside of urban areas, but it still trails television as the primary source of news and information for most Russians. Much of the time Russians spend online is on social media sites, consuming entertainment content, or carrying out basic tasks, such as banking. Indeed, the majority of Russians still watch some form of national TV news programme at least two to three times a week.

State control over information

The regime exerts control over information not just through ownership of key assets, but also via direct orders from the top about which stories to cover and how to do so. Leaked documents reveal that top government officials meet representatives from the three national television networks in the Kremlin every week. Direct telephone lines between the Kremlin and these networks also allow for the communication of official talking points about the day's current events. There are also strict limits on foreign entities owning media assets and setting editorial policy.

These concerted efforts result in a very tightly controlled messaging apparatus squarely operating in the government's interests. First, news programmes portray Putin in an unequivocally positive light. Through relentless daily coverage, he is held up as a dedicated public servant working tirelessly to ensure political and social stability and resolve the country's many challenges. News programmes rarely wade into nuanced discussions or debates over domestic policy.

State media is particularly mobilized during events of government failure, working to deflect blame from Putin personally and point the finger at both insubordinate officials and foreign enemies as the real saboteurs of the country's welfare. In the rare instances that opponents of the regime make the news, they are often painted as self-interested criminals or even enemies of the state. Otherwise, stop lists are used by the Kremlin to identify which politicians and public figures can appear and in what format on television. The aim is alternately to ignore or discredit any possible opposition to the regime, undermining the possibility of alternative views reaching the masses.

The fear of crossing the government has also created new norms of self-censorship among journalists. By undermining professional norms regarding journalistic integrity, the regime encourages self-selection of compliant journalists into the state-owned sector who understand the type and tone of reporting that will be expected of them. Journalists and management who refuse to toe the party line can be fired at will. In the 2010s, for example, top editors at several of Russia's most popular and credible media outlets (Lenta.ru, RBC.ru, and *Kommersant*) all either lost or quit their jobs over conflicts with owners about having published politically sensitive stories and investigations.

The appeal of propaganda

Why do Russians tune into content with such an obvious and heavy bias towards the regime? Over the last decade, social scientists have exploited detailed public opinion polling, including the use of survey experiments, to tease out the appeal and effectiveness of state propaganda. First, in contrast to the gray stolid news broadcasts of the Soviet era, current state-controlled channels are modern media conglomerates deploying state-of-the-art technology to attract viewers and readers. Media holdings, backed by government resources, have invested heavily in increasing the production value of content they offer to Russian consumers. Rather than rely on imported foreign content as was the norm in the 1990s, under Putin creative personnel have enjoyed large budgets to craft original serials, reality shows and news programmes that genuinely appeal to the median Russian consumer. When Russians tune in for entertainment content, the integral part of this multi-billion dollar business, they generally stay for and consume the news programming that accompanies it.

Second, state media emphasize strongly patriotic and positive overtones to the information delivered. This resonates with Russians' preference for politically like-minded information. Watching the news extol the government for stabilizing and developing the country, even if reality is far more nuanced, provides citizens with a warm glow and even emotional gratification. In that sense, the Kremlin gives media consumers what they want: a rosy, almost unconditionally optimistic vision of Russia's future that stands in stark contrast with domestic or foreign alternatives that view their journalistic obligations as being more critical towards government more generally. The regime also promotes its conception of national identity and patriotism through choreographed political events and relentless propagandizing by showmen such as Dmitriy Kiselev and his long-running Sunday night news programme. Using a variety of showman techniques, Kiselev deftly uses sensationalism to arouse audiences' emotions as well as to trot out more radical views than those commonly held in society. His approach can be especially effective in imparting state-preferred frames about current events.

Finally, propaganda may be effective in Russia because it deftly mixes fact and fiction. A central trade-off for non-democratic regimes which manipulate the media is how far to push the truth. Propaganda that is clearly at odds with reality will repel viewers and possibly turn them against the government. Instead, Russian state media carefully calibrate their news coverage to align with the limited information citizens have about the world around them. Russian stories on economic topics hew closer to the truth. Coverage of foreign relations, especially concerning the United States and the West, bends and even completely falsifies reality to fit the Kremlin's political objectives. State-owned media do report on bad news and crises in the country, but are quick to blame insubordinate, corrupt officials or external actors, while shielding the president from blowback.

Independent media under siege

Independent media outlets struggle to compete with these powerful headwinds behind the propaganda machine. During the first two Putin administrations, the government tolerated a small degree of alternative media coverage, as long as its audience did not grow too markedly and question the regime's hold on power. One such channel, *Dozhd'* (TV Rain), delivered modern, attractive and independent news to a largely urban audience on cable subscriptions. But gradually that sense of tolerance gave way to an increasingly hostile work environment. Journalists who investigate corruption among public officials run significant personal risks; from 1992–2022, the Committee to Protect Journalists documented 106 Russian journalists killed, imprisoned, or gone missing as retribution for their investigative activities. State pressure on advertisers severely limits the amount of commercial funding available to pay personnel and reach audiences. Since 2012, dozens of journalists and outlets, including TV Rain, have been labelled 'foreign agents', a burdensome designation that requires intrusive financial reporting and the affixing of a label to all content produced under threat of heavy fines. In 2014, TV Rain was forcibly taken off the air and forced to migrate online, severely limiting its audience and advertising revenue.

The growth of the Internet in Russia beginning in the mid 2000s instilled new hope that Russians might access independent sources of information online, perhaps hosted by foreign service providers further from the grasp of government authorities. In fact, initially the regime perhaps underestimated the potential of the Internet to increase Russians' access to independent information and viewpoints as well as organize collective action, such as protests. In the wake of the 2011 parliamentary elections, which were widely considered fraudulent, citizens flocked to foreign social media (such as Facebook and Twitter), as well as more popular domestic networks such as VKontakte and Odnoklassniki to express their frustration with ballot box fraud, rampant corruption and other societal problems. Opposition activists, and in particular Alexei Navalny, quickly built a significant support base with their creative and compelling grasp of the potential of new media to reach younger, more critically inclined Russians. A number of intrepid investigative outlets, including *Vazhnye Istorii*, *The Insider*, and *Proekt*, began publishing a slew of well-researched, polished, and accessible online exposés of corruption and malfeasance within the Russian government.

Besieged by an array of criticism, the regime began cracking down and asserting control over the wild and potentially threatening Internet. To begin with, officials opted for a more legalistic approach to regulating internet media. A series of laws were passed that allowed authorities to punish journalists, bloggers, and even regular citizens for posting content deemed as 'extremist', containing 'unreliable information', or expressing 'blatant disrespect' for government authorities. The regulatory agency in charge of mass media, Roskomnadzor (an abbreviation for the Federal Service for Supervision of Communications, Information Technology, and Mass Media), began experimenting with blacklists of banned websites and media outlets as well as ramping up its monitoring capacity of all speech online. Alongside selective censorship, the government employed an army of pro-regime bloggers, social media influencers, and trolls to overwhelm the RuNet by creating confusion over information sources and distorting opposition messaging.

Finally, the Kremlin was also keen to bring to heel the social media networks that enabled opposition activity to flourish. The Yarovaya law, passed in 2016 forced all internet companies to store their data in Russia as well as make it available to law enforcement authorities upon request. VKontakte founder Pavel Durov was pressured into selling his shares and relinquishing control over his company, which ultimately ended up in the hands of Gazprom, a state-owned corporation, and Vladimir Kiriyenko, the son of one of Russia's top state officials. Many Russians also frequent news aggregators, such as Yandex and Lenta.ru, whose algorithms and editorial policies as of late are believed to be subject to state intervention and strict policing of content deemed as extremist, illegal, or just undesirable for the regime. This 'sovereign Internet' strategy allows the government to begin filtering and monitoring all information flows within the country, while preventing access to alternative viewpoints.

Media consolidation during wartime

In the run-up to Russia's 2022 all-out invasion of Ukraine, the regime bounded past the old model of selective censorship towards a new and even more aggressive approach towards both independent media outlets and Western social media networks. The regime has kicked its propaganda efforts into overdrive to paint the war as an existential and necessary defensive step taken by Russia to protect itself against foreign interests and demilitarize its neighbour, Ukraine. So far this whitewashing of Russia's role in the conflict appears to have resonated with a substantial part of Russian society.

In addition, new so-called 'war censorship laws' have essentially prohibited any content seen as discrediting (i.e. criticizing) any actions taken by the Russian military or other state organs. These restrictions even allow punishment for any individual who reposts banned materials or refers to the 'special military operation' as a war. In response, dozens of media outlets stopped operating in Russia and fled abroad to places such as Riga, Vilnius and Prague, where many continue to publish stories critical of the regime and its war. Popular online newspapers *Meduza* and *Proekt* have been punished even further as 'undesirable organizations', meaning that any persons promoting their articles or donating money could theoretically face prison sentences. State-owned media have at times aired opinions surprisingly critical of certain aspects of Russia's military strategy, but that criticism has so far not been allowed to touch Putin personally.

Fearful of Russians accessing information challenging the regime's version of events in Ukraine, authorities also began implementing in earnest their version of the China's Great Firewall. By July 2022, Roskomnadzor had blocked nearly 100 media outlets targeting Russian audiences, as well as officially banning Facebook, Twitter, and Instagram from the country. At the time of writing in 2023, Russians could still access these resources using VPNs, but the government had taken a huge step towards the Chinese model by introducing a powerful and sophisticated filtering system to manage access to information. However, so far both YouTube and Telegram, two sites very popular in Russia that host content critical of the regime, are both available, suggesting there are still some constraints on how far the government will go in cutting its citizens completely off from the Western world.

The repressive state

Beyond the information environment, the Russian government has come to rely on a powerful and largely unchecked repressive apparatus to cement the regime's grip on power. As a former KGB officer, Putin has made no secret of his affinity for the security services, for both their perceived loyalty to a strong Russian state and their willingness to carry out targeted repression of potential opponents, media outlets, and non-government organizations.

Rise of the siloviki

Upon taking office, Putin immediately began filling vacant government positions with *siloviki*, a term originating from the Russian word for 'force' (*sila*) signifying individuals with past work experience in one of Russia's so-called force ministries (e.g. those authorized to use violence and coercion in the name of the state). The most prominent siloviki are agents from the Federal Security Service (FSB), the successor to the Soviet-era KGB secret police and spy agency. The FSB has ascended into what has been termed a 'New Nobility' – an elite position, for the agency reigns supreme over other government organs (Soldatov and Borogan 2010). But other heavyweights include the Federal Protective Service (FSO), which assumes responsibility for Putin's personal security while also performing important intelligence-gathering activities, the Prosecutor General's Office, military intelligence (GRU), and the Foreign Intelligence Service (SVR). Observers have noted that officials from the Interior Ministry and the various branches of the military appear to rank lower in prestige but also firmly qualify as organs of the siloviki ethos.

Putin's rise to power in 1999 saw a dramatic increase in the number of top state officials drawn from the ranks of these force ministries. Many commentators saw in the rise of the siloviki a wholesale transformation of Russian officialdom, whereby veterans of the secret services and military would accumulate unrivaled political and economic power. Sergei Ivanov, a former intelligence officer of the KGB became deputy prime minister during

Putin's first term and then Chief of Staff during his third. Nikolai Patrushev worked with Putin himself in the Leningrad KGB during the Soviet Union, before later being appointed head of the FSB and chairman of the Security Council. Siloviki were also used to help the centre re-establish control over unruly regions in their capacity as presidential envoys to newly created federal districts. Although some scholars have argued that the presence of siloviki in government peaked during Putin's second presidential term, the continued influence of a small number of men with security backgrounds continues to be felt across the political and economic spectrum.

Putin not only tapped the security services for personnel, he invested massive budgetary resources into returning them to prominence within the Russian state. Much of that money went towards recruitment and rearmament, especially in the case of the Ministry of Defence, which overwent an overhaul worth over $300 billion beginning in 2009. Other reorganization efforts went into positioning the FSB as first amongst equals. Under Putin, the FSB has absorbed other agencies, acquired new foreign intelligence-gathering powers, and was able to place counterintelligence officers across the Russian government.

Under Putin, new security agencies appeared on the scene, boasting close ties to the President and a mandate for preserving the political order. In 2007, the Investigative Committee assumed its role as the main federal investigative authority in the country, wielding new powers to investigate corruption, foreign agents and terrorism (among other crimes), committed by regular citizens, businesspeople and especially officials from other security services, the wider federal bureaucracy and regional and local governments. Its head Aleksandr Bastrykin attended university with Putin and now reports directly to him.

Next came the creation of the National Guard of Russia in 2016, made up of troops from the Ministry of the Interior. Tasked with maintaining social order (read as clamping down on social unrest), Putin appointed his former bodyguard Viktor Zolotov as director. Zolotov's close personal ties to the Kremlin have led many to speculate about the National Guard operating as a sort of praetorian guard bent on protecting Putin from any threats, either from the masses below or from within his elite coalition. The National Guard oversees the OMON riot police which have been used frequently to quash demonstrations across the country as well as rapid reaction teams to respond to other types of social disorder. Following these reorganizations, the broad Russian intelligence and security community now comprises nine major agencies; although precise estimates of personnel are impossible to come by, over one million officers may now work for some type of force ministry or security agency, a number that excludes the formal Russian armed forces.

Empowered with larger budgets and trust from above, security services in Russia have taken a new place as an elite vanguard of stability and order. Siloviki view themselves as the front lines protecting the government against perceived external and especially internal threats. Fending off these challenges, in their view, requires a strong and highly centralized state where paramount authority is given to large and well-resourced security and defence agencies. Blame for the tumult of the 1990s is assigned to a combination of freewheeling oligarchs, corrupt officials, and external forces, in particular the West, trying to exploit the country's wealth and deprive it of status as a great power. Restoring Russian greatness not only means protecting the country's political interests, but also empowering a strong role for the state in the economy to ensure that the economic interests of the nation are defended.

However binding this commitment to a strong Russian state seen as being besieged by internal and external forces, there are fewer other ideological tenets binding the siloviki into a coherent group. Some factions with the broader security array have also developed a close relationship with the Russian Orthodox Church. But Russia's repressive apparatus is wide and broad, comprising hundreds of thousands of officers with their own sets of personal interests. The division of labour and frequently overlapping responsibilities across many agencies has generated strong internal rivalries. In some instances, these conflicts can spill over into overt hostilities. Agencies compete with one another for both access to budget resources and rent-seeking opportunities outside the state, for example, attractive private enterprises to pressure and expropriate. Instead, the security services have been able to accumulate vast power and influence across the Russian state because of their immunity from public oversight and external control. Their mutual interest is in preserving the status quo and preventing any kind of political, institutional or economic reform that might weaken their grip on rent streams or hold them accountable for unlawful activities. Protecting their spheres of influence against outside interference is paramount, as is punishing defectors and other people viewed as traitors to the broader community.

Importantly, the regime has developed a very specific legislative base to sanction its attacks on its opponents. Its strategy best resembles the idea of 'rule by law', where legal instruments are used to arbitrarily repress individuals and groups based on their perceived threat to the regime, rather than any true criminal or treasonous behaviour. This stands in contrast to what is referred to in democratic states as the 'rule of law', which holds that all entities within a society are accountable to the same legal tenets and treated equitably before the law. The arbitrary and even random application of the law in Russia instils a culture of fear, whereby people internalize the abuse of the judicial system by the broader government to achieve its political objectives. Authorities regularly hand down excessive punishments following minor legal infractions in order to demonstrate the high costs of activism against the regime and undermine the capacity of rivals to organize against it.

Repression under the Putin era first began to be used in earnest against Yeltsin-era oligarchs who still commanded disproportionate influence in the early 2000s. The most cited example of this harsh pivot away from the oligarchs was the takeover of Russia's largest oil company Yukos and the imprisonment of its CEO Mikhail Khodorkovsky in 2004. The arrest of Khodorkovsky sent a chilling message to the rest of Russia's oligarchic class, which had since 1991 enjoyed the most prominent economic perches in the country. Oligarchs were made to understand that they could keep their vast commercial holdings only on the condition of loyalty to the Putin regime. By funding opposition parties and even hinting at presidential ambitions, Khodorkovsky had seemingly violated that implicit deal and then paid a very steep price. Although individual oligarchs still command personal fortunes of billions of dollars, their ability to enjoy that wealth depends on their willingness to play ball with the government, such as by developing and exploiting political connections to the siloviki, contributing financially to government-approved causes and projects, and most recently endorsing Russia's invasion of Ukraine.

Taking their place is what Daniel Treisman has described as a new set of economic elites, the 'silovarchs' (a combination of the words silovik and oligarch), who took control over the commanding heights of the Russian economy, both through connections and repression (Treisman 2007). These individuals viewed themselves as stewards of 'state capitalism', where only veterans of the force ministries could be trusted to direct economic activity in support of national interests. Igor Sechin, head of Russia's now largest oil company Rosneft, for example served in military intelligence during the 1980s, while Vladimir Yakunin took over Russian Railways after a long career in the KGB during the Soviet era. Their rise has increasingly led to a much more hostile business environment, as security officials enjoy wide scope to harass businesses, raid companies, and even jail businesspeople, all to get their hands on lucrative economic assets. Silovarchs with close personal ties to Putin himself have prospered the most, building new empires on the back of access to public procurement and protectionist policies. By expropriating assets and developing new political-economic networks with connections to the security services, these individuals have largely replaced the Yeltsin-era oligarchs at the top of Russia's power vertical.

Keeping down the opposition

Repression is also used to keep the coalition of political elites intact. Agencies such as the Investigative Committee and the FSB have used their investigative powers to go after officials across the federal bureaucracy, ostensibly on an anti-corruption campaign but frequently targeting elites encroaching on certain economic spheres of influence or displaying insufficient loyalty to the regime. The arrest and imprisonment of Minister of Economic Development Alexei Ulyukaev in 2016 on bribery charges is often seen as a bellwether for economic interests with close ties to the security services targeting a more liberal official to access a wider rent stream. Criminal investigations have also been brought against lower-level officials throughout the country, with dozens of governors and hundreds of mayors being arrested, detained, and often sentenced to significant jail terms, again often under the aegis of an anti-corruption campaign.

State-directed repression also does not respect international borders. The Russian government has shown less restraint targeting high-profile defectors who have been viewed as cooperating with the West and betraying Russian interests. In 2006, former FSB officer Alexander Litvinenko was poisoned in London, England. UK criminal investigators have publicly identified two Russian nationals acting at the behest of the Russian government in carrying out this 'state execution', but to date have been unable to complete their extradition and bring them to trial. In 2018, two Russian intelligence agents attempted to assassinate another defector Sergei Skripal and his daughter, using a chemical nerve agent in Salisbury, England. These actions publicly demonstrate the costs of crossing the regime, helping prevent defections even during times of economic and political crisis when discontent within elite ranks has surely grown.

Alongside the repression of elites, the security services also began constructing a vast surveillance and repressive apparatus for targeting potential political opposition. Rather than label the political opposition using ideological or even religious terminology, the Kremlin has exploited a combination of anti-extremism, anti-terrorism, and anti-corruption laws to roll back political rights and repress challengers. Any threats to the regime, real or imagined, are deemed socially dangerous and worthy of especially harsh treatment. Targets have included nationalists of various stripes, adherents of religious groups such as Jehovah's Witnesses and Islamic activists, and of course civic activists, in particular those who organize and participate in mass demonstrations. New legislation has effectively shut down any space for regime opposition. All protests involving more than one individual must be approved in advance, or are otherwise suppressed. The same foreign agent laws described above as being used to punish independent media have destroyed the funding and operational bases for countless civil society organizations in Russia.

Repression of the opposition can also take on a variety of quasi-legal forms. Undercover agents and moles penetrate civic and religious groups, gathering information and even sabotaging organizational efforts from within. The government's much-heralded investment in digitalization has not passed by the security agencies, who have powerful surveillance tools at their fingertips to track both online and offline activity of individuals and groups which are deemed to be threatening. FSB officers exploit a complex nationwide system entitled the System for Operative Investigative Activities (SORM) to tap phone conversations, intercept emails and text messages, and track most digital activity by Russian citizens.

Other tactics are much less subtle and much more aggressive. The OMON riot police enjoy free rein to suppress any unsanctioned protests; heavy-handed treatment of protestors can lead to physical injury in addition to fines and short-term arrests. Activists have also reported police brutality and torture within the Russian prison system. Just as with journalists, civic activists are vulnerable to physical assault and even assassination by actors most likely supported by the regime. In February 2015, opposition leader Boris Nemtsov was horrifically gunned down just steps from the Kremlin, demonstrating the impunity of certain actors within Russian society to carry out political assassinations with near-complete impunity.

As with the crackdown on independent journalists, the regime escalated its aggressive stances towards civil society and opposition groups throughout the 2010s and especially in the wake of the 2022 all-out invasion of Ukraine. Following his marked growth in popularity during the 2011–12 protest cycle, Alexei Navalny and activists from his Anti-Corruption Foundation have sat squarely in the crosshairs of the regime. Even though his criticism has been overtly political and Navalny himself has run against the regime at the ballot box, the Kremlin has pursued false criminal charges accusing Navalny of embezzlement, slander, stealing donations, and ultimately extremism. After a series of show trials featuring falsified accusations and evidence, Navalny was hit with sentences totalling over twelve years, much of which has been served so far in particularly brutal conditions of solitary confinement. By criminalizing opposition based on charges purportedly unrelated to politics, the regime attempts to further discredit the opposition and paint them as corrupt, self-interested actors in the service of external enemies (Rogov 2018).

Moscow's increasingly aggressive actions towards Ukraine have coincided with the effective end of open opposition politics and independent civil society within Russia. Navalny's foundation is far from the only civil society group targeted by the crackdown. NGOs such as the Moscow Helsinki Group, Memorial, and the Sakharov Center have all been closed down. Opposition figures such as Ilya Yashin and Vladimir Kara-Murza face extraordinarily harsh sentences for opposing Russia's war in Ukraine. According to the NGO OVD-Info, which runs the PolitPressing.org site, as of 2023, there are over 2,000 victims of political repression in Russia, most of whom are currently in prison. Speaking out against the regime in any form now carries the threat of serious punishment, serving to force opponents to flee abroad and mostly silence what remaining dissent exists in the country.

Managing elections

The third key tool in the Putin's strategic authoritarian arsenal has been a readiness to engage in both overt and more subtle types of electoral manipulation to prevent challengers from accessing key political positions. Electoral fraud comes with serious trade-offs for the regime. On one hand, undermining electoral integrity helps deliver preferred outcomes at the ballot box and allows the regime to maintain power. This can be especially critical during times of crisis when the regime's declining popularity might otherwise compel voters to propel opposition groups to power. Electoral fraud has been a critical factor behind the sizeable margins that regime-affiliated candidates have secured since the early days of the Putin's first term as president. The regime goes to great lengths to avoid having to share power and rents with the opposition, as well as giving them the chance to govern and demonstrate a political alternative to the current elites in office.

But just as repression and censorship can backfire politically, electoral fraud can also threaten the regime's hold on power. Opposition groups can exploit electoral abuses to mobilize citizens onto the streets, while embarrassing revelations of ballot box fraud hurt the regime's image among even its most fervent supporters (Reuter and Szakonyi 2021). It is believed that much of the motivation behind the Kremlin's authoritarian turn beginning in the mid-2000s stemmed from a fear of being toppled by mass demonstrations propelled by accusations of electoral fraud, that is, the contagion from the Colour Revolutions that toppled national leaders in Georgia, Ukraine, and Kyrgyzstan. Blatant fraud carries serious downside risks.

Moreover, cancelling elections altogether, which the regime has experimented with at the regional and local levels, deprives the government of many critical benefits while also contradicting government propaganda that Russia is still in many ways a democracy. Elections provide policymakers with concrete information about public preferences and levels of support, perhaps more reliably than opinion polls alone. Forcing elites to compete in open contests also helps the regime identify and promote capable leaders who demonstrate loyalty by adopting ruling-party banners. Winners can access the spoils of government and grow more invested in supporting the regime in the long run. Finally, the Russian population has come to expect at least some degree of open competition for leadership posts, and may withdraw its support for the regime if manipulation is seen as going too far. Holding and winning elections can help maintain and increase regime legitimacy.

The basics of electoral fraud

Thus, the Kremlin has tried to tread carefully when it comes to electoral manipulation, combining deliberate and impactful fraudulent tactics with significant investment in concealing their use from the wider public. Electoral fraud has been implemented in close coordination with their other authoritarian tactics described so far in this chapter. Restricting independent media prevents voters from learning the real weaknesses in electoral processes. Repressing civil society and opposition groups and severely limiting most forms of protests limits the potential fallout from the ballot box being exposed publicly. So far, this strategy has undermined the opposition's ability to organize mass protests against electoral fraud in a repeat of the 2011–12 electoral cycle.

How does electoral fraud work in Russia? Many tactics are implemented long in advance of the actual voting on election day. Opposition candidates struggle to reach the ballot and register their candidacies. Onerous signature and document requirements allow authorities to deny registration based on minutiae and bureaucracy. Electoral laws automatically disqualify millions of Russians from even seeking office based on criminal records or political associations, with some persistent challengers facing abuse and assault even for testing these restrictions. For those candidates allowed to run, the regime makes sure that financing only flows to those affiliated with the regime. Businesspeople and other wealthy individuals are pressured not to make donations to opposition campaigns, while United Russia can tap administrative resources to reach voters and fund advertising expenditures. Finally, state-owned media provide gushing coverage for regime-affiliated candidates and slander challengers, if they receive any airtime at all.

Even the most manipulated elections still require some voters to turn out and cast votes. Regimes depend on some level of actual voter mobilization to demonstrate popularity and engage with their core supporters; otherwise electoral results can appear blatantly manufactured and disconnected from reality. Mobilization in Russia unfolds on multiple fronts. Employers regularly appeal to their workers to vote, offering a combination of carrots and sticks in exchange. Precincts are often established in the workplace itself, allowing employers to monitor turnout closely. Budgetniki, that is people directly on the government payroll such as teachers, doctors, and bureaucrats, can face pressure from their superiors not only to turn out but also mobilize their networks. Party activists also take to the streets, going door to door, distributing flyers, and much less often buying votes with cash or material goods. Turnout in Russian elections can vary generally, depending on how many levers the regime pulls to activate its core electorate.

Election day results are the product both of that widespread mobilization and a number of illegal schemes orchestrated by the regime to manipulate the vote. Through its influence within municipal governments, United Russia often directly controls the staffing of poll workers, who face intense pressure from above to deliver the preset vote percentage on behalf of regime candidates. Blatant electoral fraud, such as ballots being stuffed into urns or final tallies being falsified, is often captured in videos and pictures from election monitors. Another widespread scheme is the use of multiple voting (or 'carousels'), whereby voters are either allowed to vote several times at one precinct, often using absentee ballots, or ride pre-arranged buses to vote at a number of polling stations throughout election day. Vulnerable populations, such as prisoners, patients in psychiatric hospitals, and university students may also be coerced into voting. Other groups facing pressure to vote may have to submit pictures of their ballot taken with a mobile phone in order to demonstrate they followed through with directives.

Fraud exposed

Detecting and preventing election fraud is something of a cat-and-mouse game between the regime and a small group of election monitors, academics, and independent analysts. For example, by detecting anomalies in the numerical digits of vote counts submitted by polling stations, sophisticated econometric analysis has uncovered that a substantial share of votes cast in the twenty-first century for Putin and United Russia have been fraudulent. Other empirical work relies on citizens directly sharing data about when and how manipulation occurs. Each election the country's most prominent monitoring organization, Golos, hosts an online portal where citizens from across the country can report electoral violations. Local civil society activists, including from Golos, are also deployed to precincts to monitor elections firsthand and issue reports about problems relating to electoral integrity. Analyzing the presence of monitors within precincts, academics have established, for example, that not only were approximately a quarter of votes stolen during the 2011 Duma elections in Moscow, but such citizen initiatives helped ensure more free and fair elections.

Over time, however, the regime has cracked down on independent election monitors and restricted access to the underlying data in order to suppress any leakage of evidence relating to electoral violations. Viral videos of electoral fraud helped propel the 2011–12 protest wave, something the regime was loathe to see repeated. Conscious of the potential for negative publicity, the regime then invested in superficial efforts to convince the population that it takes these issues seriously. Afterwards, video cameras were installed in thousands of precincts country-wide and equipped to simultaneously broadcast the vote count online. And any poll workers caught engaging rarely if ever face legal consequences for their actions.

Difficulties coordinating thousands of election administrators and preventing illegal actions from reaching the public may have prompted the Kremlin to extend one of its favourite new initiatives – digitalization – to the electoral sphere. Beginning in 2020, citizens were allowed to cast votes electronically through an ostensibly secure online portal with identity verification. Introduced during the coronavirus pandemic, electronic voting was heralded as a way for voters to remain at home, socially distanced, while still casting their ballots. However, both the opacity around the actual implementation of electronic voting and the overtly pro-regime bias so far in the electronic votes cast have raised considerable concern that it is just one more weapon in the regime's arsenal of fraud. For example, in the 2021 Duma elections, tallies from electronic voting delivered last-minute victories to United Russia candidates. Not only did the Kremlin refuse to acknowledge the suspicious vote drop, but electronic voting will continue to roll out across the country and potentially be in use during elections at all levels in the coming years.

Russia falls squarely within the camp of electoral autocracies, failing to meet minimum standards of free and fair elections but still allowing managed and sometimes unpredictable competition. Elections are still used to select leaders at many levels of government, though recent reforms have increasingly replaced elected positions with political appointees in executive posts in Russia's regions and cities. The big fear among supporters of democracy is, however, not whether elections will continue to happen in the future, but rather whether the expansion of electronic voting will give the regime free rein to manipulate outcomes without any fear of exposure.

Conclusion

Putin's brand of authoritarianism leans on several pillars to secure popular legitimacy, prevent the emergence of challengers, and maintain a firm grip on power without abrogating elections. The media is tightly controlled through state ownership of key assets, while government agencies closely monitor and filter all information flowing through the once mostly unregulated Russian Internet. Security agencies have received significant investment in resources, personnel and mandate, without any third-party monitoring to hold the state accountable for violating human or political rights. Finally, elections are now a finely stage-managed affair with fewer and fewer opportunities for opposition candidates to reach the ballot and citizens to ensure that their votes are being counted fairly.

Putin with his regime closely resembles a new breed of 'information autocrats' who rely more on controlling the popular narrative than repression to remain in power (Guriev and Treisman 2022). Russia's 2022 all-out invasion of Ukraine may have partly changed that calculus, because even amidst an escalated propaganda offensive on the domestic front, the government has increasingly turned to overt repression to prevent dissent from bubbling to the surface. Russia may now have joined the ranks of closed authoritarian states such as China, with few institutional safeguards to protect openness and the free expression of alternative voices within society.

Questions for discussion

1 What are the obstacles that independent journalists face doing their work in Russia?
2 Why do Russian citizens often trust information from state-owned outlets, even when they recognize that it may be biased?
3 What does the term 'rule by law' signify and how is it applicable to the Russian government's approach towards repression?
4 How united are the siloviki in their approach to their governance roles?
5 Why are the ruling authorities careful to avoid blatant electoral fraud wherever possible?

Recommended readings

Frye, Timothy, Reuter, Ora John, and Szakonyi, David. 2014. 'Political Machines at Work: Voter Mobilization and Electoral Subversion in the Workplace.' *World Politics*, 66(2), pp. 195–28.

Oates, Sarah. 2016. 'Russian Media in the Digital Age: Propaganda Rewired.' *Russian Politics* 1, No. 4: 398–417.

Proekt Media. 2022. 'Novy Mir: A Guide to Russian Media in the Times of Total Censorship.' See www.proekt.media/en/guide-en/russian-media-after-war-en/.

Soldatov, Andrei, and Irina Borogan. 2010. 'The New Nobility: The Restoration of Russia's Security State and the Enduring Legacy of the KGB.' *PublicAffairs*.

Taylor, Brian D. 2011. *State Building in Putin's Russia: Policing and Coercion after Communism*. Cambridge University Press.

10

Federalism and Centre–Periphery Relations

Vladimir Gel'man

If one were to begin a study of Russian federalism and sub-national politics from a reading of several major official documents, such as constitutions and federal laws, it might be possible to get the impression of a very developed institutional framework of federal democracy in Russia. Indeed, this is the largest federal state in the world, which is organized around more than eighty territorial federal units (regions) and more than 19,000 municipalities of different types. According to legal frameworks, sub-national authorities in Russia enjoy a great deal of autonomy, and the division of resources and responsibilities between federal, regional, and local governments is strictly defined by countless state regulations. Moreover, it is assumed that all sub-national authorities in Russia are elected by regional and local votes on the basis of free and fair elections, with open competition among several parties and/or candidates. Such a rosy picture of law-based sub-national autonomy and democracy Russia sharply contradicts the rather grim realities. Top-down hierarchical governance from the Kremlin to remote peripheral villages, known in Russian political idiom as the 'power vertical', aims at full-scale centralized control over sub-national units and serves as a major informal mechanism of distribution of power and rents (Gel'man, Ryzhenkov, 2011). At the same time, sub-national electoral politics in Russia exhibits patterns of overwhelming domination by machine politics, and all political regimes across Russia's regions and cities are authoritarian.

The disjuncture between a façade of formal democratic institutions and the informal authoritarian core of real politics is hardly unique for sub-national politics in Russia: Politics at the nationwide level demonstrates similar trends. It is also not a country-specific and context-bounded phenomenon of Russia.

In fact, sub-national authoritarianism has been widespread in a number of Latin American countries and many cities in the United States in the twentieth century, and often persists over decades, despite major changes in nationwide politics (Gibson, 2012). Many countries across the globe have demonstrated sub-national political diversity, which opened many opportunities for sub-national comparisons in various contexts, and Russia is no exception in terms of cross-regional variations (Snyder, 2001). The hierarchy of 'power vertical' in sub-national governance is also typical for many autocracies across the globe, ranging from Central Asia to sub-Saharan Africa. However, practices of centre–periphery relations in autocracies have varied greatly. In their comparative study, Alexander Libman and Michael Rochlitz (2019) convincingly demonstrated the crucial difference between patterns of sub-national governance in Russia and China. The Chinese provincial authorities compete with one another for promotion to high-level jobs in Beijing, and excellence in their economic performance is a key criterion for upward career mobility. In Russia, regional governors have little chance of being promoted to top jobs in Moscow, while their survival in top positions depends heavily upon vote delivery for Putin and for the United Russia party (for a more detailed account, see Chapter 9 of this volume). This is why Chinese provincial leaders have had to focus their efforts on building new roads and airports, while their Russian counterparts have been interested more in stuffing ballot boxes during polls and preventing mass protests in the harshest possible way. This combination provides numerous negative incentives for sub-national politics and governance in Russian regions and cities.

What caused these mechanisms of centre–periphery relations in Russia and to what extent do they matter for the functioning of the Russian state and its political regime? This chapter seeks answers to these and other questions. After a brief historical overview of Soviet and post-Soviet federalism in Russia, it addresses major issues of territorial politics in Russia, analyzes key elements of the sub-national political order, and discusses the prospects for Russian federalism and centre–periphery relations in the wake of ongoing war with Ukraine.

Background: Soviet federalism and its legacies

According to a classical definition, 'federalism is a political organization in which the activities of government are divided between regional governments and a central government in such a way that each kind of government has some activities on which it makes final decisions' (Riker, 1975, p. 101). The present-day Russian model fits ill with this definition, and the Soviet model has little in common with genuine federalism despite the official status of the Soviet Union as a federal state. Bolsheviks first proclaimed Russia as a federation in 1918 in order to garner support from ethnic and nationalist movements, which emerged in the wake of revolution and the fall of the Russian monarchy after the end of empire. The Soviet Union was also organized in 1922 as a federation for similar reasons.

Later, the model of Soviet federalism became institutionalized on several principles. First, the Soviet Union was a multilayered hierarchical federation. On its top layer, fifteen units, organized around certain ethnic groups (such as Armenians or Uzbeks) had the highest status of 'union republics'. Second-tier units gained the status of ethnic-based 'autonomous republics' within union republics (such as Tatars or Buryats), and third-tier ethnic groups were designated around autonomous oblasts and districts within territorial units (krais and/or oblasts), which, in turn, had no special status. These statuses and units changed over time, especially in the wake of ethnic cleansings and deportations during the World War II, but have remained stable since 1957. Second, the Soviet model legally proposed an opportunity for both the free admission of union republics to the Soviet Union and for free secession. This norm was used as a pretext for the co-optation of the Baltic republics after their Soviet occupation in 1940, but none of them took the opportunity for secession seriously until the period of Soviet collapse in 1990–91 (at that time, three Baltic states, and Georgia, Armenia, and Moldova proclaimed their independence).

Third and most important, in real terms, all ethnic and territorial units of the Soviet Union were heavily penetrated by the Communist Party, which according to the Soviet constitution of 1977 was 'a ruling and guiding force of the Soviet society, the core of the Soviet political system'. The Communist Party maintained a firm, full-scale control over sub-national politics and governance through its extensive territorial networks and hierarchical subordination, so the political and economic autonomy of all republics and other units was rather limited. Sub-national Communist party bosses played a major role in the socio-economic development of respective areas, and this working experience was essential for further promotion to top careers in the Soviet hierarchy for every top official, ranging from Khrushchev to Yeltsin. Over time, the regional Communist leadership consolidated their powers in the provinces, paving the way for the emergence of sub-state dictatorships (Gorlizki, Khlevniuk, 2020).

During perestroika, Soviet federalism fell victim to three interrelated processes. First, rapid democratization, accompanied by the mass reshuffling of sub-national elites, opened new opportunities for an awakening of bottom-up social and political activism and political entrepreneurship in the provinces. Secondly, large-scale decentralization amid deteriorating economic conditions contributed to increasing grievances vis-à-vis Moscow-led policies and became a trigger event for a wave of nationalist mobilization, promoted and endorsed by ethnic elites in the republics (Beissinger, 2002). Thirdly, several ethno-territorial conflicts that had remained hidden and dormant over decades of Communist rule turned into open confrontation in various areas ranging from Transnistria to Nargorno-Karabagh. Gorbachev, in turn, was not ready to deal with these unintended consequences of his reforms. He had a poor understanding of the nature of increasing tensions, and found himself between the rock of ethnic separatism and the hard place of the survival of the Soviet state. Several proposals for reforming Soviet federalism were discussed, but not in fact implemented. After a failed attempt at a Communist coup in August 1991, former union republics proclaimed their independence, and were recognized by each other and by foreign nations. Soon after, the collapse of the Soviet state became inevitable, and in December 1991 the former Union Treaty of 1922, which served as a foundational act of Soviet federalism, was renounced by the authorities of Russia, Ukraine, and Belarus. The Soviet Union disappeared from the global map, but its legacies affected post-Soviet Russian federalism to a great degree.

From the Soviet model, Russia inherited an ethnic-based nature of federalism as well as its complex multilayered structure. According to the 1993 constitution, Russia proclaimed itself a federal state, which included six types of federal units (twenty-one republics, six krais, forty-nine oblasts, one autonomous oblast, ten autonomous districts, and two federal cities – Moscow and St Petersburg), while the total number of federal units (eighty-nine) was the highest in the world among federations. This legacy and the traumatic experience of the Soviet collapse in the 1990s contributed to many expectations that Russia might soon break up in the same way as the Soviet Union. In fact, however, these expectations proved to be mistaken, and the Russian Federation did not collapse despite the many problems faced during the post-Soviet transition. As Henry Hale (2005) convincingly demonstrated, post-Communist Russia, unlike the Soviet Union or Yugoslavia, was organized not as a subset of various peripheral ethno-territorial units around a single dominant core ethno-territorial unit at the centre, but as a rather mixed conglomerate of various units of different types (ethnic and territorial) without a core unit at the centre. Such a constellation made it unlikely that the Russian Federation would collapse along ethno-territorial lines. This style of Russian federalism prevented major violent separatist rebellions as well as collective actions against a non-existent core. Also, unlike the Soviet Union, Russia demonstrated a relatively low degree of ethnic heterogeneity, as ethnic-based regions mixed with non-ethnic territories with predominantly Russian populations. Even though some sub-national leaders in Russia attempted to gain a large degree of autonomy from Moscow soon after the Soviet collapse, even ethnic-based regions did not strive for full-scale independence. This is why, instead of major collapse, the trajectory of post-Soviet federalism in Russia resembled a pendulum-like swing.

Centre and peripheries: swings of the pendulum

The Soviet collapse in 1991 coincided with a dramatic weakening of the Russian state against a background of a deep and protracted recession. Both the fiscal and coercive capacity of the Russian state underwent major decay, and resources for the control of law and order in many provinces were almost exhausted. Under these conditions, the leadership of several ethnic republics resorted to blackmailing the federal government in Moscow, announcing drives for full-scale independence (Giuliano, 2011) while simultaneously insisting on favourable conditions of control over fiscal transfers and property rights in their respective regions. In turn, Moscow employed a policy of selective appeasement of the most rebellious regions, satisfying their demands and making major concessions, but also winning more favourable election results in exchange for the loyalty of regional elites (Treisman, 1999). Such an approach, albeit costly in economic terms, became a working compromise for a period of transition from Soviet to post-Soviet federalism and reduced the threat of potential conflicts between central and regional governments. Chechnya, with its two bloody wars (see Chapter 11 of this volume) became the only exceptional case of a violent separatist clash among Russia's regions.

During the 1990s, Russia's regions, which gained a significant degree of political autonomy from the Kremlin, established their own political regimes. The introduction of competitive elections in the regions sometimes resulted in major turnover of elites and changing constellations among the major actors. In most instances, these new political regimes belonged to the category of decentralized sub-national authoritarianism (Gel'man, 2010; Reisinger, Moraski, 2017). Before the 1999 State Duma elections, an informal coalition of regional leaders around the powerful mayor of Moscow, Yuri Luzhkov, entered the federal political arena and promoted a pre-election bloc, Fatherland – All Russia, led by the former prime minister, Yevgeny Primakov. This alliance confronted the key interests of the Kremlin, which promoted the alternative Unity electoral bloc, strongly backed by Vladimir Putin. In the end, Unity won and took over Fatherland – All Russia. It was later absorbed into a new dominant party, United Russia (Hale, 2006). But the 1999 attempt at the collective encroachment of regional elites into the domain of federal political did not go unnoticed and soon triggered a major wave of recentralization in Russia, known as the 'federal reform'.

In May 2000, soon after the beginning of his presidency, Putin reorganized federal agencies in the regions, including law enforcement offices (such as police, prosecution, and investigative bodies) and tax inspectorates. Instead of de-facto dual subordination to both their federal superiors and regional governments, which was developed in the 1990s, they were taken back under the Kremlin's unilateral control. Putin also appointed his special envoys, who were territorially grouped around eight newly-created, supra-regional federal districts. Presidential envoys requested massive revisions of regional laws and over the next couple of years brought them into conformity with federal regulations. (Later, the influence of the envoys gradually declined, but they still exist in Russia alongside the federal districts.) At the same time, Putin insisted on getting rid of top regional officials from the upper chamber of the Russian parliament, the Federation Council. (They were replaced by professional lawmakers, appointed by regional authorities with the Kremlin's consent.) Finally, a massive revision of federal regulations resulted in the recentralization of major rules and norms, including key changes to the taxation system and the organization of law enforcement agencies. These changes coincided with the beginning of a major economic recovery in Russia, with 7 per cent average annual economic growth between 1999 and 2008. The wave of recentralization was welcomed by Russian business, as it played an important role in removing many barriers for business development in Russia's regions: 'Provincial protectionism' in Russia (Sonin, 2010) came to an end. Even the number of federal units in Russia shrunk in the 2000s from eighty-nine to eighty-three, as some small autonomous districts were absorbed by larger krais and oblasts. If in the 1990s the pendulum of Russian federalism went to the point of extreme decentralization, in the 2000s it began to swing in the opposite direction (Reddaway, Orttung, 2004–05).

In September 2004, Putin announced a new stage of recentralization, which resulted in a major rearrangement of regional political institutions. De facto appointments of regional chief executives (hereafter, governors) upon presidential nomination (Reisinger, Moraski, 2017) replaced popular elections for these posts. Regional legislative elections soon came under the control of United Russia, which received a majority of seats in virtually all regional assemblies. As for the Russian cities, governors and United Russia gradually did away with popular elections of mayors and replaced them with city managers, de facto nominated by governors and appointed by local councils. Sub-national authoritarianism in Russia became heavily centralized and based upon Kremlin-controlled party politics, led by United Russia. Regional actors, in turn, had no power or resources to resist the Kremlin (Sharafutdinova, 2013). From that time, the political and administrative centralization of Russia reached a new equilibrium, and the pendulum of Russian federalism has now stopped. The 'power vertical' was consolidated around Kremlin-appointed governors, who enjoyed a certain degree of freedom in their actions in the regions as long as they could satisfy the Kremlin's political demands. This model allows the Kremlin to replace undesirable and/or inefficient regional leaders at any time, thus minimizing their disloyalty and/or poor political performance (Reuter, Robertson, 2012). The need for strengthening the 'power vertical' was and still is officially justified by Putin as an antidote to the threat of the territorial breakdown of Russia, although such a threat was greatly overestimated even in the 1990s.

Even then, regional political regimes were not unified. Some of the provinces demonstrated certain variations of local social and political activism, the Kremlin's political control over elections was imperfect in many instances, and many local governments kept their autonomy in one way or another. The unexpected wave of mass protests against fraudulent State Duma elections in December 2011 (for a detailed account, see Chapter 13 of this book) demonstrated the political limits of the 'power vertical'. Since 2012, popular elections of regional governors were reinstated in most of the regions, but their conditions did not imply full-fledged electoral competition. The new 'municipal filter', which was based upon a legal requirement of official endorsement of registered candidates for gubernatorial elections by 5–10 per cent of all councilors in municipalities across regions, effectively banned unwanted candidates from contesting elections. Using various political and institutional tricks, incumbent governors (backed by the Kremlin) retained their control over elections in a similar way to the period of gubernatorial appointments between 2005 and 2012 (Reisinger, Moraski, 2017).

By the early 2020s, Russian federalism had become more an empty shell than a substantive feature of politics and governance in the country and some observers considered these changes 'de-federalization' (Ross, 2023). Sub-national autonomy was limited in several important respects. Politically, regional governors came to serve as loyal agents of the Kremlin in charge of implementation of top-down directives and the achievement of key performance indicators set up by the presidential administration (Kynev, 2020). Economically, centralized financial and taxation models left most of the regions and municipalities heavily dependent on federal (or, in the case of cities, regional) transfers and subsidies. Administratively, major state agencies, such as the law enforcement apparatus and watchdogs responsible for oversight and monitoring, established their own 'power verticals', integrated with their Moscow-based superiors but loosely related to regional and local authorities in many provinces. Such a system of governance was criticized for its overly rigid nature and inefficiency as well as for aggravating principal–agent problems over time, especially in the wake of the COVID-19 pandemic, when the Kremlin allowed regional governments more room for policy manoeuvre in order to avoid deepening of the crisis (Busygina, Klimovich, 2022). During this time, the regional authorities de facto obtained a higher degree of autonomy from the federal government and more funding in order to mitigate the political and economic risks of the pandemic in exchange for the preservation of the status quo in respective regions at any cost. Overall, however, the Kremlin valued the loyalty of its sub-national subordinates over efficiency, and aimed at the preservation of the political status quo over growth and development. From this perspective, the 'power vertical' sounds like a perfect fit to pursue these goals.

In 2020, Russia adopted (via popular voting) new constitutional amendments aimed at continuing status quo in the country for an indefinite period. Among many other changes, the legal autonomy of local government was eliminated, and the governance of Russian cities and villages was recognized as a part of the 'power vertical', which officially received constitutional status as a 'unified system of executive authority'. While the continuity of top-down hierarchy was expected to be a mechanism for governing Russia for many decades, if not centuries, the full-scale Russian invasion of Ukraine in 2022 posed new major challenges to federalism and centre–periphery relations in the country.

From the Kremlin to *Glubinka*: actors and factors of sub-national politics

One of the most persistent elements of centre–periphery relations in Soviet and post-Soviet Russia is a great degree of spatial inequality. To some extent, the nature of this inequality is structural: resource-rich areas such as the Yamal-Nenets district, a centre of Russian gas production, are much wealthier than remote rural territories such as Chita. The spatial inequality emerged and developed both as a by-product of long-term historical patterns of demography and mobility in Russia and as side effects of Soviet spatial planning over decades (Hill, Gaddy, 2003). The geographical diversity of Russia has also coincided with the sectoral diversity of its economy, as many regions and cities are heavily dependent on certain major enterprises, which are not only key taxpayers but also key providers of jobs and social services.

The Russian economic geographer Natalia Zubarevich summarized the divisions between different spatial layers of development with the concept of 'four Russias' (Zubarevich, 2013). According to her classification, the key factors of spatial inequality in Russia are the size of settlements and their geographic position (which also include access to natural resources and the location of major enterprises and transportation routes). This is why the most developed and prosperous 'Russia-1' category is grouped around big cities and agglomerations with more than 500,000 residents. The mid-developed 'Russia-2' category is based upon medium-sized cities, often locked within industrial mono-towns. Badly underdeveloped 'Russia-3' includes small towns and rural peripheries; and 'Russia-4' represents many ethnic peripheries, where low levels of economic development coincide with the persistence and/or reemergence of traditional social order (Lazarev, 2023). These patterns of spatial inequality emerged during the Soviet era and were reproduced over time. While the relative wealth in Moscow (at least, before 2022) was largely comparable with that in major European cities, small towns and villages in some areas of provincial Russia (colloquially labelled as *glubinka*, or 'deep Russia') were not so far from their counterparts in sub-Saharan Africa in terms of relative poverty. This is why the social and spatial diversity of Russia provides fertile ground for diversity in its sub-national politics and governance.

Still, the Kremlin largely perceived the political diversity of Russia's regions and cities as a nuisance at best. There are two reasons for these perceptions. First, the experience of decentralization in the 1990s was clearly identified by Russia's elites as a source of major threats because of risks of major disorder and lack of control, while the Soviet experience of a centralized hierarchy of governance was perceived as a role model for twenty-first century Russia. Second, the top-down chain of command considered the subordination and submission of lower layers of the 'power vertical' as a top priority for governing the state in the most suitable way for the Kremlin (Gel'man, Ryzhenkov, 2011). This is why the building and maintenance of a hierarchy from the top state officials to public schools in remote areas is an essential part of the Russian political regime. The sub-national diversity did not disappear, and some regions and cities still maintain a degree of autonomy, either because of their primary importance for the country (the city of Moscow being a prime example), or because of close relationships between their leaders and the Kremlin (e.g. Chechnya). Beyond these special cases, control, cooptation, and coercion serve as three major tools of sub-national politics and governance in Russia.

The Kremlin has effectively used both administrative and economic levers of control over Russia's regions and cities. Administratively, regional governors were subordinated to the presidential administration. Similarly, law enforcement agencies, state watchdog services, and state-controlled enterprises were fully integrated into respective hierarchies of their sectoral 'power verticals'. The regulatory framework of rules and norms in Russia, especially during the 2010s, shifted toward increasing the density of state regulations and their decreasing quality. As a result, not only were the centralized law enforcement apparatus and state watchdogs greatly empowered vis-à-vis regional and local actors, but the regulatory burden of economic agents dramatically increased. These regulatory practices imposed major constraints on regional and local authorities (Gilev, Dimke, 2021), as they were faced with many risks of punishment for numerous real and/or imagined violations. Street-level bureaucrats in Russian regions and cities have to respond to these regulations via their over-compliance or 'creative compliance' (aimed at demonstration of adherence to top-down requests), which satisfies federal and/or regional superiors' demands for control but also aggravates problems of imperfect performance of the 'power vertical'.

The Kremlin's economic control over the regions (and regions' control over municipalities) became even more important in the wake of financial recentralization that took place in Russia during the 2000s. Fiscal transfers served primarily political purposes, as rewards and punishments for regional and/or local chief executives (Treisman, 1999; Starodubtsev, 2018), and other instruments of regional policy, such as state programmes of territorial development, in many ways performed similar functions. Pouring money into lower layers of the 'power vertical' is often driven by local-level capacities to deliver votes for Putin and/or United Russia. However, the political loyalty of local authorities has no impact in terms of the delivery of public goods (such as the repair of roads and rehousing of residents from dilapidated buildings) in municipalities across Russia (Zavadskaya, Shilov, 2021).

Regional governors serve as major nodes in sub-national networks of political and administrative 'power verticals'. Their rule, however, differs from that of late-Soviet sub-state dictatorships (Gorlizki, Khlevniuk, 2020), not only because of the electoral nature of sub-national authoritarianism in Russia (Gel'man, 2010; Reisinger, Moraski, 2017), but also because of the poor institutionalization of Russia's national-level political regime (for a detailed account, see Chapter 8). A major reshuffling of the composition of Russian governors occurred in 2010, when long-standing and powerful regional leaders, such as Yuri Luzhkov (Moscow), Mintimer Shaimiev (Tatarstan), and Murtaza Rakhimov (Bashkortostan), were replaced by younger and less autonomous state officials. Later on, the Kremlin developed a practice of appointing as new governors those state officials who were not rooted in respective regions and only sporadically linked with their elites (they were colloquially known as 'varangians') (Kynev, 2020). Such a practice strengthened mechanisms of control over regions, but were hardly productive in terms of improving the quality of sub-national governance, as most of these governors – unlike their predecessors, Soviet regional Communist leaders (Gorlizki, Khlevniuk, 2020) – expected short terms in office and lacked career incentives to invest resources and efforts in regional development.

City mayors, especially in the regional capitals and some other big cities, often became the most important actors of sub-national politics after governors, given the socio-economic importance of respective cities. From the 2000s, the Kremlin, alongside regional governors, attempted to limit their influence through the replacement of popular elections for mayors by the appointment of city managers or by delegating the functions of mayors to chairs of local councils (controlled by governors and/or by United Russia). Despite some local resistance, popular elections for city mayors were eliminated in almost all regional capitals of Russia. Moreover, city mayors often became the targets of criminal investigations, conducted by Russian law enforcement agencies due to the various instances of misconduct: About 10 per cent of mayors of Russian big cities were arrested in the 2000s to the 2010s. While opposition-backed mayors were much more likely to be

arrested, their vote delivery for United Russia had no impact on immunity
against criminal charges (Buckley et al., 2022). Overall, the role of city
mayors had greatly diminished by the 2020s amid institutional and personnel
changes.

Elections held in the regions – both sub-national and national – were still
a major source of legitimacy for the Russian regime, and the Kremlin paid
careful attention to their conduct and vote delivery. In many provinces,
especially in ethnic republics and rural areas, a mechanism of vote delivery
for both the Kremlin and incumbent governors had been established since
the 1990s, and over time this developed into a full-scale political machines.
Some of these regions, which demonstrated overly high numbers of votes for
Putin and United Russia (in the North Caucasus, in particular), were dubbed
'electoral sultanates'. Regional authorities played a major role in this tendency
(Golosov, 2011), as they effectively used institutional manipulation (e.g.
numerous changes to regional electoral systems), political pressure for the
mobilization of voters, and – last but not least – electoral fraud. This is why
instances of incumbent losses in gubernatorial elections after their
reinstatement in 2012 became rare. The coming introduction of electronic
voting practices in Russia's regions (proposed by 2024) places elections in
question. The first large-scale testing of the system in the city of Moscow
during the 2021 State Duma elections was heavily criticized due to a lack of
transparency, with results fully contradicting the results of voting by paper
ballots held simultaneously.

Regional legislatures (which bear various official titles like legislative
assembly, Duma, State Council, etc.) are subordinated vis-à-vis regional
governors in institutional terms, as the design of executive-legislative
elections in most of the regions is somewhat similar to the institutional
design at the federal level (see Chapter 8 of this book). While in the 1990s
the composition of regional legislatures varied from region to region, by the
2010s efforts by the Kremlin and governors had resulted in a stable majority
for United Russia in all regional legislatures (Golosov, 2011). By early 2023,
71.5 per cent of all Russian regional lawmakers belonged to United Russia.
At the same time, regional legislatures gave representation to other 'systemic'
parties than United Russia, including the KPRF (13.2 per cent of all regional
lawmakers), LDPR (6.1 per cent), A Just Russia (SR) (5.8 per cent), among
others. These mechanisms of power-sharing contributed to cooptation of
the regional opposition into the 'power vertical', in particular because some
posts were assigned to representatives of these parties and resulted in a
decline in popular protests in the regions (Reuter, Robertson, 2015).

Legislative assemblies in the regions also serve as major arenas of lobbyism of different sorts, and in this respect remained important sites of policymaking and informal bargaining of political and economic actors.

Regional business people were deeply involved in sub-national politics, especially via nomination of their candidacies to regional assemblies and local councils. As David Szakonyi (2020) demonstrated, such a format of political participation is the least risky mechanism of political investment vis-à-vis other formats of political lobbying of their interests in terms of balancing costs and benefits. While being elected to regional assemblies or becoming city mayors, business people mostly intend to satisfy the interests of their own companies – especially in sectors of the economy such as construction and agriculture. Sensitive policy areas such as urban development and land use became priorities in this respect and such an encroachment of economic actors into sub-national politics resulted in a certain fusion between state officials and business actors for the sake of rent seeking. As a result, business people as mayors and deputies were often interested in the development of economic infrastructure of regions and cities at the expense of resolving social problems – they preferred to cut taxes, reduce barriers for business, and improve the quality of roads, whilst paying less attention to education and public health, let alone quality of governance. In other words, profits for regional business people often brought losses for voters and for respective regions and cities.

Civil society organizations emerged in the 1990s mostly at the sub-national level and played an important role in various fields, ranging from social policy to environmental protection. These NGOs enjoyed a level of autonomy until the 2000s, when regional authorities (following the approach of the Kremlin) established regional Public Chambers (consultative bodies) as instruments of their cooptation. Further developments in the 2010s, such as the distribution of state grants to NGOs that were loyal to the authorities and vicious attacks on disloyal NGOs (some of them were labelled 'foreign agents'), changed the landscape of relations between state and civil society in the regions. The response of regional NGOs to these challenges heavily depended upon respective sectors: While the activities of many human rights and environmental organizations were curtailed and some even ceased to exist, providers of social services often benefited from changing patterns of social policy in Russia and the outsourcing of certain activities to NGOs. Overall, however, independent civil society NGOs lost any impact on sub-national politics in Russia in the wake of authoritarian centralization.

While institutionalized forms of civic participation in Russia's regions and cities were faced with major obstacles, regional protests were visible through the entire post-Soviet period. During the 1990s, most forms of bottom-up activism such as ethnic movements (Giuliano, 2011) or strikes (Robertson, 2011) were effectively mobilized by sub-national elites and used as a bargaining chip vis-à-vis the Kremlin. The centralization of governance in Russia put an end to these practices. Meanwhile, the new wave of protests, which emerged in many regions and cities in 2011–12, contributed to attempts at cross-regional coordination of protest activism (Dollbaum et al., 2018). Even though these attempts were later curbed, as federal authorities extensively used coercion against provincial protesters, sub-national protests in Russia did not disappear. Major local environmental protests, which emerged in Arkhangelsk oblast and Bashkortostan, and urban protests against the predatory practices of local developers (such as housing renovation in Moscow) gained nationwide visibility, although most of these instances could be described as NIMBY (Not in My Back Yard) protests. None the less, various forms of local activism remain an important part of sub-national politics in Russia.

Russian federalism goes to war

Since 2014, Russian geopolitical adventures have played an important role in further transforming federalism and centre–periphery relations. The very logic of the territorial expansion of Russia greatly contributed to both the composition of the Russian Federation and the mode of centre–periphery relations. In 2014, as a response to the overthrow of Viktor Yanukovych in Ukraine, the Russian authorities initiated the annexation of Crimea (for a detailed account, see Chapter 15 of this book). This peninsula was taken over by Russia through a referendum of local residents, conducted in March 2014 with major Kremlin support. While, according to official numbers, almost 97 per cent of Crimean voters approved of joining the Russian Federation, the Russian parliament immediately adopted this decision and took the Republic of Crimea and the federal city of Sevastopol as two new federal units of Russia. In the next several years, these units were integrated into Russia in administrative, political, and economic terms under the guise of a 'return' of areas that had historically belonged to Russia in both pre-Soviet and Soviet times (until 1954, when Crimea was transferred to Ukraine).

The new round of Russian aggression towards Ukraine in 2014 included the formation of the self-proclaimed separatist Donetsk and Luhansk 'people's republics' (DNR and LNR, respectively), which served as Russian proxies, controlled by the Kremlin. However, at that time these two areas were not absorbed into Russia along the Crimea model: They remained unrecognized puppet states until the launch of full-scale war against Ukraine in February 2022. Amid the bloody military invasion, many areas of southern and eastern Ukraine turned into a battlefield. Russia seized a significant part of Ukrainian territory, but failed to increase its territorial control. By September 2022, the initial Russian offensive was exhausted, and the Ukrainian military launched its counteroffensive. As the Kremlin's plans to take over major Ukrainian cities became unrealistic, Russia attempted to integrate occupied territories, using the Crimean experience of a popular vote to join Russia. The referendums were held not only in the Russian-occupied parts of Donetsk and Luhansk oblasts, but also in the Russian-controlled areas of Kherson and Zaporizhzhia oblasts of Ukraine, which had been captured and occupied during the first week of the 2022 invasion. Under Russian occupation, it is no surprise that the referendums were arranged to support the Kremlin's policy, and absolute majorities were declared in favour of joining Russia. On 30 September 2022, Vladimir Putin officially announced that these four regions (DNR, LNR, Kherson, and Zaporizhzhia oblasts) had joined Russia. The Federal Assembly adopted them as new federal units, in spite of the fact that Russia did not have full control over any of these regions. Proclaiming these occupied territories as parts of the Russian Federation was probably perceived by the Kremlin as a potential bargaining chip for further negotiations with Ukraine.

Whatever the reasons for the new constitutional changes in Russia, driven by the official increase in the number of federal units to eighty-nine, they had limited impact on the military conflict. In November 2022, Ukraine liberated Kherson from Russian troops. Not only had attempts at the further integration of the new occupied areas into the Russian Federation become illusory, but the territorial integrity of Russia (including its control over Crimea) was called into question, to put it mildly. While the future of the post-2014 territorial extensions of Russia will depend upon further developments on the battlefields and the outcomes of an ongoing war, Russian federalism as such experienced a new exogenous shock.

Since the beginning of the war, Russia's regions have borne the major burden not just in terms of the mobilization of soldiers and related administrative machinery, but also in terms of performance in their respective areas, heavily affected by the war in terms of economic and technological problems and human losses. As in the period of the COVID-19 pandemic, the Kremlin opted for de facto decentralization of regional governance, aimed at diminishing the negative effects of war. At the same time, the increasing regional inequality greatly influenced the grim harvest of military mobilization, as the share of killed and wounded Russian soldiers, drafted from small towns, rural areas, and ethnic peripheries ('Russia-3' and 'Russia-4') was much higher than that from 'Russia-1'. Certainly, rising war-driven problems over time are likely to increase tensions between the Kremlin and the regions and contribute to provincial grievances in ways recalling the 1990s (Giuliano, 2011), but it is too early to say to what extent these tendencies may change mechanisms of regional governance and the performance of the 'power vertical'.

Conclusion

The trajectory of centre–periphery relations in Russia over the last several decades has been very uneven. From a very high degree of centralization during the Soviet decades, Russia shifted into major decentralization in the 1990s and then again to recentralization in the 2000s and further strengthening of the 'power vertical' in the 2010s. The diversity of regional politics, typical for the period immediately following the Soviet collapse, turned into greater uniformity in the 2000s and 2010s, but still not to the extent of the top-down Communist practices of sub-national governance in the Soviet Union. Regional and local elections, very much non-democratic and largely unfair, perform functions of legitimation of sub-national regimes, which are currently muddling through the country's numerous political and economic problems. Overall, the current model of centre–periphery relations and sub-national governance in Russia has proved to be imperfect but relatively stable and it tends to maintain the status quo as much and as long as possible.

However, any major political changes – whenever and however they occur – will inevitably affect federalism and centre–periphery relations in Russia. At present, the nature of these potential changes is not obvious. Although some critical observers perceive the existing model of centre–periphery relations in Russia as an incomplete collapse of an empire and welcome its further territorial disintegration, there are more reasons to expect that present-day Russia has no potential for these developments despite numerous problems, and even its possible military defeat would not destroy the Russian Federation. Meanwhile, there are few reasons to regard the possible decentralization of Russia as a magic bullet against authoritarianism: Such a move without full-scale nationwide democratization may only further empower regional and local strongmen. The territorial dimension of politics and governance will inevitably continue to loom large in a country as big and diverse as Russia, and its regions and cities are destined to remain sources of both many advances and many setbacks.

Questions for discussion

1 Why did Russia, unlike the Soviet Union, not disintegrate as a federation in the 1990s?
2 What have been the major effects of the recentralization of Russia since the 2000s?
3 What are the major sources of diversity of sub-national politics in Russia?
4 What are the key strengths and weaknesses of the hierarchy of sub-national governance in Russia?
5 How has the military conflict with Ukraine affected Russian federalism?

Recommended readings

Hale, Henry E. 2005. 'The Makeup and Breakup of Ethnofederal States: Why Russia Survives Where the USSR Fell.' *Perspectives on Politics*, Vol. 3, No. 1.
Gel'man, Vladimir, Ryzhenkov, Sergei. 2011. 'Local Regimes, Sub-national Governance and the "Power Vertical" in Contemporary Russia.' *Europe-Asia Studies*, Vol. 63, No. 3.
Gilev, Aleksei, Dimke, Daria. 2021. 'No Time for Quality: Mechanisms of Local Governance in Russia.' *Europe-Asia Studies*, Vol. 73, No. 6.
Golosov, Grigorii. 2011, 'Regional Roots of Electoral Authoritarianism in Russia.' *Europe-Asia Studies*, Vol. 63, No. 4.
Sharafutdinova, Gulnaz. 2013. 'Gestalt Switch in Russian Federalism: The Decline of Regional Power under Putin.' *Comparative Politics*, Vol. 45, No. 2.

11

Chechnya

Marat Iliyasov

It would be no exaggeration to state that Chechnya has been a major force shaping Russian domestic politics and its relations with the West since the collapse of the Soviet Union in 1991. Indeed, this small republic of the Russian Federation has disproportionate significance and capacity to make international headlines, which often bring it to the centre of the world's attention. This significance of this republic, with a population of just 1.5 million, justifies a separate chapter on Chechnya in this textbook.

Today, Chechnya is known for its suppressive authoritarian regime run by Ramzan Kadyrov. The regime is notorious for unconditional support for Russian president Vladimir Putin, participation in Russian military actions around the world, violations of human rights, and extrajudicial killings. Few people would have thought that Chechnya would be the way it is now in the early 1990s, when the republic was trying to achieve its independence from Russia. At that time, it became renowned for the intensity of its resistance to post-Soviet Russia, which was to a large extent determined by the nation's collective memory.

However, prior to 1991, Chechnya was largely unknown outside of the Soviet Union. Within the USSR, the Chechens were mostly known from classical Russian literature. Every Soviet schoolchild had to learn by heart the 'Cossack's Lullaby' by Mikhail Lermontov, which had a line about 'a sly Chechen who crawls over the riverbank and sharpens his dagger'. Such fear-inspiring imagery extended through the poetry of Alexander Pushkin and novels by Leo Tolstoy. And outside of the school curriculum, Chechens were known throughout the Soviet Union as 'people not to mess with', because neither prison nor capital punishment could stop them from breaking the law if their honour was at stake.

It was during the liberalization politics of perestroika (restructuring) and glasnost (openness) in the late 1980s that the name Chechnya was first brought to international attention. As did other nationalist movements at that time, Chechen nationalists cheered Boris Yeltsin's invitation for them 'to swallow as much sovereignty as one can'. These words, uttered in the context of a struggle for power between Yeltsin, then President of the Russian Soviet Federative Socialist Republic (RSFSR) and Mikhail Gorbachev, then president of the USSR, placed the formal leaders of the Chechen-Ingush Autonomous Soviet Socialist Republic – a small, peripheral region inside of the RSFSR – between a rock and a hard place. They needed to maintain their own power and control over the region, appease Chechen nationalists, and choose between Yeltsin and Gorbachev. In this situation, they declared sovereignty, elevating the autonomous republic's status to the level of other Soviet republics in 1990.[1]

However, this move did not satisfy Chechen nationalists, who demanded full secession from the Soviet Union. Their revolt against the official and still largely Soviet power brought them control over the republic, which they utilized to organize presidential elections in the autumn of 1991. The winner of these elections, a Soviet General of Chechen origin, Dzhokhar Dudayev, immediately declared Chechnya's full independence. This decision would have lasting repercussions, unlocking a chain of events that would lead the Chechen nation into two wars with Russia (1994–96 and 1999–2009) and the eventual establishment of an oppressive, Moscow-backed regime that has been in power in the republic since date. As a consequence of the wars and the Kadyrov regime's repressions, up to 20 per cent of the Chechen nation (250,000–300,000 people) left the republic and settled, mostly, in Europe. Many of them bear the traumatic experience of wars and the desire to retaliate against Russia and the pro-Russian Chechen regime, which explains the flow of Chechen volunteers to Ukraine and Syria, where they have fought against Russia since 2014.

This chapter provides an overview of the recent history of Chechnya, focusing on the events that led up to the Russo-Chechen wars and their outcomes, such as the increased international significance of the republic. It begins with a brief outline of the origins of Chechnya and continues with an overview of the history of Russo-Chechen interaction through the last 250 years. Through the lens of the nation's collective memory, the chapter explains the Chechen desire for an independent state and Chechens' determination to protect their freedom. It concludes with an assessment of possible developments in future Russo-Chechen relations.

Who are the Chechens?

There are fewer than two million Chechens in the world and around 60–70 per cent of them live in Chechnya, which is situated in the northeastern part of the Caucasus mountain range between the Caspian and Black Seas. The territory amounts to 6,700 square miles, the size of which is between the smaller US states of Connecticut and New Hampshire. Chechens are native to this territory, which has been populated for more than 40,000 years. Their language belongs to the family of Caucasian languages together with Circassian, Georgian, and some languages spoken in neighbouring Dagestan.

As is the case with other small nations, Chechens try to emphasize and amplify their own historical significance. One common claim is that Chechens can trace their roots back to ancient Mesopotamia. While this view rests on shaky foundations, it is widespread among the population, as well as being supported to some degree by Georgian historian Giorgi Anchabadze (2009, 15). In his book *The Vainakhs,* a term used to refer to Chechens and Ingush, Anchabadze asserts that the native tongue of the ancient Transcaucasian/Mesopotamian state Urartu, which was situated mostly in the eastern part of modern Turkey, was close to the Nakh-Dagestanian family of languages. The Chechen language also belongs to this group of languages, unique to the Caucasus.

However, a linguistic analysis conducted by Joanna Nichols in the 1990s reports the opposite. According to her research, neither the Chechen nor other languages of the Nakh-Dagestanian family have relations to any other language group either in or out of the Caucasus. The same analysis emphasizes that Nakh-Dagestanian languages are among the oldest spoken languages in the world. In Nichols' (1995) estimation, a distinct form of the Chechen language existed as early as 6,000–8,000 years ago.

The first written mention of Chechens can be found in works of Georgian, Greek, and Armenian historians. Anchabadze (2009, 31) refers to Georgian medieval Chronicles (*Kartlis Tskhovreba*) by Leonti Mroveli (written between the ninth and fourteenth centuries) to support the view that Chechens are native to the Caucasus region. He includes stories about military alliances that existed between Georgians and Chechens, who were then known as Durdzuks. Greek sources, such as *Geography* by Strabo (first century BC), also mention tribes that lived in the territory of today's Chechnya, referring to them as Gargars. This word is still used in a slightly different form in the modern Chechen language, meaning kinfolk. The

Armenian work of ancient geography *Ashkharatsuyts*, which was written in the seventh century, mentions the Nakhchmatyan people, a name which translates as 'Chechen-speaking' in the modern Chechen language.

It is only in the seventeenth or eighteenth century that the ethnonym 'Chechen' appeared in the historical record, as well as in common use, mainly in the Russian language. It is not clear how and under what circumstances the descriptor Chechen was first adopted by the Russians and everyone else thereafter. One of the more credible theories suggests that it was used in a slightly different form by the neighbouring nations of the North Caucasus. For instance, Kabardians used the term 'Shashan' and the Ossetians 'Sasan' to refer to the Chechen language, territory, and people. An alternative theory proposes that the name was chosen due to contact with a tribe that lived in the town Chechen-aul. However, it is almost impossible to find strong proof to support these or other theories. It is similarly difficult to explain the origin of the ethnonym *Nokhchi* (plural) or *Nokhchuo* (singular), which Chechens still use to identify themselves. This ethnonym relates to the word '*nakh*' (Chechen for 'people'). Such a reference is quite common for many ancient peoples, who in this way distinguished themselves from others – 'the people' from those who were not.

Chechen quest for independence

The political reintroduction of the ethnonym Nokhchi happened in the 1990s. After declaring independence from the former Soviet Union and Russian Federation alike in 1991, the Chechen nationalist leadership adopted two official names for the republic. For the international audience, Chechnya became the Chechen Republic Ichkeria and for a domestic audience, Nokhchi-Chuo – the place of the Chechens. This section provides an overview of some of the history of Russo-Chechen interaction that later contributed to the events that led to the declaration of Chechnya's sovereignty. The section explains the reasons behind this move and analyzes further political developments in the republic.

Chechens in the Russian Empire and Soviet Union

Clashes between Chechen tribes and Russian troops became quite frequent after the Persian March by Peter the Great in 1722. The Empire had plans to expand to the south, and the North Caucasus was on its way. Steadily encroaching, the Empire eventually provoked widespread armed resistance among the local population that encompassed the whole North Caucasus. The uprising began in 1785 under the leadership of a Chechen who became known as Sheikh Mansur (Sheikh as religious title and Mansur as Victorious – Arabic). The insurgents were initially encouraged by the Ottoman Empire, which had recently been defeated by Russia in the 1768–74 war and wanted to retake the lost territory of Crimea. However, the new war that the Ottomans started in 1787 was not successful either. They lost battle after battle in Eastern Europe and the Balkans and hence were unable to support Sheikh Mansur, whose forces were eventually defeated in 1791. He was captured by Russian troops in the fortress Anapa on the shores of the Azov Sea and jailed in the Schlisselburg fortress on the shores of Lake Ladoga, near St Petersburg. The defeat of the Ottomans in 1792 and the annexation of Georgia in 1801 determined the fate of the North Caucasus. The Russian Empire could no longer afford to have an uncontrolled territory that separated it from Transcaucasia.

The war against the North Caucasian peoples, known as the Caucasian War, began in 1801 and lasted until 1864. If this 'was the longest and costliest' war for Russia (Derluguian 2005, 359), the cost for North Caucasians was even higher. The main anti-imperial force – consisting of Chechens – ended its resistance only when the war reduced their population by more than 60 per cent to a mere 115,000 people. Even then, many Chechens refused to accept the conquest. Professor Pavel Kovalevsky, who analyzed the political situation in the Caucasus after the conquest of Chechnya, wrote: 'In 1859 the Chechens were defeated. Defeated, but not subdued; subdued, but not appeased' (1912, 12).

The Bolshevik coup in 1917, which is known as the October Revolution in Russian historiography, provided Chechens with the opportunity to restore their independence. Together with the other North Caucasian nations, part of the Chechen elite announced the creation of the independent state *Gorskaya Respublika* (the Mountain Republic) in 1917. This republic existed for several months and was destroyed by the Bolsheviks who set out to reconquer the North Caucasus in 1918. The resistance was fierce and long. Some parts of the territory resisted efforts to establish Bolshevik rule until 1925. There were regular rebellions against a regime that many Chechens perceived as being foreign and unjust, and these continued until the 1940s.

Probably, this stubborn resistance that Chechen nationalists demonstrated placed the nation on the Soviet list of untrustworthy peoples ('*neblagonadezhnye*' – Russian). Like other people of the North Caucasus such as the Ingush, Karachay, Balkars, and Kalmyks, the Chechens were accused of collaboration with the Nazis and deported several thousand miles away from their homeland to Central Asia in 1944. Bearing in mind the level of collaboration among Russians, this was a disproportionate punishment which resulted in the death of approximately half of the Chechen population, who succumbed to diseases and hunger during the journey and in its immediate aftermath. This loss and a sense of injustice reinforced the hatred that many Chechens felt for the Soviet state, which they considered to be another form of the same Russian Empire that had conquered and colonized Chechnya. The reaction to the deportation and the Chechen attitude towards the Soviet Union is vividly described by Alexander Solzhenitsyn in his *Gulag Archipelago*. He writes that the Chechens were 'openly hostile to the authorities and despised everyone who was not' (1973, pp. 420–21).

The Chechens' situation gradually started to improve after the death of Joseph Stalin (1878–1953). The de-Stalinization policy initiated by the new Soviet leader Nikita Khrushchev in 1956 included a partial restoration of the rights of deported peoples. The Chechen-Ingush Autonomous Soviet Socialist Republic (ASSR) that had existed 1936–44 was restored and the Chechens were allowed to return home in 1957. Most of them did. Moreover, most of the Chechens and the Soviet regime learned to cohabit. The authorities did not try to break or assimilate the nation and the rebellions against the regime ceased. This was the beginning of the most peaceful thirty years that the Chechens had enjoyed during the last 250 years.

This peaceful cohabitation continued until the late 1980s when perestroika and glasnost triggered a resurgence of nationalist movements all over the periphery of the Soviet Union. In this, Chechnya followed the example of the Baltic States, to which it was comparable according to population size, strength of ethnic and religious identity, and negative attitudes towards the Russian state due to lived experiences.

Chechen nationalists sought full secession from the Soviet Union and Russia alike and justified it with three main reasons. First, full independence would make it possible to nurture ethnic traditions, religion, and culture. Second, it would facilitate faster economic growth through political control over an oil-rich republic, and enhanced trade and interaction with technologically advanced countries. The most important of the reasons, which resonated with the population's sentiments, was the prevention of the possible repetition of the Deportation. Indeed, for many Chechens, the new Russian Federation was not much different from the Russian Empire or the

Soviet Union. Therefore, many were suspicious about the democratic future of Russia and supported the idea that international recognition of Chechnya would increase the nation's security. Other ethnic groups of the Russian Federation that had similar experiences of living in the Soviet Union, however, did not follow the example of the Chechens. The following reasons explain this choice: (1) a lack of demographic and economic capacity (e.g. Ingush); (2) weak national consolidation of multiple ethnic groups (e.g. Dagestanis); (3) geographic location with no international borders and a higher level of integration (e.g. Tatars).

The first war of 1994–96

The first attempt to force Chechnya back into the Russian fold was made immediately after the Chechen revolution that brought down Soviet structures of power in the republic in the summer of 1991. The news regarding presidential elections that followed in Chechnya and the subsequent declaration of independence by the Chechen nationalist leadership was received negatively in Moscow. The parliament of the Russian Federation, led by ethnic Chechen Professor Ruslan Khasbulatov, declared the results of the elections illegitimate and President Boris Yeltsin issued a decree announcing a state of emergency in Chechnya. The Russian government sent an elite military regiment to Chechnya to reverse the situation, but the recently formed Chechen national guard blocked the troops upon their landing in the capital city Grozny, disarmed them, and sent them back to Moscow. The Russian political elite led by Yeltsin then realized that they needed to find a more effective solution to the question of Chechen independence. Concern with Chechnya, however, was suspended due to the more urgent need to consolidate political power in Moscow, on which the Russian elite were then focused. The deteriorating economic situation, shattered by the collapse of the Soviet Union, was another matter requiring attention.

A return to the Chechen question occurred in late 1994. The Russian military secretly joined local opposition forces in an attempt to overthrow Chechen President Dzhokhar Dudayev that November, but the coup failed miserably. Dudayev offered to return captured soldiers and officers in exchange for official recognition that the Russian government had been involved in this affair. Moscow responded with an ultimatum – Dudayev had to declare Chechnya a part of the Russian Federation and step down from his post. Both parties were ready for war. Chechen nationalists did not want to give up on their independence and Russia needed a quick and victorious war to distract its population from domestic problems. The war that began on 11 December 1994 turned into an eighteen-month-long disaster, which ended with a Russian military defeat in August 1996.

This war was a combination of noble and ignominious behaviour on both sides. On the one hand, Chechens and Russians still did not dehumanize each other and were often in communication over war-related questions, such as prisoner exchanges or a truce. On the other hand, both sides demonstrated cruelty which escalated as the war continued. The war also witnessed many crimes, which were later repeated by the Russian military in wars with Georgia in 2008 and Ukraine starting in 2022. These crimes included indiscriminate bombing, the use of civilians as human shields, regular marauding and harassing of the population, and mass murder. In addition, the Russian military started a lucrative business which consisted of detaining people and demanding ransoms even for the dead bodies of detainees who had sometimes been tortured to death. In part, this cruelty on the Russian side related to the practice of hiring mercenaries, many of whom were criminals recruited from prisons. This practice later grew into an enterprise, which is known today as the Wagner private military company. The Chechens responded to this cruelty twice by attacking Russian cities in the neighbouring regions of Stavropol and Dagestan and taking hostage the civilian population there. These attacks on Budennovsk in 1995 and Kizliar in 1996 were later classified as a new type of terrorism. The distinct features of the new terrorists were the readiness to sacrifice life, a lack of interest in money or safe passage, and the demand to stop the war.

The military operation conducted by the Chechen forces in August 1996 and the context of presidential elections that Yeltsin aimed to win, forced the leadership of the Russian Federation to accept a peace brokered by the OSCE. In September 1996, Chechen and Russian military commanders signed a peace agreement, which became known as the Khasavyurt Accords. A peace treaty was signed by the reelected President of Russia Boris Yeltsin and just elected President of Chechnya Aslan Maskhadov in 1997. This provided an informal recognition of Chechnya as an independent state. The formality had to follow a referendum, which the sides agreed to hold in the republic in 2001.

The second war of 1999–2009

The political process of Chechnya becoming a fully recognized state was interrupted in 1999 by the second Russian invasion. Russia justified this by accusing Chechens of the invasion of Dagestan in August 1999 and the terrorist attacks that hit Russia right after it in September of the same year. The significance of these two events necessitates a closer look at both.

The roots of the first are related to the interwar period and the political situation in Chechnya at this time. Undoubtedly, the Chechen success in the first war of 1994–96 encouraged separatist tendencies among different ethnic groups in the Russian Federation and some other parts of the world. In Chechnya's neighbour, multiethnic Dagestan, proponents of separatism logically grounded their views in Islam over ethnic nationalism. Feeling unwelcome in the homeland, the leaders of Dagestani political Islam (Salafism/Islamism) relocated to the de facto independent Chechnya and operated from there in 1996–99. They were hosted by Chechen politicians who did not manage to secure the leading role in the post-war Chechen government. Most prominent among them were Shamil Basayev and Movladi Udugov. The former was the most notorious warlord in Chechnya, who forced the Russian government into a truce by taking hostages at a maternity hospital in Budennovsk in 1995. Udugov had achieved fame as a minister of information who outmanoeuvred Russian propaganda efforts during the war. Both ran for the Chechen presidency and lost to Aslan Maskhadov – the commander-in-chief of the Chechen forces. Even if not excluded, both felt dissatisfied with the government positions offered by Maskhadov and sought other opportunities to satisfy their ambitions. The Dagestani Salafist movement that sought independence from Russia and the creation of an Islamic state provided them with such an opportunity. They planned their leadership in a united state of Chechnya and Dagestan, which they envisioned in the aftermath of Dagestan becoming independent. Dagestani Salafists were convinced that the population of the republic was ready to rebel and claim independence from the Russian Federation. As proof, they would point to the formation of an enclave of four small towns (with a total population of around 5,000) in mountainous Dagestan, which was ruled by Islamists. This enclave, which is situated not far from the border with Chechnya, later became known to the public as Qadar zone. Surprising, as it may seem, Dagestani Islamism was viewed positively by some Russian politicians. Then prime minister of Russia, Sergei Stepashin, personally visited Qadar zone a few months before the unrest in 1999 and praised the order that he observed there. Moreover, he expressed a desire that some practices of the Islamists would become more widespread. This fact later contributed to the popular conspiracy theory that Islamism in the North Caucasus was encouraged by Russia as part of preparation for the second war in Chechnya. This theory also links this preparation with the ascent to power of Vladimir Putin, who was the director of the FSB in 1998 and was appointed as prime minister immediately following the start of fighting in Dagestan.

In August 1999, the Dagestani Islamists began the rebellion. Around 2,000 Chechen volunteers, many of whom were jobless after the war, gladly responded to the call of Basayev and joined him in support of this rebellion. Unfortunately for the planners, the rebellion did not spread across the republic and after around five weeks of fighting the Chechen forces withdrew from Dagestan. The Russian military was ready to follow them into Chechnya, but they needed the Russian population's support for the action – this was a lesson learned from the first war, which was very unpopular in Russia. The necessary support was galvanized by a wave of explosions in apartment buildings that shocked Russia in September 1999. The first three explosions occurred while the fighting between Chechen-Dagestani Islamists and the Russian military was still going on in Dagestan. A car bomb, which exploded near an apartment building in the Dagestani city Buynaksk on 4 September, killed more than fifty people. Three more explosions at apartment complexes followed in Moscow (8 and 13 September) and Volgodonsk (16 September). In total, they killed more than 300 people and wounded more than 1,700. In terms of their scale and impact, these explosions are often compared with the 9/11 attacks in the United States. It is widely believed that the next in this chain of explosions was supposed to happen in Ryazan on 22 September, but was prevented by sharp-eyed citizens, who noticed suspicious looking men bringing sacks into the basement of a building. The alerted police found and disarmed a powerful hand-made bomb and arrested the suspects, who happened to be Russian Federal Security Service (FSB) officers. The incident was analyzed later in a book by a former FSB officer, Alexander Litvinenko, who became a defector. He was later poisoned and murdered in London by a former colleague. In his book, Litvinenko claimed that the explosions were a part of an elaborate cover-up operation by the FSB, the goal of which was to stir up popular anger against the Chechens and justify a new invasion. Before his death, he directly accused Putin of ordering these terrorist attacks.

Despite the controversy and the lack of evidence of guilt in the bombing, Russian propaganda managed to convince the population that Chechen terrorists were behind the explosions (Wilhelmsen, 2016). The country was ready for the second war, which was the first major act by Putin in his new capacity as Russian prime minister. His decision to start the war in September 1999, his public response to the international criticism, and other conduct created Putin's image of a tough politician – decisive, determined, and ready to restore Russia's might. His popularity soared and assured an easy victory in presidential elections after Boris Yeltsin vacated the position on New Year's Eve 1999–2000. Moreover, this image persisted and combined with already traditional vote manipulation to help Putin repeat his electoral success again and again.

Unlike the first war, the second had few of the elements of noble behaviour between enemies towards one another and was much more brutal. Officially, the Kremlin called this war a counter-terrorist operation, which became a self-fulfilling prophecy. The brutality of the war, the weak central command, and a lack of resources quickly pushed the Chechen side to adopt terrorist methods, including a new tactic for the Chechens – female suicide bombing. The first suicidal attacks happened on the territory of the republic and targeted either military or governmental buildings of the Russian administration. However, terrorism quickly spilled over the borders of the republic and encompassed the whole of Russia. Two of the most notorious attacks repeated the pattern that had proved effective during the first war. Shamil Basayev, who was the architect of the attack on Budennovsk maternity hospital in 1995, claimed responsibility for both, which did not remove the widespread suspicions that the Russian security service played some role in organizing them. The first attack targeted the Moscow Dubrovka theatre in 2002, and the second was on a school in the North Ossetian town Beslan in 2004. Both aimed to bring an end to the war in Chechnya, but – unlike Budennovsk – both failed as the Russian government refused to negotiate with the attackers. Both ended up with the deaths of hundreds of hostages.

Another important difference between the first and second wars in Chechnya was the Russian military and political strategy. In its second war, Russia avoided direct military clashes with Chechen troops and relied on their preponderance in heavy weaponry and dominance in the air. Moscow was also much more successful in implementing the political component of their war strategy. The Russian strategists chose to rely not on opposition to the nationalist regime, which was unpopular among the population, but on more influential collaborators and defectors from the Chechen resistance. The use of defectors also allowed Russia to present the conflict as a Chechen domestic issue – the policy that became known as 'Chechenization' of the conflict (Souleimanov, 2015).

What do Chechens remember?

Scholars agree that collective memory is a powerful tool, which helps to determine a group's identity. The power of collective memory derives from the sentiments that it attaches to historic events. The stronger the sentiment about an event, the stronger the memory about it. Therefore, it is more likely that a collectivity would remember events that provoke strong feelings such as hatred, fear, humiliation, or pride. Clearly, collective memory shapes an attitude towards the source of these feelings. As the previous section demonstrates, the main historical events that shaped Chechen collective memory are related to interactions with Russia. Hence, to understand what Chechens are, what their attitudes towards Russia are, and what prospects there are for future relations between the two nations, it is important to learn what most Chechens remember. The study of Chechen collective memory is also crucial for such understanding, because the nation does not have a well-researched or written history. Before the Russian conquest, the most important events in the history of the individual Chechen tribes/clans/societies would be memorialized by folk singers or transmitted orally from generation to generation in the form of legends. The spread of literacy (using Georgian and/or Arabic scripts) in the late Middle Ages encouraged many Chechen families and clans to write down historical events and legends in family or clan chronicles called *Teptars*. Most of these chronicles were lost in the Deportation of 1944. They were collected by the Russian military and burnt on the central square of the capital city, Grozny. However, the Chechens preserved their history in part through the tradition of memorizing one's paternal ancestry line back through at least seven generations. This custom, which encourages remembering over a long period, also makes collective memory a much more powerful determinant of Chechen identity than written history.

Memory of resistance to the Russian Empire (1785–1917)

In chronological order, the first collective memory of the Chechens relates to the heroes that led popular resistance to the Russian Empire. One of them is Sheikh Mansur (1760–94). The available knowledge about him is limited to his personal traits and qualities. He was a good orator, charismatic, religious, and a brave military leader who managed to unite many North Caucasian ethnic groups in their fight against the Russian Empire in 1785–91. It is not so well known among Chechens that he was from a village called Aldy (part of today's Grozny), that his Chechen name was Ushurma, and that he was around twenty-five years of age when he won his first victory against Russian troops. The widespread knowledge about Sheikh Mansur emphasizes three things, which reflect Chechen traditional values: (1) he did not surrender; (2) he cherished honour more than life; and (3) he betrayed neither his nation nor cause.

The hero of the later period, the Caucasian War of the nineteenth century, is a Chechen warrior Baysangur. He was one of the top generals of Imam Shamil, who led the Chechen and Dagestani state Imamat (which Chechen and Dagestani Salafists were trying to revive in the late 1990s) and the resistance to the Russian Empire. A widespread narrative about him claims that having lost an eye, a leg, and an arm in the war, he continued fighting the Russians even after the surrender of Imam Shamil in 1859.

The memory of the Caucasian War is also imbued with tragedy. Even though not widely remembered, many Chechens know the name of Alexei Yermolov, who was a particularly cruel general who commanded the Russian troops in Chechnya in 1818–26. A memorial built to him during the Russian Empire and restored by the Soviets in the capital city Grozny was regularly vandalized and destroyed by Chechens, despite efforts by the Soviet authorities to protect it.

Another tragic memory is the massacre of Dady-yurt, which was destroyed completely by a Russian raid in 1819. A prominent Chechen narrative about this episode commemorates the village's brave defenders, all of whom died. It also recalls the story of women who were captured in that raid. When the convoy of Russian soldiers was escorting the captive women across a bridge over the River Terek, the women jumped into the river and dragged their captors with them so that they would also drown. This incident was memorialized in present-day Chechnya with the 2013 establishment of the Day of the Chechen Woman and the opening of a monument where the massacre took place. It is ironic that the construction of the monument, which was initiated by the nationalists, was finished by the current Chechen pro-Russian government.

Memory of the Deportation of 1944

Undoubtedly, the most significant event for the Chechens in political and emotional terms is the memory of the Deportation. All Chechens know about this tragedy, which began on 23 February 1944. In a planned operation, within a week the Soviet secret police NKVD (later KGB/FSB) stationed in the republic for this particular purpose deported the entire Chechen and Ingush population to Central Asia. Eyewitnesses to this tragedy recall that in some towns that day the Russian military started festivities to celebrate Red

Army Day. The music and dances attracted people, who were suddenly herded into barracks and stables. Simultaneously, the NKVD proceeded with mass arrests across the republic, hunting down all Chechens and Ingush. Then the detained people were systematically transported to train stations, where they were put on train carriages and sent away to Central Asia. According to eyewitnesses, people were allowed to have 50 pounds of luggage to take with them.

The NKVD reports boast that the operation went smoothly. Indeed, caught by surprise, the Chechens demonstrated little resistance, which was effectively suppressed. To stay within the schedule, old and sick people who were difficult to transport were simply killed and dumped in nearby lakes. In the mountainous village Khaibakh, more than 700 people were locked in stables and burnt alive.

The documents from the secret Soviet archives found by Nikolay Bugai in the 1990s confirmed that the Chechens lost more than 40 per cent of their population during the three-week journey to Central Asia and in the first year in exile (Bugai 1992). Most of them succumbed to epidemic diseases, which spread due to a lack of food, water, and sanitation. Upon arrival, many deportees were simply deposited off the trains onto the steppe in the cold with no food or shelter. Many survived thanks to the help of the local population.

Stories about the Deportation survive in every Chechen family and are transmitted from generation to generation. The loss of their homeland, the inhumane attitude of the Soviet NKVD police, and the death of the population turned this experience into a collective trauma for the Chechens, and has prompted the slogan 'never again' on an emotional level. The fear of its repetition was the driving force behind the Chechen decision to secede from Russia in 1991 and to defend its declared independence by armed resistance (Williams 2000).

Memories of the wars of 1994–96 and 1999–2009

Both the Russo-Chechen wars of 1994–96 and 1999–2009 are well remembered by the Chechen population due to their recency. Every Chechen over the age of twenty will have some direct experience.

The memory of the first war revolves around the tragedy of the town of Samashki, where more than 100 civilians were murdered by Russian troops in 1995. This massacre dwarfed all other experiences, including abductions, torture, and mass killings of detained civilians during that war.

Glorified memories of the first Russo-Chechen war are borne out of the unprecedented resistance and brilliance of the military operations of Chechen forces. The former recalls the resistance of the Chechen warriors in the town of Bamut, where they held out against Russia's siege for one and a half years. The latter reflects victory against one of the most militarily potent states in the world in 1996. These memories of tragedy and glory are nurtured by the Chechen online community, which regularly posts videos and reading materials about these events.

The second war of 1999–2009 is remembered by Chechens mainly in tragic terms. It witnessed more Samashki-like massacres of the civilian population in Alkhan-yurt in 1999 and Aldy in 2000. In both cases, the troops killed around fifty civilians to punish these towns for hosting Chechen warriors. However, the quintessence of the tragedy of the second war in Chechnya became the murder of Elsa Kungayeva. The eighteen-year-old woman was abducted, raped, and killed by drunk Russian Colonel Yuri Budanov in early 2000. This crime was one of the very few committed by the Russian military that ended up in court. The power of this memory became obvious in 2018, when the corpse of Yusup Temirkhanov, who killed Budanov to avenge this crime that was so traumatic for all Chechens, was brought to funerals in Chechnya. The hometown of Temirkhanov could not accommodate all the people, who came to pay their last respects to this new hero of the Chechen nation.

The current regime in Chechnya

One more memory, highly contested by the political elite in Chechnya, relates to the controversial legacy of the founder of the current regime Akhmat Kadyrov. He was appointed as an acting head of the Chechen administration by Moscow during the first months of the second Russo-Chechen war in 2000. As the mufti (religious leader – Arabic) of independent Chechnya, he had once encouraged people to join jihad (holy war – Arabic) against the Russians during the first war of 1994–96. But he started collaborating with the Russian Federation at the beginning of the second Russo-Chechen war in 1999. Kadyrov's choice made it possible for Russia to implement the Chechenization policy and to justify the reincorporation of the republic into the Russian Federation by organizing a sham referendum on Chechnya's Constitution drafted with the blessing of the Kremlin.

In 2004, during the celebratory parade on the Victory Day of 9 May, Akhmat Kadyrov was assassinated in a targeted explosion. His son Ramzan, who was twenty-eight years old at that time, was not an obvious choice for the succession. First, he was two years younger than the minimum age required by the new Chechen Constitution. Second, there were more experienced and deserving Chechen politicians with good connections in Moscow as well as powerful support among numerous kinfolk and comrades in arms.

However, his loyalty to Putin was unquestionable and this determined his career. After the initial appointment as a first deputy to the prime minister of Chechnya, Ramzan Kadyrov worked hard making himself indispensable as the only ruler who could suppress the armed resistance and keep Chechnya calm. In 2007, he was appointed to the position of head of the republic, after a stint as Chechen prime minister. Kadyrov reinforced his position by removing all the potential contenders along with those known to be critics of Putin and himself. Most of them died at the hands of assassins. For instance, a famous journalist, Anna Politkovskaya, was killed at the entrance to her house in Moscow in 2006. A member of the lower chamber of the Russian Duma and a potential replacement of Kadyrov, Ruslan Yamadayev, was assassinated in the centre of Moscow in 2008. His younger brother Sulim, a decorated hero of Russia who had accused Kadyrov of this assassination and promised to take revenge, was killed in Dubai half a year later. The Dubai police accused Kadyrov's cousin and member of the Russian Parliament Adam Delimkhanov of ordering this assassination, but he remained free. Over the following years, several more opponents of Kadyrov and Putin were killed in Russia, across the Europe, and in Turkey, supposedly on the orders of Kadyrov . The most prominent of these was the leader of Russia's opposition, Boris Nemtsov (1959–2015).

After his years in power, Kadyrov maintained the trust of Putin and ensured singlehanded control over Chechnya. In exchange for personal loyalty and keeping Chechnya calm, the Kremlin has supported Kadyrov politically and the republic financially. Moreover, Russia does not interfere in Chechnya's domestic affairs. The republic is largely considered to be Kadyrov's personal domain. Meanwhile, Kadyrov consistently reaffirms his readiness to die for Putin and threatens all opponents of the Russian leader on the international and domestic stage. He further demonstrates his loyalty to Putin by sending Chechen troops to support Russia's actions abroad. By the order of Kadyrov, Chechen military personnel participated in the annexation of Crimea, the battle for the Donbas region, Russia's involvement in Syria since 2014, and the invasion of Ukraine from 2022.

However, neither the Kremlin's support nor the brutality of his rule ensures Kadyrov's legitimacy in the eyes of the population, which he tries to win through several means. He is engaged in a self-legitimization effort by promoting a cult of personality around his late father, which translates into his own right to inherit the rule. Furthermore, he promotes himself as a leader who rebuilt the republic and made it a 'safe haven' where the population is free to practice Islam and to follow ethnic traditions, which was not possible during Soviet times. His focus on ethnic and Islamic values, however, became the backcloth for numerous violations of human rights, the imposition of a dress code for women, the adoption of elements of Sharia law in Chechnya's legal system, and the persecution of LGBTQ people. Even though Kadyrov's role at the federal level remains fairly insignificant, his control over the most rebellious republic of the Russian Federation highlights his political significance for the Kremlin.

Conclusion

Due to warlike interactions with Russia, the last 250 years have been the most thoroughly researched period of Chechen history. Scholars emphasize that since the conquest of the North Caucasus in 1864, Chechens have never abandoned their dream of independence. They have also never missed an opportunity to restore it, placing these attempts in wider contexts such as the crushing of the Russian Empire or the collapse of the Soviet Union. The driving force behind this quest has been the nation's collective memory.

The collective memory of the Chechens comprises a mixture of glory and tragedy, but it was the experience of tragedy that pushed the nationalist agenda to the fore and encouraged the desire to secede from Russia in 1991. This move, based on the experience and memory of the Deportation, which was recognized as an act of genocide by the European Parliament in 2004, determined the further political development of the Russian Federation. The decision to start the first war in Chechnya in order to bring it back into the Russian fold shook the weak foundation of nascent Russian democracy, whereas the second invasion drove Russia's fast backsliding into authoritarianism. Moreover, it brought to the fore dormant imperial ambitions, which resulted in further aggression against Georgia in 2008 and Ukraine in 2022.

Both these latter wars reinforced a negative attitude towards Russia among some Chechens and added to existing memories of glory and tragedy. However, it was once again the memory of tragedy that determined the participation of veterans of both Chechen wars in the Russo-Ukrainian war. The flow of volunteers that started in 2014 became much more pronounced with the beginning of the full-fledged military campaign in 2022. For many, the war in Ukraine was an opportunity to settle scores and to retaliate for the suffering that the Chechen nation had experienced at the hands of the Russian military. Not to miss this chance, many exchanged the comfort and safety of Europe for military fatigues and the risk of being killed. Moreover, the Chechen battalions in Ukraine harbour ambitions to liberate Chechnya. The Ukrainian legislators support these ambitions and the hopes of the Chechen nationalists by recognizing Chechnya as an occupied territory. It is difficult to predict whether the aspiration to liberate Chechnya will be fulfilled, but the attempt could certainly take place due to the authoritarian style of Kadyrov's rule, which is often compared to Stalin's times. The participation of the Chechen volunteers in the war in Ukraine and the battalions named after Sheikh Mansur and Dzhokhar Dudayev demonstrates that collective memory could play a significant and perhaps decisive part in such an attempt.

A change in the state of affairs between Russia and Chechnya could also be triggered by Kadyrov's loss of political support from the Kremlin. The overreliance on Kadyrov, who often demonstrates his independence in decisions, sometimes seems more a burden than a boon for many Russian politicians. However, this initiative will hardly come from Putin, who appreciates loyalty in people above other qualities.

Box 11.1 Brief chronology of Chechen political history

1801–1864 – The Caucasian War
1917–1918 – Independent Mountain Republic
1925 – Soviet power established in Chechnya
1944 – Deportation of the Chechens to Central Asia
1957 – Chechens return from exile
1991 – Dzhokhar Dudayev becomes the first president of Chechnya and declares republic's independence
1994 (Dec) – The First Russo-Chechen War begins
1996 (April) – President Dudayev killed

1996 (Aug) – Military defeat of the Russian troops in Chechnya
1996 (Sept) – Khasavyurt Peace Accords
1997 – Chechen presidential elections won by Aslan Maskhadov
1997 – Peace Treaty signed by the presidents Aslan Maskhadov and Boris Yeltsin
1999 (Sept) – Beginning of the Second Russo-Chechen War
2000 – Akhmat Kadyrov appointed as new head of administration in Chechnya by Moscow
2003 – The new Constitution of Chechnya and sham elections bring the republic back into the Russian Federation
2004 – Akhmat Kadyrov assassinated during 9 May Victory Day Parade
2005 (March) – President Maskhadov killed
2007 – Ramzan Kadyrov officially becomes the new head of the republic
2009 – Cancellation of the counter-terrorist operation in Chechnya
2014 (onwards) – Chechens participate on both sides of the war in Ukraine and in various militant groups in Syria
2022 – Ukraine recognizes Chechnya as an occupied territory.

Questions for discussion

1 What were the main reasons for the Russo-Chechen wars?
2 Why did the Chechen resistance resort to terrorism, and what were the aims of the terrorist attacks?
3 Is a renewed Chechen insurrection possible?
4 How typical is Chechnya as a republic in the Russian Federation?
5 Is Chechnya now more a source of political stability for Russia's regime or instability?

Recommended readings

Lazarev, Egor. 2023. *State-building as Lawfare. Custom, Sharia, and State Law in Postwar Chechnya*. Cambridge University Press. UK.
Murphy, Paul J. 2011. *Allah's Angels: Chechen Women in War*. Naval Institute Press.
Satter, David. 2016. *The Less You Know, the Better You Sleep: Russia's Road to Terror and Dictatorship Under Yeltsin and Putin*. Yale University Press.

Schaefer, Robert W. 2011. *The Insurgency in Chechnya and the North Caucasus: From Gazavat to Jihad*. Santa Barbara, Denver, Oxford: Praeger Publishers Inc.

Ware, Robert Bruce. 2009. 'Chechenization: Ironies and Intricacies.' *The Brown Journal of World Affairs*, 15(2), 157–69.

12

Inequality and Marginalized Groups

Jeremy Morris

This chapter covers major issues of relevance to understanding the positioning of vulnerable groups such as the working poor, migrants, and pensioners. Topics covered include inequality and poverty; race and migration; material life strategies and social mobility; state–society relations; the relevance of personal networks. Thematic discussions are prefaced by sections on the social history of transition from communism after 1991, and the social meaning of 'Putinism'. A final section briefly covers broader processes and questions of how 'marginalized' social groups relate to the political regime and seek to overcome disorganization and atomization.

The long transition from communism: loss of social state guarantees

The retrospective imagining by ordinary Russians and politicians alike of the 1990s as a socio-economic disaster for the majority is now so entrenched as a defining raison d'être of Putin's rule that the actual experience of the monumental changes deserves careful examination. Setting aside political turmoil, the following experiences were commonly formative, and striking for their relative suddenness: sharp rises in visible inequality and social differentiation; downward social mobility into poverty; erosion of a social safety net without concomitant or sufficient development of a 'third' sector of charities and NGOs; exploration of novel and unwelcome forms of getting by, such as market trading; female unemployment and underemployment; wage arrears in industry; a sharp rise in social despair and destructively maladaptive behaviours – especially among men. While not losing sight of the fact that these issues were not experienced universally, they are especially pertinent to more vulnerable groups such as those with fewer economic and educational resources, rural people, single-parent families, and ethnic minorities.

While Soviet society was much more divided by 'class', income, and demographic outcomes like mortality and morbidity than many people in the West imagined, real levels of inequality were modest in comparison to other advanced countries. The late USSR could be compared in this regard to social democratic Sweden, or the welfare state society of the UK (Haynes 2013). Regardless of how inequality is measured, it cannot be overemphasized that despite tangible social stratification in the late USSR, the abruptness of transition to market capitalism led to a wholesale shock to society – psychological as much as material. Families, almost in 'real time' experienced the threat of complete destitution as shortages of goods in the 1980s gave way to hyperinflation in the early 1990s and the disruption of supply chains. Savings were wiped out as ordinary people scrambled, often too late, to buy durable goods – still in short supply. Existing stratification cruelly played a role as those with some insider knowledge or connections via organizations like the Communist Youth League (*Komsomol*), could anticipate such changes and position themselves to better weather them. Two friends with similar middle-class work, credentials, and status in 1989 might experience jarringly opposite trajectories: one going to work in a bank thanks to her connections, the other forced to sell evening newspapers on the metro or her book collection in an open-air market to supplement her inadequate salary. Not only this, but the luckless faced a further shock: loss of the social state. The albeit rickety cradle-to-grave welfare system from the USSR they had grown up with effectively ceased to exist because the Russian economy was in free-fall and lacked tax receipts with which to fund expenditures. Social expenditures on pensions halved between 1990 and 1992. Family allowances effectively disappeared except for the poorest. Furthermore, a large part of social expenditure in the USSR was delegated to factories, employers, and enterprises. With few exceptions, such as parts of the military industrial complex or other key sectors, employers severely cut back on social spending – estimated by the World Bank as a reduction in 60–70 per cent in spending between 1991 and 1992, equivalent to up to 10 per cent of family income.

Further, the state de facto reneged on many social guarantees by delegating and 'decentralizing' delivery of welfare to regional level government where few resources were available (Cook 2007, 66–67). It is no exaggeration to state that the more vulnerable were effectively abandoned to rely on their own resources, leading to what Michael Burawoy and his Russian colleagues (2000) called household 'involution': defensive and risky strategies of minimalist survival such as market and long-distance trade as individual 'entrepreneurs'. Women were forced into dangerous and exploitative positions on the front line of the new economy, buying and selling petty commodities.

Writing about the Moscow middle-class, anthropologist Nancy Ries (1997) showed that even among this stratum, the transition period was characterized by narratives of hopelessness and despair, and even a kind of gallows-humour fatalism accompanying social dislocation. A further strand of social research relating to the sudden immersion of people into marketized relations detailed how alien and traumatic this process was. Anthropologist Caroline Humphrey (1999) illustrates the triple blow dealt by transition. First, expectations of social support to get through crisis were not met with action. Secondly, there was a naïve expectation fostered at all levels that transition would magically create an abundant consumer society for all, and yet a tiny new rich (the so-called 'New Russians') and a mass poor emerged instead. Third, the process of being ejected from secure jobs in the Soviet period to precarious ones such as retail was experienced as humiliating and bewildering. This was because 'trade' had historically been seen as morally reprehensible in the Soviet period, as well as because of the sudden visibility of organized crime and corrupt police which fed off market activities. Furthermore, traders were visible targets for ordinary people to hold responsible for Russia's misfortune. Memorably, Humphrey called the experience of the 1990s a crisis of values leading to a 'culture of disillusionment' (1995). In a controversial intervention, researchers writing for the leading British medical journal *The Lancet* linked mass privatization in the early 1990s with an increase in male mortality rates of 12 per cent due to 'psycho-social stress' made worse because of the relative absence of social support organizations, outcomes worse than any other postcommunist state (Stuckler at al. 2009). Life expectancy for men fell to 58 by 1999, leading to reports that up to ten million men were 'missing', due to demographic collapse.

Researchers have also broken down the experience of the 1990s to show how dislocation was disproportionately borne by vulnerable groups such as women, older and rural people, and the working class. Anthropologists observed that women were the primary victims of 'structural adjustment' because employment cuts came first to light industry and service sectors where they were disproportionately employed. Sexual discrimination and violence increased, new forms of sexualization of women in popular culture, along with increasing 'retraditionalization' of gender roles, proved a reversal of the USSR's limited advances in women's rights and opportunities (Ashwin 2000). Older people saw their already meagre pensions eroded by inflation, and many relied on social support. In the countryside, the collapse of collectivized farming created mass rural unemployment and migration. In the labour market, particularly in industry, job insecurity and wage arrears became near universal experiences for workers. Enforced 'unpaid' leave, and non-payment of wages, sometimes for months in a row, were enterprise tactics for forestalling bankruptcy – at the expense of their own employees. At times workers were paid 'in kind' because of the lack of currency in firms and many workers resorted to cultivating kitchen gardens as an insurance policy against starvation. This multifaceted form of economic exploitation exacerbated societal insecurity, making planning and investment harder, both for individuals at the level of the household, as well as firms themselves. The most vulnerable workers – in the many single-industry company towns – faced a dilemma: to take risks in migrating to better prospects, or to stick loyally to a non-performing firm in the hope of better times. The 'decaying paternalism' of moribund industrial enterprises made it hard to leave because workers valued even the meagre social benefits such as workplace canteens which remained after communism (Friebel and Guriev 2000).

The legacy of 'Soviet man' or Soviet 'mentality'

The charge of a more general paternalistic mentality among many Russians, and the idea that social contract is today impossible because of 'clientelist' expectations, especially among the less resourced in society, finds its origin in influential theories of maladaptation to postcommunism: specifically to the idea of a liberal market-based form of social intercourse. Most pertinent to this chapter is the idea that authoritarianism and incomplete transition to a normative political economy (with less corruption and more democracy) are the fault of those with less social, economic, and educational capital. This framing has been observed in different postcommunist societies, but in the Russian case is most associated with the idea of *homo sovieticus* proposed by sociologist Yuri Levada and his team from the 1980s: a trope of people 'damaged' by the Soviet system and incapable of refashioning themselves according to, or even understanding Western, liberal ideals (Sharafutdinova 2019, p. 174). Less commented on is that a key maladaptive characteristic of *homo sovieticus* carries strongly classed perspectives relating to stereotypes of Russian peasants and lower orders: 'the cunning people', 'simple people', those in a subordinate social positioning.

Homo sovieticus is translated quite unequivocally today in classed language about ordinary Russian people as 'cattle' who mindlessly chew the inadequate feed (both material and rhetorical) provided by their patron-owner – the Russian authoritarian state – and now go willingly to slaughter in Ukraine. In popular liberal imagination the 'cattle' are contrasted to the 'intelligentsia' and 'active' parts of the population. Prominent literary critic Dmitry Bykov famously pronounced about the 2011–12 protests that those participating wanted to show each other that they were not cattle: passive, prone to rumour, basely cunning, and immune to notions of what is noble in life. Samuel Greene (2019), along with Gulnaz Sharafutdinova, critique generalizations based on maladaptive *homo sovieticus*. Greene focuses instead on the need to pay closer attention to 'common-sense, locally grounded, defensive, and slowly changing guideposts for navigating uncertainty' among Russians and how social incentives towards dispositions like 'agreeableness' are more relevant than generalizations about political 'culture'. His approach takes inspiration from earlier critics who use the concept of 'vernacular knowledge' to describe how communities take strategic actions which are defensive, internal, local, and slow paced (Aronoff and Kubik 2012). Understandably, relatively less visible or rapid examples of social agency might then be reinterpreted as merely maladaptive. Greene also reanalyzes Levada's material to note the development of strong prohibitions against breaches of interpersonal trust in contrast to breaches of impersonal, generalized trust. One conclusion is that strategic social action is possible in Russia but is local and limited. Citizens can become active, but to assess impact we need to look carefully and via a range of methodologies.

The social meaning of early Putinism

As many commentators have noted, the timing of Putin's rise to power was highly serendipitous because his first two terms as president coincided with, rather than facilitated, sustained economic growth and much higher real incomes, even for the poorest. Poverty rates fell from 38 per cent in 1998 to 10 per cent in 2004. Nonetheless the vast majority continued to complain of high levels of inequality and worsened life-chances (Rutland 2008). Putin's rhetoric of rebuilding state capacity to fulfil social guarantees in housing, health, pensions, and education was effective until the global financial crisis after 2008, not so much because of targeted actions in these areas, but because the oil wealth Russia garnered in these years had a general 'lifting all boats' effect. State agencies did benefit from much-increased resources both in absolute and relative terms. However, more significantly, the waged incomes of more vulnerable groups were for the first time keeping up with inflation. Crucially, the kind of social mobility last experienced by the poor in the Soviet period seemed once more possible because of opportunities offered by new positions in state bureaucracies and a growing consumption and service economy. Labour migration was also significant to social mobility, whether from ethnic minority areas in the Caucasus, or from the declining monotowns all over Russia. Migration, even to dirty, risky, and dangerous jobs in construction or even informal taxi-driving in Moscow and other large cities was effectively a step up the socio-economic ladder for many.

While the first decade of the 2000s often saw effective propagandizing of Putin's first terms as heralding 'stability', the return to the semblances of a law-based order, and the return of the socially interventionist state, the actual experience of vulnerable groups was equivocal. While poverty declined, inequality rose faster in this period as the differences between earned incomes among the 'working poor' (in Russia, most of the population) and a small number of well-paid city-dwellers (perhaps 10–20 million people) widened (Remington 2012). In Russia, the working poor could be defined as those who own no assets apart from their home and live pay cheque to pay cheque, taking loans to buy big-ticket items like cars, or even holidays and furniture. By the end of the decade, a relatively junior office job in Moscow might pay $1,000-equivalent a month, while manual labourers in regions considered themselves lucky to earn $400. Inequality measured by the GINI index remained as high in Russia as it was the 1990s and was comparable to the figure in the United States, a notoriously unequal advanced economy. But wealth and income polarization in Russia are far worse than in the US. The top 1 per cent hold 70 per cent of assets; the top 5 per cent, 80 per cent (Pavlovskaya 2018, 90). Russia by 2007 had become a country where 10 per cent of the population received half of all income;

a resource-rich country full of poor people who owned no assets beyond their poorly maintained inherited Soviet apartments.

Pensions continued to lag inflation outside large cities. Despite the depredations of the 1990s and so-called 'withdrawal of the state', in 2003, 100 million people still received some kind of social benefit and 24 per cent of households received non-monetary services or goods (Remington 2012, 48). In the name of efficiency and modernization, the regime soon set to work converting these in-kind benefits to cash sums in the so-called *lgoty* (benefit) reforms. A typical example was the withdrawal of the right to free prescription medicines for the chronically ill, or free urban transit cards for pensioners in exchange for much less valuable cash assistance. For example, if one considers that most pensioners were forced to continue working or had post-retirement 'careers', the loss of free transit cards had a significant negative effect on their real incomes – up to 10 per cent of income for poor households (Wengle and Rassel, 2008). A key part of the social safety net for the most vulnerable was removed, although overall these benefits had been ineffective because of their untargeted distribution, often tied to status (e.g. parents of disabled children), not actual need. The monetization reforms provoked the first significant protests against Putin's government and forced minor concessions. Later, particularly after 2008, the reduction in subsidies to communal services and utilities also had a significant impact on what were now falling incomes, meaning that in the 2010s households were spending up to a quarter of income on necessities like heating and obligatory apartment maintenance, while income used on discretionary items like recreation did not change over the same period. The relative share of social expenditure by the government was little changed, other than pensions, and even decreased in the crisis year of 2009 (Kulmala et al. 2014).

The equivocal nature of early reform extended to those policies designed as socially, or demographically supportive. A good example was the flagship pronatal policy from 2006 which offered relatively large cash payments to parents for the birth of a second child. This 'maternal capital' programme was designed to reverse the precipitous decline in fertility since its peak in 1987 (2.2 births per woman). By 1999 there were only 1.2 births per woman, lower even than Italy (famous for its low fertility) and well below the population replacement rate. Having more than one sibling had become a marked rarity among children growing up in the late 1990s and 2000s, and often a sign of poverty. The 2006 policy raised rates, but only temporarily, to 1.8 births. In 2020 the rate had fallen back to 1.5. Why did the policy fail? Like the monetization of benefits reform before it, the maternal capital grant could not compensate for the costs of a second child for poorer, or even middle-class families. It was overly bureaucratic in administration and came with strings attached (although less complex to claim than other benefits); it was a 'one off', not 'cash-convertible', and it was only claimable three years after the birth. In a sense, the benefit encapsulated the conditional and even fickle instrumental relationship between the newly minted Russian state and its citizens. It followed the pattern of belated, inadequate, and patch-work rebuilding of the social contract. Russians reacted in an economically rational way, by not having second children: The grant did not nearly meet projected expenses of raising a child, especially considering the lack of extensive, high-quality, or affordable pre-school childcare and the lack of accompanying measures to protect women's employment rights while on maternity leave (on paper, strong, in reality, weak). Since 2007 other pro-family policies have followed a similar pattern: one-time payments and small allowances which expire while the child is still quite young.

The failure of Putin's government to think more deeply about measures to ameliorate the conditions of Russia's working-poor majority is no better symbolized than by the failed pronatal policy. Designed as a response to charges that the state had abandoned families, and that it was complicit in the 'genocide' of the Russian population, it was a keystone of Putin's commitment to the renewal of the 'social state'. Article Seven of the 1993 Russian Constitution (still present in the 2020 revision) stipulates that state policy aims at establishing strong social security guarantees to ensure a 'worthy life' and protect people's labour and health through a minimum wage and extensive benefit system. Yet from the first, policies were designed and presented within a narrowly monetaristic and pragmatic framework – a technocratic problem to solve; the duty of the state towards women was expressed in populist, even liberal tones by Putin, but revealed a relatively detached (no consistent family allowance was considered), piecemeal, and conditional idea of state–social contract (Rotkirch et al. 2007). The social Darwinist instinct of the new, 'self-made' Russian elite, implanted through the desperate experiences of the 1990s, was arguably visible in both the *lgoty* and pronatal policies. Fiscal probity from the state, and boot-strapping and self-help among the misfortunate, were more important than the idea of a comprehensive welfare, let alone social, state – once so crucial to communist legitimacy. These tendencies in social policy to underestimate, or even ignore, the issues of poverty and inequality only accelerated after the initial shock of the global financial crisis subsided in the early 2010s. Yet the idea of social rights and protection by the state from the vicissitudes of the market remained powerful political ideals for the majority (Bindman 2018).

We can also refer to the prospects for even more vulnerable social groups such as the disabled and people in need of social care (children and older people). In the case of children left without parental care, Russia made rapid moves to deinstitutionalize care after 2012 and shift to a fostering model (Kulmala et al. 2017). This was due to changing attitudes, social policy, and material factors, but overall it saw an alignment with global trends in ameliorating the harm of institutional care to children. A measure of the prominence of child protection in Russia was the emergence of pressure groups against 'juvenile justice' and in favour of traditional family hierarchy. In this policy innovation, as with others, the question of causation is open to debate. Some observers see the extension of harsher fiscal consolidation in nearly all realms, which could be termed 'austerity' politics (Zubarevich 2016). Others, more positively, see changes as an overdue acknowledgement of how the Soviet state tried to do too much and failed in the process. Finally, some took the view that the Russian state made a virtue of its limited social capacity by becoming a network manager in a flexible and hybrid, yet still authoritarian approach to governance (Berg-Nordlie et al. 2018). For example, it might be that a grassroots NGO that takes the initiative in provision for AIDS patients is then subordinated and regulated by state bodies. Other hybrid institutions of care include 'veterans' committees (open to more than just former military service persons), often attached to municipal government. Symbolic support to provide 'ontological security' via a continuity of rituals from the Soviet period (such as celebrating festivals) is as important as material aid. In parallel with the above processes, the severe curtailment of foreign NGOs accelerated in the period after 2012, creating new gaps in provision for the vulnerable, for example for disabled people (Hartblay 2020), but also providing openings for indigenous forms of hybrid state–society initiatives.

Prospects for social reproduction after the global financial crisis (2008–present)

After sociologist Pierre Bourdieu (1984), a 'capitals' approach to social reproduction refers to how people remain in the same class as their parents because they fail to accrue enough economic, cultural, human, and social resources to break through to the next level in a stratified society. A secondary meaning of social reproduction refers to how much work in remaking society is relegated to the household sphere and unnoticed by economists and policymakers alike because it is carried out by women and other devalued or subordinate people, is unwaged, or undervalued. Essentially, key costs of reproducing labour power are excised from the picture. Both these meanings gain greater relevance in the straightened economic circumstances of working-poor Russians and other vulnerable groups in the period after 2008. Investment of individuals' capitals became riskier and harder, and the returns less certain, resulting in limited social mobility. Further, as Russian governments found it harder to sustain both economic development and rebuilding a military and security state, they embraced a politics of economic austerity (limiting social spending) and rhetoric of social Darwinism (every man and woman for themselves) already widespread among the smaller part of society that had done well since the 1990s. Olga Shevchenko (2015, p. 59) memorably summarizes the 'cult of the winner' among such groups: an 'aggressive emphasis on personal autonomy and self-sufficiency... a moral legitimation of inequality, and an aggressive pursuit of self-interest'.

Symptomatic of the deterioration of the living standards for the majority, inequality, poverty, and social stratification increased in the 2010s and 2020s, apart from two periods where the government took action. In 2009 Russian GDP fell more than any advanced economy, by 8 per cent, and the government took stimulative fiscal measures – but these mainly helped the corporate sector and assisted individual households only indirectly. They did not prevent large-scale layoffs and the traditional methods of devolving economic pain to the lowest rung: by forcing workers into long periods of unpaid leave and paycuts. Without effective trade union action, made all-but-illegal since 2001, there were few forms of collective action workers could resort to. Nonetheless, labour sociologists recorded increases in industrial strife in this period. During the COVID-19 pandemic too, direct aid to businesses was extended to maintain employment, but once again 'socio-demographic measures' such as direct payments to furloughed workers were insignificant compared to other advanced economies. Overall, almost all workers dependent on a monthly wage experienced the period as one of stagnation at best, and for many, inflation and the lowering of the value of the ruble meant in real terms their incomes declined. By 2017, for the first time in post-Soviet history, polls reported that a majority were more concerned with economic reforms and social justice than political stability, a rising trend. To put these changes in perspective, 40 per cent of the population reported that they struggled to afford new clothing, and the lowest paid spent 80 per cent of their income on food alone. In dollar terms, average wages fell by 40 per cent between 2013 and 2016 while in cities, the real costs of energy, transport, and food were comparable to much richer European countries while inflation remained stubbornly high. Finally, in 2018 the government raised the retirement age significantly, prompting protests and some adjustment to the policy.

Scholars offer different political interpretations based on this period of Putin-era stagnation. Samuel Greene (2017) argued that ordinary Russians were still able to compartmentalize economic woes and loyalty to the regime, particularly towards Putin personally. Greene's main question was: Why wasn't there more economic protest and opposition? The conundrum could find different answers: a repeat of 'involution' of the 1990s, outlined above; that more assertive foreign policy by the Russian state provided a compensatory feeling of national pride; the decimation of civil society, unions, and independent media meant that Russians, especially the most vulnerable, felt so atomized that no joined-up action was imagined possible. Bryn Rosenfeld (2017) found that middle-class groups with family incomes dependent on state employment were less likely to engage in anti-regime protests. Some Russian observers argued that Russia had become a neo-feudal state where people were clearly marked by 'caste', or social estate, and the idea of service for reward replaced the concept of social mobility. Ilya Matveev (2019) argued that Russia exhibited hybrid characteristics of state capitalism and neoliberalism, where government interventionist policy favours large conglomerates (many of which are partly state-owned) and new elites at the expense of a diverse, healthy economy and growth that might benefit all. Ordinary people are subject to the naked law of the market, a shrinking, more 'efficient', and conditional public welfare sector, while insiders become a rentier class, reproducing themselves through unearned wealth.

Networks, informality and economic rationality among vulnerable groups

In examining inequality, the uneasy social compact, and absence of meaningful contract, some scholars highlighted the continued relevance and large size of the informal economy in Russia (Morris and Polese 2013). In the classic trifecta of 'exit, voice, and loyalty' proposed by economist Albert Hirschman (1970) to describe the possible responses to decline, the informal economy as 'exit', whether in day labouring, migration, personal services such as car repair, home hairdressing or nail salons, or simply market trade, remained viable and even desirable to the more vulnerable of both genders because informality not only provided a (usually secondary) income, but also allowed the hiding of some income or assets from the state and taxation. The exploration of how prominent the informal economy in Russia remained, even after many economic reforms and supposedly pro-entrepreneurial steps like the introduction of a low flat-tax on income early in Putin's first term, highlighted not only mistrust of the state, but the importance of personal networks and favours as a particularly Russian form of social capital, for the poorest as much as other social classes. *Blat*, discussed in Chapter 7, was prominent as a form of long-term favour exchange involving goods and services rather than cash in the Soviet economy of shortage, but remains relevant and 'monetized' today (Ledeneva 1998).

Along with reciprocity, scholars explored in detail how networks of mutual aid and resilience operated among the poorest, particularly denizens of the declining company towns where underemployment and low wages were acute problems (Morris 2016). Key questions asked were: To what extent did such practices extend beyond survival and generate further social and economic capital? Was it possible for vulnerable groups to willingly internalize 'marketized selves' in an era of global neoliberal diffusion? These topics were a return to difficult issues examined by sociologists during the previous crises of the 1990s – such as the debate about whether vegetable plots could be a genuine survival resource for the poorest in Russia because the high costs of tending plots outweighed their benefits. Nancy Ries (2009) later insisted that economic rationality of Russian survival strategies should be contextualized in a deeper understanding that the state is an unreliable social guarantor and that 'potato ontology' (growing some root-crop come what may) provides psychological reassurances that if the worst happens poorer people can survive on their own resources.

Informality and the secondary or 'black' economy is also relevant when examining the subaltern positioning, yet ubiquity of Central Asian migrants in the Russian Federation, particularly because of the political implications of migrants' increasing visibility and the association of immigration and illegal or illicit work. It is often forgotten that a legacy of economic growth under Putin was also the development of an enormous remittance economy as millions of migrants with precarious documentation settled in Russia from former Soviet republics and sent back earnings to their homelands. By 2005 the official counts of migration flows were unreliable; fewer than 200,000 foreign workers from the CIS had residence and work permits, but the real figure employed was likely at least two million. Research on the trades taken up by migrants shows forms of ethnic clustering and co-dependence. For example, Rustamjon Urinboyev (2021) shows how Uzbek construction workers in Moscow from a single area in the Ferghana valley rely on their co-ethnics for almost all services and even resort to a parallel shadow legal order to solve disputes. Caste, class, and ethnicity are overlayed. For example, outside Moscow, Uzbeks with more complete documentation live comfortably as a labour aristocracy in some informal trade contexts, supervising the spade work of Tajiks, who represent a day-labouring underclass and who live in terrible conditions with very low pay. While sex workers are mainly an export from the former Soviet space to the West, many trades in large cities in Russia are both feminized and ethnicized – women from former Soviet republics taking jobs as waitresses, shop assistants, cleaners, and care workers. In all these cases, incomplete knowledge of the law and language means that these workers can be coerced into a grey zone of employment and part of their wages stolen on the pretext that they are not quite legal. By 2019 there were likely seven million labour migrants in Russia, the majority from three Central Asian countries: Kyrgyzstan, Tajikistan, and Uzbekistan. Shakedowns of the latter two groups by corrupt police using ethnic profiling has been an ever-present hazard, compounding the open racism and xenophobia experienced at every step. Kyrgyz nationals in theory have equal labour rights but still experience police extortion (Eraliev and Urinboyev 2020).

The treatment of migrants shows how endemic corruption in Russia, which targets the most vulnerable, operates at multiple levels of interaction, from police to higher bureaucracies. It is not only tolerated by society at large, but even contributes to a hybrid form of state capacity: for example, in the simultaneous formal and informal practices of immigrant control (Schenk 2021). Corruption affects all strata in Russian society but in different ways, and it can tell us a lot about relative degrees of social marginalization, as well as about state–society relations. A beat or traffic policeman may be embedded in a web of corrupt dependencies, extracting economic rents in the form of bribes from migrants or ethnic Russian market traders and 'paying upwards' (called *otkat* in Russian) a large sum to his superiors. In professions (as in politics) it is more accurate to talk of clientelism (a mutual relationship between superiors and subordinates where each benefits at the expense of outsiders), but exploitation and social harm are still ever-present. Take for instance the still widespread practice of doctors and others paying kickbacks to gain favourable hospital positions (meaning many may be incompetent), and highly differential treatment by medical professionals based on the imputed wealth of patients. Similarly, corruption exacerbates regional inequalities. A cancer patient in Moscow might access good treatment without any need to make informal payments. A similar patient in a provincial city might feel obligated to pay locally for 'better' treatment even though no quality oncology equipment even exists in her region, the funds for them having been embezzled, or simply absent. Corruption is just one issue, but it works in concert with the others highlighted in this chapter such as the intentional rhetoric of an uncaring state, fiscal austerity, and neglect of social protection, the high cost of essential services (utilities) provided by opaque privatized entities, and increased 'milking' of the population via hefty fines and charges for all manner of infractions. The overall effect for the more vulnerable is a message of a hostile and predatory state from which it makes sense to distance oneself. Social disappointment is compounded because of the still widely shared expectations of state and corporate paternalism among elements of society with fewer resources, stemming from the late Soviet model outlined above. In the final section we look more generally at concepts such as paternalism and atomization in society.

Conclusion

Among the many threads in this chapter, it is worth pulling further on two: the idea that less resourced Russians still default to paternalistic relations with sources of authority – both political and economic – and so they choose unrequited 'loyalty'; or that because they find themselves in a relatively hostile and unsupportive state, they unintentionally sustain the regime by choosing 'exit' (political quiescence) over 'voice'. Both these perspectives are implicit in many scholarly approaches to Russian society (see respectively Gudkov 2015, and Gel'man 2010 for emblematic examples). The war on Ukraine tends to exacerbate these views. It is certainly true that sociology proposes a link between exploitation and marginalization, and 'alienation' and 'anomie'. The more extreme a modern consumption-capitalist system becomes, the more prominent feelings among the less resourced of powerlessness, isolation, and self-estrangement, leading to political atomization and an inability to even imagine oneself as a political subject rather than a subordinate or supplicant in a system of patronage, or allocation based on caste membership. Does the legacy of paternalism and the current socially hostile state mean Russians with fewer resources are a priori demobilized and politically atomized, easy prey to populist nationalism, or even fascistic rhetoric?

More applied searches for sources of agency among the marginalized in Russia have been carried out. In a paper aptly titled: 'Beyond loyalty and dissent', Karine Clément and Anna Zhelnina (2020) argue that various modalities of pragmatic everyday politics are possible in Russia. They echo Greene, arguing that intense activity is possible where people see the possibility of changing their immediate material environment and that this is a way of overcoming atomization and the prior impossibility of imagining a 'social' world. They point to the relevance of other research on marginalized and vulnerable communities which finds sources of 'small politics' and 'non-indifference'. Research on activism tends to focus on high-resource groups in metropolitan settings such as those involved in supporting Alexei Navalny in his political strategies to unseat Putin. But there is increasing attention to low-level activism, such as among pensioners organizing against housing demolition or local people protesting trash dumping and pollution, showing that the marginalized can mobilize rapidly in particular circumstances and with the help of new social media (Sundstrom et al. 2022, Poupin 2021, Morris et al. 2023).

Questions for discussion

1 Why is inequality in Russia such an important topic in relation to politics?
2 How have vulnerable categories of citizens fared since 2000?
3 How has the nature of the social state changed over the period since 2000?
4 What are the different ways Russians think about the role of the state in the life of the individual?
5 How do questions about social adaptation relate to political questions such as those about atomization?

Recommended readings

Bindman, Eleanor. 2017. *Social Rights in Russia: From Imperfect Past to Uncertain Future*, Routledge. [Chapter 4: The development of social rights in Russia.]

Clément, Karine, and Zhelnina, Anna. 2020. 'Beyond Loyalty and Dissent: Pragmatic Everyday Politics in Contemporary Russia.' *International Journal of Politics, Culture, and Society* 33: 143–62.

Greene, Samuel A. 2017. 'From Boom to Bust: Hardship, Mobilization & Russia's Social Contract.' *Daedalus* 146(2): 113–27.

Kay, Rebecca. 2012. 'Managing Everyday (In) Securities: Normative Values, Emotional Security and Symbolic Recognition in the Lives of Russian Rural Elders.' *Journal of Rural Studies*, 28(2): 63–71.

Morris, Jeremy. 2011. 'Socially Embedded Workers at the Nexus of Diverse Work in Russia: An Ethnography of Blue-collar Informalization.' *International Journal of Sociology and Social Policy*, Vol. 31 No. 11/12: 619–31.

13

Protest and Civil Society

Katerina Tertytchnaya

Mass protest is one of the most consequential actions individuals can undertake in order to influence political change. Civil society, the sphere in which non-governmental organizations, voluntary associations, and movements operate, is also important for ensuring the representation of citizens' interests. Understanding the dynamics of protests and civil society in authoritarian settings like Russia has been a central focus of research in comparative politics. For example, researchers have asked who organizes and who participates in protests in Russia and what motivates people to join civil society organizations. Scholars of Russian politics have also sought to understand how legal restrictions and the repression of civil society have impacted political participation in the country. To answer these questions, researchers have created new protest-event catalogues that provide information on the location and size of protest events taking place across Russia, fielded real time, on-site surveys of individuals taking part in protests, and engaged in participant observation – immersing themselves in the day-to-day activities of Russian activists.

In this chapter, we will consider developments in contemporary Russian protests and civil society, with a focus on the period between the large electoral protests of 2011–12 and the months that followed Russia's invasion of Ukraine in February 2022. As the ensuing discussion will show, the invasion of Ukraine coincided with the tightening of political control and the escalation of repression within Russia. The crackdown on civil society and opposition networks with the ability to coordinate mass protest, already under way since the early 2010s, also accelerated after the invasion of Ukraine.

To better understand the development of Russian protests and civil society, we will adopt a wide lens. To place contemporary developments in context, we will briefly review protests that took place from the late Soviet period through the 1990s and early 2010s. The discussion will also consider some of the laws that the Russian authorities adopted to regulate protest and civil society. As we will see, repressive legislation has limited opportunities for successful collective action and constrained the development of an independent civil society.

In the second part of the chapter we will focus on some of the largest and most consequential protests of the last decade. Several protest waves occupy centre stage in the discussion that follows: the electoral protests of 2011–12; the 2018 protests against the reform of the pension age; the 2021 protests in support of Russian opposition leader Alexei Navalny; and, finally, the protests that followed Russia's invasion of Ukraine. Relying on new data and evidence from protest catalogues, the discussion of protests that followed the invasion of Ukraine shows how, in response to new legislation that criminalized dissent, large street protests gave way to symbolic forms of resistance, such as painting graffiti or laying flowers at war monuments.

Russian protest since the late Soviet period

In the late 1980s, mass protests taking place in Russia and across the USSR's other republics played an important role in the union's downfall. Demonstrators taking to the streets of Russia during this period advanced a range of nationalist, socio-economic, and political demands – asking, for example, for the establishment of a multi-party system and greater political freedoms. It is precisely the growth of demonstrations that had encouraged local authorities to adopt new laws and regulations that would allow them to regulate protest. In 1987, the Moscow City Soviet was one of the first local authorities to adopt new regulations on protest (Beissinger 1990, p.52). The Moscow city authorities did so in response to protest by Crimean Tatars in Red Square in the summer of 1987. According to new rules, protest organizers had to notify the city authorities of their intention to stage a protest and had to apply and secure parade permits ahead of certain protest. New regulations also specified fines for those violating protest regulations and set certain areas, such as the Red Square, as 'out-of-bounds' for protest. In response to growing demonstrations, new, all-union rules on protest were adopted by mid-1988 (Sharlet 1990). Of note, until new laws on protest were passed in

2004, Russian protest continued to be regulated largely according to a decree of the Presidium of the USSR Supreme Soviet adopted in 1988.

During the 1990s Russian citizens could participate in protest freely. Protest permits were granted readily to both supporters and opponents of the ruling regime. Protest grew during the late Yeltsin period (Robertson 2010, p.7). Faced with economic decline and unpaid wages, Russian citizens, mainly workers, staged strikes, demonstrations, hunger strikes, and blockades. Yet, crucially, protests under Yeltsin remained isolated and were poorly coordinated. To some extent, the lack of coordination was due to the fact that in the 1990s Russia lacked independent organizations and social movements that could inspire and sustain coordinated street action. For example, labour unions, which were dependent on state patronage, did not take a decisive role when it came to protest coordination. Protest levels during the 1990s also varied greatly by region. Using daily reports on protest from the Russian Interior Ministry, Graeme Robertson (2010) has shown that while in some regions local elites actively encouraged protest, using them as leverage against federal authorities, in other regions protest was actively discouraged.

In the 2000s protest tactics changed. Strikes, common in the 1990s, were replaced by demonstrations and marches (Robertson 2010). The geography of protests was also different, with growing numbers of protests taking place in Moscow and St Petersburg as opposed to other regional centres. Protest activity grew in the second half of the 2000s. Those taking to the streets advanced a range of demands. For example, while some demonstrators called for greater protection of the environment and green spaces, others asked for revisions to government policies and opposed the authorities' plans for social and economic reform. Plans to replace social benefits such as housing maintenance and free public transport with cash payments triggered one of the largest protest waves of this period. In January 2005 pensioners, war veterans, people with disabilities, and many others participated in demonstrations, blocked highways, and paralyzed traffic. These protests were the largest show of discontent during Putin's first five years as president. Bringing together a coalition of groups, from liberals to communists, protests against the monetization of social benefits showed how attempts at social reform could spark mass protest across the country. On this occasion, faced with growing mobilization, regional officials were quick to accommodate some of the protesters' demands. For example, some regions announced that they would maintain access to free public transport.

Analyzing data on Russian protests that took place from 2006 onwards, studies have shown important differences in the ways that the Russian authorities respond to protests depending on the types of grievances they advance. Protests advancing political demands – for example, calling for regime change or policy reform, condemning corruption, or asking for free and fair elections – were more likely to face repression than protests advancing social or economic demands. It is estimated that approximately one in three political protests faced some type of disruption across 2006–17 (e.g. Lankina and Tertytchnaya 2020). The Russian authorities remained more tolerant of socio-economic as opposed to political protests even in the period that followed the invasion of Ukraine, a time of renewed protest repression within Russia. Differentiation in the Russian authorities' response to protests advancing political and other types of demands may stem from a range of factors. In general, as socio-economic protests do not typically attribute blame vis-à-vis the national government as political protests do, they may be perceived as less threatening for power holders. Observing socio-economic protests may also allow the Kremlin to better identify and address citizens' grievances while also monitoring the performance of local officials. The Russian authorities may also have aimed to signal that as long as citizens shy away from participating in protests that advanced political demands, they should be less concerned about arrests.

The electoral protest of 2011–12

In response to electoral manipulations in the December 2011 parliamentary election, tens of thousands of citizens attended demonstrations in Moscow and other Russian cities. Demonstrations continued after Vladimir Putin's victory in the first round of the March 2012 presidential elections. On 6 May 2012, on the eve of Putin's third inauguration as President of Russia, thousands of protesters gathered in Bolotnaya square in Moscow, a short walk away from the Kremlin. Demonstrators called for political change and demanded Putin's resignation. Although the Bolotnaya protest was mainly peaceful, the authorities used isolated acts of violence to describe it as a 'mass riot'. Hundreds of demonstrators were arrested on that day, while dozens of them were charged with various crimes. Their trials, which received widespread coverage in the press, were used to portray demonstrations against the authorities as 'undesirable' and 'threatening' for Russian society in general.

To quickly monitor arrests during the electoral protest of 2011–12, volunteers set up *OVD-Info*, an advocacy group and independent media project. In collaboration with other organizations, such as the Human Rights Center *Memorial*, OVD-Info helps provide legal assistance to those arrested during protest and shares information on the number of individuals who reach out asking for legal advice through either Telegram or OVD-Info's hotline. To date, OVD-Info remains one of the most comprehensive and trustworthy sources of information about arrest and repression in contemporary Russia.

The Kremlin's response to the protests of 2011–12 combined repression with propaganda. To communicate that the authorities enjoyed widespread support, the Kremlin manipulated the framing of online and offline protest news, stigmatizing protest organizers and participants. The Kremlin also mobilized its own supporters. Pro-regime rallies took place across Russia. Onsite surveys of protesters taking part in pro- and anti-regime protest across 2011–12, with protesters interviewed while participating in the protests, have improved our understanding of protesters' identity and allowed important insights into their political views. For example, such surveys have shown that regime opponents and supporters were generally supportive of street action and defended people's right to take to the street (Smyth et al. 2013). Surveys of protesters taking to the streets over the course of the 2011–12 electoral protest wave have also improved our understanding of demonstrators' profiles. For example, Rosenfeld (2017) has shown that while the opposition movement drew support from members of the middle class who were employed in the private sector, Russia's public-sector middle class was more likely to stay at home during the protests.

Increasing restrictions on protest and civil society following the 2011–12 protests

According to commentators, Russia's 'snow revolution', as the electoral protests of 2011–12 were described, melted quickly with the spring. Nonetheless, the protests were a watershed moment. Among the biggest anti-government rallies in Russia's post-Soviet history, the protests of 2011–12 highlighted society's potential to unite and mobilize around political causes. In their aftermath, the Russian authorities adopted a far more adversarial approach towards protest policing and civil society. For example, legislative reforms enacted as early as in the summer of 2012 limited opportunities for successful collective action and constrained the development of an independent civil society. New legislation also increased the penalties for organizing and participating in unauthorized protests, those taking place without the authorities' prior approval. The so-called 'Lugovoi' Law, adopted in 2013, also empowered the authorities to block – within twenty-four hours and without a court order – online sources that disseminated calls for mass riots, extremist activities, or participation in mass protest events that had not secured authorization.

The obstacles that protest organizers have had to overcome in order to organize lawful protests have continued to increase since 2012. In the aftermath of Crimea's annexation, for example, in March 2014, it was decided that protest participants could be held criminally liable if they breached protest regulations more than twice within 180 days, a charge that could lead to five years' imprisonment. Amendments passed in December 2020 also expanded the definition of 'public event' requiring authorization by the local authorities to include single-person pickets held consecutively in the same location. While up to this point queues to picket could be organized in response to 'breaking-news' events and did not require the authorities' approval, legislation passed in 2020 did not recognize consecutive single-person pickets as truly single person. The year 2020 also saw the introduction of new responsibilities for protest organizers, including requiring the organizers of protests with over 500 participants to provide their bank details as part of the event notification submitted to the local authorities. Protest organizers were also banned from receiving funding from foreign states, organizations, or citizens, entities labelled as 'foreign agents'; minors; or anonymous donors. These reforms inevitably increased the costs of crowdsource funding for protest.

New laws coming into force following the full-scale invasion of Ukraine in February 2022 created insurmountable obstacles to protests. By banning any references or activities that 'discredited the armed forced of the Russian Federation', including protests against their deployment in Ukraine or calls for them to be withdrawn, new legislation effectively criminalized anti-war protests. The invasion also ushered in a new wave of administrative and criminal prosecutions of civil society organizations and activists. Amid growing fears of prosecution, civil society leaders and environmental and social movement activists who had the capacity to coordinate nationwide protest fled Russia. What is more, in the aftermath of Russia's invasion of Ukraine, some of Russia's last remaining independent media outlets, such as

TV Rain, Tomsk TV2, and Echo of Moscow were blocked by Roskomnadzor, the public media regulator. Restrictions on independent news outlets and civil society organizations that traditionally collected and reported information on acts of dissent taking place across Russia also hindered researchers' ability to monitor and analyze Russian protest and other acts of resistance.

Civil society under attack

As civil society organizations began to grow in the early 1990s, they were left largely unchecked by the state, with little by way of legal oversight. Non-governmental organizations' efforts to secure financial aid from the international community were encouraged and even supported. When Putin came to power in 2000, formal structures were established to enable contact between the state and the thousands of new organizations that began to emerge in different parts of the country. For example, the establishment of the federal Public Chamber in 2005 offered opportunities for improved communication between civil society and state bodies. In 2007, the state introduced programmes of financial support for civil society organizations both through ad-hoc and competitive grant programmes led by the Ministry of Economic Development. Starting in the mid-2000s, however, the authorities began to place restrictions on civil society organizations. New regulations also gave the state significant control over the activities of non-governmental organizations. For example, a federal law coming into force in 2006 limited the funding that non-governmental organizations could receive from abroad, cutting off support that the sector had come to rely on through the 1990s.

The introduction of the 'Foreign Agents Law' in 2012 enabled the authorities to designate organizations that received funding from abroad as foreign agents. This label subjected targeted organizations to extensive monitoring on the part of the state. Organizations with a foreign agent status were required to register with the Ministry of Justice and would be subject to regular additional audits and scrutiny of their spending. Using the law to label NGOs as foreign agents, the authorities not only attempted to prevent targeted groups from engaging in activities critical of the government, but also sought to discredit them in the eyes of the public. Federal legislation went further still in 2015 by empowering authorities to classify certain organizations as 'undesirable'. The activities of these organizations could be rendered illegal. For example, in July 2015 Russian law enforcement officials raided the offices and homes of staff of *Golos*, a local non-governmental organization that monitors elections. The Committee Against Torture was also forced to cease operations after the Ministry of Justice listed it as a foreign agent.

The introduction of laws restricting the activities and funding of non-governmental organizations had a profound impact on the development of civil society in Russia. According to research, the Kremlin's approach effectively divided civil society organizations into two groups. For socially oriented organizations, successfully co-opted by the Kremlin, structures were created to allow them to flourish by delivering services on behalf of the state and carrying out meaningful projects in the community. The authorities not only refused to collaborate with organizations perceived as having hostile political goals, but also subjected them to restrictive legal requirements (e.g. Bogdanova et al. 2018).

Civil society organizations were therefore faced with a choice: They could either continue to engage politically and risk facing repression, or change focus and collaborate with the state. As a result, many political organizations ceased to exist, while those which refused to concede their political raison d'être moved abroad. Russia's full-scale invasion of Ukraine, which coincided with a renewed attack against civil society organizations, saw several organizations, including the Human Rights Centre *Memorial*, liquidated for allegedly violating the foreign agent legislation. In the aftermath of the invasion of Ukraine, the assault against civil society was complete – several non-governmental organizations were destroyed, their members were forced into exile, and their funding was cut off.

Protests after Bolotnaya

In the period between the electoral protests of 2011–12 and the 2018 presidential election, people continued to take to the streets across Russia. Although several of the protests taking place this period were concentrated in Moscow and St Petersburg, the two cities with federal status, regions outside of Moscow and St Petersburg featured significant volumes of protest activism as well. Prior to Russia's invasion of Ukraine in February 2022, Russia's Southern and North Caucasus federal districts witnessed the lowest levels of protests. Nonetheless, areas in the North Caucasus – Dagestan, Chechnya and Karachayevo-Cherkessia – shared some of the highest protest suppression rates across the country.

Several of the protests taking place from 2012 onwards were organized to express dissatisfaction with deteriorating living standards and poor social services. Socio-economic protests, often led by opposition parties loyal to the Kremlin such as the Communist Party of the Russian Federation (KPRF) and other grass-roots movements, primarily targeted employers and the regional authorities. Russians also continued to protest against the authorities' plans for social and economic reform. Consider, for example, the truckers' protests of 2015–16. In late 2015 and early 2016, Russia's long-distance truckers protested against the imposition of a new road tax on trucks weighing over twelve tonnes. This tax was to be collected by a new electronic monitoring system, *Platon*, owned by individuals close to Vladimir Putin. In addition to calling for the system to be scrapped, aggrieved truckers also expressed concerns relating to deteriorating living and working conditions, poor road infrastructure and economic decline. The protesters' demands were almost exclusively economic in nature – the truckers themselves repeatedly denied that they had anything to do with politics and even appealed to the federal authorities for help. Over time, however, the truckers' protests took on a more political dimension. Some of the truckers called for the resignation of the government and one of their leaders even announced his intention to run for president. Overall, however, the truckers' protests were short-lived. Protest activity dwindled after the authorities offered some concessions, such as a temporary decrease in the freight tax and a reduction in the penalty for non-payment. These protests illustrated how precarious social and economic reform could be for the Kremlin. The adoption of reforms that impacted people's daily lives negatively could lead to the eruption of widespread protest. The truckers' protests also highlighted how protests with socio-economic demands could become politicized, with demonstrators advancing demands for broader political change. Yet, connections between social groups taking to the streets and opposition groups and parties that were able to translate social and economic grievances into political demands were rare.

Occupying centre stage in discussions of protests in the period between the presidential elections of 2012 and 2018 were protests led by opposition leader Alexei Navalny and his team. Navalny, an outspoken blogger, anti-corruption campaigner, and one of Putin's fiercest critics, played a leading role in the election protests of 2011–12. Through his online activity he encouraged many Russians to take to the streets, addressed the crowds during protests, and was himself arrested several times. Navalny also managed to run as a candidate in Moscow's 2013 mayoral election and was the most serious challenger to the Kremlin-backed mayor Sergei Sobyanin. In late 2016, he announced his intention to run as a candidate in the 2018 presidential election. His campaign, coordinated by ninety-two regional offices across Russia's eleven time zones, was supported by 200,000 volunteers.

To elevate their campaign's agenda to public consciousness and generate support, Navalny and his supporters staged a series of nationwide protests in 2017 and 2018. The first of these, taking place on 26 March 2017, followed the release of a documentary film that accused then Prime Minister Dmitry Medvedev of embezzlement. Further nationwide 'days of protest' followed on 12 June 2017 and 7 October 2017. The anti-corruption protests of 12 June 2017 were the largest. It is estimated that on that day, between fifty and ninety-eight thousand demonstrators took to the streets across 207 localities. There were 1,700–1,805 arrests. Local authorities refused to authorize several of the protests taking place during this time. To secure authorization for their protests, Navalny's supporters were often forced to accept restrictions on the manner in which they could demonstrate, or were compelled to revise the time or the location of the protest. For example, to secure authorization for a proposed protest against government corruption on 12 June 2017, protest organizers in Kazan, in the Republic of Tatarstan, had to agree for the protest to take place at 7 a.m. Such restrictions, which also involved pushing protests to less visible public spaces on the outskirts of cities, served to undermine protesters' ability to generate awareness of their demands.

The anti-corruption protests of 2017 did not persuade the Kremlin to allow Navalny to compete in the 2018 election. Yet the protests succeeded in politicizing parts of Russia's younger population, especially those in the provinces. They also created the potential for sustained political activism even after Navalny's presidential campaign had ended (Dollbaum et al. 2018). As we will see in the sections that follow, Russians continued to take to the streets after Putin's 2018 re-election to the presidency. More often than before, people took to the streets in order to express their frustration with abuses of power, such as politically motivated arrests, as well as to ask for free and fair elections.

Russian protests since the presidential election of 2018

The pension reform protests of 2018

Shortly after Putin's re-election to the presidency in March 2018, the Russian government announced plans to raise the pension age from sixty to sixty-five for men and from fifty-five to sixty-three for women. These plans were unpopular. Opposition parties loyal to the Kremlin, such as the Communists, and others who opposed the authorities adamantly agreed on the need to protest against the Kremlin's plans. As such, protest against the raising of the pension age represented a rare opportunity for Russia's' opposition forces to coalesce, bring large numbers of people to the streets, and pose an even greater threat to the authorities. Nevertheless, street coalitions were rare. On some occasions, protests against the increase in the retirement age led by different groups were even in direct competition, taking place on the same day and with the same demands, just in different locations of the same locality.

According to the Institute of Collective Action (IKD), the Communist Party of the Russian Federation, at the forefront of the protests, organized approximately two in three of the pension protests. Navalny supporters and trade unions staged approximately 10 and 9 per cent of the protests, respectively. Other political parties and associations, such as the Liberal Democratic Party of Russia (LDPR), Yabloko, and A Just Russia, organized a smaller share of all events. It is estimated that between July and September 2018, thousands took to the streets to demand that the government abandon its pension reform. Early protests, scheduled for 1 July 2018, took place under the shadow of restrictions on protests imposed as a result of Russia hosting the 2018 FIFA World Cup. The number of protests against the increase of the retirement age across Russia, as well as the number of protest participants, increased once restrictions on protest were lifted. The weekend of 28 and 29 July 2018, for example, saw some of the largest protests in the country. On 28 July 2018 alone, more than 10,000 protesters attended a rally in Moscow.

The lack of coordination and agreement over a common set of demands were some of the anti-pension reform movement's key weaknesses. Reacting to the movement's lack of unity, the Kremlin accused opposition parties of staging protests for their own political gains, unable to offer credible alternatives to the pension reform. Even though the protests did not prevent the increase in the pension age, voters did punish the party of power, United Russia, in the regional elections of September 2018.

Protests advancing political demands continued unabated in subsequent years. For example, in June 2019 Russian reporters staged a series of single-person pickets to express their anger at the unlawful arrest of Russian investigative journalist Ivan Golunov. Golunov, who investigated state corruption and illicit business practices, was arrested on fabricated drug chargers. In the summer of 2019, forming queues to stage a single-person pickets was one of the few forms of protest available to citizens who wanted to protest against 'breaking news' events. Single-person pickets at the time did not require prior authorization. This changed in 2020. A few weeks after the protests in support of Ivan Golunov, in July–August 2019, protesters again took to the streets of Moscow after the authorities refused to allow most independent candidates to run in the Moscow City Duma Election. Protests demanding open city elections, several of which were not authorized by the authorities, were met with arrests and police brutality.

Protests during the COVID-19 pandemic

As part of Russia's response to the pandemic, regional governors and city mayors were tasked with restricting public assembly and banning mass gatherings in the form of protests, sports events, and concerts. Although these restrictions did not specifically target protests, once the worst of the first wave of the pandemic had passed, by approximately June 2020, restrictions on assembly began to be used selectively. Music events and other gatherings were allowed to go ahead, while local authorities used the pandemic and threats to public health as a pretext to deny protest organizers the right to go ahead with planned action. Nonetheless, by the summer of 2020, protest activity grew. Several of the protests happening in the second half of 2020 were organized by residents of the far eastern city of Khabarovsk. Protesters took to the city's streets to express their opposition to the arrest of Sergey Furgal, Khabarovsk governor and member of the right-wing opposition Liberal Democratic Party. Protests in support of Furgal continued across 2020–21. This makes them one of the longest protest cycles in Russia's recent history.

Moreover, local restrictions on mass gatherings often outlasted other public health regulations relating to the pandemic. For example, at a time when bars and nightclubs in Moscow reopened, it was against the law to hold even a single-person picket – a form of protest with no risk of spreading the virus, as according to federal law, picketers holding single-person events had to be at least fifty metres away from each other. Restrictions on protests continued to be enforced selectively. Events endorsed by the regime, such as the celebration of the anniversary of the annexation of Crimea in March 2021, were permitted to go ahead uninterrupted. Protests organized by the opposition were banned. For example, in July 2020, the authorities cited the severity of the country's epidemiological situation in order to deny authorization for protests organized by the 'No!' campaign against amendments to the Russian constitution. Citing concerns about the spread of the coronavirus in Russia, the authorities also denied authorization for events organized in support of Alexei Navalny upon his return to Russia from Germany in January 2021. As these protests unfolded, the authorities even accused protest organizers and participants of deliberately contributing to the spread of coronavirus across Russia. We now turn to these protests in detail.

Protests in support of Alexei Navalny

On 17 January 2021, Alexei Navalny, a prominent Russian opposition politician introduced earlier in this chapter, was arrested in Moscow's Sheremetyevo airport. Navalny was returning to Russia from Germany, where he had spent five months recovering from being poisoned with a nerve agent. In response to Navalny's arrest, his team announced two weekends of protests, scheduled for 23 and 31 January 2021. Calling for Navalny's release and expressing broader discontent with the clampdown on civil and political freedoms in Russia, protests taking place in January 2021 across Russia were some of the largest demonstrations against Putin's rule.

Most of the protests during this period had not secured the authorities' approval to go ahead. Even before Navalny's team could apply for a protest permit in Moscow, the city authorities issued a statement advising that all and any notifications for protests submitted by Navalny supporters would be rejected on the basis of city-wide regulations that barred mass gatherings. Restrictions on mass gatherings had been re-introduced in response to the second wave of the pandemic in November 2020. The country's deteriorating epidemiological situation was also cited as a pretext for banning protests in places where local Navalny teams had applied for permission to protest, such as the cities of Vladimir, Belgorod, and Irkutsk.

Despite restrictions and the lack of prior approval, demonstrations in support of Alexei Navalny were held across Russia from January to February 2021, from Kaliningrad to Vladivostok. The first day of nationwide protests took place on 23 January 2021. These protests attracted tens of thousands of participants. Protesters returned to the streets of Russia on 31 January. To dampen protest attendance, the authorities shut down seven central metro stations in Moscow and blocked off streets. *Nevsky Prospekt*, St Petersburg's main avenue, was also shut down. Thousands of demonstrators faced arrest and police brutality. Onsite surveys of those participating in the January protests have shown that Navalny's attempted poisoning and subsequent arrest not only exacerbated underlying frustrations with the regime, but also mobilized old and new constituencies (Erpyleva and Zhuravlev 2021). In the lead-up and aftermath of these protests, the police detained several members of Navalny's team and other well-known activists. Searches of 'Team Navalny' headquarters and of individuals' homes were also used to intimidate protest organizers and their families.

On 4 February 2021, Leonid Volkov, Navalny's chief of staff, announced that protests would be suspended until the spring and the summer. In Volkov's own words, the continuation of protest would lead to the campaign's offices being paralyzed, making it impossible to continue campaigning ahead of the 2021 parliamentary election. Yet, when news broke of Navalny's deteriorating health, protesters returned to the streets. While protest turnout did not match those of earlier demonstrations, the police crackdown was harsh. According to estimates, approximately 1,500 people were arrested on a single day alone.

The 2021 crackdown on civil society dismantled Alexei Navalny's Anti-Corruption Foundation and other independent civil society organizations, such as *Memorial*, which had the capacity to coordinate further national protests. In the aftermath of the winter protests, and a few short months ahead of the parliamentary elections of September 2021, a court in Moscow also banned Navalny's Anti-Corruption Foundation and regional offices with immediate effect. Designated as 'extremist', organizations linked to Navalny were ordered to cease all activities, putting anyone continuing to work for them at risk of imprisonment. In these circumstances, Navalny-linked organizations were forced to disband, later relaunching only abroad. By knocking Navalny himself and his organizational network out of action, the Russian authorities had incapacitated a potent protest force.

Protesting the invasion of Ukraine

When news of Russia's invasion of Ukraine broke out, many Russians took to the streets to express their opposition to the invasion and to Putin. According to estimates from OVD-Info, between 24 February and 13 March 2022, at least 498 demonstrations took place across 154 cities. While the number of protest participants remains unclear, it is estimated that 15,000 people were detained across these protests. This was approximately the number of protesters who contacted OVD-Info for legal advice during this period. The police responded with excessive force to the anti-war protests, beating and manhandling peaceful demonstrators. Anti-war protesters taking to the streets during this period faced arrests and police brutality. It is estimated that the police responded with violence, beatings, and arrests in up to a staggering 92 and 98 per cent of anti-war protests taking place in February and March 2022 respectively (Tertytchnaya 2023).

Those injured during anti-war protests were refused medical assistance, while several police stations did not allow detained protesters to access legal advice. Arrested demonstrators also reported experiencing torture and ill-treatment, including sexualized police violence, at the hands of the authorities. Within weeks of the invasion, the majority of civil society leaders and activists were either detained or had fled the country.

The news of partial mobilization in September 2022 was again met with a surge in acts of dissent, especially in the ethnic republics of the North Caucasus. Ethnic republics, some of the hardest hit by casualties in Ukraine, were also disproportionately affected by partial mobilization. Reports suggest that women repeatedly gathered outside military recruitment centres in Grozny and Makhachkala to express their opposition to the invasion and to the draft. Other citizens in the North Caucasus engaged in acts of resistance such as road closures. Yet, protests against the draft were poorly coordinated and failed to build momentum. While unsuccessful at shaping Russians' views of the war or government policy, women's anti-war activism and growing mobilization in the ethnic republics could have long-lasting consequences. As Guzel Yusupova (2023) reminds us, such acts of resistance were especially meaningful for individuals who engaged in them and for targeted communities. In a similar vein, anti-war mobilization in the ethnic republics emphasizes the importance of better understanding the origins and consequences of protest mobilization across Russia and how people in Russia's regions most affected by war casualties and the draft feel about the invasion and the authorities.

A year after the invasion of Ukraine, at the time of this writing, a Russian anti-war movement had failed to materialize. Developments already reviewed in this chapter, including escalating repression, the dismantling of opposition networks, as well as the state's brutal response to protest staged in support of Alexei Navalny in 2021 and against the invasion of Ukraine in early 2022 may partly account for this. The onset of the invasion also coincided with a broader decline in Russians' willingness to take to the streets. Within the first months of Russia's invasion of Ukraine, the share of Russians willing to participate in political protests shrank. Nationally representative surveys of voting-age respondents, fielded by reputable polling firms such as the Levada Centre, suggest that just 9 per cent of Russians reported that they would be willing to participate in political protests if they were to take place in the country in May 2022, down from 18 per cent in February 2022.

Nonetheless, citizens continued to express their opposition to the war, even if in subtle and symbolic ways. Although less visible than street protests, symbolic acts of resistance have been widespread. For example, since the early days of the invasion, citizens have replaced price tags on supermarket shelves with anti-war messages. An Instagram page titled '*malenkii piket*', or little protest, has recorded over 1,000 miniature figurines placed across Russia holding tiny placards with anti-war slogans. In a similar vein, reacting to indications that referring to the invasion as 'invasion' or 'war' would breach laws against the spread of 'false information', citizens began using the formulation 'Net V***e' on posters, censoring the slogan No War ['Net Voine']. In one case, a woman in Tyumen was charged with discrediting the armed forces for writing 'Net V***e' on the pavement of a city square, but argued in court that she had in fact meant 'Net Voble' – no to a type of fish known in Russian as *vobla*, and in English as the Caspian roach. Following the publicity around this case, images of fish became a veiled symbol of anti-war sentiment, appearing on posters, graffiti, and online spaces. The '*Net Voine*' expression has been taken up even more obliquely in references to the number of letters in the slogan. For example, some posters have featured only ellipses, with three and five dots used in sequence. To express their opposition to the invasion, Russians also engaged in other forms of resistance, such as open letters, train derailments, and even arson. To this day, members of Russia's Feminist Anti-War resistance movement walk through central city squares dressed in black and holding white flowers, in remembrance of the invasion's casualties. To spread awareness of atrocities committed in Ukraine, members of Russia's feminist anti-war resistance movement also distribute leaflets with anti-war messages and leave anti-war messages on banknotes.

Demonstrations organized to express support for the invasion grew in the spring of 2022, largely as a response to widespread anti-war protest. These events, covered extensively by local and federal media, aimed to portray a country that was rallying around the president and the war. Pro-war meetings were organized by local authorities, war veterans, and other pro-regime civil society organizations, such as the Young Army Cadets National Movement. True to its identity as an opposition force loyal to the Kremlin, the Communist Party of the Russian Federation also offered its full support to the invasion of Ukraine and led pro-war protests during the country. About a quarter of all pro-war demonstrations occurring during February 2022–23 were organized by the communists (Tertytchnaya 2023).

Conclusion

Following the invasion of Ukraine, the Russian authorities moved swiftly to criminalize anti-war protests. As the costs of protest participation increased, visible street protests gave way to more subtle and symbolic acts of resistance. As this chapter shows, attacks against civil society and opposition leaders had been on the rise long before the invasion. Laws intended to crack down on the opposition and to restrict independent civil society organizations – revised in the aftermath of the electoral protests of 2011–12 and following the annexation of Crimea – have only multiplied in recent months. Recent developments, combined with the attack on independent media and free speech have also made Russian protests and acts of resistance harder to study. Yet, the need to monitor acts of dissent across Russia, including symbolic acts of resistance, has never been greater.

Questions for discussion

1 Under what conditions should autocrats be more fearful of protests?
2 Why do the Russian authorities use the law to manage dissent?
3 Why did an anti-war movement fail to materialize in the aftermath of Russia's invasion of Ukraine?
4 Are street protests more consequential than other types of political action?
5 In what ways is Russia representative of other electoral autocracies in the ways it manages protest?

Recommended readings

Dollbaum, Jan Matti, Lallouet, Morvan, and Ben Noble. 2021. *Navalny: Putin's Nemesis, Russia's Future*? C Hurst & Co Publishers Ltd.
Frye, Timothy, and Ekaterina Borisova. 2019. 'Elections, Protest and Trust in Government: A Natural Experiment from Russia.' *The Journal of Politics* 81:3, 820–32.

Lankina, Tomila and Katerina Tertytchnaya. 2020. 'Protest in Electoral Autocracies: A New Dataset.' *Post-Soviet Affairs.* 36(1), pp. 20–36.

Lerner, Alexis, M. 2021. 'The Co-Optation of Dissent in Hybrid States: Post-Soviet Graffiti in Moscow.' *Comparative Political Studies.* 54(10), pp. 1757–85.

Smyth, Regina. 2020. *Elections, Protest, and Authoritarian Regime Stability. Russia 2008–2020.* Cambridge University Press.

14

Climate Change

Debra Javeline

Like all countries, Russia is being transformed by global climate change. In some Russian regions, these transformations are even greater than the global average. Nevertheless, Russia's political leaders largely ignore the need to address climate change and often assert that climate change brings net benefits to the country. The unwillingness of Russia's government to address climate change has implications for domestic politics, economics, health, and human safety and also threatens international efforts to address the climate emergency.

This chapter reviews the impacts of climate change on Russia and Russia's minimalist response. It then situates Russia's domestic climate inaction in the context of global climate governance. The chapter ends with an analysis of the climate impacts of Russia's war in Ukraine.

Russia in the context of global climate change

The Earth has warmed more than 1°C above preindustrial levels and is on track to reach 1.5°C by 2040 (IPCC 2018). The warming is already resulting in catastrophic impacts across the planet. Ecosystems have changed, limiting the services they provide to humans, such as water resources and food. Heatwaves, droughts, wildfires, heavy precipitation events, and rising sea levels threaten humans globally (IPCC 2018).

Russia is warming more than twice as fast as the planet as a whole, and its Arctic region is warming nearly four times faster (Rantanen et al. 2022).

Given that much of the country's historical climate has been frigid and inhospitable, warming might seem appealing. For example, Russian agriculture might seem to benefit from warmer temperatures by increasing crop yield. However, warming is only one dimension of climate change, which also involves increasingly frequent and long-lasting droughts, wildfires, and floods, changing soil properties, and other impacts that diminish crop yield, and the aggregate results of these positive and negative impacts are unclear. Similarly, Russia's urban residents might seem to benefit from warmer winters that reduce need for heating and improve hydropower generation, but these benefits are likely offset by the harmful climate impacts of flooding and damage to buildings, roads, sewage systems, and other infrastructure (Anisimov and Kokorev 2017; Katsova et al. 2022).

Most other impacts of climate change are unequivocally negative for Russia. Indeed, Russia's geography makes it especially vulnerable to climate change. Some 10 per cent of the country is tundra – the flat, treeless Arctic region with permanently frozen subsoil called permafrost. Warming disturbs this permanence and changes life for inhabitants who now live on unstable ground. Other distinctive aspects of Russia's geography lend themselves to distinct climate impacts, such as burning Arctic peatlands (Witze 2020). Throughout the country, heatwaves, wildfires, and floods have caused, and will continue to cause, deaths and property destruction. Human health impacts from climate change include infectious diseases from flooding, the revival of so-called 'zombie viruses' from thawing permafrost, and the wider transmission of diseases carried by ticks, mosquitos, and other insects (Alempic et al. 2022; Revich et al. 2019, 2022). Impacts on infrastructure also result from flooding and thawing permafrost, with the latter causing soil instability and damaging building foundations, pipelines, roads, health care facilities, and public utilities (Revich 2020; Savilov et al. 2020; Hjort et al. 2022).

Russia is partly responsible for the global changes that are so affecting its own country. Scientists attribute global temperature increase to the emission of greenhouse gases, predominantly carbon dioxide (CO_2), methane (CH_4), and nitrous oxide (N_2O). These emissions result from human activities, such as electricity, heat, transportation, industry, agriculture, and deforestation, or the clearing of trees that would otherwise serve as a carbon sink, meaning that they take carbon dioxide from the atmosphere and sequester (or store) it. Russia's expansive forests are the largest in the world, covering approximately half of the country with an estimated 640 billion trees, or more than a fifth of the world's trees, and the carbon sequestration of Russia's forests helps counteract climate change (Pearce 2021). However, Russia is currently the world's fourth largest emitter of greenhouse gases and the third highest CO_2 emitter in history (Zagoruichyk 2022). Its per capita emissions are lower than those of the United States, but higher than those of China and the EU (Kozin 2021). Planetary health, including the health of Russians, depends on Russia's leaders taking action to combat climate change.

The government's weak *mitigation* response

The international community calls for measures to mitigate climate change, or reduce greenhouse gas emissions (IPCC 2018). Such measures include decreased reliance on fossil fuels, shifting agricultural practices that release excess carbon dioxide, methane, or nitrous oxide, and protecting forests, peatlands, and other ecosystems that historically have served as carbon sinks. To date, very few mitigation measures have been implemented in Russia. Russia's climate inaction persists despite the passage in 2009 of a Climate Doctrine and the 2009 creation of a position as advisor to the president on climate.

The Russian state owns or controls most Russian energy companies and is a major exporter of oil and gas. The revenues from these exports – as well as the exports from carbon-intensive industries such as metallurgy, fertilizer production, and chemicals – power the federal budget (Makarov et al. 202: 1251). As a result, the Russian economy depends on the continued global reliance on fossil fuels (Gustafson 2021). For Russia's current political leaders, whose interests intertwine with the interests of the nation's business elites, political power also depends on continued global reliance on fossil fuels and the revenue generated from that dependence.

Russian political leaders thus prefer to downplay or ignore the negative impacts of climate change on Russia, sometimes flatly denying the existence of climate change while claiming that it is a Western trap for Russia and sometimes simply remaining silent about the crisis. As recently as 2019, President Vladimir Putin claimed that 'no one knows the true cause of climate change' and that humanity's impact on the global climate 'is very difficult, if not impossible' to determine (Zagoruichyk 2022). Mainstream political parties in Russia ignore climate change; green political parties or opposition parties with a green agenda fail to get public support and have not proposed concrete policies beyond declaring the need to address climate change (Semenov 2021). The silence extends to the legislature, where neither the Duma nor Federation Council entertain meaningful debate on climate change, let alone pass legislation to require or encourage mitigation (Semenov 2021).

To the extent that climate change is acknowledged, powerful officials have tried to find paths for fossil fuel business-as-usual. One prominent Energy Ministry official advocates for pushing through big fossil fuel extraction projects while the opportunity still exists (Ministry of Energy 2020) – that is, before a global clean energy transition makes such extraction unprofitable – and the Ministry of Foreign Affairs advocates for climate change perspectives that allow fossil fuel extraction (Dobrovidova 2021). Russian political officials also prefer to emphasize the perceived advantages of climate change for Russia, including the supposed increase in agricultural yield, improved living conditions in formerly brutal climates, and in particular the commercial and industrial opportunities afforded by a year-round sea route in a melted Arctic Ocean (Lustgarten 2020).

While Russia's forests play an important global role in carbon sequestration, Russia uses these natural processes largely as an excuse for continued greenhouse gas emissions, 'counting' the sequestration as an offset or credit (Pearce 2021). Russia is on track to increase its emissions due to expanded production of gas, oil, and coal, which together provide more than 60 per cent of electricity generation in the country (Zagoruichyk 2022). Russia will thus likely continue to be a major source of the emissions that cause the country so much harm.

Russia's scientists are actively studying climate change and its impacts on Russia. The key agency conducting this important analysis is the Ministry for Natural Resources and the Environment (MNRE), and especially the MNRE's Federal Service for Hydrometeorology and Environmental Monitoring (*Rosgidromet*). These state-sponsored scientists produce sophisticated reports, including estimates of potential economic losses from climate change amounting to 1–2 per cent of GDP (Gusev 2016: 45). However, scientists are largely marginalized in Russian policymaking (Korppoo 2016, Katsova et al. 2022), and it is unclear whether their reports have any impact.

Russian citizens have not elevated climate change as a priority, and many share the suspicions of Russian policymakers that international climate diplomacy is an anti-Russian Western-led conspiracy (Tynkkynen and Tynkkynen 2018: 1115; Korppoo 2020: 119–20). Environmental issues such as local pollution, forest fires, or flooding drive at least 10 per cent of protests in Russia (Lankina 2018), but protesters rarely link these concerns to climate change. Should more citizens become climate-concerned, protest remains unlikely due to decreasing tolerance for public activism by Russia's wartime authorities.

Russia would benefit greatly from forward-thinking political officials who initiate plans to diversify the Russian economy in anticipation of a post-carbon future. Such diversification is imperative for the country's long-term economic sustainability and may also matter even in the short term of the next decade, because climate change poses threats to Russia's prime revenue generator: the production and distribution of fossil fuels. Climate change impacts, such as sea shore erosion, fires, and extreme precipitation events, cause damage to ports and oil and gas infrastructure, and while permafrost thaw and ice melt enable access to previously inaccessible and cost-ineffective extraction fields, thaw and melt also jeopardize extraction (Hjort et al. 2022; Katsova et al. 2022, 310–11).

Diversifying the Russian economy would require identifying strengths in industry, science, or other economic spheres that are unrelated to fossil fuels (Henderson and Mitrova 2020). So far, Russia's leaders have shown little interest in identifying such strengths, let alone promoting renewable energy sources such as wind power (Henderson and Mitrova 2020; Koch and Tynkkynen 2021). (Renewables currently account for less than 1 per cent of electricity generation in the country, and there are no investments or other signs that this sector will grow in the near future.) Additional motivation for economic diversification might have come from Western sanctions that followed Russia's invasion of Ukraine, potentially showing the precariousness of banking the country's entire economy on fossil fuel exports. However, sanctions seem to have motivated only a desperate search for alternative buyers (Morozov 2020; Babaeva 2022; Galaktionov 2022).

The government's weak *adaptation* response

Russia would also benefit from forward-thinking political officials who initiate and implement proactive measures to reduce the country's vulnerability to climate impacts. This process of vulnerability reduction is known as adapting to climate change. By not adapting, and by not even acknowledging the high risks of climate change, the country's political leaders fail to ensure or at least maximize the protection of Russia's people and property. For example, disaster prevention is not a priority in Russia, and while competent post-disaster management generates public support (Lazarev et al. 2014), such competent management will be in short supply as disasters increase in frequency and intensity.

To be fair, most of the world's governments have implemented few adaptation measures, and most of the world's 8 billion people are vulnerable to some climate impacts. There is little evidence anywhere of 'transformational adaptation', or responses to climate change that go beyond incremental changes to more fundamental changes of socio-ecological systems (Berrang-Ford et al. 2021). Rewarding disaster management, especially the delivery of disaster relief spending, over disaster preparedness is an unfortunate feature of even the most democratic political systems (Healy and Malhotra 2009). These perverse incentives make adaptation planning and implementation difficult.

Still, even in this global context of unpreparedness, Russian unpreparedness is notable. The United Nations Environment Programme (UNEP) publishes an annual assessment called the Adaptation Gap Report. In the 2021 report, Russia is mentioned for finally having produced its first National Adaptation Action Plan, and Eastern Europe more generally is listed as a region where little adaptation is taking place (UNEP 2021: 21, 40). This minimal progress – or 'Too Little, Too Slow', as the 2022 Adaptation Gap Report is titled – puts people and property at serious risk (UNEP 2022a).

Russia may face heightened challenges from adaptation deficits if the country becomes a target destination for migrants from poor communities in the aftermath of disasters or fleeing other environmental conditions (Blondin 2019; Sagynbekova 2021). The World Bank estimates that 3.7 million climate migrants might soon arrive in Russia from Central Asia, Eastern Europe, and elsewhere (Clement et al. 2021). Russian Deputy Prime Minister Viktoria Abramchenko acknowledged this climate migration as 'inevitable' (TASS 2021), but climate migration is not a policy priority nor even mentioned in the limited adaptation planning that Russia has pursued.

There are some small versions of adaptation plans for specific economic sectors in Russia. Specifically, the Russian government approved ten plans to adapt to climate change in: transport, fuel and energy, construction and housing, agriculture and fishing, environmental management, healthcare, the Arctic, civil defence and emergency situations, industry and trade, and sanitation and public health (TASS 2022). There are also government-sponsored efforts to reduce the country's vulnerability that are not labelled as adaptation. For example, in the name of national food security, the Russian government invests in seed technologies for Russia's main crops, wheat, barley, sugar beets, and potatoes (Dobrovidova 2019). If successful, these technologies could also serve as adaptation to harmful climate change impacts. Specific Russian regions – including Belgorod, Volgograd, Vologda, Kemerovo, Kursk, Penza, and the illegally annexed Crimea – have developed plans to address climate vulnerabilities, such as water scarcity and extreme weather impacts, and other regions are following suit (TASS 2022).

However, opportunities to adapt are more frequently lost, as public health plans or strategic plans for specific cities do little more than acknowledge climate change or fail to mention it at all (Revich et al. 2020; Revich 2021). Documents that acknowledge climate change, report adaptation needs, and even describe plans for addressing those needs are not backed by financing and are rarely implemented (Moe et al. 2022).

Like for mitigation, the minimal acknowledgement that adaptation is necessary, and the resulting deficiency of actual adaptation, stem from Russian elites' commitment to short term personal gain. Such neglect will prove costly for Russia, as evidenced by recent responses to deadly climate events. For example, in 2001, the Lena River flooded and killed eight people, infected 39,000 people with hepatitis A, thanks to the overwhelmed sewage system, and damaged 20,000 properties, twenty-six schools, seven healthcare facilities, and public utilities and transportation infrastructure. Rather than think about long-term adaptation, the authorities quickly rebuilt the city on the same vulnerable food plain at 400 times the cost of preventive measures (Anisimov and Kokorev 2017). Given the high probability of future flooding, such rebuilding is commonly labeled 'maladaptation', or action that increases risk of adverse climate-related outcomes, rather than decreases risk.

Russia and global climate governance

It is common to hear climate change described as a collective action problem – indeed, *the single greatest* collective action problem of all time (e.g. Ostrom 2009). The logic of collective action theory involves free riding. In the context of climate change, free riding manifests in the desire to benefit from a stable climate without making any sacrifices to achieve that stability. Every country presumably wants to free ride off the efforts of other countries. Seen through the lens of collective action theory, Russia's minimal climate actions are designed to outmanoeuvre other countries, encouraging reductions in greenhouse gas emissions elsewhere, while Russia itself continues to produce an outsize portion of global emissions.

Some scholars now challenge this paradigm and describe climate change as distributive conflict between holders of fossil fuel assets, also known as climate forcing agents, and climate vulnerable agents (Aklin and Mildenberger 2020; Colgan et al 2021). The battle to retain their political and economic advantages drives the climate forcing agents to deny the existence of climate change and obstruct climate action. The distributive conflict model recognizes that 'climate policies create new economic winners and losers' (Aklin and Mildenberger 2020) and that the losers are staving off the time when asset revaluation threatens their very existence (Colgan et al. 2021). Seen through the lens of distributive conflict, Russia's minimal climate actions are designed to postpone as long as possible any loss of resources and power for the nation's corporate and political elite and for the country itself.

Whether Russia engages in free riding or distributive conflict, Russia's actions have resulted in minimal contributions to international mitigation efforts. The United Nations Framework Convention on Climate Change (UNFCCC) was established at the first Earth Summit in Rio de Janeiro in 1992, and starting in 1995, almost all countries of the world have met annually under the auspices of the UNFCCC at the Conferences of Parties (COP). At the third COP in 1997, countries adopted the Kyoto Protocol, which set obligations for the reduction of greenhouse gas emissions by industrialized countries. Russia ratified both the UNFCCC and the Kyoto Protocol, but only after delays of two years and seven years respectively, signalling its lukewarm commitment (Zagoruichyk 2022).

Russia had little to lose and something to gain from ratifying the Kyoto Protocol. Because another climate action laggard and sometime obstructionist, the United States, refused to ratify, Russia's ratification became critical to the very existence of the Protocol, and it could bargain with other countries diplomatically and boost its image as a good global citizen and partner in international affairs (Henry and Sundstrom 2007). The negotiations ended with terms that benefited Russia by requiring little sacrifice, specifically the choice of the year 1990 as the base year for emissions targets. In 1990, the USSR was on the brink of collapse, and over the next decade, economic collapse followed, including the shutdown of many Soviet-era industries. With fewer factories burning fossil fuels, this incredibly difficult post-Soviet economic period unintentionally saw reduced greenhouse gas emissions. By negotiating successfully for 1990 as the benchmark year at a time when its emissions were already significantly lower, Russia could actually increase emissions and still claim compliance with its Kyoto commitments. Indeed, that is what Russia did. In the post-Kyoto period, Russia became the world's largest exporter of natural gas, second largest exporter of oil, and third largest energy consumer (Henry and Sundstrom 2007, p. 47).

For the past few decades, Russia has continued to walk a fine line in engaging in international mitigation discussions without actually taking significant steps to reduce emissions of greenhouse gases. Its strategy has been to deny climate change or argue that Russia is already doing its part (Tynkkynen and Tynkkynen 2018; Godzimirski 2022; Korppoo 2022). Climate policy in the 2010s included national targets for the reduction of greenhouse gas emissions but again left loopholes for Russia to increase emissions (Gusev 2016).

In 2015, the 196 parties, or member countries of the UNFCCC, participated in COP21 in Paris and adopted the landmark Paris Agreement, which aims to limit global temperature increase to below 2°C above pre-industrial levels, and preferably below 1.5°C. Each country would determine its own emissions targets, or nationally determined contributions. Russia ratified the Paris Agreement, but again only after a delay, this time four years. In 2020, Russia pledged to keep emissions 30 per cent below 1990 levels by 2030, using 'the maximum possible absorptive capacity of forests and other ecosystems'. As with the Kyoto Protocol, Russia's Paris Agreement pledge is unambitious, given the 1990 reference date and the focus on forests and other ecosystems as carbon sinks, which together allow the country to meet its targets without actually reducing fossil fuel use or other carbon-emitting practices (Gusev 2016; Zagoruichyk 2022). The motivations behind Russia's climate inaction are again financial: If all nations kept their pledges and reduced emissions as promised in the Paris Agreement, Russia's economy would suffer (Makarov et al. 2020).

The climate impacts of Russia's war in Ukraine

Climate change is increasingly regarded as a threat multiplier for violent conflict (e.g. Hendrix and Salehyan 2012; Koubi 2019; von Uexkull and

Buhaug 2021). While not a primary motivator of Russia's invasion of Ukraine, climate change factored into the conflict. Crimea, the first region of Ukraine to be attacked in 2014, relied for 70–85 per cent of its water on the North Crimea Canal. In response to Russia's illegal seizure and annexation, Ukraine dammed the Canal, leaving Russian-occupied Crimea dependent on limited local water sources. Higher temperatures and decreased rainfall caused pollution, drying rivers, and near-empty reservoirs and cost the Russian government billions of rubles for reservoir reconstruction and the building of water treatment and desalination plants across Crimea (Vynogradova 2020). When Russia invaded Ukraine again in 2022, one of its first acts was to blow up the dam and then to try to take the Ukrainian province of Kherson, partly to control the Canal and therefore steady water availability for Russian-controlled Crimea (Troianovski 2021; Rutland 2022). In this sense, resource diminishment exacerbated by climate change could be said to play a role in hostilities between countries.

In turn, the hostilities exacerbate climate change. War is carbon-intensive due to exploded munitions, missiles, and mines, fires burning infrastructure and forests, and emissions from broken gas lines. Even before any shots are fired, military vehicles such as tanks, personnel carriers, and aircraft burn extraordinary amounts of carbon-emitting fuel, with jet fuel being particularly 'dirty', and the defence industry emits greenhouse gases in the production and distribution of missiles, munitions, vehicles, and other supplies (Simon 2022). During Russia's war so far, leakage from the Nord Stream 1 and 2 pipelines released large amounts of methane, a greenhouse gas more potent than carbon dioxide, in quantities that exceed emissions from warfare (de Klerk et al. 2022).

When the war ends, rebuilding Ukraine will also be carbon-intensive. It will require heavy machinery, the production of cement and concrete to replace demolished residences and other buildings, and the transportation of materials to construction sites. Although rebuilding could potentially include low-carbon construction materials that act as carbon sinks, the sheer scale of renovation driven by such widespread destruction will likely encourage use of traditional construction methods (de Klerk et al. 2022). Combining these emissions from war preparation, actual warfare, and anticipated post-war reconstruction, estimates as of November 2022 are that seven months of Russia's aggression resulted in at least 100 million additional tCO_2e (tonnes of carbon dioxide equivalent), which, for reference, is the same amount as emitted by The Netherlands during that same period, and is likely a significant underestimate (de Klerk et al. 2022).

War has other environmental impacts with likely implications for climate change. Russian forces have conducted military activities such as missile strikes and heavy shelling that resulted in fires and the release of toxic industrial chemicals (UNEP 2022). A cruise missile hitting hazardous waste facilities has led to excess ammonia in soil and river water and compromised drinking water for some residents, further diminishing the limited resource, and Ukrainian tailing storage facilities containing over six billion tonnes of industrial waste may also pose risk to air and water from chemical pollution (UNEP 2022). Missile strikes have damaged oil refineries and other infrastructures for oil and gas processing, in some cases forcing a halt in operations that might seem consistent with mitigation goals. However, attacks on oil and gas facilities typically involve the burning of these targets, suggesting no benefit for climate change mitigation, only harmful releases without actually helping meet Ukrainian energy needs. Disruption to Ukraine's agricultural sector has also resulted in a decrease of greenhouse gas emissions (UNEP 2022, 27), but hardly seems a desirable means. Given Ukraine's important role in providing corn, wheat, and barley for export, as well as fertilizers, Russia's war has dangerously increased the cost of living across the globe and caused an additional 47 million people to face acute hunger (UNEP 2022, 27). The war has disrupted global biodiversity conservation, including protection of Russia's forests and peatlands, and thus disrupted related climate change mitigation efforts (Gallo-Cajiao et al. 2023).

The United States and Western Europe may decide to boost military spending in order to retain a strong presence in the region, meaning continued use of fossil fuels above levels planned when these countries committed to the Paris Agreement. Moreover, energy security has reemerged as a priority for countries that once depended on Russian fossil fuels, and this concern may distract attention from the climate crisis (Simon 2022). In some cases, countries may rely more heavily on coal as a substitute for natural gas, slowing progress toward a clean energy transition (de Klerk et al. 2022).

Russia's isolation from the international community has dangerous implications for global mitigation efforts. Its pariah status means it no longer has incentives to cooperate on international climate policy as it did for the Kyoto Protocol or the Paris Agreement. Given Russia's continued status as the world's fourth largest emitter of greenhouse gases, Russia's noncooperation could slow or derail the collective efforts of other countries (Overland 2022).

Rejection of Russian fossil fuels by other nations is perhaps the only potential positive contribution of Russia's war to global mitigation efforts. The war put the spotlight on European dependence on Russia, especially the precarity of reliance on Russian natural gas during the cold European winters when Russia could just cut supplies. This heightened awareness, as well as sanctions on Russian oil, petroleum products, and coal, has strengthened the case for renewable energy sources, which are increasingly cost-effective and secure (Overland 2022). Substituting domestic fossil fuels for Russian fossil fuels, and reversing progress on mitigation, remains a climate-threatening option for many nations (Bennhold and Tankersley 2022), but it is also possible that Russia's invasion may accelerate the clean energy transition.

Conclusion: Russia's future in a changed climate

As Russia continues on its current fossil-fuel-dependent path, the country experiences short-term financial gain that disproportionately benefits the country's political and corporate elite. The gain also provides enough revenue for the current provision of social welfare benefits and therefore seems to generate public acceptance of the government path or at least seems to minimize public opposition. However, Russia's short-term financial gain masks long-term problems for its economy and for the health and well-being of its citizens, who will be increasingly vulnerable to the impacts of climate change with few plans to reduce those vulnerabilities.

Because of the close relationship between fossil fuels, business, and political power in Russia, economic and ecological problems will at some point become political problems. When – not if – oil and gas revenues decline, and when – not if – catastrophic climate change impacts upend the lives of unprecedented numbers of Russian citizens, existing Russian political institutions and leaders will need to respond in some way but will likely be ill-equipped. The consequences of such instability in a climate-changed Russia are unclear but have great potential to result in power struggles and other problems that distract further from mitigation and adaptation efforts. Thus, the fate of Russia will shape the fate of the global climate, and vice versa.

Questions for discussion

1   How is Russia vulnerable to the impacts of global climate change? Which vulnerabilities are common to other countries, and which are unique to Russia?

2   Why do Russian authorities downplay the impacts of climate change to their country and the world?

3   Why has Russia engaged in past international efforts to mitigate climate change, and what are the prospects for current and future participation in such efforts?

4   How does Russia's war in Ukraine influence global climate change, and how does climate change factor into the war?

5   Assuming Russia's political authorities wanted to address climate change, what steps would they need to take to reduce the country's emissions of greenhouse gases (mitigate) and reduce the country's vulnerability (adapt)?

Recommended readings

Gustafson, Thane. 2021. *Klimat: Russia in the Age of Climate Change.* Cambridge: Harvard University Press.

Henry, Laura A., and Lisa McIntosh Sundstrom. 2007. 'Russia and the Kyoto Protocol: Seeking an Alignment of Interests and Image.' *Global Environmental Politics* 7(4): 47–69.

Makarov, Igor, Henry Chen, and Sergey Paltsev. 2020. 'Impacts of Climate Change Policies Worldwide on the Russian Economy.' *Climate Policy* 20, No. 10: 1242–56.

Tynkkynen, Veli-Pekka, and Nina Tynkkynen. 2018. 'Climate Denial Revisited: (Re)contextualising Russian Public Discourse on Climate Change During Putin 2.0.' *Europe-Asia Studies* 70, No. 7: 1103–20.

Korppoo, Anna. 2022. 'Russian Discourses on Benefits and Threats from International Climate Diplomacy.' *Climatic Change* 170: 1–24.

15

Russia's Invasion and Ukraine's Resistance

Maria Popova and Oxana Shevel

Russia's invasion of Ukraine did not start on 24 February 2022, but almost exactly eight years earlier in 2014. At that time, undercover Russian forces took control of Crimea and, soon after, harnessed local protests in Donbas and instigated an armed challenge to the central government in Kyiv. Over the next eight years, Russia hoped to use fighting in Donbas and peace negotiations known as the Minsk process to vassalize a destabilized and weakened Ukraine. Ukraine focused on reforming its state institutions to withstand Russia's aggression and moved closer to Euroatlantic integration. The West condemned Russia's illegal annexation of Crimea and pledged solidarity with Ukraine, but hoped to forge compromise through the Minsk process and normalize relations with Russia.

Instead of gradual normalization, 2022 brought a major escalation in Russia's aggression against Ukraine. In the early hours of 24 February that year, Russia launched a full-scale invasion and aimed straight for the capital Kyiv. In a long speech on the eve of the invasion, Russian President Vladimir Putin announced a 'special military operation' that sought to 'de-Nazify' and 'de-militarize' Ukraine. This was to be done by removing Ukrainian President Volodymyr Zelensky's elected government and disabling the Ukrainian military, which Putin claimed was perpetrating 'genocide' against the Russian-speaking population of Donbas. According to Putin, Russia's actions were in self-defence, because Ukraine posed a threat to Russian security – allegedly due to NATO plans to use it as a staging ground for attacking Russia (Putin 2022). The whole world was shocked to see Russia embark on a war of conquest against its sovereign neighbour.

Many were also shocked to see that Ukraine mounted a quick and fierce resistance. Russia's expectation, expressed frequently by propagandists on prime-time TV, was that the 'special military operation' would be over in a matter of days, not only due to Russian military might, but also because Ukrainians would welcome Russian troops who came to 'liberate' them from Zelensky's purportedly 'Nazi' rule. Russia had been pushing the false narrative about the Ukrainian government being a 'Nazi junta' both to Russian citizens and to the world, despite the far right's tiny representation in Ukrainian politics and Zelensky's moderate political views and Jewish background. Western governments and pundits also expected Ukraine to fall quickly to Russia's invasion. The discussion focused on how Russia would run occupation authorities and how much of a guerilla insurgency Russia might face because the overwhelming assumption was that Kyiv would fall rather quickly and the Ukrainian army would be defeated by Russia's (Kagan 2022).

Ukraine quickly delivered a shocker. President Zelensky refused an evacuation offer from concerned Western partners and chose to rally Ukrainians to defend their country. On 26 February, he recorded a defiant selfie video from central Kyiv. His message to Ukrainians and to the world was loud and clear: 'I am here. We are not putting down arms. We will be defending our country' ('I'm here': Zelenskyy's message to his people Saturday morning' 2022). Ukrainians from all corners of the country heard him and acted in unison, flooding army recruitment offices to volunteer to serve and jumpstarting volunteer organizations to help with logistics, crowdfunding, and humanitarian aid.

The Ukrainian army and territorial defence units quickly stopped Russia's attempt to capture Kyiv, and by the end of March, Russian forces had no choice but to withdraw from the capital region. After the blitzkrieg attempt on the capital had failed, in April Russia refocused its efforts on capturing territory in the east and south of the country. Far from overpowering its opponent, the Russian army suffered more losses just in the first few months of the Russo-Ukrainian war than the USSR had suffered in a full decade of war in Afghanistan (Carbonaro 2022). Russia managed to occupy swaths of eastern and southern Ukraine, and in the fall of 2022 it attempted to formalize the conquest by announcing the annexation of four Ukrainian regions: Donetsk, Luhansk, Kherson, and Zaporizhzhia, none of which it controlled fully. Russia's strategy was to use nuclear saber-rattling to convince both Ukraine and its Western partners that once it formally laid claim to these regions, it would defend them as Russian territory, with nuclear escalation if necessary, in line with its military doctrine.

Ukraine called this bluff and in late fall 2022 liberated areas both in the east and in the south. Russian troops, which had occupied nearly 25 per cent of Ukraine's territory since 2014, ceded nearly half of the 2022 gains and retreated. No escalation followed (Breteau 2022). Despite a partial mobilization campaign and a recruitment effort in Russian prisons run by the Wagner group (a mercenary outfit run by Putin's then-protégé Yevgeny Prigozhin), Russia's winter offensive failed to achieve significant results. Instead, both the army and Wagner lost tens of thousands of troops in a battle for the small city of Bakhmut, which was entirely destroyed in the fighting. As this textbook goes to press in fall 2023, Ukraine's army is in the midst of a counteroffensive aimed at liberating all of Ukraine's territory from Russian occupation, while Russia maintains its ambition to conquer Ukraine. Both the maximalist goals of Russia's invasion and the capacity and intensity of Ukraine's resistance surpassed expectations.

What explains Russia's decision to attempt this anachronistic, illegal war of imperialist conquest to end Ukrainian statehood? What enabled Ukraine's army and society to stop the military onslaught despite the obvious disparity in size and resources between invader and invaded? Why was a diplomatic solution not possible before Russian tanks started rolling across the border?

The key to understanding Russia's full-scale invasion of Ukraine is the dramatic divergence between the two countries since 1991. As Ukraine consolidated a competitive political regime and moved towards democratic consolidation, in Russia, Putin slowly suppressed and co-opted any potential opposition and consolidated an autocracy. As Ukraine gradually committed to a distinctive self-conception of the Ukrainian nation and independent statehood, the Putinist regime's obsession with resurrecting the Russian or Soviet empire – and especially with recapturing its crown jewel, Ukraine – grew. Reconquering Ukraine was the lynchpin of the reimperialization drive and initially Russia sought to achieve it through non-military means. As the various non-military levers failed to destroy the democratic and Western-aligned Ukrainian civic nation, Russia escalated to full-scale invasion in order to destroy the 'anti-Russia' version of Ukraine that it deemed hostile and unacceptable. Ukraine, on the other hand, increasingly came to perceive the prospects of becoming a Russian vassal and a part of the 'Russian World' (a term popularized in Russia during the Putin years) as a veritable nightmare and resisting incorporation became existential. After 2014, the will to defend the state and nation from Russia's aggression became a shared goal for Ukrainians from all regions of the country.

How did Russia and Ukraine become so different and why did this divergence lead to the 2022 war? The answer to this question lies less in the domain of international politics and Russia-NATO tensions and more in the dynamics of domestic politics in Russia and Ukraine. The Russian invasion of Ukraine in 2022 was the culmination of two mutually reinforcing processes that played out in bilateral relations since the late Soviet period – Russia's revanchist, re-imperialization drive vs. Ukraine's solidifying commitment to independence. After the dissolution of the USSR, Russian elites expected, if not to restore formal control over the former Soviet states, then at least to be *primus inter pares* and still the centre of gravity of the region. Meanwhile, Ukrainian elites took independence to heart and continued the centrifugal trajectory of the late 1980s that rent the USSR asunder. The more Russia attempted to re-vassalize Ukraine, the more Ukraine became determined to prevent it, and the more Ukraine deflected re-integration attempts, the more Russia became committed to not letting Ukraine slip away. Regime divergence both fed on and exacerbated the process – a democratizing Ukraine entrenched its commitment to independent statehood and a pro-European orientation, while autocratizing Russia slipped further into imperial revanchism and anti-Westernism.

This escalatory cycle put the two countries on a collision course, especially after the 2004 Orange Revolution in Ukraine, and first led to violence in 2014 when Russia invaded Ukraine in the aftermath of the Euromaidan change of government. Russia's annexation of Crimea and the insurgency it jumpstarted in Donbas escalated the divergence between the two states even further. After an unsuccessful eight-year campaign to use the Donbas conflict to undermine Ukrainian statehood and cut off Ukraine's path towards Europe, eventually Putin decided on a full-scale invasion as the only solution to his 'Ukraine problem'.

Russia in the 1990s: Re-imperialization drive vs. capacity

Was post-communist Russia always imperialist? After all, in the late 1980s and the early 1990s under Yeltsin's leadership, Russia not only accepted but seemingly spearheaded efforts to bring down the Soviet empire. Under Yeltsin's leadership, Russia declared sovereignty from the USSR before Ukraine did, Yeltsin co-authored the Belavezha accords that disbanded the

USSR, and he urged autonomous republics within Russia itself to 'take as much sovereignty as [they] can swallow' (Kochnev 2020). During his first presidential term, Russia gradually withdrew its troops from Eastern Europe and the Baltics. It recognized the borders of most newly independent states, and with it implicitly acquiesced to millions of ethnic Russians and Russian-speakers being left outside of Russia by the USSR collapse. And in 1993, when other post-Soviet states pursued slower marketization reforms than Russia, Yeltsin favoured destroying the ruble zone that bound Russia to its former vassals economically to push through his shock therapy programme (Johnson 2018, 89). Yet what looks on the surface like deliberate steps to dismantle the Soviet empire and release the former vassals, on closer examination, was instead mainly strategic maneuvering by Yeltsin vis-a-vis his main rival Gorbachev or vis-a-vis political challengers within Russia. Despite these strategic steps, Yeltsin and most of the liberal elites in his camp held an ingrained assumption that Russia would continue to be at the centre of a wide sphere of influence, whatever the formal arrangement.

In the waning years of the USSR, Yeltsin's main political goal was to get the upper hand in his power struggle with Gorbachev. In the context of Yeltsin and Gorbachev's long, well-documented competition, Russia's declaration of sovereignty from the Soviet Union and the devolution of sovereignty to Russia's regions was Yeltsin's way of weakening Gorbachev's control over the state hierarchy. The dissolution of the union state itself was not Yeltsin's objective. After Yeltsin emerged as the most powerful figure not only in Russia but in the Soviet Union as a whole following his role in the defeat of an August 1991 anti-Gorbachev coup, keeping the union together in fact became one of Yeltsin's main concerns (Plokhy 2014, p. 173). It was only after Ukraine declared independence and refused to stay in the union that Yeltsin was forced to endorse the disbanding of the USSR. Yeltsin could not imagine a union without Ukraine, as he explained to United States President George Bush on the eve of Ukraine's December 1991 independence referendum that overwhelmingly confirmed Ukrainians' commitment to leave the USSR (Plokhy 2014, 295). When Yeltsin eventually took part in disbanding the Soviet Union behind Gorbachev's back when he signed the Belavezha agreement in December 1991, he still hoped to negotiate a new union deal with Ukraine directly (Plokhy 2014, p. 296).

Post-1991, Yeltsin prioritized market reform and state modernization over preserving the empire. Russian state weakness meant that imperial restoration had to cede precedence to more pressing problems. It would thus be misleading to characterize as examples of anti-imperialism moves that

Russia took when its hand was forced by international and domestic constraints. For example, when in 1993-1994, Russia withdrew its troops from the Baltic States, which the USSR had first occupied in 1940 and again at the end of World War II, it delayed and withdrew only in response to an American threat to cut financial aid Russia desperately needed to avoid economic collapse. Seemingly anti-imperialist Russian moves co-occurred with imperialist ones in other parts of the former USSR, further underscoring that anti-imperialism was reluctant, strategic, and limited, rather than deliberate and consistent. As Russia was preparing to withdraw troops from the Baltics, it was sending troops to intervene in other parts of the former USSR – Moldova and Georgia, both governed by leaders Russia perceived as 'anti-Russian'.

Moreover, even if Yeltsin were convinced that Russia had to 'rid itself of its imperial mission' (Yeltsin quoted in Colton 2008, 266), his position was not shared by the majority of Russian elites. His de-imperializing moves were vehemently opposed and obstructed by other political actors within Russia. For example, while Yeltsin's team wanted to scrap the ruble zone in order to speed up Russian economic reforms, the Central Bank of Russia (CBR) clashed with the executive, undermined its efforts, and fought fiercely to keep the ruble zone together. The ruble zone only fell apart when the majority of the newly independent states defied the CBR and issued their own currencies instead of ceding their monetary sovereignty to Russia (Johnson 2018, 91). The nationalists and the Communists in the Russian parliament resented Yeltsin's de-imperialization steps with even more passion than did the technocrats and perceived them as weakness or even outright treason. In 1996 the State Duma, the lower house of the Russian parliament, voted overwhelmingly to annul the Belavezha accords. In 1999, Yeltsin was nearly impeached by the Russian parliament for signing the accords (Colton 2008, 429).

In other words, post-1991, imperialism had to be reconciled with other objectives of the Russian state, such as consolidating political authority at home and strengthening the economy through international cooperation. Even as Yeltsin chose nation-building over empire-saving (Szporluk 1989), Russia saw itself as *primus inter pares* in the post-Soviet space, a role that many of the newly independent states feared and resented (President of the Republic of Estonia 1994). Imperialist goals sometimes ceded priority to other objectives, but they were always in the background and anti-imperialism as a stand-alone goal never developed. Instead, three dynamics defined relations between Russia and its neighbours in the post-Soviet era.

First, Russia always perceived the former Soviet states as not fully 'foreign'. It coined the term 'near abroad' to refer to the post-Soviet states, distinguishing them from 'truly' foreign 'far abroad' states and connoting a diminished type of sovereignty. Russia expected the 'near abroad' to remain within its sphere of influence, to display loyalty in international politics, and to steer clear of domestic policies that Russia perceived as 'anti-Russian'. In essence, Russia expected the former Soviet states to behave like its vassals. Russia's imperialism towards the former Soviet republics thus differed from Western European imperialism as it was not driven primarily by the desire to extract economic resources from the colonies, but by deep-seated entitlement to control them politically in perpetuity.

Second, Russia did not always pursue re-imperialization with the same methods and had somewhat different levels of tolerance based on the perceived historical and identity connection and geopolitical importance of its neighbouring states. Ukraine and Belarus, the two Slavic nations that Russia perceived as 'fraternal', were of critical importance, with Ukraine the more important of the two.

Third, the reality of formally independent statehood and Russia's expectation of vassalism were in inherent conflict. Independent statehood implies final authority on all matters of domestic and foreign policy. It also demands policy measures – especially urgent for new states – that legitimate the existence of a separate sovereign state and underscore its distinctiveness. Such state and nation-building policy measures include the creation of state symbols, defined borders, national citizenship, historical myths and heroes, official language, and more. But any such policies can be potentially interpreted as 'anti-Russian' if they conflict with what Russia sees as contrary to its interests and its own interpretations of the relevant histories and current identities.

The escalatory cycle of Russian re-imperialization and Ukrainian independence: From 1991 Soviet collapse to 2004 Orange Revolution

In Russia-Ukraine relations, these three dynamics together produced an escalatory cycle. The more Russia sought to fulfill its vision of restoring control over Ukraine (formally or informally), the more Ukraine pulled away and tried to consolidate real, rather than nominal, independence from Russia. The central place that Ukraine occupied in Russia's national imaginary and its geopolitical centrality to any future Russia-led polity meant that Russia cared most about Ukraine's political trajectory relative to the rest of the post-Soviet states. The escalatory cycle was thus the most obvious and the most consequential in Russia-Ukraine relations, eventually leading to the current war.

How did this process unfold? To formally dissolve the USSR in December 1991, Yeltsin secretly got together with the leaders of Ukraine and Belarus (Leonid Kravchuk and Stanislav Shushkevich, respectively) and agreed to create a loose association they called the Commonwealth of Independent States (CIS), an entity most other post-Soviet states quickly joined. The elites of independent Russia operated under the assumption that the CIS would be a new format for maintaining Russia's leading role among the post-Soviet states: While nominally independent, the successor states would continue to be tightly bound to each other economically, politically, and geostrategically. They would retain a common currency; the armed forces would be under joint command; and CIS citizenship would replace Soviet citizenship. A 1992 friendship treaty draft that Russia offered Ukraine illustrates the scope of Russia's vision. The Treaty on Friendship, Cooperation, and Partnership envisioned unification in all crucial policy domains – joint customs, taxation, trade, military, and foreign policy – and spoke of a 'single regional military-strategic space' (Kuzio 2022, 139). Over time, many in Yeltsin's camp reasoned, the former Soviet republics would gravitate back to Russia, which would become an attractive centre due to its successful marketization reforms.

However, from the very start, Ukraine resisted Russia's assumption that the two states would remain inextricably tied and Ukraine would continue to be Russia's 'little brother'. Ukraine's defiance started out as moderate and mostly driven by Ukrainian elites – an informal alliance of nationalists and national democrats ideologically committed to Ukrainian independence and former communists and new economic elites who favoured independent statehood as a means of increasing their political and economic power and international standing. Ukrainian society was divided on its future relationship to Russia. Majorities in the predominantly Russian-speaking south and east of the country favoured closer relations with Russia. But majorities in the predominantly Ukrainian-speaking west, as well as many Russian-speakers in the central regions and in the country's urban centers, including the capital city, favoured independence and a pro-Western rather than a pro-Russian orientation.

Societal divisions affected the balance of power between political forces for and against vassalism. Ukrainian governments changed, but each struck a similar balance – while giving a nod to the pro-Russian electorate and to Russia itself by falling short of implementing the ideal policies of the ideologically-driven Ukrainian nation-building elites, the governing 'centrist' elites – themselves primarily Russian-speaking and often coming from southeastern regions – still facilitated the strengthening of the state and national identity. Citizenship, language, and historical memory policies emphasized the distinctiveness of the Ukrainian nation and de-emphasized cultural and political links with Russia. Russia resented and strenuously objected to all these domestic Ukrainian policies. In the international arena, Ukrainian governments under the first two presidents, Leonid Kravchuk and Leonid Kuchma, forged a 'multi-vector' foreign policy through which Ukraine was to serve as a bridge between the West and Russia. Russia, however, kept pushing for more control over Ukrainian domestic and foreign policies. Still, through the 1990s and early 2000s, Russia's interference was moderate and limited to economic pressure through energy blackmail, leveraging media resources, and meddling in Ukrainian elections.

Russia's interference was moderate due to multifaceted domestic crises and the weakness of the Russian state in the wake of the USSR's demise. Moreover, Russia's elites were optimistic that even limited economic and diplomatic pressure to increase integration through the CIS framework would suffice to reverse the separation process and bring Ukraine back under control. During the 1990s, Russia managed to keep Ukraine largely within its geopolitical orbit, and regime divergence between the two states was not significant. Signing the Budapest Memorandum in 1994, Ukraine agreed to relinquish its nuclear warheads and transfer them to Russia, thus giving up any plausible chance of developing a nuclear deterrent and entrusting its security, in part, to Russia. In 1997, Ukraine and Russia divided the Black Sea Fleet and Ukraine agreed to allow Russia to keep its fleet in Sevastopol, Crimea. Still, Ukraine was governed by elites who adeptly resisted Russia-led initiatives to re-establish political and security-sphere integration among the post-Soviet states, but sought to build partnership with both Russia and the West.

On New Year's eve 1999-2000, Yeltsin resigned, whereupon then-Prime Minister Vladimir Putin became acting president. Putin then easily won an early presidential election and immediately set out to strengthen the state.

He quickly centralized power in the presidency by clipping the wings of the main alternative loci of power: regional elites and 'oligarchs' (big politically engaged businesspeople) who had become synonymous with the 1990s and Yeltsin's weak second presidency. Putin also re-started the war in Chechnya to re-establish Moscow's authority over the breakaway region, which made it abundantly clear to other regions in Russia that the age of sovereignty was over. The establishment of a 'power vertical' (a term referring to strong centralized authority) quickly and significantly reduced political competition.

At the same time, political competition only strengthened in Ukraine. The 2004 Ukrainian presidential election was extremely close and it pitted two very different candidates against each other: Viktor Yanukovych, a pro-Russian candidate with a murky past in the lawless early post-Soviet years, and Viktor Yushchenko, a pro-Western reformist promising to clean up Ukrainian politics, strengthen the Ukrainian nation, and bring Ukraine closer to the West. Massive electoral fraud and manipulation in favour of Yanukovych brought thousands of Ukrainians onto the streets in a protest dubbed the Orange Revolution. After 21 days of peaceful resistance, the outcome was the reversal of the manipulated results, a clean repeat run-off, and Yushchenko's victory.

Russia could not conceive of the Orange Revolution as the mobilization of Ukrainian civil society and instead interpreted it as a Western plot against the pro-Russian candidate and thus against Russia itself. The Orange Revolution, together with other colour revolutions in Georgia and Kyrgyzstan, triggered Russian paranoia about an expansionist West supposedly trying to encroach on Russia's rightful backyard and steal its vassals. The imperial lens that Russia used obscured the straightforward evidence that the colour revolutions were above all domestic phenomena. The inherent instability and political competition in hybrid political regimes created uncertainty for the ruling elites and an opening for popular action (Hale 2005). These mobilizations were motivated by demand for free elections and driven by local civil society, rather than nefarious Western interference.

The Orange Revolution was a critical juncture, one which not only entrenched Ukraine's democratic regime trajectory but also hastened Russia and Ukraine's divergent trajectories in many policy realms. President Yushchenko introduced legislation that recognized the 1932-33 famine (the Holodomor) as a genocide against Ukrainians. Russia strenuously objected, insisting that the famine was 'a common tragedy of the Soviet people'. Yushchenko also angered Russia by reaching out to the Ecumenical Patriarch in Istanbul in his attempt to foster the formation of an Orthodox church in Ukraine independent from Moscow. Russia's wrath was even greater when the Yushchenko administration (unsuccessfully) sought legislation to grant veteran status and benefits to members of the Organization of Ukrainian Nationalists (OUN) and the Ukrainian Insurgent Army (UPA), two nationalist organizations that during and after World War II had fought Soviet forces in attempting to establish an independent Ukraine.

In foreign policy, Yushchenko became the first Ukrainian president who rejected the multi-vector policy and sought to put Ukraine on a path towards European integration. In 2007, Yushchenko managed to open negotiations with the European Union on an Association Agreement between Ukraine and the EU, one comprehensive and ambitious enough that it could lead to a membership perspective for Ukraine. Yushchenko was equally ambitious when it came to NATO integration and launched Ukraine's NATO membership bid by applying for a Membership Action Plan. However, NATO collectively rebuffed Ukraine's NATO aspirations at the 2008 Bucharest Summit. While the George W. Bush administration advocated for Ukraine (and Georgia's) NATO accession, France and Germany rejected the suggestion and thus Ukraine only received a non-committal assurance that its bid would be considered some day.

The next phase in the escalatory cycle: The 2014 Euromaidan and the start of Russia's war against Ukraine

Russia did not lash out militarily against Ukraine following its unsuccessful NATO bid in 2008. This time, it wasn't state weakness and domestic crisis that constrained Russian imperialist appetites, but the reasonable expectation that Yushchenko would lose office in upcoming elections and could be replaced by a pro-Russian president. Indeed, due to infighting within the Orange coalition, Yushchenko's inability to end corruption, and controversial cultural policies, the 2010 presidential election was won by the loser of the Orange Revolution election, the pro-Russian Yanukovych. Russia's goal to vassalize Ukraine was back on track. Yanukovych quickly set out to emulate Russia's political model and started reversing the Orange-era's democratic gains and Ukrainization policies. The Holodomor interpretation was brought closer to Russia's preferred reading and other memory policies also started to inch closer to what Russia wanted. Yanukovych also changed the legal status of the Russian language, granting it official status in many regions and urban centres. Russia got a thirty year extension on its Black Sea Fleet lease in Ukraine. And finally, Yanukovych communicated to NATO that Ukraine was no longer interested in membership.

At the same time, Yanukovych's pro-Russian policies were still constrained by pushback from the substantial pro-Western constituency that had strengthened during the Orange era. Vibrant political competition meant that Yanukovych could not pull out from the negotiations with the EU that Yushchenko had started. In the fall of 2013, the negotiations came to an important milestone: Ukraine was invited to sign the Association Agreement at the EU Vilnius summit. Russia was unwilling to accept Ukraine's decision to pursue a foreign policy that would decisively remove it from the Russian World. And Russia was developing new ways to promote this World: A couple of years earlier, in 2011, it had formed the Eurasian Customs Union (later expanded to become the Eurasian Economic Union). This was envisioned as a mirror image of and alternative to the European Union. Ultimately, Moscow's hope was that it would reunite its former vassals and preclude them from joining the EU.

To thwart Ukraine's efforts to pursue European integration, in 2013 Russia decided to send a clear signal to Ukraine that signing the Association Agreement would be a 'suicidal step' (Glazyev quoted in D'Anieri 2019, 200). To illustrate the threat, in the summer of 2013 Russia started a trade war through which it aimed to pressure the Ukrainian government to abandon the idea of signing on the dotted line with the EU. The pressure campaign continued with a secret meeting between Putin and Yanukovych in November 2013 at which the Russian president managed to strongarm the Ukrainian leader to renege on signing the agreement at the last moment. This abrupt change of course triggered social mobilization in Ukraine against the Yanukovych government and Russia's meddling. Thus began the Euromaidan protest movement, which started immediately after the failed signing and quickly ballooned after Yanukovych's forces applied escalating violence to suppress it (the term *maidan* in Ukrainian refers to the public squares in which the protests took place). The murder of dozens of protestors by government security forces in February 2014 led to the crumbling of Yanukovych's regime and he fled to Russia.

Russia again interpreted Ukrainians' popular mobilization through an imperial lens. Just like it saw the Orange Revolution as a Western plot against the pro-Russian candidate Yanukovych, it saw the Euromaidan as a 'Western coup' against then-president Yanukovych. In both cases, instead of recognizing the agency and grievances of Ukrainians, Russia concluded that the West was orchestrating events to 'steal' Ukraine from its rightful 'owner', Russia. In this frame, Russia labeled the new Ukrainian government 'an illegal fascist junta' and started a disinformation campaign aimed at delegitimizing it in the eyes of the Ukrainian, Russian, and Western publics.

To understand why Russia lashed out after Yanukovych's ouster and used military aggression, rather than the non-military toolkit still available to it, we need to focus on the escalatory cycle between Russia's aim to control Ukraine and Ukraine's commitment to avoiding this domination. Patiently waiting for Ukraine's political process to bring another Russia-friendly president to power was, after the Euromaidan, a riskier strategy because the new central government was the most pro-Western, and hence to Russia, the most 'anti-Russian' in Ukraine's history. The lesson that Russia took away from this watershed moment was that the non-military pressure tactics it had used to try to keep Ukraine in its sphere of influence were insufficient and Ukraine was slipping away more decisively than ever. The past levers included economic carrots and sticks, the weaponization of gas deliveries, an extensive network of agents of Russia's influence in civil society and state institutions, and saturation of Ukraine's information space with Russian and pro-Russian media. A pro-Russian president with a parliamentary majority and a sizeable pro-Russian electorate were additional avenues for Russia's influence in Ukraine, and yet all those had proven insufficient to prevent the Euromaidan's victory. To establish control over Ukraine, Russia concluded that more decisive and aggressive steps were necessary.

Russia's military action started from Crimea. Overnight, almost immediately following Yanukovych's flight from the country, Russian troops without insignia (dubbed 'little green men') took over state institutions and military bases on the peninsula. The operation proceeded quickly and efficiently, in part because Russian troops were already present in Crimea through Ukraine's prior agreement to host Russia's Black Sea Fleet, and in part due to the element of surprise. Ukraine did not manage to react militarily to defend its territory. The army was in shambles after years of corrupt management and was not prepared to defend Ukraine from Russia. State power was profoundly destabilized following the Yanukovych regime's implosion, and the West strongly encouraged Ukraine to restrain its reaction. Given the confluence of those factors, Russia moved incredibly quickly to grab Crimea. Within two weeks it staged a 'referendum', which did not meet any minimum standards for a free plebiscite but supposedly showed that the Crimean population preferred to separate from Ukraine and join the Russian Federation.

While Crimea was the only Ukrainian region with a Russian ethnic majority population (54 per cent), this exceptional status does not fully explain either why Russia attacked or why it took Crimea so easily. Russia's goal in taking Crimea was neither to 'protect' ethnic Russians and Russian speakers from the new Ukrainian government, nor to respond to a supposed local desire to be in Russia. Surveys of Crimean residents conducted in the years before the Euromaidan showed that a growing majority viewed autonomy within Ukraine as the best status for their region, while a shrinking minority wanted annexation by Russia (International Republican Institute, Baltic Surveys/The Gallup Organization, and Ukraine 2013). Opinion polls conducted shortly before the annexation likewise showed that only a minority of Crimeans favoured leaving Ukraine and joining Russia (Kyiv International Institute of Sociology 2014a). Rather, Putin's goal was to destabilize the pro-Western government in Kyiv and even to hasten central state collapse, which would halt Ukraine's drift towards Europe and put it back on a path towards vassalization by Russia (Popova and Shevel 2023).

In pursuit of this goal, after annexing Crimea, Russia launched what it called the 'Russian Spring' project aiming to leverage dissatisfaction with the post-Euromaidan government in southeastern Ukraine in order to destabilize the new government in Kyiv. The most directly affected regions were Odesa, Kherson, Mykolayiv, Zaporizhzhia, Kharkiv, Dnipropetrovsk, Donetsk, and Luhansk, which Russia began to collectively call *Novorossiya* (New Russia), employing tsarist-era terminology. Russia sought to amplify local dissatisfaction with the change of government in Kyiv and instigate a regional rebellion. The overall plan was to use the threats that southeastern regions might secede and that Ukraine might break up to force the central government to agree to a 'federalization' of the country that would give 'Novorossiya' the power to veto central government policies. In this vision, 'Novorossiya' might be either a single political entity if it could be created, or, failing that, a series of separate 'people's republics' in individual southeastern regions.

The 'Russian Spring' failed almost everywhere in 'Novorossia' because Russia misjudged popular opinion in these regions. Moscow assumed that Russian-speakers there were not only angry with the change of government in Kyiv but would also want their region to secede from Ukraine. But support for secession has been a minority view (Kyiv International Institute of Sociology 2014b), and only in eastern Donbas (parts of Donetsk and Luhansk oblasts) has Russia's plan partly succeeded. Donetsk and Luhansk 'people's republics' (sometimes referred to by their Russian-language initials DNR and LNR) were proclaimed, and armed insurgency challenged the central government militarily. The interim Ukrainian government responded by launching what it called an Anti-Terrorist Operation (ATO), a military campaign to restore Ukrainian territorial integrity in Donbas. As the Ukrainian military began to gain advantage on the battlefield by late summer 2014, Russia, while continuing to deny involvement, resorted to sending significant numbers of regular troops to stave off the military defeat of the 'people's republics'. Russia's direct military intervention turned the tide. To avoid losing even more territory, Petro Poroshenko (elected the new president of Ukraine shortly after the Euromaidan) was forced to sign two disadvantageous accords in Minsk in September 2014 and again in February 2015. These negotiations over the war in Donbas became known as the Minsk process.

Post-Euromaidan developments illustrate the escalatory cycle between Russian imperialism and Ukraine's determination to safeguard its independent statehood. Russia's aggression against Ukraine in Crimea and Donbas aimed to prevent Ukraine from leaving Russia's orbit, but instead accelerated this very process. The Ukrainian government did not get scared out of pursuing a pro-Western policy course, and Ukrainian citizens came to support this course in growing numbers. In 2014, Russia attacked Ukraine which was a neutral state with less than a third of the population favouring NATO membership and only a slight majority preferring to join the EU rather than the Russia-led Customs Union. Russia's 2014 aggression, instead of forcing Ukrainians to accept that they were in Russia's sphere of influence, increased support for EU and NATO membership in all regions of Ukraine. Support for EU membership, which in May 2013 was 41.7 per cent, by May 2014 increased to 50.5 per cent, while support for joining the Customs Union declined from 32.1 to 21.4 per cent (Razumkov Center 2014). Support for Ukraine's membership in NATO also increased decisively. By late 2014, 46 per cent favoured Ukraine's membership in NATO (KIIS poll cited in Popova and Shevel 2023, 220).

Reflecting this evolving popular sentiment, elections in the post-Euromaidan period produced majorities for pro-Western parties and politicians, in contrast to previous legislatures divided on whether to support closer ties with the West or Russia. Ironically, Russia enabled this new political reality: Voters in the annexed Crimea and in the parts of Donbas controlled by the 'people's republics' – historically Ukraine's most Russia-leaning regions – could no longer vote in Ukrainian elections. By taking some 12 per cent of the Ukrainian electorate – consisting of the most pro-Russian voters – out of the electoral equation, Russia had made the formation of a pro-Russian Ukrainian government virtually impossible.

The new electoral geography and shifting public opinion in Ukraine also meant that those post-Euromaidan policies that most infuriated Russia could now be voted in with relative ease in the parliament and no longer generated strong opposition in society. These included enshrining the goal of NATO membership in the constitution, accelerating Ukrainization through an amended language law, giving rise to an Orthodox church independent from Moscow, and launching 'decommunization' policies aimed at purging Ukraine's public spaces of Soviet-era references and symbols. In addition, Ukraine signed the Association Agreement with the EU, which Yanukovych and Russia had sought to prevent. As part of the new close relationship with the EU, Ukraine started implementing a series of reforms of its state institutions (police, courts, local government, etc.) that put it on track to meeting EU membership criteria. Defence cooperation with NATO, the newly found state commitment to strengthen the military to defend against Russia's ongoing aggression in Donbas, and a steady flow of volunteers committed to defending their country fostered the reform and modernization of the Ukrainian armed forces. In virtually every aspect of domestic and foreign policy, rather than returning to the Russian World, Ukraine was drifting further away from it with each passing year.

In 2019, the next round of competitive presidential elections resulted in another turnover in power. Volodymyr Zelensky defeated Poroshenko and was inaugurated as Ukraine's sixth president. Zelensky promised to continue necessary reforms to facilitate Ukraine's EU accession, especially by tackling political corruption more effectively than had his predecessor Poroshenko. Zelensky, a Russian-speaker from the south of Ukraine, also declared his intention to reach an agreement with Russia on Donbas as well as Crimea. Russia's response to Zelensky's victory was to up the pressure to force its preferred outcome regarding Donbas. Just days after Zelensky was inaugurated, Russia extended Russian citizenship to all residents of the LNR and DNR, intentionally complicating the re-integration of Donbas into Ukraine. With an inexperienced and conciliatory-talking president in office in Ukraine, Russia's goal of leveraging Donbas to restore its influence over Kyiv finally looked within reach. In the wrangling over Minsk implementation, Russia has been pressuring Ukraine to prioritize amending its constitution and granting vaguely defined 'special status' to Russia's proxies, the DNR and the LNR. If 'special status' was secured before Ukrainian state control returned to Donbas through free elections and restoration of Ukrainian control of the Russia-Ukraine border, Russia would wield de-facto veto power over policies of the central government though its proxies. If the DNR and LNR could leverage their constitutionally-guaranteed 'special status' to block central government policies Russia disliked, Ukraine was back on the vassal track.

But even an inexperienced Ukrainian president seeking a compromise with Russia quickly realized the danger posed by Russia's reading of the Minsk agreements. Ukrainian voters were also opposed to giving Russia's proxy 'republics' in Donbas special status. While a majority in Ukraine supported a negotiated resolution to the conflict in Donbas, less than a quarter were in favour of giving the LNR/DNR the powers that Russia demanded (Razumkov Center 2020). The Minsk process deadlocked again, and Russia was denied its objective of vassalizing Ukraine despite the change from Poroshenko to Zelensky in Kyiv. Zelensky's promise to reduce the outsized role of oligarchs in Ukrainian politics additionally undermined Russian covert influence in Ukraine. A series of steps by the Ukrainian government against Viktor Medvedchuk – a leader of a pro-Russian party in parliament, an oligarch, a personal friend of Putin's, and a long-standing conduit of Russian influence in Ukraine – sent a clear signal to the Russian regime that Ukraine was continuing its trajectory of distancing from Russia.

The road to Russia's 2022 full-scale invasion of Ukraine

Russia responded to its failure to leverage the Minsk agreements to vassalize Ukraine by escalating its methods of pressure. Military action was implicitly threatened in the fall of 2021, when Russia amassed over 100,000 troops along its border with Ukraine. Russia also attempted to blackmail the West into 'delivering' a vassalized Ukraine when it presented unrealistic demands to the NATO alliance. Russia wanted the US to sign a treaty – the text was prepared by Russia and handed to the US in December 2021 – that would result in the withdrawal of NATO weapons and troops from the post-Communist NATO member states, a ban on further NATO expansion, and a ban on all military cooperation between NATO and post-Soviet non-NATO countries, such as Ukraine. Russia viewed post-Soviet states as only nominally independent and believed itself entitled to have final say in these state's foreign policy decisions. By taking its demands for NATO only to the

US, Russia revealed that it likewise saw central and even western European NATO member states as only nominally independent from the US. The US could not consider agreeing to these demands, which flew in the face of both the principle of collective decision making within NATO and the principle of sovereignty and sovereign states having the right to decide their foreign policy alliances.

Russia's escalation and attempt to blackmail the West failed, and so did its efforts to cow Ukraine. Ukraine, convinced that Russia's ultimate goal was vassalizing the country, saw Minsk implementation on Russia's terms and neutrality as steps towards this goal. Conceding neutrality after the annexation of Crimea and the loss of territory in Donbas would have been a creeping loss of sovereignty, while acquiescing to separatist entities holding veto power over a swath of state policies would have cemented this sovereignty loss.

The Zelensky government's resistance to Russia's demands reflected the preferences of Ukrainian society, where the majority saw these steps as unacceptable surrender to Russia. Russia's aggression eroded pro-Russian attitudes in Ukraine and by early 2022, 62 per cent nationwide, with a majority in every region except the east, were in favour of Ukraine's membership in NATO (Rating Group 2022a). A majority was also against satisfying Russia on Minsk – just 11 per cent believed that Ukraine should be implementing the Minsk agreement (Rating Group 2022b). Zelensky trying to push through these measures would have likely led to street protests and political instability. Putting together the super-majority in the legislature required to amend the Constitution most likely would have been impossible. Trying but failing to do this would have not only denied Russia what it was seeking, thus putting the Russian invasion back on the agenda, but also left Ukraine facing the invasion with a less trusted government, a weakened state, and a more divided society.

The full-scale war has become the final rupture in the Russia-Ukraine relationship. Ukrainians are fully united around the goal of leaving the Russian World and its autocratic form of government and joining the West and strengthening their democracy. Large majorities in each region of the country want to win the war, enter the EU and NATO, maintain democracy, strengthen the Ukrainian language, separate from Russia culturally, and see themselves as members of the civic Ukrainian nation, rejecting belonging to any sort of 'imagined community' with Russia.

Meanwhile, the Russian regime is digging a deeper hole of authoritarianism and imperialism. Repression is reaching Stalin-era levels (with methods including show trials, lengthy sentences, and snitching on neighbours and acquaintances) and dissidents are either in prison or in exile. While it is hard to gauge the exact level of popular support in Russia for the war against Ukraine due to methodological challenges of conducting polls in authoritarian settings, surveys consistently indicate stable majority support for the war (about 65 per cent) and stable, limited opposition (about 20 per cent) (Pop-Eleches, et al, 2023). A widespread myth of 'imperial innocence' (Kassymbekova and Marat 2022), TV propaganda, and an atomized, apathetic society have all combined to produce this compliant majority. The anti-war movement is confined to the margins and thus easily suppressed through repression or drained through emigration. The majority does not agitate for escalating the war, but also does not call for ending it. They simply follow regime cues. Russian society is thus highly unlikely to force the regime to end the invasion. For their part, Ukrainians see not just the Russian regime but Russian citizens as responsible for the war. As a result, 77 per cent of Ukrainians now hold negative views of Russians (Razumkov Center 2023), and just 9 per cent view only Putin and the Russian leadership negatively without having similarly negative opinions of Russian society as a whole (Smola 2023).

Could the full-scale war have been avoided?

While the war in 2022 was another step in the escalatory cycle, in the thirty year period since the Soviet Union's dissolution, there have been several critical junctures when developments in either Ukraine or Russia could have unfolded along different trajectories and could have avoided the 2022 collision. The logic of an escalatory cycle between re-imperialization and independence centres on the compatibility between Russia's and its neighbours' foreign and domestic policies. When the vassals pursue parallel foreign policy and refrain from emphasizing 'anti-Russian' identities domestically, Russia does not need to exert its imperial power (Popova and Shevel 2023). Such compatibility could have potentially arisen at several points. In the early 2000s, Ukraine's democratic breakthrough could have failed. Had Yushchenko died from the dioxin poisoning that put him in intensive care and disfigured him right before the 2004 election, the Orange Revolution that served as an empowering precedent for Ukrainian civil society and a decisive pro-Western turn for Ukraine would likely not have taken place. Once victorious, pro-Russian president Yanukovych, whose authoritarian impulses were well-established, would have started building an authoritarian regime in Russia's image as early as 2005, and he could have succeeded. An authoritarian Ukraine would have pursued a more pro-Russian course in both foreign and domestic politics. As the Belarus example shows, Russia could have pursued reintegration with a pro-Russian Ukraine without the need for military aggression.

It is harder to imagine a realistic scenario under which Russia could have fully accepted the sovereignty of its former vassal. Such acceptance would have entailed Russia fully recognizing Ukraine's right to design and implement domestic policies without pressure or endorsement by Russia. Russia's full acceptance of Ukraine's sovereignty would have meant that Ukraine was free not to take Russia's preferences into consideration, even if Russia did not like the policies Ukraine chose to pursue. Such acceptance also would have avoided the zero-sum perspective Russia developed with regard to its own and the West's purported competition for control of Ukraine – this perspective can be summarized as 'either we control it, or they do, Ukraine as nobody's vassal or proxy cannot exist'. Only a Russia fully committed to respecting Ukraine's independent statehood and distinctive identity would have avoided a collision course with non-vassalized Ukraine. However, Russia entered the post-Soviet era entirely lacking a history of a non-imperial identity, greatly complicating the creation of a non-imperial identity post-1991 both as a set of state policies and as an idea internalized by society.

Had Russia managed to build and consolidate a democracy, the democratic system could have mediated Russia's imperial impulses and prevented military aggression. Sustained democratic competition and regular free elections could have increased the number of voices influencing the policy making process. Even if many, or even most, of these voices shared imperialist goals, there would have been disagreements over the means toward these ends. Such an environment would have reduced the likelihood of military aggression because advocates of alternative goals and methods could have expressed their criticisms openly and influenced the policy making process. For example, in a competitive political system, the only major politician who gravitated towards anti-imperialism, Boris Nemtsov, would have stood a chance of gaining political power through elections and not being murdered for his opposition stance. Even among those favouring the restoration of the USSR or the Russian empire, the advocates of military aggression would have had to compete with those favouring non-military means towards similar goals. Instead of invading Ukraine, Russia could have ended up pursuing the vision of Anatoly Chubais, for example, who in the early 2000s called for the creation of a Russia-centred 'liberal' economic empire in the former Soviet space. Finally, a competitive regime may also have produced economic diversification and rule of law, which would have incentivized Russia to place more emphasis on international cooperation than on controlling neighbours in pursuit of imperial domination.

None of these hypothetical counterfactuals came to pass. Ukraine did not develop into a pro-Russian autocracy and Russia neither entrenched political competition capable of moderating its imperialist impulses nor constructed an anti-imperial identity. The peak of competitive politics in Russia came during the problematic 1996 contest between an unpopular Yeltsin committed to further reforms and a revanchist Communist Party leader, Gennady Zyuganov, who promised to bring back the USSR. Democratic competition has been on the decline ever since. By 2014, Ukraine and Russia stood starkly apart. Ukraine was fully committed to independence and increasingly oriented to the West, while Russia was entrenched in the belief that a fully independent Ukraine seeking Western integration was not the outcome of complex domestic processes within Ukraine but an anti-Russian project engineered by the West. One way or the other, Russia was determined to destroy the Ukraine that it came to see as 'anti-Russia'.

Could a different Western policy have averted Russia's aggression against Ukraine?

The only realistic potential way to have averted war would have been for the West to choose containment of Russia over continued engagement with it in response to earlier instances of Russian aggression. In the aftermath of Russia's invasion of Georgia in 2008 and of Ukraine in 2014, some argued that the West pushed Russia too much and disregarded its legitimate interests in preserving influence in the post-Soviet space that it has dubbed its 'near abroad'. Instead, however, the West should have drawn a very different lesson. The West should have worried not about provoking Russia, but about Russia's being bent on restoring the vassal status of its neighbours who were left out of the EU and NATO. The events of 2008 and 2014 were the first steps in Russia's aggressive re-imperialization drive. Had the West switched from engaging to containing an increasingly belligerent Russia, this may have prevented the 2022 war.

Western containment could have included several elements, such as systematic measures to counter Russia's malicious efforts to undermine Western democracies through interfering in elections, launching disinformation campaigns, and engaging in illegal party financing. The US opted for a 'reset', but it could have instead imposed extensive sanctions on Russia after its invasion of Georgia in 2008. A determined Western response to that military aggression could have given Russia pause and deterred it from attempting an opportunistic land grab again, this time in Ukraine in 2014. Instead, the weak and muddled Western reaction in 2008 led Russia to the natural conclusion that it could escalate its aggression in the neighbourhood because the West was on the decline, divided, and ultimately neither willing nor able to prevent Russia from re-establishing dominance over its neighbours. The West's introspection after the 2008 financial crisis and focus on domestic reforms to overcome consequences of the crisis further strengthened Russia's belief that the time was right, and opportunity costs were low, to re-vassalize the post-Soviet region.

In 2014, the West had another chance to change course and prevent further Russian escalation, and this chance too was missed. Had the West imposed more extensive sanctions after 2014 and united to isolate Russia, it could have made the costs of Russian imperialism prohibitively high and this could have deterred the 2022 Russian full-scale invasion of Ukraine. Among concrete steps, Europe, and especially Germany, could have made a political commitment and taken practical steps to reduce energy dependency on Russia. But instead Europeans only increased this dependency by proceeding with Nord Stream 2 pipeline construction. The West should have also more extensively armed Ukraine and trained its military to send a clear signal to Russia that overrunning Ukraine militarily would be prohibitively costly. Instead, the West feared that arming Ukraine would provoke Russia and rationalized this policy with arguments – soundly discredited since the February 2022 invasion – that arming Ukraine would not make a difference on the battlefield.

After 2014, a narrative gained significant attention that depicted aggressive Western expansionism into the former Communist bloc involving the luring into NATO of, first, Eastern European states, and ultimately post-Soviet states too, including Ukraine (Mearsheimer 2014). This narrative is unconvincing. First, the West did not lure the East Europeans into NATO.

Those Eastern Europeans who made it into NATO pushed hard for it and had to overcome initial Western skepticism about their membership. An overlooked consequence of NATO's and the EU's eastward expansion is that it increased stability and promoted partnerly relations between Russia and its former Soviet bloc vassals. Being now secure as Euro-Atlantic alliance members, the former vassals could – and most did – develop and maintain cooperative relations and economic ties with Russia without fearing a loss of sovereignty.

Second, rather than ignoring Russia's concerns, the West in fact prioritized them over the security concerns of Eastern Europe, Georgia, Moldova, Ukraine, and others as it was seeking Russia's cooperation in the international arena. The West strove to include Russia in Europe's security architecture, often over the objections and security concerns of the Eastern Europeans. The West also downplayed Russian aggression in the early 1990s in Moldova, Georgia, and Chechnya. The optimistic thinking in the West was that engagement with Russia through trade and other forms of cooperation would benefit everyone. After 2001, the West also sought to secure Russia's cooperation in mitigating global problems such as conflicts in the Middle East and Afghanistan, the threat of Islamic terrorism, and Iran's nuclear programme. Rather than seeing Russia as an adversary, the West treated Russia as a geopolitical and economic partner, and repeatedly tried to restore friendly relations after each setback. During the 2000s, the EU and Russia intensified trade and economic ties, especially in energy, worked on harmonizing trade regulations to remove trade barriers, and Western leaders regularly welcomed Putin in European capitals as a friendly partner.

Finally, Russia's full-scale invasion of Ukraine sought to prevent not NATO expansion but the loss of Ukraine as its vassal. With France and Germany firmly opposed to Ukraine's NATO membership, the prospect of Ukraine entering NATO any time in the foreseeable future, if at all, was non-existent. Russia, of course, knew this. It escalated militarily, eventually launching a full-scale invasion of its neighbour, in response to the prospect of Ukraine signing an economic agreement with the EU that would have locked it on a trajectory towards Europe and ended Russia's hope of anchoring Ukraine in the Russia-led economic union. It had objected to a broad range of Ukrainian domestic politics ranging from decentralization reforms and local governance to media and education legislation. Had security fears caused by NATO expansion been Russia's primary motive, Moscow would have reacted differently to Sweden and Finland entering the alliance since the start of the invasion. Russia barely objected to this major expansion of the alliance, and instead of fortifying its 830 miles borders with the new NATO member Finland, Russia instead pulled out some of its troops from the border, relocating them to Ukraine. Nor did Russia fortify Kaliningrad, a Russian enclave surrounded by NATO.

That Russia's primary concern and objectives are not NATO but the eradication of a distinct Ukrainian identity and independent statehood is further evidenced by the widespread and systematic destruction of all manifestations of Ukrainian identity in the occupied territories. Russian occupying forces change place names, destroy monuments and Ukrainian books in libraries, arrest and torture people for speaking Ukrainian, and use the education system and deportations to Russia as means to erase the young generation's Ukrainian identity. Russian state-controlled TV regularly broadcasts genocidal rhetoric against Ukrainians, advocating their forced conversion into their allegedly 'true' Russian identity or, failing such conversion, outright extermination. None of these policies and goals are about Russia's military security but about its desire for domination, informed by imperial identity and geopolitical goals.

Conclusion

In sum, over the last three decades, the Russian-Ukrainian relationship was characterized by an escalatory cycle that led to increasing divergence between the two countries in multiple dimensions: identity conceptions, regime dynamics, and geopolitical orientation. In Russia, the state and the nation became increasingly conceptualized in civilizational-imperial terms, whereas Ukraine solidified a distinct Ukrainian identity committed to independent statehood. Under Putin's rule, Russia consolidated an increasingly repressive and personalist authoritarian regime that felt threatened by Ukrainian democracy's progress. Robust civil society and vibrant political competition flourishing in Ukraine looked like a nightmare scenario from the perspective of Russia's authoritarian regime. In foreign policy, Putin's Russia became increasingly anti-Western and bent on asserting Russia's dominance over the post-Soviet states, first and foremost Ukraine, at the same time as Ukraine committed to a European path. Russia's imperial vision came to dominate policy-making vis-a-vis Ukraine as Ukraine increasingly slipped away from Russia's grasp.

The methods Russia used to pressure Ukraine to change course escalated from diplomatic pressure, energy flow carrots and sticks, information warfare, and cyber-attacks to military aggression. In Ukraine, each escalation of pressure by Russia prompted an ever increasing share of Ukrainians to shift from pro-Russian and towards pro-Western positions, and to embrace stronger Ukrainian civic identity. As a result, while each Ukrainian incumbent sought to balance between a pro-Russian and a nationalizing or pro-Western position, the context changed over time. Each pro-Western incumbent became bolder in pursuit of Euro-Atlantic integration, while each pro-Russian incumbent was less in step with public opinion. This trend in turn boosted Russia's paranoia that the West was stealing Ukraine. The result of this escalatory cycle of divergent trajectories was the emergence of two incompatible domestic equilibria: Russia became committed to resetting Ukraine as a loyal vassal, while Ukraine became convinced that it had to leave Russia's sphere of influence altogether and join the West.

Russia's objective of destroying Ukrainian state independence means that until and unless Russia's leadership abandons this goal, independent Ukraine will remain in danger. Measures such as a ceasefire or a peace agreement that rewards Russia with Ukrainian territory may stop fighting temporarily but they will not amount to a lasting peace or a stable security architecture. Only Ukraine's accession to NATO and the EU and its decisive geopolitical recategorization from a 'gray zone' between Russia and the West into a full-fledged member of the Euro-Atlantic community will guarantee Ukrainian sovereignty and return stability to Europe.

Discussion questions

1 If Putin were to leave the political scene tomorrow, what do you expect would happen to Russia's war effort? What about Russia's policy towards Ukraine?

2 Can Russia overcome its legacy of imperialism? If so, how? If not, why not?

3 Should Ukraine be admitted to NATO? Why or why not? If yes, when?

4 Which past Western policy would you have changed, and how, to have had the best chance of preventing the Russo-Ukrainian war?

5 Are Ukraine and Russia likely to have adversarial relations after the war? Why or why not? What are some factors that will likely continue affecting relations between these two countries?

Suggestions for further reading

1. D'Anieri, Paul. 2007. *Understanding Ukrainian Politics: Power, Politics, and Institutional Design*. Armonk, N.Y.: M.E. Sharpe Inc.
2. Dragneva-Lewers, Rilka, and Kataryna Wolczuk. 2015. *Ukraine Between the EU and Russia: The Integration Challenge*. Palgrave Macmillan.
3. Hale, Henry, and Robert Orttung, eds. 2016. *Beyond the Euromaidan: Comparative Perspectives on Advancing Reform in Ukraine*. Stanford: Stanford University Press.
4. McFaul, Michael. 2018. *From Cold War to Hot Peace. An American Ambassador in Putin's Russia*. Boston: Houghton Mifflin Harcourt.
5. Popova, Maria, and Oxana Shevel. 2024. *Russia and Ukraine: Entangled Histories, Diverging States*. Polity Press.
6. Plokhy, Serhii. 2023. *The Russo-Ukrainian War: The Return of History*. WW Norton.

16

Russian Foreign Policy

Kathryn Stoner

Russian foreign policy has evolved considerably since the collapse of the Soviet Union in 1991 and the end of the Cold War. During the late 1980s Soviet, and then Russian foreign policy thereafter in the 1990s, was focused on integration with the outside world, beginning with landmark nuclear arms control agreements and other decisive movement toward cooperation with Europe and the United States. Even the first two terms of Vladimir Putin's presidency of Russia (2000–08) can mostly be characterized as seeking further cooperation and integration with the US and Europe. There was considerable collaboration with the US (and NATO's) war in Afghanistan after 11 September 2001. Between 2008 and 2012, when Dmitry Medvedev 'castled' the offices of prime minister and president with Putin, Russian relations with the US and NATO allies were at their most constructive.

Strikingly, however, and perhaps in reaction to changing domestic politics (the regime became more repressive at home), Russia became more aggressive abroad following Putin's return to the presidency in the spring of 2012. Since then, Russian foreign policy has become more assertive against the collective West, and its interests extend far beyond its immediate neighbourhood. This chapter examines this dramatic trajectory of changing Russian foreign policy – a path that has moved from cooperation to confrontation with Western powers. We begin first with an examination of this evolution, noting how the autocratic nature of the political regime under Vladimir Putin's twenty-three-year tenure as leader has influenced a shift in foreign policy priorities. We then take a tour around the world to see how and where Russian foreign policy has evolved, and the tools Russia's leaders have come to use in advancing their preferences.

The evolution of Russian foreign policy after the Soviet collapse

The current territory that constitutes modern Russia is far smaller than was the Soviet Union, although Russia today is nonetheless the largest country by territory on the planet, spanning eleven time zones, and having no fewer than fourteen international borders. In contrast to the Cold War period, post-communist Russia's global influence in the twenty-first century lacks a strong motivating ideological component in the way that the spread of communism was a central tenet of Soviet foreign policy. While geostrategic interests also mattered to be sure, Soviet decision making abroad was also guided by the exigency to perpetuate Marxist-Leninist regimes in opposition to capitalism.

In contrast, the current Russian regime, under Vladimir Putin's leadership, does not look to Marxist-Leninism for guidance in determining its foreign policy. Putin has attempted to establish Russia as the tip of the spear of a group of socially conservative, 'illiberal' regimes opposed to American global aggression, but Russia today is not the head of a global movement in the way that the USSR was of communism.

The Soviet Union built alliances and helped domestic actors establish communist regimes in the six Warsaw Pact countries – Bulgaria, Czechoslovakia, East Germany, Hungary, Poland, and Romania. Soviet allies that constructed communist systems included Afghanistan, Angola, Benin, the Congo, Cuba, Ethiopia, Guinea, Kampuchea, Laos, Mongolia, Mozambique, Nicaragua, North Korea, North Vietnam, and Yemen. Soviet allies whose regimes were not completely socialist or communist at the height of the Cold War in 1980 included Algeria, Ghana, Guinea, India, Iraq, Lebanon, Libya, Madagascar, Mali, Panama, and Syria. Yugoslavia and Albania, though not in the Warsaw Pact or Eastern Bloc, were socialist countries. Under Nikita Khrushchev and Mao Zedong in the 1960s, the Soviet Union and China had a serious falling out over communist doctrine and policy toward the US and remained more enemies than friends until well after the Soviet collapse in 1991.

The 'communist international' of countries was more than just a set of like-minded leaders with planned economies and politics dominated by a communist party. Rather, it was a network of economic, political, and military relationships vital to the survival of communism worldwide, and to the survival of the Soviet Union itself. This in no way resembles what contemporary Russia's leadership has sought to pursue globally.

The global footprint that post-communist Russia inherited from the Soviet Union shrank almost to within its own borders as Boris Yeltsin struggled with difficult domestic economics and politics through the 1990s. But as Russia's economy stabilized in the ensuing decades, Putin's Russia extended its web of political, economic, and strategic contacts worldwide. Whereas during the late Cold War, the Soviet Union was a somewhat conventional and predictable enemy, Russia, after more than two decades under Vladimir Putin's leadership, is anything but conventional in its approach to foreign policy.

The influence of domestic politics on Russia's foreign policy

The unpredictability of Russian foreign policy decisions may stem from the nature of its domestic political system. Over time, it has gone from being an unconsolidated, often fractious, but open and pluralistic political system in the 1990s, to a 'managed democracy' in the early 2000s, then a 'competitive authoritarian' system after 2012, to what is now a highly personalistic, repressive autocracy.

As the system has become more closed and repressive, it has become increasingly difficult for observers to know exactly how foreign policy decisions are made. We have good reason to think that the decision to invade Ukraine in 2022 was made by a small group around the President that includes the head of the Federal Security Service (FSB is the Russian acronym), the head of the Foreign Intelligence Service (or SVR in Russian), and the chairman of the Russian Security Council, all of whom had careers in the Soviet intelligence services as did Mr Putin prior to the collapse of the USSR.

Other decisions, like the Syrian Special Operation of 2015, also appear to have been made by President Putin, but in a more normal policy process that involved the Chief of the General Staff, the Minister of Defence, as well as the Russian Security Council. It is clear, however, that when it comes to big foreign policy decisions, little happens without Putin's involvement and express approval. This is the nature of personalist autocracies.

The Russian legislative branch (or Duma) is now clearly little more than a rubber stamp in facilitating the president's decisions, although this was not always the case. In the twenty-three years that Putin has ruled Russia, decision making has become increasingly opaque and narrowed to a small group of influencers around the president. All are loyalists, are of about the same age (early seventies), and appear to hold the same world view as Putin – that Russia is under constant threat from the liberal West, and that it must leverage the power resources that it has to disrupt global politics and prevent the US in particular from containing its ambitions on its borders, and further afield.

What tools does the regime use to promote its foreign interests?

Russia's foreign policy tools are many and varied. It has significant 'hard power' resources like its military. And it is, of course, the only country on earth (to date) that can deliver a nuclear warhead to any major American city on the tip of an intercontinental ballistic missile (ICBM) in under thirty minutes. The Strategic Arms Reduction Treaty ('New START' treaty), which went into effect in 2011 (and extends currently until 2026) between Russia and the US limits each of the two signatories to 1,550 strategic (generally long range) nuclear warheads and bombs. Russia, however, has many more tactical (or shorter range) nuclear weapons than does the US, and there is currently no treaty in force that limits these or calls for an inspection regime as does New START. In February of 2023, President Putin announced the suspension of the New START treaty.

In sum, Russia has very significant nuclear capabilities in its hard power arsenal. Ideally, these are useful only as a deterrent and would not be used in war, although President Putin has threatened to use a low-yield weapon in Ukraine should the Russian homeland be directly threatened during the course of Russia's war there. Whether he would truly employ even a small nuclear weapon in Ukraine remains to be seen.

Beyond nuclear weapons, Russia has significant conventional military capabilities on land, sea, and in the air. The military underwent a comprehensive reform after about 2010 and transitioned from the Soviet conscript-based model to a contract-based system, where members of the military sign up for a set number of years. The armed forces have purportedly been redesigned and slimmed down to fight modern, electronic based warfare, rather than a large continental conflict which was the force structure under the Soviet system. Thus, Russia has about 1,000,000 uniformed members of the military, and only about 100,000 of them are supposed to be conscripts serving for only a year.

In practice, we have seen rather poor performance by the Russian military in its 2022 war in Ukraine, but that appears to be a problem of execution, supplies, management, and organization as opposed to a lack of capacity on paper to wage war. The corruption that is endemic in other Russian bureaucracies appears to be just as present and problematic in executing policy within various branches of the military.

Russia also has significant tools of 'soft' power to attract populations in other countries to its culture and foreign policy preferences, and 'sharp' power or cyber based resources to poke or prod leaders and populations abroad towards a particular perspective on an issue of importance to Russia's leadership.

In addition to tactics that in the past might have been called propaganda, Russia's soft power resources include an array of tools of good will, including the provision of aid and emergency services to foreign countries during natural disasters, the establishment of cultural centres in Europe and the US, and the use of pan-Slavism and the Russian Orthodox religion in countries that share both traits with Russia. For Russian policymakers, soft power is not so much a passive power of attraction, as an active campaign to wage friendship in the service of specific policy goals. It is designed to get others to want the outcomes that Russia wants.

Sharp power is a term meant to capture the ways in which countries like Russia and China use information technology and traditional media to manipulate, confuse, or distract a target population (Walker and Ludwig 2017). The Russian leadership under Putin has established new media resources that present news and information from a distinctly pro-Russian perspective, like Sputnik and the international television company RT (formerly known as Russia Today). The most notorious example of cyber-based sharp power is the 2016 US presidential election where not only was information stolen from the Democratic National Committee through an email phishing operation and then released at just the right point in the campaign to try to discredit Hilary Clinton's candidacy, but bots and trolls using fake social media accounts planted stories or laundered and amplified certain messages until they were picked up by a targeted group. This is all in an effort to manipulate the information environment of an adversary to present narratives that are more beneficial for Russian interests.

Finally, the Russian regime uses the significant economic resources it has amassed from energy exports and leverage over the production, sale, and movement of oil, gas, and other commodities including aluminum, agricultural fertilizer, wheat, and precious metals, as tools of its foreign policy. It has also used its ownership of or political influence over some of the largest oil and gas suppliers in the world as instruments of its foreign policy. The next section of this chapter explores where and how Russia has deployed these resources abroad.

Where in the world is Russia?

In 2014, President Barack Obama infamously referred to Russia as a 'regional power, that is threatening some of its immediate neighbors – not out of strength, but out of weakness' (Obama 2014). To some degree, the spread of the Kremlin's geographic influence might surprise some readers who, like President Obama, have mistaken Putin's Russia for nothing more than a regional power. On the contrary, however, Russia is far more than that – the regime under Vladimir Putin has established itself as a major global influencer and disrupter.

Russia and other formerly Soviet republics

The collapse of the Soviet Union in December 1991 created fifteen independent countries, of which Russia was the largest economically, geographically and in terms of population. Given its geographic dimensions, relative population size, gross domestic product (GDP), and historical legacy as the seat of both the Russian and Soviet empires, it is not surprising that modern Russia should have significant influence over the politics and economies of the other fourteen post-Soviet states. But Russia's contemporary leadership has sought and maintained more control over some former Soviet states than others, and their success in different countries has been highly varied. Indeed, it is safe to conclude that Russian power even in this traditional sphere of influence has fluctuated – relative to the highly centralized Soviet period, of course, but also across time and geography since the Soviet collapse. While Russia's geographic size is staggering, and its economy relative to that of its post-Soviet neighbours is also immense, these alone are not the sole influences on the patterns of its relations within its immediate neighbourhood. The degree to which the political systems of the other former Soviet states are open or more autocratic, or whether the populations are predominantly ethnically Slavic appear to make a difference in how Russia interacts with them. Beyond Ukraine (covered separately in this volume), Russia has sought increased political influence in the domestic politics and economics of the other former Soviet republics – especially those that could infect Russian society with democratic aspirations that might damage the stability of Putin's autocracy.

The six more politically liberalized or liberalizing states of Estonia, Latvia, Lithuania (all of which are now members of the European Union and of NATO), Moldova, Ukraine, and (until recent backsliding) Georgia have received rather different treatment from Russia than have the autocratic regimes of the five Central Asian states of Kazakhstan, Uzbekistan, Kyrgyzstan, Tajikistan, and Turkmenistan. Similarly, Belarus, governed by dictator Alyaksandr Lukashenka since 1994, has been ever-more closely aligned with and controlled by Russia under Putin, especially after Lukashenka was almost deposed by public protests in 2020–21 over an evidently fraudulent presidential election. Putin offered Russian security assistance and provided logistical support in putting down mass strikes within Belarus, effectively ensuring that Lukashenka would stay in power and precluding any sort of Belarusian copy of the Ukrainian 2014 Revolution of Dignity. In winter 2021–22, Russian forces gathered and staged part of their attack on Kyiv and northern Ukraine from Belarusian territory, and in 2023, Russia transferred S-400 missiles to Belarus while retaining operational command of the systems. Putin also redeployed nuclear weapons in Belarus, again while maintaining Russian operational control.

In the South Caucasus, Armenia and Azerbaijan, countries with regimes not quite as autocratic as Belarus' and those of the Central Asian countries, are kept in Moscow's political and economic orbit through heavy Russian involvement in their economies. Armenia too is a member in Russian-led trade organization (the Eurasian Economic Union), the Collective Security Treaty Organization (CSTO), and with Azerbaijan is a 'Dialogue Partner' of the Shanghai Cooperation Organization (SCO), primarily a security organization, where Russia shares leadership with China.

In comparison, Russia's relationship with the more politically open countries (Latvia, Lithuania, Estonia, Ukraine, Moldova, and, until recently, Georgia) has often been antagonistic and even punitive, especially as Russian domestic politics under Putin's long rule has become more autocratic. Russian policies in these states have often been geared toward changing their political orientations to better serve Russian (read Putin's autocratic regime's) interests. The levers Russia has used have capitalized on some of the still existing Soviet-era legacy infrastructure in oil, gas, and electricity provision, although over time, these mechanisms of control have gradually dissolved as the Baltic states in particular have updated their systems to become more independent of Russia influence. But between 2000 and 2006 alone, Russia cut off oil and gas deliveries in the Baltics at least forty times, usually in response to government policies in these countries that Russia wanted changed (Stoner 2021, p. 38).

Under Putin, Russia has used similar control over Ukrainian gas supplies to try to change its politics in the early to mid 2000s but to little avail. In all six of these countries, however, Russia has used control over business elites, especially in the energy sector, sometimes (although not always) of Russian descent, to exercise its economic and political influence. Russia has also used its cyber capabilities to try to disrupt the economies of these countries through denial-of-service attacks on their banking systems and government websites, as well as trying to use 'sharp' power tools to feed false information to mass publics about mistreatment of ethnic Russians on their territories.

Georgia, Ukraine, and Moldova, unlike the three Baltic countries, have all been subject to Russian military incursions and occupations since the Soviet collapse as well. A small group of about 1,500 Russian troops have occupied the breakaway region of Transnistria in Moldova since 1992; Russia has occupied two regions of Georgia (South Ossetia and Abkhazia) following an invasion and short war with Georgian forces there in 2008, and as discussed in greater detail in Chapter 15 in this volume, Russia illegally annexed the Crimean peninsula from Ukraine in 2014, and supported and supplied a civil war in the eastern Donbas region of Ukraine through early 2022. That was followed by its full-blown attempted invasion of the rest of Ukraine that began on 24 February 2022. In autumn of 2022, Putin announced the official annexation of four more provinces of Ukraine (Zaporizhzhia, Donetsk, Luhansk, and Kherson), even though the Russian military did not actually occupy or control all of this territory.

Nonetheless, as with the two regions of Georgia that it occupies, and in Transnistria in Moldova, the Russian government has handed out Russian passports to citizens of these regions. Ukrainians refusing Russian citizenship were reportedly forcibly deported.

In sum, Russian foreign policy toward its fourteen neighbours that had themselves also been republics of the Soviet Union has evolved since 1991. Increasingly, however, Vladimir Putin has pressed for greater integration among Slavic republics (like Belarus and Ukraine) and Moldova, and sought to discourage, or even use force to prevent them from seeking membership in NATO or the European Union.

Russia and Europe

Beyond the countries that were formerly, like Russia, part of the Soviet Union, contemporary Russian foreign policy has been influential and disruptive across Europe. Following the collapse of communism in 1989, the countries of formerly communist Eastern Europe had become Ground Zero – not for the 'end of history' of the exploitation of man by man as envisioned by communists in Russia one hundred years earlier, but for the end of Marxist-Leninist forms of government themselves. Virtually all had opted instead in favour of liberal democracy (at least initially) and that very capitalist system that Marx had so maligned more than a century earlier. But the struggle over Eastern Europe turned out not to have ended in a full victory for democracy. Elections of far-right governments in Poland and Hungary in 2010, and their rollback of many of the rights and freedoms those states had embraced twenty years earlier, have eroded the resiliency of their transformations. Under Putin, Russia has also made efforts to entice other Central European governments away from the influence of the EU and encouraged internal political dissent in others in attempts to divide European unity.

There are geostrategic reasons behind this, of course. Russia has long had an historical and security interest in Eastern Europe. The Russian Empire fought wars with Sweden, the Habsburgs, and the Ottomans over these 'lands in between' Russia proper and what is now a reunited Germany in the West (Orenstein 2018). As the new Russia emerged from its post-Soviet reform hangover, these interests were revived, although competition with Western Europe in this region was not inevitable. Rather, there was a conscious choice under Putin not to join Europe, even when given opportunities to do so. After Putin reassumed the Russian presidency in 2012, the broader region that lies between Russia's western borders and Germany's east evolved into a central battleground for political and economic influence between Russia on the one hand, and Europe and the US on the other.

Russian foreign policymakers became increasingly exercised about NATO expansion, although Yeltsin had come to grudgingly accept it. His concern had been that the US and Europe were hedging on the success of Russia's nascent democracy by installing a security buffer in Eastern Europe. Opponents within the Russian Ministry of Defence and Ministry of Foreign Affairs pointed in the mid-1990s to a verbal promise allegedly made to Mikhail Gorbachev by George H. W. Bush's secretary of state, James Baker, in February 1990, that the alliance would expand 'not one inch eastward' once

Germany had been reunited, necessarily including what had been communist East Germany into NATO (Sarotte 2021). Whether or not such promises were made, they were not written down, and became largely irrelevant as more liberal and democratic governments came to power in the six countries of the former Warsaw Pact. From an American and Western European perspective, these were sovereign states, the democratically elected leaders of which could make foreign policy decisions on behalf of their people independent of Russian input. Therefore, when Poland, Hungary, and the Czech Republic asked to join and then were accepted to NATO in 1999, it was their right to do so.

Russia had been invited to join the North Atlantic Cooperation Council in 1991 and would join the Euro-Atlantic Partnership Council by 1997. On a parallel track, initially intended to replace NATO expansion, integration into European security structures was the idea behind NATO's 'Partnership for Peace' programme that included Russia and virtually every other former communist country in Eastern Europe as well as Armenia, Azerbaijan, Belarus, Georgia, Moldova, Ukraine, and the five former Soviet republics of Central Asia. In the late 1990s too, Boris Yeltsin sent Russian peacekeepers to work with NATO forces in the Balkans. The 1997 NATO-Russia Founding Act formalized relations, and in 2002 the NATO-Russia Council was established as a permanent consultative forum. Russia was an ally and Europe was there to help it recover from communism and rejoin the society of free, prosperous countries. All of this would unravel, however, with the Russian annexation of the Crimean Peninsula from Ukraine in March of 2014 and the re-invasion of Ukraine by Russian forces in 2022.

With the addition in 2004 of former Soviet republics, and now sovereign countries, Estonia, Latvia, and Lithuania, as well as the Eastern Bloc countries of Bulgaria, Slovakia, and Slovenia, NATO reassurances did little to soothe the concerns of the Russian political and military establishment. They were acutely aware of the fact that, as of 2004, NATO forces sat a mere 120 km from St Petersburg. Putin also apparently truly believed, as Yeltsin had, that Russia should be able to join NATO as a full member. If Russia was not the intended focus of NATO expansion eastward, as Western leaders argued, then why could Russia not become a full member and partner? In July 2001, Putin said of NATO, 'We do not see it as an enemy. We do not see a tragedy in its existence, but we also see no need for it', and he argued that Russia should be included in a new single security and defence space in Europe

(Putin 2001). Over time, however, perceptions of the EU and NATO among Putin and other members of Russia's foreign policy and defence establishment shifted. They began to see the EU not as a trading zone of free countries, nor NATO as a security organization with which Russia could (and did) cooperate under Yeltsin, during most of Putin's first and second terms, and under Medvedev's presidency of Russia between 2008–12; instead, the Russian leadership saw them now as institutions specifically designed to isolate and contain Russia. By February 2007, Putin complained loudly and clearly for the first time at the Munich Conference on Security Policy about NATO expansion.

As NATO expanded through Eastern and Central Europe, Russian interests abroad expanded significantly as well. In some parts of the world, this was a reinvigoration of old Soviet ties, but in others, the relationships were new. While undoubtedly, Europe is where Russia's involvement is most obvious, especially in formerly communist countries like Hungary, for example, it has also sought to influence politics and publics in West European democracies like France, Italy, Germany, and even the UK during Brexit. Following Putin's 2012 return to the presidency, Russian foreign policy became ever-more focused on disrupting and ideally breaking up the NATO alliance and dividing the European Union. Poorer European states were also increasingly vulnerable to Russian influence. Europe's relative strength in comparison to Russia's is only in its unanimity. Thus, promoting divisive politics in some countries, including right-wing populist movements, has been one of the Kremlin's methods of trying to tear some EU members away. Russian companies were also heavy investors in some of the newer members of the EU like Bulgaria and Hungary, and under right-wing prime minister Victor Orbán, Hungary has been an enthusiastic partner to Russia. But beyond Hungary, under President Putin's leadership, Russia has invested in other right-wing populist political forces like Marine Le Pen's National Front in France and the nationalist UKIP during the Brexit campaign, in an effort to disrupt European unity.

As we have seen since Russia's full-scale invasion of Ukraine in 2022, Europe was especially vulnerable to Russian influence in the energy sector. Indeed, until 2022, when EU sanctions cut off Russian gas and oil imports into most of Europe, Russia was the main supplier of both commodities to the EU. But since 2022, in an effort to prevent proceeds from the sale of energy exports flowing into Russia to fund its war on Ukraine, the EU has dramatically curtailed its reliance on Russian suppliers of energy, effectively eliminating Europe as a market for Russian oil and natural gas, and also preventing Russian policy actors from using energy as a weapon to manipulate European politics.

Nonetheless, within individual European countries, as in countries in its more immediate neighbourhood, under Vladimir Putin, Russia has developed alliances and chains of dependency with the goal of disrupting politics and eroding European unity. It has used a diversity of methods to do so in what some scholars have referred to as a 'hybrid war', where the emphasis is on an indirect or 'non-linear' package of tools, including but not limited to military means, to interrupt the domestic politics of other countries. This toolset has included cyber technology and traditional media used to influence or confuse countries' information environments, inserting intelligence assets or 'agents of influence' into important positions, financing opposition politicians, and bribing or discrediting elected governments in Western Europe. These tools are not entirely new: They are akin to many of the tactics the KGB used in Western Europe during the Cold War, the difference being, perhaps, less in the array of tools used to exercise influence over European politics and more in the guile (and occasional sloppiness) with which contemporary Russia has done so.

Perhaps more damaging to the unity of Europe is the support of illiberal politicians. Since Putin's return to the Kremlin in 2012, his administration has put great effort into cultivating their rise, especially in Hungary. Under Prime Minister Victor Orbán, Hungary received the dubious honour of first place in the category of democratic recession in Europe. Hungary passed laws on non-governmental organizations (NGOs) that imitated restrictions in Russia introduced a few years earlier. Orbán has also imitated the Putinist use of legislative fiat and arbitrary fines to effectively shut down opposition political parties to tip the scales in favour of his own Fidesz Party. Orbán's decidedly pro-Russian bent followed a 2009 meeting with Putin; after becoming Hungary's prime minister in 2010, he emphasized economic opportunities for Hungary not just in the EU, but also to the east in Russia. Within Eastern Europe, Orbán has become a leading proponent of illiberalism – the idea that elections are held only to legitimize the status quo dominance of one party, and that there need not be institutional independence for courts, opposition political parties, or the media. This line of thinking echoes sentiments and policy within Russia and is presented as an alternative to the perception of the rest of Europe as placing excessive emphasis on personal rights and freedoms to the detriment of a cohesive social fabric.

Russia and the Middle East and North Africa

While Russian involvement in the Middle East is not new, given significant historical interests in the region by both Soviet and imperial actors, Russia under Vladimir Putin has re-established a striking and influential presence in the region. The policy scope of Russia's renewed involvement and influence in the Middle East and North Africa (MENA) parallels the same three general themes seen in Europe: energy, comprising oil and gas, but also nuclear power; non-energy trade, especially considering that the sale of Russian weaponry is greater in the Middle East than in Europe; and finally, the buttressing of Russia's own national security and autocratic durability, specifically with the aim of countering American influence and presenting itself as an alternate pole of global power.

In understanding the domain and scope of Russia's activity in the Middle East, the region can be reasonably organized into four groups. The first three groups – Syria, Iran, and Iraq; Turkey and Israel; and Egypt, Libya, Morocco, and Tunisia – form a set of their own, as states that are primary interests for Putin's regime in military and political security terms (although Russia also has some nuclear and other energy interests in Iran and Iraq). The fourth group – Saudi Arabia and the Gulf States – are in the Putin regime's sights primarily because of their role in global energy markets.

Of particular note, Russia in the twenty-first century has become uniquely able to balance relations with states that are usually adversaries, such as Iran and Israel or both of those countries and Saudi Arabia. While the US has chosen clear sides and is a staunch adversary to Iran but an unfailing ally of Israel, Putin's Russia has become a simultaneous partner to both – something even the Soviet Union failed to do. Some observers attribute this to a strictly transactional approach to dealing with Middle Eastern regimes. That is, successive dealings between Putin's regime and different leaders in the Middle East are not tied together with the intent of building long-term alliances based on shared philosophical beliefs or worldviews. Instead, areas of cooperation are relatively narrow and unmoored from moral judgments or requirements for further interaction. In a sense, this is an advantage not just over the US, which has traditionally (although not always, of course, in its dealings with countries like Saudi Arabia or Iran under the Shah, for example) tied respect for human rights and liberalized politics to support for its allies, but also over the Soviet Union, since there is no concerted ideological war to wage for the allegiance of the citizens or leaders of these states.

Russia's main military footprint in the Middle East has been in Syria since 2015. This was also the first time Russian forces were on active deployment (beyond peacekeeping missions in the former Yugoslavia) outside the territory of the former Soviet Union. In September 2015, as the extremist group ISIS moved further into a Syria already splintered into warring factions of the regime's opponents, the Russian military moved in to buttress Syrian President Assad's forces.

The impressively rapid mobilization of Russian forces in Syria also announced to the world – and to Russian citizens back home via daily updates on the conflict by state-controlled news services – that the Russian military was strong and battle-ready, with new weapons systems and capabilities. Indeed, Syria turned out to be a testing ground for a new cohort of young Russian officers who gained serious combat experience. The engagement also provided state-owned Russian arms exporters with an opportunity to exhibit new weapons they were eager to sell elsewhere in the Middle East and beyond. Private Russian mercenaries known as the Wagner Group, operated by Putin associate Yevgeny Prigozhin, also emerged in Syria (and later Libya, and elsewhere), and became notorious owing to their brutality and recruitment of Russian convicts to serve in the war in Ukraine in 2022.

The Syrian conflict also buttressed ties between Russia under Putin and Iran's theocracy, as its troops battled on the ground in Syria supported by Russian aircraft. Iran has also supplied Russia with drones during its renewed conflict in Ukraine.

Russia and Sub-Saharan Africa

Contemporary Russia's spreading global influence has moved southward from the MENA region into parts of sub-Saharan Africa, too. As in the Middle East, both the imperial and Soviet periods initially established a presence in much of Africa. The Soviet Union was a developmental model for liberation movements in some postcolonial African states. The Soviets also provided military aid and had signed agreements with a majority of African countries for technological and economic assistance. In this period, a reported 25,000 Africans were trained at Soviet universities or technical academies as well by the early 1980s (Stoner 2021, 103).

In 2015, with Russian influence in the Middle East greatly enhanced through its intervention in Syria, sub-Saharan Africa gained new importance for Russia, appearing as a priority area in a national security document emphasizing trade potential; economic, military and technical cooperation; and opportunities for educational aid.

In what should now be a recognizable theme to the reader, Russia's interests in Africa are in natural resources extraction; the marketing and control of transportation routes; trade in arms sales; security on the continent that would require military cooperation, education, and humanitarian needs; and the provision of materials for infrastructural development, including roads and nuclear power plants. Among these, arms sales have been an easy way for Russia to enter or re-establish trade relations with many African states. Somalia, an old Soviet ally, for example, needed Russian weapons in its battle with Al-Shabaab. In return, Russia has become a partner in developing oil, gas, and uranium. In Ethiopia, Russia has invested in the energy sector; similarly, Uganda, another former Soviet ally and sometimes US partner, sought Russian assistance in infrastructure development and an emerging energy sector. In Kenya, the biggest East African economy, Russia has re-emerged as a key trading partner. The Russian government has cancelled billions in former Soviet debt extended to African countries and in return, Russian companies (often owned or controlled by Putin's cronies) have gained contracts for infrastructural development across the continent.

The goals for Russian foreign policy on the African continent are largely economic, especially in the wake of the sanctions imposed on some of the jewels of the Russian economy, frequently under the control of businesses tied tightly to Putin himself. In some cases, too, it is less expensive to mine and market African natural resources, like oil and precious minerals, than in Russia. Here too we have seen private mercenaries tied to the Wagner Group appear to market diamonds or provide security services. In addition, the continent is home to one billion consumers with emerging technology needs and interests that Russian companies are happy to try to serve as they look for new markets to replace those that were closed to them after 2014 and further rendered out of reach by the tight sanctions regime that followed the 2022 invasion of Ukraine.

Some of Russia's biggest companies have projects in Africa, including a set that are state-owned or very closely tied to the state like Gazprom, Lukoil, Alrosa, Renova, Rusal, RosAtom, and Norilsk Nickel, among others. Such projects exist in South Africa, Libya, Angola, the Democratic Republic of the Congo, Togo, Botswana, Nigeria, Ghana, and Namibia. Big projects have focused on diamond extraction in Angola, gas pipeline construction in Nigeria, nickel mining in Botswana, oil deposit exploration in Côte d'Ivoire and Ghana, precious mineral mining in South Africa, and oil extraction in Equatorial Guinea.

Russia and Latin America

As in other regions, Putin's Russia has sought to rebuild Soviet-era relationships and establish new partners in Latin America. Beyond Cuba, the Soviet Union was not all that active in the region during the Cold War. The Soviets did provide some support to leftist regimes in Nicaragua and El Salvador, for example, but these were not fully communist regimes and did not have close trade and security ties with the USSR, as did Cuba under Castro. But after the global financial crisis of 2008, clear signs of Russian engagement in Latin America emerged. These relationships continued to blossom in the decade that followed, and especially as Russian companies sought to avoid isolation in the wake of US and European sanctions after 2014 that intensified after February 2022.

Echoing its push into the Middle East and Africa, in Latin America, Russian interests have coalesced around energy, arms sales, and infrastructure development deals. As was the case in sub-Saharan Africa, Putin forgave almost all of Cuba's Soviet-era debt. In 2017, Rosneft signed agreements with Brazil for a controlling stake in drilling for oil in the Amazon Basin. Putin also requested that Ecuador, Brazil, Argentina, and Chile provide agricultural products to Russia, replacing those that would normally have come from the EU but were under Russian countersanctions.

In 2000, total trade between Russia and all of Latin America was only about $3 billion; Russia's imports were largely agricultural and food products, while it supplied Latin American militaries with new tanks, helicopters, and surface-to-air missiles. This changed with Russia's re-engagement with the region, such that according to one estimate, little more than ten years later Russian–Latin American trade had grown to as much as $24 billion (Stoner 2021, 107).

Most significant in Russia's projection of influence in Latin America is its relationship with Venezuela, the recipient of the most notable arms deals. Under Nicolas Maduro, Venezuela became increasingly dependent on Putin's Russia, especially since the crash of oil prices in 2014. American sanctions on both countries also arguably drove them into one another's arms, as they have looked for new partners for their energy products. In 2016, as collateral for a $1.5 billion loan, Rosneft took a 49.9 per cent stake in Venezuela's state oil company's refining subsidiary, Citgo, based in the United States (Stoner 2021, p. 108). In the spring of 2020, Rosneft's assets in Venezuela were transferred to an entity wholly owned by the Russian state. Despite heavy sanctions on Venezuela by the US against the state-owned Petroleos de Venezuela (PDVSA), Putin's Russia managed to keep Venezuelan oil on international markets. Indeed, Russian support effectively saved the Maduro government from complete collapse in 2019. That spring, amid rumours of an armed American intervention, Secretary of State Mike Pompeo announced with some certainty that the embattled Venezuelan leader was preparing to flee Caracas as violent protesters demanded his ouster in favour of opposition leader Juan Guaidó. But Russia's leadership sent two military planes with Russian military 'technicians' to intervene; evidently the US backed away, and Maduro remained in power. Putin's regime also used its chair at the table in the United Nations Security Council to protect Venezuela and Nicaragua against further sanctions, as well as providing other financial avenues to lessen the impact of American and EU sanctions.

Russia and Asia

Moscow's increasing and intensifying relationships across Asia are too numerous to explore in significant depth here. Indeed, renewed Russo-Sino relations alone are worthy of a book in and of themselves. But since 2012, the current Russian regime has sought to grow and diversify its trade linkages across Asia, as well as to create chains of economic and strategic dependencies and connectivity that make it difficult for the US or Europe to isolate Russia internationally. Chinese-Russian economic and military cooperation has grown significantly since the early 2000s such that by 2019, Dan Coats, then director of US National Intelligence, testified to the Senate Select Committee on Intelligence that 'China and Russia are more aligned than at any point since the mid-1950s' (Coats 2019).

Even before Russian forces emerged from their bases in Sevastopol in Crimea in 2014 and the ensuing sanctions imposed on parts of the economy, Putin's Russia had begun closer economic and strategic collaboration with China under President Xi Jinping. This was an axis of mutual convenience to be sure, and came at a time when relations with the US were in sharp decline for both Russia and China.

As in other areas, under Putin, Russian interests in China were guided by energy supply, non-energy trade, military sales and cooperation, regional security issues like North Korea, the South China Sea, and, more recently, transportation and trade routes opening in the Arctic.

Given the size of the Chinese economy and population relative to Russia's, it is often argued that Russia is the weaker partner in any relations with

China. The asymmetry in these traditional measures of global power is obviously true, but while Russia's population is smaller, it is richer per capita than China's, its nuclear arsenal is larger, its military technology is superior, and its weighty influence in energy markets – control and ownership of vast energy resources and energy transportation networks – all help to bring some balance to the relationship.

Nonetheless, there are clear areas where Putin's Russia must contend with China – for example, with respect to the latter's Belt and Road Initiative (BRI) and the possibility of pulling Russia's Central Asian partners out of its economic orbit. Perhaps to try to mitigate Russian concern in 2015, Xi agreed to coordinate with Russia on Central Asian investments with the Eurasian Economic Union (EEU). Russia and China also jointly founded the Shanghai Cooperation Organization (SCO), and despite predictions of conflict rather than comity, there is growing evidence that they cooperate in the contemporary international environment more than they directly compete.

Beyond stability and security in the greater Eurasian landmass, the policy areas where Russian and Chinese interests now more closely converge are in security and trade. China has purchased S-400 anti-missile defence systems from Russia, as well as Su-35 jets. According to SIPRI, about 12 per cent of Russia's weapons sales went to China between 2013 and 2017 (Saalman 2017, 26).

All of this is in rather stark contrast to Soviet-Sino relations that progressively worsened under Stalin and Mao, culminating in a break in the 1970s. Indeed, there is no ideological component in Chinese-Russian relations in the twenty-first century; the blossoming relationship between Putin's Russia and contemporary China is pragmatic. The Russian regime needs Chinese markets and foreign investment to keep its economy growing and society stable, especially during its ongoing war in Ukraine, while China needs Russia's energy and weaponry. There are shared interests in exploring the Arctic for new energy sources, as well as in forging new, more direct trade routes through there. There are shared security interests in Central Asia. Both need new allies who might support their respective new territorial claims in the South China Sea for China and Ukraine in the case of Russia. China abstained from the United Nations Security Council resolution condemning Putin's seizure of Crimea in 2014, the only member (other than Russia, which vetoed it) to do so, and behaved the same way when Russia invaded Ukraine in 2022. Its trade with Russia has increased since then, taking advantage of the Russian need to replace lost European energy markets in oil and natural gas.

As with states in the Middle East that have long had adversarial relationships with one another, as noted earlier in this chapter, in Asia and South Asia, Russia under Putin has proven able to balance constructive relationships with traditional rivals in the region. With respect to India, contemporary Russia has sought to continue its large volume of weapons sales, while at the same time balancing this with expanding relations with China, long an adversary to India. In part, Putin's Russia has sought this balance working through several regional trade and security organizations like the Shanghai Cooperation Organization (SCO); the Association of South East Asian Nations (ASEAN), through which Russia has sought to develop further trade ties with growing economies in South Asia like Vietnam as well as with South Korea and Japan; and the Collective Security Treaty Organization (CSTO), which includes Armenia, Belarus, Kazakhstan, Kyrgyzstan, Russia, Tajikistan, and the two observer states of Serbia and Afghanistan. Since the mid-2000s, the CSTO, which Russia leads, has sought closer ties and cooperation with the SCO in the areas of counterterrorism, anti-narcotics trade, arms trafficking and transnational crime, for example.

Despite this comity with regional organizations and within the UN, contemporary Russia has had to seek balance in its blossoming trade and political relationships with China and with its relations with India. The volume of trade between India and post-Soviet Russia has been much smaller than it has become with China. Indian investment in Russia has also been relatively limited, although it has been in vital areas of mutual interest like defence, pharmaceuticals, diamonds, and non-fossil fuels energy sectors – as in India's agreement in 2017 to have Russian firms build twelve nuclear power plants.

Since 2014, India has not only continued its high volume of defence purchases from Russia, but it has also increased investment in Russia's Arctic oil interests, purchasing a $1.27 billion (15 per cent) stake in the Vankor oilfield, for example, at a time when the West imposed sanctions on companies exploring there (Stoner 2021, 113). Further, Rosneft and India's Essar agreed in 2015 to refine 100 million tons of oil in India over a ten-year period, and Rosneft gained a 49 per cent stake in the shares of the refinery and a chain of more than 3,000 gas stations in India. Russia has maintained its position as India's main supplier of defence equipment – supplying as much as 56 per cent of Indian military-technical equipment between 2015 and 2019, and that high figure was actually a decrease from 74 per cent in the preceding four-year period (Weseman et al. 2020). As with Turkey, Saudi Arabia, and elsewhere, Russia has also supplied India with S-400s. Russia is not, however, just a military supplier to India; by 2017, Putin's Russia had licensed some of its military technology for India to develop fighter jets, tanks, ammunition, and helicopters.

Despite this close cooperation in the defence field, other areas of trade and security cooperation between India and Russia were more aspirational and prospective until Russia's invasion of Ukraine in 2022. Whereas until then, the volume of trade and investment between the two was relatively low and focused on construction, pharmaceuticals, and transport, after 2022, India has increased its purchases of Russian energy in particular – a much-needed boost to Russia's budget given the loss of European markets for gas given the stiff sanctions regime. But even before Russia's invasion of Ukraine and India's move to rapidly scale up its purchase of Russian energy, India's Narendra Modi and Putin had pledged to increase trade between the two countries by three times the 2018 volume, to $30 billion by 2025. India's growing energy needs are an important market for Russian firms, especially with the loss of European markets after the 2022 invasion of Ukraine.

Russia's renewed relations with India, not dissimilar from those with China, have provided avenues by which to avoid the full impact of Western sanctions initiated in 2014 and expanded after 2022 on its economy while also representing large new markets for Russia more generally. Russia under Putin has thus far deftly managed the political and strategic tensions simmering between these Asian powerhouses to further its global interests. Moreover, Putin's regime has sought to partner with them in strategic areas to make them 'force multipliers' for the promotion of Russian foreign policy interests.

Conclusion

Russian foreign policy reach and scope by 2023 had expanded dramatically in comparison to the 1990s. The policy areas in which Putin's Russia exercises its influence have been focused on energy, trade, and national security. Russia's growing presence in the Global South, and its deepening cooperation with China and India, have provided the regime with the opportunity to promote the narrative at home that under Putin's leadership, Russia had reclaimed its status as a global power, 'as a strong state – a country that others heed and that can stand up for itself' (Putin 2008).

Questions for discussion

1 Would a different regime type in Russia – democracy for example – lead to a less aggressive and more cooperative foreign policy with the West?
2 Did the expansion of NATO lead to a true security crisis for Russia?
3 Should we consider Russia today a 'great power'?
4 Does Russia represent an existential threat to the US and Europe?
5 How different are the goals of Russian versus Soviet foreign policies?

Recommended readings

Giles, Keir. 2023. *Russia's War on Everybody and What it Means for You.* London: Bloomsbury Academic.
Renz, Bettina. 2018. *Russia's Military Revival.* Medford, MA: Polity Press.
Sarotte, M. E. 2021. *Not One Inch: America, Russia, and the Making of Post-Cold War Stalemate.* New Haven: Yale University Press.
Stent, Angela. 2019. *Putin's World: Russia Against the West and with the Rest.* New York: Twelve Press.
Stoner, Kathryn. 2021. *Russia Resurrected: Its Power and Purpose in a New Global Order.* New York: Oxford University Press.

Notes

Chapter 4

1. See www.pewresearch.org/global/2022/06/22/ratings-for-russia-drop-to-record-lows/.
2. See chrome-extension://efaidnbmnnnibpcajpcglclefindmkaj/https://freedomhouse.org/sites/default/files/inline_images/2004.pdf.
3. See http://en.kremlin.ru/events/president/news/19243.
4. See http://en.kremlin.ru/events/president/news/19243.
5. See https://jamestown.org/program/russian-ethnic-minorities-repudiate-proposed-law-russian-nation/.

Chapter 5

1. Parts of this chapter were first published at Der Pragmaticus Verlag AG, www.derpragmaticus.com, @2022.

Chapter 6

1. See the Central Bank of Russia's statistical reports at www.cbr.ru/eng for useful historical data. Since the Russian invasion of Ukraine in February 2022, the CBR's statistics have become less reliable.
2. See http://en.kremlin.ru/events/president/transcripts/24080.
3. Vladimir Putin, Meeting with Valdai International Discussion Club participants, 25 October 2012, http://eng.kremlin.ru/news/4564.

Chapter 11

1. The Soviet Socialist Republics were considered independent states and formally had a right to secede from the Union. Smaller territories, such as autonomous republics or districts (usually, parts of the Union republics), had a lower status and could not secede from the Union.

References

Chapter 1

Barry, Ellen. 2009. 'Putin Plays Sheriff for Cowboy Capitalists.' *The New York Times*, 4 June 2009, sec. Europe. www.nytimes.com/2009/06/05/world/europe/05russia.html.

Colton, Timothy J. 2017. 'Paradoxes of Putinism.' *Daedalus* 146(2): 8–18.

Colton, Timothy J. 2018. 'Regimeness, Hybridity, and Russian System Building as an Educative Project.' *Comparative Politics* 50(3): 455–73.

Colton, Timothy J., and Henry E. Hale. 2014. 'Putin's Uneasy Return and Hybrid Regime Stability: The 2012 Russian Election Studies Survey.' *Problems of Post-Communism* 61(2): 3–22.

Dawisha, Karen. 2014. *Putin's Kleptocracy: Who Owns Russia?* New York: Simon & Schuster.

Frye, Timothy. 2021. *Weak Strongman: The Limits of Power in Putin's Russia*. Princeton: Princeton University Press.

Frye, Timothy, Ora John Reuter, and David Szakonyi. 2014. 'Political Machines at Work: Voter Mobilization and Electoral Subversion in the Workplace.' *World Politics* 66(2): 195–228.

Gans-Morse, Jordan. 2017. *Property Rights in Post-Soviet Russia: Violence, Corruption, and the Demand for Law*. Cambridge, United Kingdom: Cambridge University Press.

Gel'man, Vladimir. 2015. *Authoritarian Russia: Analyzing Post-Soviet Regime Changes*. Pittsburgh: University of Pittsburgh Press.

Guriev, Sergei, and Daniel Treisman. 2019. 'Informational Autocrats.' *Journal of Economic Perspectives* 33(4): 100–27.

Hale, Henry E. 2011. 'The Myth of Mass Russian Support for Autocracy: The Public Opinion Foundations of a Hybrid Regime.' *Europe-Asia Studies* 63(8): 1357–75.

Hale, Henry E. 2015. *Patronal Politics: Eurasian Regime Dynamics in Comparative Perspective*. New York, NY: Cambridge University Press.

Hale, Henry E., Ora John Reuter, Bryn Rosenfeld, David Szakonyi, and Katerina Tertytchnaya. 2022. 'Russia May Be about to Invade Ukraine. Russians Don't Want It to.' *The Washington Post*, 14 February 2022, sec. The Monkey Cage.

www.washingtonpost.com/politics/2022/02/11/russia-may-be-about-invade-ukraine-russians-dont-want-it/.

Johnson, Juliet. 2000. *A Fistful of Rubles: The Rise and Fall of the Russian Banking System*. Ithaca: Cornell University Press.

Kara-Murza, Vladimir. 2018. 'In Russia, a Democratically Elected Mayor Finally Succumbs to Putinism – The Washington Post.' *The Washington Post*, 5 April 2018. www.washingtonpost.com/news/democracy-post/wp/2018/04/05/in-russia-a-democratically-elected-mayor-finally-succumbs-to-putinism/?utm_term=.c8deeac0f5fe.

Laruelle, Marlene. 2017. 'The Kremlin's Ideological Ecosystems: Equilibrium and Competition.' 493. PONARS Eurasia Policy Memo. Washington, DC: George Washington University. www.ponarseurasia.org/memo/kremlins-ideological-ecosystems-equilibrium-and-competition.

Magyar, Bálint, and Bálint Madlovics. 2021. *The Anatomy of Post-Communist Regimes: A Conceptual Framework*. Budapest: Central European University Press.

McAllister, Ian, and Stephen White. 2008. '"It's the Economy, Comrade!" Parties and Voters in the 2007 Russian Duma Election.' *Europe-Asia Studies* 60(6): 931–57.

Morar', Natalia. 2007. 'Chernaia Kassa Kremlia.' *The New Times*, 10 December 2007.

Petrov, Nikolay, Maria Lipman, and Henry E. Hale. 2014. 'Three Dilemmas of Hybrid Regime Governance: Russia from Putin to Putin.' *Post-Soviet Affairs* 30(1): 1–26.

Reuters. 2015. 'Russia's Nabiullina Named Central Bank Governor of 2015 by Euromoney', 16 September 2015. www.reuters.com/article/russia-cenbank-euromoney/russias-nabiullina-named-central-bank-governor-of-2015-by-euromoney-idUSL5N11M1X420150916.

Sakwa, Richard. 2010. 'The Dual State in Russia.' *Post-Soviet Affairs* 26(3): 185–206.

Sharafutdinova, Gulnaz. 2020. *The Red Mirror: Putin's Leadership and Russia's Insecure Identity*. Oxford, New York: Oxford University Press.

Stoner-Weiss, Kathryn. 2001. 'The Russian State in Crisis: Center and Periphery in the Post-Soviet Era.' In *Russian Politics: Challenges of Democratization*, edited by Zoltan Barany and Robert G. Moser, 103–34. New York: Cambridge University Press.

Taylor, Brian D. 2018. *The Code of Putinism*. New York: Oxford University Press.

Tubridy, Mack. 2022. 'One Mayor Down', *Russia.Post*, 21 December 2022, https://russiapost.info/regions/tomsk, accessed 9 March 2023.

The Economist. 2008. 'Mechel Bashing', 31 July 2008. www.economist.com/node/11848486.

Chapter 2

Alexopoulos, Golfo. *Illness and Inhumanity in Stalin's Gulag.* New Haven: Yale University Press, 2017.

Applebaum, Anne. *Red Famine: Stalin's War on Ukraine.* New York: Doubleday, 2017.

Barnes, Steven A. *Death and Redemption: The Gulag and the Shaping of Soviet Society.* Princeton: Princeton University Press, 2011.

Baron, Samuel H. *Bloody Saturday in the Soviet Union: Novocherkassk, 1962.* Stanford: Stanford University Press, 2002.

Bittner, Stephen V. *The Many Lives of Khrushchev's Thaw: Experience and Memory in Moscow's Arbat.* Ithaca: Cornell University Press, 2008.

Cameron, Sarah. *The Hungry Steppe: Famine, Violence, and the Making of Soviet Kazakhstan.* Ithaca: Cornell University Press, 2018.

Conquest, Robert. *The Harvest of Sorrow: Soviet Collectivization and the Terror Famine.* New York: Oxford University Press, 1986.

Conquest, Robert. *The Great Terror: A Reassessment.* Oxford: Oxford University Press, 2008.

Davies, Sarah and James Harris. *Stalin's World: Dictating the Soviet Order.* New Haven: Yale University Press, 2014.

Dobson, Miriam. *Khrushchev's Cold Summer: Gulag Returnees, Crime, and the Fate of Reform after Stalin.* Ithaca: Cornell University Press, 2011.

Fainberg, Dina and Artemy Kalinovsky, 'Stagnation and its Discontents: The Creation of a Political and Historical Paradigm', in eds. Dina Fainberg and Artemy Kalinovsky, *Reconsidering Stagnation in the Brezhnev Era: Ideology and Exchange.* Lanham: Lexington Books, 2016.

Fitzpatrick, Sheila. *Stalin's Peasants: Resistance and Survival in the Russian Village after Collectivization.* Oxford: Oxford University Press, 1999.

Fitzpatrick, Sheila. 'Revisionism in Soviet History.' *History and Theory*, Vol. 46, No. 4 (2007): 77–91.

Fitzpatrick, Sheila. *On Stalin's Team: The Years of Living Dangerously in Soviet Politics.* Princeton: Princeton University Press, 2015.

Fitzpatrick, Sheila. *The Russian Revolution*, 4th edition. Oxford: Oxford University Press, 2017.

Friedrich, Carl J. and Zbigniew K. Brzezinski. *Totalitarian Dictatorship and Autocracy.* Cambridge, MA: Harvard University Press, 1965.

Goldman, Wendy Z. and Donald A. Filtzer. *Fortress Dark and Stern: The Soviet Home Front During World War II.* Oxford: Oxford University Press, 2021.

Gorlizki, Yoram and Oleg V. Khlevniuk. *Cold Peace: Stalin and the Soviet Ruling Circle, 1945–1953.* Oxford: Oxford University Press, 2005.

Graziosi, Andrea. 'The Uses of Hunger: Stalin's Solution of the Peasant and National Questions in Soviet Ukraine, 1932 to 1933', in *Famines in European*

Economic History: The Last Great European Famines Reconsidered, eds. Declan Curran, Lubomyr Luciuk, and Andrew Newby. London: Routledge, 2015.

Lenin, Vladimir. 'Last Testament', December 1922. Online: www.marxists.org/archive/lenin/works/1922/dec/testamnt/index.htm.

Lenin, Vladimir. 'The Question of Nationalities or "Autonomisation"', 31 December 1922. Online: www.marxists.org/archive/lenin/works/1922/dec/testamnt/autonomy.htm.

Lenoe, Matthew E. *The Kirov Murder and Soviet History*. New Haven: Yale University Press, 2010.

Khlevniuk, Oleg. V. *Master of the House: Stalin and His Inner Circle*, trans. Nora Seligman Favorov. New Haven: Yale University Press, 2008.

Khlevniuk, Oleg. V. *The History of the Gulag: From Collectivization to the Great Terror*. New Haven: Yale University Press, 2013.

Kibita, Nataliya. *Soviet Economic Management Under Khrushchev: The Sovnarkhoz Reform*. London: Routledge, 2015.

Kotkin, Stephen. *Magnetic Mountain: Stalinism as a Civilization*. Berkeley: University of California Press, 1997.

Kotkin, Stephen. *Armageddon Averted: Soviet Collapse, 1970–2000*. Oxford: Oxford University Press, 2009. Online: www.marxists.org/archive/lenin/works/1920/lwc/ch03.htm.

Kozlov, Denis and Eleonory Gilburd. *The Thaw: Soviet Society and Culture during the 1950s and 1960s*. Toronto: University of Toronto Press, 2013.

Malia, Martin. 'Leninist Endgame.' *Daedalus*, Vol. 121, No. 2 (1992): 57–75.

Malia, Martin. *The Soviet Tragedy: A History of Socialism in Russia, 1917–1991*. New York: Free Press, 1994.

Martin, Terry. *The Affirmative Action Empire: Nations and Nationalism in the Soviet Union, 1923–1939*. Ithaca: Cornell University Press, 2001.

Merridale, Catherine. *Ivan's War: Life and Death in the Red Army, 1939–1945*. New York: Metropolitan Books, 2006.

Miller, Chris. *The Struggle to Save the Soviet Economy: Mikhail Gorbachev and the Collapse of the Soviet Union*. Chapel Hill: University of North Carolina Press, 2018.

Naimark, Norman M. *Stalin's Genocides*. Princeton: Princeton University Press, 2010.

Naumenko, Natalya. 'The Political Economy of Famine: The Ukrainian Famine of 1933.' *The Journal of Economic History*, Vol. 81, No. 1 (2021): 156–97.

Nove, Alexander. 'Victims of Stalinism: How Many?' in *Stalinist Terror: New Perspectives*, eds. J. Arch Getty and Roberta Manning. Cambridge: Cambridge University Press, 1993.

Pipes, Richard. *The Russian Revolution*. New York: Vintage, 1991.

Plamper, Jan. *The Stalin Cult: A Study in the Alchemy of Power*. New Haven: Yale University Press, 2012.

Schattenberg, Susanne. *Brezhnev: The Making of a Statesman*. London: Bloomsbury, 2021.

Shearer, David. *Policing Stalin's Socialism: Repression and Social Order in the Soviet Union, 1924–1953*. New Haven: Yale University Press, 2009.

Stalin, J. V. 'Marxism and the National Question', 1913. Online: www.marxists.org/reference/archive/stalin/works/1913/03a.htm.

Suny, Ronald Grigor. 'Toward a Social History of the October Revolution.' *The American Historical Review*, Vol. 88, No. 1 (1983): 31–52.

Tumarkin, Nina. *The Living & The Dead: The Rise and Fall of the Cult of World War II in Russia*. New York: Basic Books, 1994.

Weiner, Amir. 'Saving Private Ivan: From What, Why, and How?' *Kritika: Explorations in Russian and Eurasian History*, Vol. 1, No. 2 (2000): 305–36.

Weiner, Amir. *Making Sense of War: The Second World War and the Fate of the Bolshevik Revolution*. Princeton: Princeton University Press, 2001.

Wheatcroft, Stephen G. 'The Turn Away from Economic Explanations for Soviet Famines.' *Contemporary European History*, Vol. 27, No. 3 (2018): 465–69.

Viola, Lynne. *Peasant Rebels Under Stalin: Collectivization and the Culture of Peasant Resistance*. Oxford: Oxford University Press, 1996.

Yurchak, Alexei. *Everything Was Forever, Until It Was No More: The Last Soviet Generation*. Princeton: Princeton University Press, 2005.

Zubok, Vladislav M. *A Failed Empire: The Soviet Union in the Cold War from Stalin to Gorbachev*. Chapel Hill: University of North Carolina Press, 2009.

Zubok, Vladislav M. *Collapse: The Fall of the Soviet Union*. New Haven: Yale University Press, 2021.

Zubkova, Elena. *Russia After the War: Hopes, Illusions and Disappointments, 1945–1957*. London: Routledge, 2015.

Zubkova, Elena. 'The Rivalry with Khrushchev', in *Nikita Khrushchev*, eds. William Taubman, Sergei Khrushchev, and Abbott Gleason. New Haven: Yale University Press, 2000.

Chapter 3

Ekiert, Grzegorz, and Stephen E. Hanson. 2003. 'Time, Space, and Institutional Change in Central and Eastern Europe'. In *Capitalism and Democracy in Central and Eastern Europe: Assessing the Legacy of Communist Rule*, ed. G. Ekiert and S. E. Hanson. Cambridge: Cambridge University Press.

Frye, Timothy, Ora John Reuter, and David Szakonyi. 2014. 'Political Machines at Work: Voter Mobilization and Electoral Subversion in the Workplace'. *World Politics* 66 (2): 195–228.

Hale, Henry E. 2015. *Patronal Politics: Eurasian Regime Dynamics in Comparative Perspective*. New York: Cambridge University Press.

Kopstein, Jeffrey S., and David A. Reilly. 1999. 'Explaining the Why of the Why: A Comment on Fish's "Determinants of Economic Reform in the Post-Communist World"'. *East European Politics and Societies and Cultures* 13(3): 613–24.

Kotkin, Stephen, and Mark R. Beissinger. 2014. 'The Historical Legacies of Communism: An Empirical Agenda'. In *Historical Legacies of Communism in Russia and Eastern Europe*, ed. M. R. Beissinger and S. Kotkin. New York: Cambridge University Press.

Lankina, Tomila V. 2004. *Governing the Locals: Local Self-Government and Ethnic Mobilization in Russia*. Lanham, Maryland: Rowman and Littlefield Publishers.

Lankina, Tomila V. 2022. *The Estate Origins of Democracy in Russia: From Imperial Bourgeoisie to Post-Communist Middle Class*. Cambridge: Cambridge University Press.

Lankina, Tomila V., and Alexander Libman. 2021. 'The Two-Pronged Middle Class: The Old Bourgeoisie, New State-Engineered Middle Class and Democratic Development'. *American Political Science Review* 115(3): 948–66.

Laruelle, Marlene. 2008. *Russian Eurasianism: An Ideology of Empire*. Washington, DC: Woodrow Wilson Center Press with Johns Hopkins University Press.

Libman, Alexander, and Anastassia V. Obydenkova. 2021. *Historical Legacies of Communism: Modern Politics, Society, and Economic Development*. New York: Cambridge University Press.

Lincoln, Bruce W. 2007. *The Conquest of a Continent: Siberia and the Russians*. Ithaca, New York: Cornell University Press.

McMann, Kelly M., and Nikolai V. Petrov. 2000. 'A Survey of Democracy in Russia's Regions'. *Post-Soviet Geography and Economics* 41(3): 155–82.

Mironov, Boris N. 2015. *Rossiyskaya imperiya: Ot traditsii k modernu*. Vol. 2. St Petersburg: Dmitriy Bulanin.

Neumann, Iver B. 1996. *Russia and the Idea of Europe: A Study in Identity and International Relations*. London; New York: Routledge.

Neumann, Iver B. 2008. 'Russia as a Great Power, 1815–2007'. *Journal of International Relations and Development* 11(2): 128–51.

Pop-Eleches, Grigore. 2007. 'Historical Legacies and Post-Communist Regime Change'. *The Journal of Politics* 69(4): 908–26.

Pop-Eleches, Grigore, and Joshua A. Tucker. 2017. *Communism's Shadow: Historical Legacies and Contemporary Political Attitudes*. Princeton, New Jersey: Princeton University Press.

Rosenfeld, Bryn. 2021. *The Autocratic Middle Class: How State Dependency Reduces the Demand for Democracy*. Princeton, New Jersey: Princeton University Press.

Sidel, John T. 2021. *Republicanism, Communism, Islam: Cosmopolitan Origins of Revolutions in Southeast Asia.* Ithaca, New York: Cornell University Press.

Simpser, Alberto, Dan Slater, and Jason Wittenberg. 2018. 'Dead But Not Gone: Contemporary Legacies of Communism, Imperialism, and Authoritarianism.' *Annual Review of Political Science* 21(1): 419–39.

Soldatov, Andrei, and Irina Borogan. 2022. *The Compatriots: The Russian Exiles Who Fought Against The Kremlin.* New York: Public Affairs.

Soroka, George, and Félix Krawatzek. 2021. 'When the Past is Not Another Country: The Battlefields of History in Russia.' *Problems of Post-Communism* 68(5): 353–67.

Wittenberg, Jason. 2012. 'What is a Historical Legacy?' Berkeley: University of California. Unpublished manuscript.

Chapter 4

Alexseev, Mikhail A., and Henry E. Hale. 2016. 'Rallying 'Round the Leader more than the Flag: Changes in Russian Nationalist Public Opinion 2013–14.' *The New Russian Nationalism: Imperialism, Ethnicity and Authoritarianism 2000–2015.* 192–220.

Anderson, Benedict. 2020. 'Imagined Communities: Reflections on the Origin and Spread of Nationalism.' *The New Social Theory Reader.* Routledge. 282–88.

Baiburin, Albert. 2012. 'Rituals of Identity: The Soviet Passport.' *Soviet and Post-Soviet Identities.* 91–110.

Beissinger, Mark R. 2009. 'Nationalism and the Collapse of Soviet Communism.' *Contemporary European History* 18(3). 331–47.

Billig, Michael. 2005. *Banal Nationalism.* London.

Bonikowski, B. 2016. 'Nationalism in Settled Times.' *Annual Review of Sociology,* 42(1), pp. 427–49.

Brandenberger, D. 2002. *National Bolshevism: Stalinist Mass Culture and the Formation of Modern Russian National Identity, 1931–1956* (Vol. 93). Harvard University Press.

Budryte, Dovile. 2017. *Taming Nationalism? Political Community Building in the Post-Soviet Baltic States.* Routledge.

Condor, Susan. 2000. 'Pride and Prejudice? Identity Management in English People's Talk About "this Country".' *Discourse and Society,* 11(2): 75–205.

Dannreuther, Roland, and Luke March. 2010. 'Tatarstan: Islam Entwined with Nationalism.' *Russia and Islam.* Routledge. 119–37.

Daughtry, J. Martin. 2003. 'Russia's New Anthem and the Negotiation of National Identity.' *Ethnomusicology* 47.1: 42–67.

Etkind, Alexander. 2013. *Warped Mourning*. Stanford University Press.

Elcheroth, Guy, and Stephen Reicher. 2017. *Identity, Violence and Power*. Palgrave Macmillan.

Ejdus, F. 2018. 'Critical Situations, Fundamental Questions and Ontological Insecurity in World Politics.' *Journal of International Relations and Development*, 21(4), pp. 883–908.

Fabrykant, M. and Magun, V. 2019. 'Dynamics of National Pride Attitudes in Post-Soviet Russia, 1996–2015.' *Nationalities Papers*, 47(1), pp. 20–37.

Fox, Jon E., and Cynthia Miller-Idriss. 2008. 'Everyday Nationhood.' *Ethnicities* 8.4: 536–63.

Gellner, E. 2008. *Nations and Nationalism*. Cornell University Press.

Gel'man, Vladimir. 2020. 'The Politics of Fear: How the Russian Regime Confronts its Opponents.' *Russian Social Science Review* 61.6: 467–82.

Goode, J. Paul. 'Russia's Ministry of Ambivalence: The Failure of Civic Nation-building in Post-Soviet Russia.' 2019. *Post-Soviet Affairs* 35.2: 140–60.

Goode, J. Paul, David R. Stroup, and Elizaveta Gaufman. 2022. 'Everyday Nationalism in Unsettled Times: In Search of Normality During Pandemic.' *Nationalities Papers* 50.1: 61–85.

Gudkov, Lev. 2005. 'The Fetters of Victory: How the War Provides Russia with its Identity.' *Osteuropa* 5: 4–6.

Graney, Katherine E. 2009. *Of Khans and Kremlins: Tatarstan and the Future of Ethno-federalism in Russia*. Lexington Books.

Hale, Henry E. 2004. 'Divided we Stand: Institutional Sources of Ethnofederal State Survival and Collapse.' *World Politics* 56.2: 165–93.

Hale, Henry E., and Marlene Laruelle. 2020. 'Rethinking Civilizational Identity from the Bottom up: A Case Study of Russia and a Research Agenda.' *Nationalities Papers* 48.3: 585–602.

'Hidden Resistance to the Russian-Ukrainian War Inside Russia.' *Russian Analytical Digest* # 291, 27 January 2023.

Hirsch, F. 2014. *Empire of Nations. In Empire of Nations*. Cornell University Press.

Hobsbawm, E. J. 2012. *Nations and Nationalism since 1780: Programme, Myth, Reality*. Cambridge University Press.

Horvath, Robert. 2013. *The Legacy of Soviet Dissent: Dissidents, Democratisation and Radical Nationalism in Russia*. Routledge.

Khalid, Adeeb. 1999. *The Politics of Muslim Cultural Reform: Jadidism in Central Asia*. Vol. 27. University of California Press.

Kolstø, Pål. 2019. 'Dmitrii Medvedev's Commission Against the Falsification of History: Why Was It Created and What Did It Achieve? A Reassessment.' *Slavonic and East European Review* 97.4: 738–60.

Kolstø, P. 2016. *The Ethnification of Russian Nationalism. The New Russian Nationalism*, 44.

Laruelle, M. 2009. *In the Name of the Nation: Nationalism and Politics in Contemporary Russia*. Springer.

Laruelle, M. ed. 2009. *Russian Nationalism and the National Reassertion of Russia* (Vol. 4). London: Routledge.

Laruelle, M. 2019. *Russian Nationalism: Imaginaries, Doctrines, and Political Battlefields* (p. 256). Taylor & Francis.

Lieven, D. C. B. 2002. *Empire: The Russian Empire and its Rivals*. Yale University Press.

Malešević, S. 2019. *Grounded Nationalisms: A Sociological Analysis*. Cambridge University Press.

Malinova, Olga. 2021. 'Framing the Collective Memory of the 1990s as a Legitimation Tool for Putin's Regime.' *Problems of Post-Communism* 68.5: 429–41.

Mitrofanova, Anastasia. 2016. 'Russian Ethnic Nationalism and Religion Today.' *The New Russian Nationalism: Imperialism, Ethnicity and Authoritarianism 2000–2015*: 104–31.

Morozov, Viatcheslav. *Russia's Postcolonial Identity: A Subaltern Empire in a Eurocentric World*. Springer, 2015.

Morris, Jeremy. 2022. 'Russians in Wartime and Defensive Consolidation.' *Current History* 121.837: 258–63.

Norris, Stephen M., and Willard Sunderland, eds. *Russia's People of Empire: Life Stories from Eurasia, 1500 to the Present*. 2012. Indiana University Press.

Robinson, Paul. *Russian Conservatism*. Northern Illinois University Press, 2019.

Rowley, David G. 1997. 'Aleksandr Solzhenitsyn and Russian Nationalism.' *Journal of Contemporary History* 32.3: 321–37.

Sharafutdinova, G. 2020. *The Red Mirror: Putin's Leadership and Russia's Insecure Identity*. Oxford University Press.

Shterin, Marat. 2001. 'New Religions in the New Russia.' 310–21.

Slezkine, Y., 1994. The USSR as a Communal Apartment, or How a Socialist State Promoted Ethnic Particularism. *Slavic Review*, 53(2), pp. 414–52.

Smyth, Regina, and Irina Soboleva. 2014. 'Looking Beyond the Economy: Pussy Riot and the Kremlin's Voting Coalition.' *Post-Soviet Affairs* 30.4: 257–75.

Suny, Ronald Grigor, and Terry Martin, eds. 2001. *A State of Nations: Empire and Nation-making in the Age of Lenin and Stalin*. Oxford University Press.

Suny, Ronald Grigor. 2001. 'The Contradictions of Identity: Being Soviet and National in the USSR and after.' *Soviet and Post-Soviet Identities*: 17–36.

Urban, Michael. 1994. 'The Politics of Identity in Russia's Postcommunist Transition: The Nation against Itself.' *Slavic Review* 53.3: 733–65.

Walker, Shaun. 2018. *The Long Hangover: Putin's New Russia and the Ghosts of the Past*. Oxford University Press.

Wijermars, Mariëlle. 2018. *Memory Politics in Contemporary Russia: Television, Cinema and the State*. Taylor & Francis.

Wood, Elizabeth A. 2011. 'Performing Memory: Vladimir Putin and the Celebration of World War II in Russia.' *The Soviet and Post-Soviet Review* 38.2: 172–200.

Yusupova, Guzel. 2022. 'How Does the Politics of Fear in Russia Work? The Case of Social Mobilisation in Support of Minority Languages.' *Europe-Asia Studies* 74.4: 620–41.

Chapter 5

Antola Swan, Alessandra. 2016. 'The Iconic Body: Mussolini Unclothed.' *Modern Italy*, 21, no. 4: 361–81.

Boatright, Robert G. and Valerie Sperling. 2020. *Trumping Politics as Usual: Masculinity, Misogyny, and the 2016 Elections.* Oxford University Press.

Chenoweth, Erica and Zoe Marks. 2022. 'Revenge of the Patriarchs: Why Autocrats Fear Women.' *Foreign Affairs*, March/April. www.foreignaffairs.com/articles/china/2022-02-08/women-rights-revenge-patriarchs.

Essig, Laurie. 1999. *Queer in Russia.* Duke University Press.

Feminist Anti-War Resistance. 2022. 'Russia's Feminists Are in the Streets Protesting Putin's War.' *Jacobin*, 27 February. https://jacobin.com/2022/02/russian-feminist-antiwar-resistance-ukraine-putin.

Johnson, Janet Elise. 2017. 'Gender Equality Policy: Criminalizing and Decriminalizing Domestic Violence.' *Russian Analytical Digest*, No. 200: 2–5.

Johnson, Janet Elise, et al. 2021. 'Mixed Signals: What Putin Says about Gender Equality.' *Post-Soviet Affairs*, 37, No. 6: 507–25.

LegitRuss: Values-Based Legitimation in Authoritarian States: Top-down versus Bottom-up Strategies, the Case of Russia', survey funded by the Research Council of Norway, Project Number 300997: www.uio.no/for-ansatte/arbeidsstotte/forskningsstotte/forskpro/prosjekter/hf/ilos/values-based-legitimation-in-authoritarian-states-top-down-versus-bottom-up-strategies.-the-case-of-russia-%28legitruss%29/index.html.

Mierzejewski-Voznyak, Melanie. 2018. 'The Radical Right in Post-Soviet Ukraine.' In: *The Oxford Handbook of the Radical Right*, ed. Jens Rydgren. New York: Oxford University Press.

Novitskaya, Alexandra, et al. 2023. 'Unpacking "Traditional Values" in Russia's Conservative Turn: Gender, Sexuality, and the Soviet Legacy.' *Europe-Asia Studies*. DOI: https://doi.org/10.1080/09668136.2023.2215484.

Perheentupa, Inna. 2022. *Feminist Politics in Neoconservative Russia: An Ethnography of Resistance and Resources.* Bristol University Press.

Riabov, Oleg and Tatiana Riabova. 2014. 'The Remasculinization of Russia?' *Problems of Post-Communism*, 61, No. 2: 23–35. DOI: 10.2753/PPC1075-8216610202.

Riabova, T. B. 2014. '"Putin vs Obama": Protivopostavlenie natsional'nykh maskulinnostei kak faktor sovremennogo rossiiskogo antiamerianizma.' *Zhenshchina v rossiiskom obshchestve*, 4: 63–71.

'Russian Church Leader Appears to Blame Gay Pride Parades for Ukraine War.' 2022. The Moscow Times, 7 March. www.themoscowtimes.com/2022/03/07/news-from-russia-what-you-missed-over-the-weekend-153-a76802.

'Signing of Treaties on the Accession of Donetsk and Lugansk People's Republics and Zaporozhye and Kherson Regions to Russia', 30 September 2022. http://en.kremlin.ru/events/president/news/69465.

Sperling, Valerie. 2015. *Sex, Politics, and Putin: Political Legitimacy in Russia.* Oxford University Press.

Sperling, Valerie. 2015a. 'Why Putin – and Some of His Female Fans – Go Shirtless.' *Huffington Post*, 17 February. www.huffpost.com/entry/putin-female-fans-shirtless_b_6664240.

Sperling, Valerie. 2022. 'Putin, Zar der Macho-Politik.' *Der Pragmaticus*, 18 July. www.derpragmaticus.com/r/putin-macho-politik/.

Sundstrom, Lisa McIntosh and Valerie Sperling, with Melike Sayoglu. 2019. *Courting Gender Justice: Russia, Turkey, and the European Court of Human Rights.* Oxford University Press.

Chapter 6

Appel, Hilary. 2018. 'How Neoliberal Reforms Lose Their Partisan Identity: Flat Tax Diffusion in Eastern Europe and Post-Soviet Eurasia.' *Europe-Asia Studies* 70: 1121–42.

Balzer, Harley. 2005. 'The Putin Thesis and Russian Energy Policy.' *Post-Soviet Affairs* 21: 210–25.

Barnes, Andrew. 2006. *Owning Russia: The Struggle over Factories, Farms, and Power.* Ithaca: Cornell University Press.

Batinti, Alberto, and Jeffrey Kopstein. 2022. 'Is Russia Really a Normal Country? A Numerical Taxonomy of Russia in Comparative Perspective.' *Constitutional Political Economy* 33: 217–32.

Blasi, Joseph R., Maya Kroumova, and Douglas Kruse. 1996. *Kremlin Capitalism: Privatizing the Russian Economy.* Cornell University Press.

Bluhm, Katharina, and Mihai Varga. 2020. 'Conservative Developmental Statism in East Central Europe and Russia.' *New Political Economy* 25: 642–59.

Gel'man, Vladimir. 2022. *The Politics of Bad Governance in Contemporary Russia.* University of Michigan Press.

Ghodsee, Kristen, and Mitchell Orenstein. 2021. *Taking Stock of Shock: Social Consequences of the 1989 Revolutions.* Oxford University Press.

Goldman, Marshall I. 2008. *Petrostate: Putin, Power, and the New Russia.* Oxford University Press.

Ickes, Barry W, and Randi Ryterman. 1992. 'The Interenterprise Arrears Crisis in Russia.' *Post-Soviet Affairs* 8: 331–61.

Johnson, Juliet. 2000. *A Fistful of Rubles: The Rise and Fall of the Russian Banking System.* Cornell University Press.

——. 2008. 'Forbidden Fruit: Russia's Uneasy Relationship with the Dollar.' *Review of International Political Economy* 15: 377–96.

Johnson, Juliet, and Seçkin Köstem. 2016. 'Frustrated Leadership: Russia's Economic Alternative to the West.' *Global Policy* 7: 207–16.

Johnson, Juliet, and David Woodruff. 2017. 'Currency Crises in Post-Soviet Russia.' *Russian Review* 76: 612–34.

Kurlantzick, Joshua. 2016. *State Capitalism: How the Return of Statism is Transforming the World.* Oxford University Press.

Mizobata, Satoshi, and Hiroaki Hayashi. 2022. 'State Capitalism in Russia', in Mike Wright et al. (ed), *The Oxford Handbook of State Capitalism and the Firm.* Oxford University Press.

Robinson, Neil. 2011. 'Russian Patrimonial Capitalism and the International Financial Crisis.' *Journal of Communist Studies and Transition Politics* 27: 434–55.

Rosefielde, Steven. 2005. 'Russia: An Abnormal Country.' *The European Journal of Comparative Economics* 2: 3.

Ross, Michael L. 2001. 'Does Oil Hinder Democracy?' *World Politics* 53: 325–61.

Shleifer, Andrei, and Daniel Treisman. 2005. 'A Normal Country: Russia after Communism.' *Journal of Economic Perspectives* 19: 151–74.

Solnick, Steven. 1998. *Stealing the State: Control and Collapse in Soviet Institutions.* Cambridge, MA: Harvard University Press.

United Nations. 2017. 'International Migration Report 2017.' New York.

Viktorov, Ilja, and Alexander Abramov. 2022. 'The Rise of Collateral-Based Finance under State Capitalism in Russia.' *Post-Communist Economies* 34: 15–51.

Woodruff, David M. 1999. *Money Unmade: Barter and the Fate of Russian Capitalism.* Ithaca: Cornell University Press.

World Bank. 2021. Russia Economic Report #46. 1 December.

Chapter 7

Barsukova, Svetlana, & Radaev, Vadim. 2012. 'Informal Economy in Russia: A Brief Overview.' *Economic sociology_the european electronic newsletter*, 13(2), 4–12.

Braguinsky, Serguey. 2009. 'Postcommunist Oligarchs in Russia: Quantitative Analysis.' *The Journal of Law and Economics*, 52(2), 307–49.

Guriev, Sergei, & Rachinsky, Andrei. 2005. 'The Role of Oligarchs in Russian Capitalism.' *Journal of Economic Perspectives*, 19(1), 131–50.

Harrison, Mark. 1985. *Soviet Planning in Peace and War, 1938–1945*. Cambridge University Press.

Harrison, Mark. 2018. 'Pripiski (Russia)' in Ledeneva, Alena (ed.) *The Global Encyclopaedia of Informality, Volume 2: Understanding Social and Cultural Complexity*. UCL Press, pp. 261–63.

Kaufmann, Daniel, & Siegelbaum, Paul. 1997. 'Privatization and Corruption in Transition Economies.' *Journal of International Affairs*, 419–58.

Ledeneva, Alena. 2009. 'From Russia with Blat: Can Informal Networks Help Modernize Russia?' *Social Research: An International Quarterly*, 76(1), 257–88.

Ledeneva, Alena V. (2013). *Can Russia Modernise? Sistema, Power Networks and Informal Governance*. Cambridge University Press.

Levin, Mark, & Satarov, Georgy. 2012. 'Corruption in Russia: Classification and Dynamics.' *Voprosy Ekonomiki*, 10, 4–29.

Yakovlev, Andrei. 2001. '"Black Cash" Tax Evasion in Russia: Its Forms, Incentives and Consequences at Firm Level.' *Europe-Asia Studies*, 53(1), 33–55.

Chapter 8

Elgie, Robert. 2011. *Semi-Presidentialism: Sub-Types and Democratic Performance*. New York: Oxford University Press.

Geddes, Barbara, Joseph Wright, and Erica Frantz. 2018. *How Dictatorships Work: Power, Personalization, and Collapse*. Cambridge: Cambridge University Press.

Golosov, Grigorii V. 2022. *Authoritarian Party Systems: Party Politics in Autocratic Regimes, 1945–2019*. Singapore: World Scientific.

Hale, Henry E. 2005. *Why not Parties in Russia? Democracy, Federalism, and the State*. Cambridge: Cambridge University Press.

Chapter 9

Guriev, Sergei, and Daniel Treisman. 2022. *Spin Dictators: The Changing Face of Tyranny in the 21st Century*. Princeton University Press.

Reuter, Ora John, and David Szakonyi. 2021. 'Electoral Manipulation and Regime Support: Survey Evidence from Russia.' *World Politics* 73, No. 2: 275–314.

Rogov, Kirill. 2018. 'The Art of Coercion: Repressions and Repressiveness in Putin's Russia.' *Russian Politics* 3, No. 2: 151–74.

Soldatov, Andrei, and Irina Borogan. 2010. 'Russia's New Nobility: The Rise of the Security Services in Putin's Kremlin.' *Foreign Aff.* 89: 80.

Treisman, Daniel. 2007. 'Putin's Silovarchs.' *Orbis* 51, No. 1: 141–53.

Chapter 10

Beissinger, Mark R. 2002. *Nationalist Mobilization and Collapse of the Soviet State*, Cambridge: Cambridge University Press.

Buckley, Noah, Reuter, Ora John, Rochlitz, Michael, Aisin, Anton. 2022. 'Staying Out of Trouble: Criminal Cases Against Russian Mayors', *Comparative Political Studies*, Vol. 55, No. 9.

Busygina, Irina, Klimovich, Stanislav. 2022. 'Pandemic Decentralization: COVID-19 and Principal-Agent Relations in Russia', *Problems of Post-Communism*, www.tandfonline.com/doi/full/10.1080/10758216.2022.2111313.

Dollbaum, Jan Matti, Semenov, Andrei, Sirotkina, Elena. 2018. 'A Top-Down Movement with Grass-Roots Effects: Alexei Navalny's Electoral Campaign', *Social Movement Studies*, Vol. 17, No. 5.

Gel'man, Vladimir. 2010. 'The Dynamics of Sub-National Authoritarianism: Russia in Comparative Perspective', in: Vladimir Gel'man, Cameron Ross (eds.), *The Politics of Sub-National Authoritarianism in Russia*, Aldershot: Ashgate.

Gel'man, Vladimir, Ryzhenkov, Sergei. 2011. 'Local Regimes, Sub-national Governance and the "Power Vertical" in Contemporary Russia', *Europe-Asia Studies*, Vol. 63, No. 3.

Gibson, Edward L. 2012. *Boundary Control: Subnational Authoritarianism in Democratic Countries*, Cambridge: Cambridge University Press.

Gilev, Aleksei, Dimke, Daria. 2021. 'No Time for Quality: Mechanisms of Local Governance in Russia', *Europe-Asia Studies*, Vol. 73, No. 6.

Giuliano, Elise. 2011. *Constructing Grievances: Ethnic Nationalism in Russia's Republics*, Ithaca: Cornell University Press.

Golosov, Grigorii V. 2011. 'The Regional Roots of Electoral Authoritarianism in Russia', *Europe-Asia Studies*, Vol. 63, No. 4.

Gorlizki, Yoram, Khlevniuk, Oleg. 2020. *Substate Dictatorship: Networks, Loyalty, and Institutional Change in the Soviet Union*, New Haven: Yale University Press.

Hale, Henry E. 2005. 'The Makeup and Breakup of Ethnofederal States: Why Russia Survives Where the USSR Fell', *Perspectives on Politics*, Vol. 3, No. 1.

Hale, Henry E. 2006. *Why Not Parties in Russia? Federalism, Democracy, and the State*, Cambridge: Cambridge University Press.

Hill, Fiona, Gaddy, Clifford. 2003. *The Siberian Curse: How Communist Planners Left Russia Out in the Cold*, Washington, DC: Brookings Institution Press.

Kynev, Alexander. 2020. *Gubernatory Rossii: mezhdu vyborami i naznacheniyami* [Russia's Governors: Between Elections and Appointments], Moscow: Liberal Mission Foundation https://liberal.ru/library/7656.

Lazarev, Egor. 2023. *State-Building as Lawfare: Custom, Sharia, and State Law in Postwar Chechnya*, Cambridge: Cambridge University Press.

Libman, Alexander, Rochlitz, Michael. 2019. *Federalism in China and Russia: Story of Success and Story of Failure?* Cheltenham: Edward Elgar.

Reddaway, Peter, Orttung, Robert W. (eds.) (2004–2005), *The Dynamics of Russian Politics: Putin's Reforms of Federal-Regional Relations*, 2 vols, Lanham: Rowman and Littlefield.

Reisinger, William M., Moraski Brian J. 2017. *Regional Roots of Russia's Political Regime*, Ann Arbor: University of Michigan Press.

Reuter, Ora John, Robertson, Graeme B. 2012. 'Subnational Appointments in Authoritarian Regimes: Evidence from Russian Gubernatorial Appointments', *Journal of Politics*, Vol. 74, No. 4.

Reuter, Ora John, Robertson, Graeme B. 2015. 'Legislatures, Cooptation, and Social Protests in Contemporary Authoritarian Regimes', *Journal of Politics*, Vol. 77, No. 1.

Riker, William. 1975. 'Federalism', in Fred I. Greenstein, Nelson W. Polsby, *Handbook of Political Science*, Vol. 5, Reading, MA: Addison-Wesley.

Robertson, Graeme B. 2011. *The Politics of Protest in Hybrid Regimes: Managing Dissent in Post-Communist Russia*, Cambridge: Cambridge University Press.

Ross, Cameron. 2023. 'Federalism and De-federalisation in Russia', in: Graeme Gill (ed.), *Routledge Handbook of Russian Politics and Society*, 2nd edition, Abingdon: Routledge.

Sharafutdinova, Gulnaz. 2013. 'Gestalt Switch in Russian Federalism: The Decline of Regional Power under Putin', *Comparative Politics*, Vol. 45, No. 2.

Snyder, Richard. 2001. 'Scaling Down: The Subnational Comparative Method', *Studies in Comparative International Development*, Vol. 36, No. 1.

Sonin, Konstantin. 2010. 'Provincial Protectionism', *Journal of Comparative Economics*, Vol. 38, No. 2.

Starodubtsev, Andrey. 2018. *Federalism and Regional Policy in Contemporary Russia*, Abingdon: Routledge.

Szakonyi, David. 2020. *Politics for Profit: Business, Elections, and Policymaking in Russia*, Cambridge: Cambridge University Press.

Treisman, Daniel. 1999. *After the Deluge: Regional Crises and Political Consolidation in Russia*, Ann Arbor: University of Michigan Press.

Zavadskaya, Margarita, and Shilov, Lev. 2021. 'Providing Goods and Votes? Federal Elections and the Quality of Local Governance in Russia', *Europe-Asia Studies*, Vol. 73, No. 6.

Zubarevich, Natalia. 2013. 'Four Russias: Human Potential and Social Differentiation of Russian Regions and Cities', in: Maria Lipman, Nikolay Petrov (eds.), *Russia 2025: Scenarios for the Russian Future*, London: Palgrave Macmillan.

Chapter 11

Anchabadze, G. 2009. *The Vainakhs*. Caucasian House, Tbilisi.

Bugai, N. 1992. '40–50-e gody: posledstviya deportatsii narodov (svidetelstvuyut arkhivy NKVD-MVD SSSR)'. *History of the USSR* 1, 122–43.

Bugai, N. 1996. *The Deportation of Peoples in the Soviet Union*. New York: Nova Science Publishers.

Kovalevsky, Pavel. *Vosstanie Chechni i Dagestana v 1877–78*. [The Upraising of Chechenia and Daghestan in 1877–1878]. Sankt Petersburg, 1912.

Nichols. J. 1995. Who are the Chechens? Linguist List: Vol. 6–22. Johanna Nichols, Who are the Chechen? (hartford-hwp.com).

Solzhenitsyn, Alexandr I. *The Gulag Archipelago. 1918–1956. An Experiment in Literary Investigation*. New York, Evanston, San Francisco, London: Harper and Row, Publishers, 2003.

Souleimanov, E. 2015. 'An Ethnography of Counterinsurgency: Kadyrovtsy and Russia's Policy of Chechenization.' *Post-Soviet Affairs*, 31(2), 91–114.

Wilhelmsen, J. 2016. *Russia's Securitization of Chechnya: How War Became Acceptable*. Routledge.

Williams, B. G. 2000. 'Commemorating "the deportation" in post-Soviet Chechnya: The Role of Memorialization and Collective Memory in the 1994–1996 and 1999–2000 Russo-Chechen Wars.' *History & Memory*, 12(1), 101–34.

Chapter 12

Aronoff, M. J. and Kubik, J., 2012. 'Homo Sovieticus and Vernacular Knowledge.' In *Anthropology and Political Science* (pp. 240–78). Berghahn Books.

Ashwin, S. (ed.) 2000. *Gender, State and Society in Soviet and Post-Soviet Russia*. London and New York: Routledge.

Berg-Nordlie, M., Holm-Hansen, J. and Kropp, S., 2018. 'The Russian State as Network Manager: A Theoretical Framework.' *Governance in Russian Regions: A Policy Comparison*, 7–42.

Bourdieu, P. 1984 [1979]. *Distinction: A Social Critique of the Judgment of Taste*, translated by R. Nice. Harvard University Press.

Burawoy. M., Krotov, P., and Lytkina, T. 2000. 'Involution and Destitution in Capitalist Russia.' *Ethnography* 1(1): 43–65.

Clément, K. and Zhelnina, A. 2020. 'Beyond Loyalty and Dissent: Pragmatic Everyday Politics in Contemporary Russia.' *International Journal of Politics, Culture, and Society* 33: 143–62.

Cook, L. 2007. *Postcommunist Welfare States: Reform Politics in Russia and Eastern Europe.* Cornell University Press.

Eraliev, S. and Urinboyev, R. 2020. 'Precarious Times for Central Asian Migrants in Russia.' *Current History* 119(819): 258–63.

Friebel, G. & Sergei Guriev, 2000. 'Should I Stay or Can I Go? Worker Attachment in Russia.' Working Papers w0008, Center for Economic and Financial Research (CEFIR).

Gel'man, V., 2010. 'Regime Changes Despite Legitimacy Crises: Exit, Voice, and Loyalty in Post-communist Russia.' *Journal of Eurasian Studies*, 1(1), pp. 54–63.

Greene, Samuel A. 2017. 'From Boom to Bust: Hardship, Mobilization & Russia's Social Contract.' *Daedalus* 146(2): 113–27.

Greene, Samuel A. 2019. 'Homo Post-sovieticus: Reconstructing Citizenship in Russia.' *Social Research: An International Quarterly*, 86(1): 181–202.

Gudkov, L., 2015. 'Russian Public Opinion in the Aftermath of the Ukraine Crisis.' *Russian Politics & Law*, 53(4), pp. 32–44.

Hartblay, Cassandra 2020. 'Disability Expertise: Claiming Disability Anthropology.' *Current Anthropology* 2020 61:S21, S26–S36.

Haynes, M. 2013. 'Social Inequality and the Continuing Russian Mortality Crisis.' *Debatte* 21(1): 25–49.

Hirschman, A. O., 1970. *Exit, Voice, and Loyalty: Responses to Decline in Firms, Organizations, and States* (Vol. 25). Harvard University Press.

Humphrey, Caroline, 1995. 'Creating a Culture of Disillusionment: Consumption in Moscow, a Chronicle of Changing Times', in *Worlds Apart: Modernity through the Prism of the Local*, ed. D. Miller.

Humphrey, Caroline. 1999. 'Traders, Disorder and Citizenship Regimes in Provincial Russia.' In *Uncertain Transition: Ethnographies of Change in the Postsocialist World*, eds. Michael Burawoy and Katherine Verdery. Lanham, Maryland: Rowman and Littlefield, pp. 19–53.

Kulmala, M., Kainu, M., Nikula, J. and Kivinen, M., 2014. 'Paradoxes of Agency: Democracy and Welfare in Russia.' *Demokratizatsiya*, 22(4).

Kulmala, M, Rasell, M, Chernova, Zh, 2017. 'Overhauling Russia's Child Welfare System: Institutional and Ideational Factors behind the Paradigm Shift.' Журнал исследований социальной политики, 15(3), pp. 353–66.

Ledeneva, A. 1998. *Russia's Economy of Favours: Blat, Networking and Informal Exchange* (Vol. 102). Cambridge University Press.

Matveev, I. 2019. 'State, Capital, and the Transformation of the Neoliberal Policy Paradigm in Putin's Russia.' *International Review of Modern Sociology* 45(1): 27–48.

Morris, Jeremy. 2016. *Everyday Postsocialism: Working-class Communities in the Russian Margins.* London: Springer.

Morris, J. and Polese, A. 2013. *The Informal Post-socialist Economy: Embedded Practices and Livelihoods.* Basingstoke: Routledge.

Morris, J., Semenov, A., Smyth, R. 2023. *Varieties of Russian Activism: State-society Contestation in Everyday Life.* Indiana University Press.

Pavlovskaya, M. 2018. 'Ontologies of Poverty in Russia and Duplicities of Neoliberalism.' In eds. S. F. Schram and M. Pavlovskaya. *Rethinking Neoliberalism: Resisting the Disciplinary Regime. London and New York*: Routledge, pp. 84–103.

Poupin, P. 2021. 'Social Media and State Repression: The Case of VKontakte and the Anti-garbage Protest in Shies, in Far Northern Russia.' *First Monday*, 26(5).

Remington, Thomas, F. 2012. *The Politics of Inequality in Russia.* Cambridge University Press.

Ries, N. 1997. *Russian Talk: Culture and Conversation During Perestroika* Cornell University Press.

Ries, N. 2009. 'Potato Ontology: Surviving Postsocialism in Russia.' *Cultural Anthropology* 24: 181–212.

Rosenfeld, B. 2017. 'Reevaluating the Middle-Class Protest Paradigm: A Case-Control Study of Democratic Protest Coalitions in Russia.' *American Political Science Review,* 111(4), 637–52. doi:10.1017/S000305541700034X.

Rotkirch, A., Temkina, A., & Zdravomyslova, E. (2007). Who Helps the Degraded Housewife? Comments on Vladimir Putin's Demographic Speech. *European Journal of Women's Studies*, 14(4), 349–57.

Rutland, P. 2008. 'Putin's Economic Record: Is the Oil Boom Sustainable?', *Europe-Asia Studies*, 60:6, 1051–1072/.

Schenk, Caress. 2021. 'Producing State Capacity through Corruption: The Case of Immigration Control in Russia.' *Post-Soviet Affairs*. 34(4): 303–17.

Sharafutdinova, Gulnaz. 2019. 'Was There a "Simple Soviet" Person? Debating the Politics and Sociology of 'Homo Sovieticus.' *Slavic Review* 78(1) 173–95.

Shevchenko, Olga. 2015. 'Resisting Resistance: Everyday Life, Practical Competence and Neoliberal Rhetoric in Postsocialist Russia.' In *Everyday Life in Russia: Past and Present,* edited by Choi Chatterjee, David L. Ransel, Mary Cavender, and Karen Petrone. Indiana University Press.

Stuckler, D., King, L., & McKee, M. (2009). 'Mass Privatisation and the Post-communist Mortality Crisis: A Cross-national Analysis.' *The Lancet*, 373(9661), 399–407.

Sundstrom, L. M., Henry, L. A., Sperling, V. 2022. 'The Evolution of Civic Activism in Contemporary Russia.' *East European Politics and Societies and Cultures*. 36(4):1377–99.

Urinboyev, R. 2021. *Migration and Hybrid Political Regimes: Navigating the Legal Landscape in Russia*. Oakland. California University Press.

Wengle, S. & Rasell, M. 2008. 'The Monetisation of l'goty: Changing Patterns of Welfare Politics and Provision in Russia.' *Europe-Asia Studies*, 60:5, 739–56.

Zubarevich, Natalya, Austerity: A Trend Across Russia's Regions (April 1, 2016). Russian Economic Developments. Moscow, 2016, pp. 87–91, Available at SSRN: https://ssrn.com/abstract=2757601 or http://dx.doi.org/10.2139/ssrn.2757601.

Chapter 13

Beissinger, M. R. 1990. 'Nonviolent Public Protest in the USSR.' 1 December, 1986–31 December 1989. National Council for Soviet and East European Research.

Bogdanova, E., Cook, L., and Kulmala, M. (2018). 'The Carrot or the Stick? Constraints and Opportunities of Russia's CSO Policy.' *Europe-Asia Studies*, 70:4, 501–13.

Dollbaum, J. M., Semenov, A., Sirotkina, E. 2018. 'A Top-down Movement with Grass-roots Effects? Alexei Navalny's Electoral Campaign.' *Social Movement Studies*, 17(5), 618–25.

Erpyleva, Svetlana and Oleg Zhuravlev. 2021. 'What's New about Russia's New Protests?' *Open Democracy*. Available online at: www.opendemocracy.net/en/odr/whats-new-in-russia-protests-2021-navalny/.

Lankina, Tomila and Katerina Tertytchnaya. 2020. 'Protest in Electoral Autocracies: A New Dataset.' *Post-Soviet Affairs*. 36(1), pp. 20–36.

Robertson, G. 2010. *The Politics of Protest in Hybrid Regimes: Managing Dissent in Post-Communist Russia*. Cambridge: Cambridge University Press.

Rosenfeld, Bryn. 2017. 'Reevaluating the Middle-Class Protest Paradigm: A Case-Control Study of Democratic Protest Coalitions in Russia.' *American Political Science Review*. 111(4), 637–52.

Sharlet, Robert. 1990. 'Party and Public Ideals in Conflict: Constitutionalism and Civil Rights in the USSR.' *Cornell International Law Journal*. 23(2), pp. 341–62.

Smyth, Regina, Anton Sobolev & Irina Soboleva. 2013. 'A Well-Organized Play.' *Problems of Post-Communism*. 60(2). 24–39.

Tertytchnaya, Katerina. 2023. 'Russian Protests Following the Invasion of Ukraine.' PONARS Eurasia Policy Memo No. 841, April 2023.

Yusupova, Guzel. 'Silence Matters: Self-Censorship and War in Russia.' PONARS Eurasia Policy Memo No. 824, January 2023.

Chapter 14

Aklin, Michäel, and Matto Mildenberger. 2020. 'Prisoners of the Wrong Dilemma: Why Distributive Conflict, Not Collective Action, Characterizes the Politics of Climate Change.' *Global Environmental Politics* 20: 4–27.

Alempic, Jean-Marie, Audrey Lartigue, Artemiy E. Goncharov, et al. 2022. 'An Update on Eukaryotic Viruses Revived from Ancient Permafrost.' *BioRxiv*, preprint, www.biorxiv.org/content/10.1101/2022.11.10.515937v1.

Anisimov, Oleg, and Vasily Kokorev. 2017. In Robert Orttung, ed. *Sustaining Russia's Arctic Cities: Resource Politics, Migration, and Climate Change.* New York: Berghahn Books.

Babaeva, Raksana. 2022. 'Zachem rossiiskie korporatsii stremitsia byt' "zelenym", RBK, 10 November. https://trends.rbc.ru/trends/green/cmrm/636cfe429a7947a52ca1808a.

Bennhold, Katrin, and Jim Tankersley. 2022. 'Ukraine War's Latest Victim? The Fight Against Climate Change.' *The New York Times*, 26 June. www.nytimes.com/2022/06/26/world/europe/g7-summit-ukraine-war-climate-change.html.

Berrang-Ford, Lea, A. R. Siders, Alexandra Lesnikowski, et al. 2021. 'A Systematic Global Stocktake of Evidence on Human Adaptation to Climate Change.' *Nature Climate Change* 11: 989–1000.

Blondin, S. 2019. 'Environmental Migrations in Central Asia: A Multifaceted Approach to the Issue.' *Central Asian Survey* 38(2): 275–92.

Clement, V., Rigaud, K. K., de Sherbinin, A., Jones, B., Adamo, S., Schewe, J., Sadiq, N., and Shabahat, E. 2021. *Groundswell Part 2: Acting on Internal Climate Migration.* Washington, DC: The World Bank.

Colgan, Jeff, Jessica Green, and Thomas Hale. 2021. 'Asset Revaluation and the Existential Politics of Climate Change.' *International Organization* 75: 586–610.

de Klerk, Lennard, Anatolii Shmurak, Olga Gassan-Ade, et al. 2022. 'Climate Damage Caused by Russia's War in Ukraine.' Initiative on GHG accounting of war, https://climatefocus.com/wp-content/uploads/2022/11/ClimateDamageinUkraine.pdf.

Dobrovidova, Olga. 2021. 'Russian Climate Scientists Upset by Ministry's Call for "Alternative" Research.' *Science* 10 June.

Galaktionov, Igor. 2022. 'Kak rossiiskaia neft' prokladyvaey dorogu v Aziiu,' BKS Ekspress, 10 August. https://bcs-express.ru/novosti-i-analitika/kak-rossiiskaia-neft-prokladyvaet-dorogu-v-aziiu.

Gallo-Cajiao, E., Nives Dolšak, Aseem Prakash, et al. 2023. 'Implications of Russia's Invasion of Ukraine for the Governance of Biodiversity Conservation.' *Frontiers in Conservation Science* 4: 989019. doi: 10.3389/fcosc.2023.989019.

Godzimirski, J. M. 2022. 'Energy, Climate Change and Security: The Russian Strategic Conundrum.' *Journal of Eurasian Studies* 13(1): 16–31.

Gusev, Alexander. 2016. 'Evolution of Russian Climate Policy: From the Kyoto Protocol to the Paris Agreement,' Centre international de formation européenne, 2 (380): 39–52. www.cairn.info/revue-l-europe-en-formation-2016-2-page-39.htm.

Gustafson, Thane. 2021. *Klimat: Russia in the Age of Climate Change.* Cambridge: Harvard University Press.

Healy, Andrew, and Neil Malhotra. 2009. 'Myopic Voters and Natural Disaster Policy.' *American Political Science Review* 103(3): 387–406.

Henderson, James, and Tatiana Mitrova. 2020. 'Implications of the Global Energy Transition.' In *The Geopolitics of the Global Energy Transition*, ed. Manfred Hafner and Simone Tagliapietre. Springer Open.

Hendrix, Cullen, and Idean Salehyan. 2012. 'Climate Change, Rainfall, and Social Conflict in Africa.' *Journal of Peace Research* 49(1): 35–50.

Henry, Laura A., and Lisa McIntosh Sundstrom. 2007. 'Russia and the Kyoto Protocol: Seeking an Alignment of Interests and Image.' *Global Environmental Politics* 7(4): 47–69.

Hjort, Jan, Dmitry Streletskiy, Guy Doré, et al. 2022. 'Impacts of Permafrost Degradation on Infrastructure.' *Nature* 3: 24–38.

IPCC, 2018: Summary for Policymakers. In: Global Warming of 1.5°C. An IPCC Special Report on the impacts of global warming of 1.5°C above pre-industrial levels and related global greenhouse gas emission pathways, in the context of strengthening the global response to the threat of climate change, sustainable development, and efforts to eradicate poverty, ed. Masson-Delmotte, V., P. Zhai, H.-O. Pörtner, et al. Cambridge University Press, Cambridge, UK and New York, NY, USA.

Katsova, V. M., et al., eds. 2022. *Tretii otsenochnyi doklad ob izmeneniiakx i ikh posledstviiakh na territorii Rossiiskoi Federatsii [Third summary document on changes and their consequences on the territory of the Russian Federation].* St Petersburg: Rosgidromet. http://cc.voeikovmgo.ru/images/dokumenty/2022/od3.pdf.

Koch, N., & Tynkkynen, V.-P. 2021. 'The Geopolitics of Renewables in Kazakhstan and Russia.' *Geopolitics* 26, No. 2: 521–40.

Korppoo, Anna. 2016. 'Who is Driving Russian Climate Policy? Applying and Adjusting Veto Players Theory to a Non-democracy.' *International Environmental Agreements: Politics, Law and Economics* 16, No. 5: 639–53.

Korppoo, Anna. 2020. 'Domestic Frames on Russia's Role in International Climate Diplomacy.' *Climate Policy* 20(1): 109–23.

Korppoo, Anna. 2022. 'Russian Discourses on Benefits and Threats from International Climate Diplomacy.' *Climatic Change* 170: 1–24.

Koubi, Vally. 2019. 'Climate Change and Conflict.' *Annual Review of Political Science* 22: 343–60.

Kozin, Daniel. 2021. 'Is Russia Finally Waking Up to Climate Change?' *The Moscow Times* 7 September, www.themoscowtimes.com/2020/03/04/is-russia-finally-waking-up-to-climate-change-a69517.

Lankina, Tomila. 2018. Lankina Russian Protest Event Dataset, https://eprints.lse.ac.uk/90298/.

Lazarev, Egor, Anton Sobolev, Irina V. Soboleva, et al. 2014. 'Trial by Fire: A Natural Disaster's Impact on Support for the Authorities in Rural Russia.' *World Politics* 66, No. 4: 641–68.

Lustgarten, Abrahm. 2020. 'How Russia Wins the Climate Crisis.' *The New York Times* 16 December, www.nytimes.com/interactive/2020/12/16/magazine/russia-climate-migration-crisis.html.

Makarov, Igor, Henry Chen, and Sergey Paltsev. 2020. 'Impacts of Climate Change Policies Worldwide on the Russian Economy.' *Climate Policy* 20, No. 10: 1242–56.

Moe, Arild, Erdem Lamazhapov, and Oleg Anisimov. 2022. 'Russia's Expanding Adaptation Agenda and its Limitations.' *Climate Policy* https://doi.org/10.1080/14693062.2022.2107981.

Morozov, Maksim. 2020. 'Transgranichnyi uglerodnyi nalog v ES: vyzov possiiiskoi ekonomike,' EKONS, 26 November. https://econs.online/articles/opinions/transgranichnyy-uglerodnyy-nalog-v-es-vyzov-rossiyskoy-economike/.

Ostrom, Elinor. 2009. 'A Polycentric Approach for Coping with Climate Change.' Policy Research Working Paper 5095, World Bank. DOI: https://doi.org/10.1596/1813-9450-5095.

Overland, Indra. 2022. 'Russia's Invasion of Ukraine: Consequences for Global Decarbonization.' *Russian Analytical Digest* 284: 2–5. https://doi.org/10.3929/ethz-b-000550755.

Pearce, Fred. 2021. 'Will Russia's Forests Be an Asset or an Obstacle in Climate Fight?,' Yale Environment 360, 15 July, https://e360.yale.edu/features/will-russias-forests-be-an-asset-or-obstacle-in-the-climate-fight.

Rantanen, M., Karpechko, A. Y., Lipponen, A. et al. 2022. 'The Arctic has Warmed Nearly Four Times Faster than the Globe Since 1979.' *Communications Earth & Environment* 3, 168.

Revich, B. A. 2020. 'Riski zdorov'ya naseleniya pri izmenenii klimata Arkticheskogo makroregiona.' *Scientific Works of the Institute of Economic Forecasting of the Russian Academy of Sciences.* https://ecfor.ru/publication/zdorove-naseleniya-pri-izmenenii-klimata-arkticheskogo-makroregiona/.

Revich, B. A. 2021. 'Izmeneniye klimata v Rossii – problemy obshchestvennogo zdorov'ya,' *Obshchestvennoye Zdorovye* 1, No. 4: 5–14. https://ph.elpub.ru/jour/article/view/31.

Revich, Boris A., Dmitry O. Eliseev, and Dmitry A. Shaposhnikov. 2022. 'Risks for Public Health and Social Infrastructure in Russian Arctic under Climate Change and Permafrost Degradation.' *Atmosphere* 13, No. 4, 28 March.

Revich, B. A., V. V. Maleyev, and M. D. Smirnova. 2019. *Izmeneniye Klimata i Zdorov'ye: Otstenka, Indikatory, Prognozy.* Moscow: Institute of Economic Forecasting, Russian Academy of Sciences.

Rutland, Peter. 2022. 'Why Crimea is the Key to the Ukraine War.' *Responsible Statecraft* 18 October, https://responsiblestatecraft.org/2022/10/18/why-crimea-is-the-key-to-the-ukraine-war/.

Sagynbekova, L. 2021. *The Impact of Climate Change Induced and Environmental Challenges on Migration Dynamics in Rural Kyrgyzstan.* Bishkek: OSCE Academy Policy Brief, https://nbn-resolving.org/urn:nbn:de:0168-ssoar-78383-6.

Savilov, Ye. D., N. I. Briko, and S. I. Kolesnikov. 2020. 'Epidemiologicheskiye aspekty ekologicheskikh problem sovremennosti.' *Gigiena i Sanitariya* 99, No. 2 www.rjhas.ru/jour/article/view/198/0.

Semenov, Andrei. 2021. 'Russian Political Forces Meet Climate Change.' Center for Strategic and International Studies, 6 April, www.csis.org/analysis/russian-political-forces-meet-climate-change.

Simon, Matt. 2022. 'Machines of War Take a Heavy Toll on Ukraine – and the Planet.' *Wired* 18 March, www.wired.com/story/machines-of-war-take-a-heavy-toll-on-ukraine-and-the-planet/.

TASS. 2021. 'Abramchenko schitayet, chto migratsiya iz-za izmeneniya klimata v Rossii neizbezhna.' *TASS* October 13, https://tass.ru/obschestvo/12649977.

TASS. 2022. 'Pravitelstvo utverdilo otraslevye plany adaptatsii k izmeneniyam klimata.' *TASS* 24 June, https://tass.ru/ekonomika/15028057.

Troianovski, Anton. 2021. 'Where Ukrainians are Preparing for All-Out War With Russia,' *New York Times*, 8 May.

Tynkkynen, Veli-Pekka, and Nina Tynkkynen. 2018. 'Climate Denial Revisited: (Re)contextualising Russian Public Discourse on Climate Change During Putin 2.0.' *Europe-Asia Studies* 70, No. 7: 1103–20.

(UNEP) United Nations Environment Programme. 2021. 'Adaptation Gap Report 2021: The Gathering Storm – Adapting to Climate Change in a Post-pandemic World.' Nairobi. www.unep.org/adaptation-gap-report-2021.

(UNEP) United Nations Environment Programme. 2022a. 'Adaptation Gap Report 2022: Too Little, Too Slow – Climate Adaptation Failure Puts World at Risk.' Nairobi. www.unep.org/adaptation-gap-report-2022.

(UNEP) United Nations Environment Programme. 2022. 'The Environmental Impact of the Ukraine Conflict: A Preliminary Review.' Nairobi.

von Uexkull, Nina, and Halvard Buhaug. 2021. 'Security Implications of Climate Change: A Decade of Scientific Progress.' *Journal of Peace Research* 58(1): 3–17.

Vynogradova, Polina. 2020. 'Backgrounder: The Water Crisis in Crimea,' *Geopolitical Monitor* 24 April, www.geopoliticalmonitor.com/backgrounder-the-water-crisis-in-crimea/.

Witze, Alexandra. 2020. 'The Arctic is Burning Like Never Before – and That's Bad News for Climate Change.' *Nature* 10 September.

Zagoruichyk, Anastasiia. 2022. 'The Carbon Brief Profile: Russia,' 22 September, /www.carbonbrief.org/the-carbon-brief-profile-russia/.

Chapter 15

Breteau, Pierre. 2022. "Nine Months of War in Ukraine in One Map: How Much Territory did Russia Invade and Then Cede?" *Le Monde,* November 25. https://www.lemonde.fr/en/les-decodeurs/article/2022/11/25/nine-months-of-war-in-ukraine-in-one-map-how-much-territory-did-russia-invade-and-then-cede_6005655_8.html

Carbonaro, Giulia. 2022. 'Russia's Death Toll in Ukraine Already the Same as 10 Years in Afghanistan.' *Newsweek*, 23 May. www.newsweek.com/russia-death-toll-ukraine-already-same-10-years-afghanistan-1708991.

Colton, Timothy J. 2008. *Yeltsin: A Life*. New York: Basic Books.

D'Anieri, Paul. 2019. *Ukraine and Russia: From Civilized Divorce to Uncivil War*. New York: Cambridge University Press.

Hale, Henry. 2005. 'Regime Cycles: Democracy, Autocracy, and Revolution in Post-Soviet Eurasia.' *World Politics* 58, No. 1: 133–65.

"'I'm here": Zelenskyy's message to his people Saturday morning.' 2022. *NBC News*, 26 February. www.nbcnews.com/video/president-zelenskyy-sends-video-to-ukrainian-people-134108741773.

IRI (International Republican Institute), Baltic Surveys/The Gallup Organization, and Rating Group Ukraine. 2013. 'Public Opinion Survey Residents of the Autonomous Republic of Crimea, May 16–30, 2013.' www.iri.org/wp-content/uploads/2013/10/201320October20720Survey20of20Crimean20Public20Opinion2C20May2016-302C202013.pdf.

Johnson, Juliet. 2018. *A Fistful of Rubles: The Rise and Fall of the Russian Banking System*. Cornell: Cornell University Press.

Kagan, Robert. 2022. 'What we Can Expect after Putin's Conquest of Ukraine.' *Washington Post*, 21 February. www.washingtonpost.com/opinions/2022/02/21/ukraine-invasion-putin-goals-what-expect/.

Kassymbekova, Botakoz, and Erica Marat. 2022. 'Time to Question Russia's Imperial Innocence.' *PONARS Eurasia Policy Memo No. 771*, 27 April. www.ponarseurasia.org/time-to-question-russias-imperial-innocence/.

KIIS (Kyiv International Institute of Sociology). 2014a. 'Dynamika stavlennia naselennia Ukrainy o Rosii ta naselennia Rosii o Ukrainy, iakykh vidnosyn z Rosieiu hotily b ukraintsi.' 4 March. www.kiis.com.ua/?lang=ukr&cat=reports&id=236&page=1&y=2014.

——. 2014b. 'Opinions and views of the citizens of Southern and Eastern regions of Ukraine: April 2014.' April 20. https://dif.org.ua/en/article/opinions-and-views-of-the-citizens-of-southern-and-eastern-regions-of-ukraine-april-2014.

Kochnev, Sergey. 2020. 'Mintimer Shaimiyev was Politically Wise, and Boris Yeltsin Wasn't a Bloodsucker.' *Realnoe Vremya*, 20 August. https://realnoevremya.com/articles/4697-all-russian-federalism-began-with-yeltsins-visit-to-tassr.

Kuzio, Taras. 2022. *Russian Nationalism and the Russian-Ukrainian War*. New York: Routledge.

Mearsheimer, John J. 2014. 'Why the Ukraine Crisis Is the West's Fault: The Liberal Delusions That Provoked Putin.' *Foreign Affairs* 93, No. 5: 77–89.

Plokhy, Serhii. 2014. *The Last Empire: The Final Days of the Soviet Union*. Basic Books.

Popova, Maria, and Oxana Shevel. 2023. *Russia and Ukraine: Entangled Histories, Diverging States*. Polity Press.

Pop-Eleches, Grigore, Isabelle DeSisto, Laura Howells, and Jacob Tucker. 2023. Russia Watcher. https://russiawatcher.com/index.

President of the Republic of Estonia. 1994. 'Address by H. E. Lennart Meri, President of the Republic of Estonia, at a Matthiae-Supper in Hamburg on 25 February 1994.' February 25. https://vp1992-2001.president.ee/eng/k6ned/K6ne.asp?ID=9401.

Putin, Vladimir. 2022. 'Transcript: Vladimir Putin's Televised Address on Ukraine.' *Bloomberg News*, 24 February. www.bloomberg.com/news/articles/2022-02-24/full-transcript-vladimir-putin-s-televised-address-to-russia-on-ukraine-feb-24.

Rating Group. 2022a. 'Dynamika zovnishniopolitychnykh orientatsii (16–17 liutoho 2022).' https://ratinggroup.ua/research/ukraine/dinamika_vneshnepoliticheskih_orientaciy_16-17_fevralya_2022.html.

Rating Group. 2022b. 'Suspilno-politychni nastroi naselennia (12–13 liutoho 2022).' https://ratinggroup.ua/research/ukraine/obschestvenno-politicheskie_nastroeniya_naseleniya_12-13_fevralya_2022.html.

Razumkov Center. 2014. 'Stavlennia hromadian do zovnishniopolitychnoho vektoru Ukrainy: rehional'nyi rozriz.' https://dif.org.ua/article/stavlennyagromadyan-do-zovnishnopolitichnogo-vektoru-ukraini-regionalniy-rozriz.

——. 2020. 'Hromads'ka dumka pro sytuatsiiu na Donbasi ta shliakhy vidnovlennia suverenitetu Ukrainy nad okupovanymy terytoriamy (liutyi 2020).' https://razumkov.org.ua/napriamky/sotsiologichni-doslidzhennia/gromadska-dumka-pro-sytuatsiiu-na-donbasi-ta-shliakhy-vidnovlenniasuverenitetu-ukrainy-nad-okupovanymy-terytoriiamy-liutyi-2020r.

——. 2023. 'Zovnishniopolitychni orientatsii hromadian Ukrainy, otsinka zovnishnioi polityky vlady, stavlennia do inozemnykh derzhav ta politykiv (liutyi-berezen 2023).' https://razumkov.org.ua/napriamky/sotsiologichni-doslidzhennia/zovnishnopolitychni-oriientatsii-gromadian-ukrainy-otsinka-zovnishnoi-polityky-vlady-stavlennia-do-inozemnykh-derzhav-ta-politykiv-liutyi-berezen-2023r.

Smola, Lidia. 2023. 'Iak ukraintsi stavliatsia do Rosii i ii hromadian? Bratamy my nikoly ne buly.' *Dzerkalo Tyzhnia*, 27 May. https://zn.ua/ukr/UKRAINE/jak-ukrajintsi-stavljatsja-do-rosiji-ta-jiji-hromadjan-bratami-mi-nikoli-ne-buli.html.

Szporluk, Roman. 1989. 'Dilemmas of Russian Nationalism.' *Problems of Communism* 38, No. 4: 15–35.

Chapter 16

Coats, Daniel R., 'Statement for the Record: Worldwide Threat Assessment of the United States Intelligence Community', for the United States Senate Select Committee on Intelligence, 9 January 2019, p. 7.

Obama, Barack, as quoted in Scott Wilson, 'Obama Dismisses Russia as "Regional Power"', *Washington Post*, 25 March 2014.

Orenstein, Mitchell. 2018. *The Lands in Between: Russia v. the West, and the New Politics of Hybrid War*. New York: Oxford University Press.

Putin, Vladimir, 'Excerpts from Transcripts from a Press Conference for Russian and Foreign Journalists, 18 July 2001', available at http://en.kremlin.ru.

Putin, Vladimir, 'Speech and the Following Discussion at the Munich Conference on Security Policy', 10 February 2007, available at http://en.kremlin.ru.

Sarotte, M. E. 2021. *Not One Inch: America, Russia, and the Making of Post-Cold War Stalemate*. New Haven: Yale University Press.

Saalman, Lora, ed., 'China-Russia Relations and Regional Dynamics: From Pivots to Regional Diplomacy.' Stockholm International Peace Research Institute, March 2017, p. 26.

Stoner, Kathryn. 2021. *Russia Resurrected: Its Power and Purpose in a New Global Order*. New York: Oxford University Press.

Walker, Christopher, and Jessica Ludwig, 'The Meaning of Sharp Power: How Authoritarian States Project Influence.' *Foreign Affairs*, 16 November 2017.

Weseman, Peter et al., 'Fact Sheet: Trends in International Arms Transfers 2019', Stockholm International Peace Research Institute, March 2020, available at https://sipri.org/sites.default/files/2020-03/fs_2003_2019.pdf, accessed 31 January 2023.

Index

The letter *b* following an entry indicates a page with a box.
The letter *t* following an entry indicates a page with a table.